PRAISE FOR *JOURNEY TO IM*

"This book is a treasure trove for teams in the social sector wanting to ma— Grounded in the science of improvement, it teaches how to understand problems, use eve—, one's skills, and learn together. The book's focus on changing inequitable systems and practices is unique in the improvement literature. By targeting examples from the social sector, it equips readers with the tools and insights needed to address pressing societal challenges. The metaphor of a journey for an improvement team following the Model for Improvement leads to learning, making changes, and getting feedback to see what works. The book makes it easy for teams to follow a map of their journey and learn their way into improvement."

—**Lloyd Provost, improvement advisor, Associates in Process Improvement; author of** *The Improvement Guide*

"Improvement science is a mindset. Its aim is to develop pathways to equity-centered systems change in education and allied disciplines. This extraordinary volume will help us use improvement science to sharpen our collaborative skills and support evidence-centered action to improve the life chances of the people we serve."

—**Louis Gomez, Professor, University of California, Los Angeles; author of** *Learning to Improve*

"This is a must-read for educators who are looking to take a scientific approach to systemic improvement. This is the invaluable guide you need in your library. You will reach for it again and again."

—**Taqwanda Hailey, chief analytics officer, Schools That Lead; former assistant head of school, Charlotte Secondary School**

"Grunow, Park, and Bennett have thought of everything, and they've packaged it neatly for easy consumption. From roles team members will play, to mindsets they will manage, to measures they must collect—this text is both relevant and comprehensive. It is a must-have introduction or reference for any improver, coach, or social sector team member seeking to systematically make the world a better place, one [PDSA] cycle at a time."

—**Brandi Hinnant-Crawford, PhD, associate professor of educational leadership, Clemson University; author of** *Improvement Science in Education: A Primer*

"Journey to Improvement offers a road map for action for those who are interested in improving organizations. It blends deep theoretical knowledge with practical advice from leading thinkers in the field of improvement science. Five stars."

—**Ben Daley, president, High Tech High Graduate School of Education**

"To advance large-scale social change, we need to develop teams with strong communication skills, emotional intelligence, and the concrete tactics and tools necessary to do the work. *Journey to Improvement* equips teams with these essentials, offering practical guidance and inspiring examples to help them achieve impact."

—**Becky Margiotta, cofounder, Billions Institute; author of** *Impact with Integrity: Repair the World without Breaking Yourself*

Journey to Improvement

A Team Guide to Systems Change in Education, Health Care, and Social Welfare

Alicia Grunow
Sandra Park
Brandon Bennett

ROWMAN & LITTLEFIELD
Lanham • Boulder • New York • London

Published by Rowman & Littlefield
An imprint of The Rowman & Littlefield Publishing Group, Inc.
4501 Forbes Boulevard, Suite 200, Lanham, Maryland 20706
www.rowman.com

86-90 Paul Street, London EC2A 4NE

British Library Cataloguing in Publication Information Available

Library of Congress Cataloging-in-Publication Data

Names: Grunow, Alicia, author. | Park, Sandra
  (Writer of Journey to improvement), author. | Bennett, Brandon, author.
Title: Journey to improvement : a team guide to systems change in
  education, health care, and social welfare / Alicia
  Grunow, Sandra Park, Brandon Bennett.
Description: Lanham : Rowman & Littlefield, [2024] | Includes
  bibliographical references and index.
Identifiers: LCCN 2023055718 (print) | LCCN 2023055719 (ebook) | ISBN
  9781538191217 (cloth) | ISBN 9781538191385 (paperback) | ISBN
  9781538191224 (epub)
Subjects: LCSH: Teams in the workplace. | Continuous improvement process.
Classification: LCC HD66 .B4443 2024 (print) | LCC HD66 (ebook) | DDC
  361.0068/4—dc23/eng/20240309
LC record available at https://lccn.loc.gov/2023055718
LC ebook record available at https://lccn.loc.gov/2023055719

Contents

Introduction

Hard work and best efforts will not by themselves dig us out of the pit.

—W. Edwards Deming 2000, 23

Improvement begins with a dissatisfaction with the status quo, a recognition that the existing outcomes are undesirable or simply not good enough. Communities experience systems intended for them but that do not meet their priorities, needs, or interests. Leaders, managers, and front-line workers are constantly negotiating unnecessary barriers that stand in the way of providing service to the people that drew them into the profession in the first place.

Improvement is also profoundly optimistic. It requires the courage to hope, to imagine, and to commit to a compelling vision of what could be. It rests on the assumption that people, learning together, can reinvent systems to achieve outcomes previously thought impossible. The fuel and energy needed for improvement comes from holding this tension, recognizing and owning the gap between the current reality and a compelling vision.

Although the courage to hold this tension is essential for improvement, it is not enough for real progress. We also need better ways of pursuing change. In the social sector (i.e., education, health care, criminal justice, and social welfare), we are better at calling out gaps than we are at closing them.[1]

Goal setting abounds; real change does not.

One of the authors[2] can remember vividly arriving early one summer at her new school. While setting up her classroom, she paused to look out the window at the courtyard where a semitruck was backing up to the schoolyard gate. The truck was partially full of what looked like piles of discarded curriculum and materials. The school doors opened, and two custodians wheeled out carts full of materials that they added to the pile in the back of the truck, returning to refill. Having just moved from a state with significantly lower per pupil funding and needing to scrounge constantly for curricular materials, the abundance of "stuff" being loaded into the truck was striking. And it filled not only the truck but also the classroom closets and school supply rooms, a treasure trove of possibilities. She would come to learn that in addition to having more "stuff," the school also had many more people—multiple literacy and math coaches, a full-time social worker, a nurse, reading specialists, a security guard, and a dedicated parent coordinator.

1

Yet somehow all these extra resources did not translate into better learning experiences for children. The school persistently underperformed academically and struggled in particular with meeting the needs of the emergent bilingual students who made up 42 percent of the population. As a teacher, she felt more alone and isolated in supporting her students' needs than she had in her previous school that had virtually none of these resources and nonteaching staff.

Behind each position and curricular program was a reform idea that presumably once held promise. Digging through the classroom closets, the school supply rooms, and that semitruck, you could piece together waves of reform that had swept through the school annually.

The image of a semitruck carrying away old programs serves as a larger metaphor for the typical churn of reform ideas in organizations, both in education and beyond. The usual strategy for reform starts with the emergence of a promising new idea, tool, or program. A small group of leaders, with the utmost of confidence, get together to hash out the details of how to roll it out quickly. Most often the change is implemented on a wide scale. In the best-case scenarios, positive changes are seen in some places. Usually, the change effort fails to meet expectations of what is imagined upon investment or close the gap between the aspirations and the current reality for most users. Very little is learned from where the ideas don't work and why. Not surprisingly, this perpetual cycle of failed top-down reform efforts also creates "change fatigue" and produces a well-earned skepticism for new reform ideas.

If you asked the leaders behind these outcomes what they hoped to accomplish, most likely they would say to get better results. And behind these efforts, you would likely find good ideas, hard work, and lots of people who really care. However, the persistent and intractable problems that plague our communities will not be solved by a few leaders coming up with an idea and mandating that everyone else implement it. Depending on the heroics of individuals trying their best to make things work on the front line is also a weak strategy. The desire and intention to improve abounds in the social sector, and that's a resource worth capitalizing on. However, what's missing is the collective skill to improve; the ability to turn the intentions, ideas, and efforts of everyone in the organization into real improvements for the children and families they serve. This requires a completely different way of thinking about and engaging in improvement.

In his book *The New Economics*, statistician and management expert W. Edwards Deming estimated that 95 percent of leaders' change efforts fail to result in an improvement (Deming 2000, 38). The book, written more than 25 years ago, did not speak exclusively to the social sector, but the 95 percent failure rate is not a bad estimate of the current state of affairs in that sector. Examples of real, sustained improvement in education, health care, and social welfare are difficult to find relative to the effort expended.

Deming attributed failed progress to the ways that organizations, and change itself, are managed. His critiques would apply to many organizations today. In short, he argued that leaders need to shift from blaming people to appreciating the role of systems in producing the current outcomes, and to shift from a top-down, compliance-oriented style of leadership to one that values learning and discovery by everyone. Only then would organizations be able to reengineer systems to produce better results.

Out of these initial ideas grew the field known as improvement science—the science of how organizations improve[3] (Langley et al. 2009; Perla, Provost, and Parry 2013).

DEFINITION OF IMPROVEMENT SCIENCE

Improvement science is an evolving field of study focused on the theories, methods, and practices that facilitate or hinder efforts to improve the performance of teams, organizations, and communities.

Improvement science

- is an applied science, primarily concerned with improving systems.
- is interdisciplinary drawing on systems thinking, psychology of change, understanding variation, and the philosophy of learning.

It contends that improvement in outcomes comes from a combination of improvement science skills and subject matter expertise.

Leaders in different sectors have taken up the ideas of improvement science at different points in history and in different parts of the world. In the early days, the work was mostly centered in agriculture and manufacturing.[4] In the late 1980s and early 1990s, a handful of health-care leaders began to invest in improvement science to improve patient outcomes (Institute for Healthcare Improvement n.d.; Godfrey 1996). Most notably, these health-care pioneers contributed to the broader field of improvement science by applying the ideas to a profession focused on caring for people. As the ideas have moved from one sector to another, figuring out how to translate and apply them has been a struggle. Every sector and organization believes that its problems are unique, and to some extent they are; yet much can be learned from the organizations that have gotten better at getting better. These organizations:

- align the efforts around the needs of the people they are trying to serve,
- shift from blaming or incentivizing individuals to appreciating how systems work and operate, and
- actively engage the people closest to the problem in learning and discovery.

Increasingly, leaders and organizations in the social sector have begun to explore how to use improvement science to transform outcomes for the populations they serve. Of primary concern for many social sector leaders is reducing or eliminating the persistent inequities found in their outcomes. Organizations are looking to improvement science for approaches that can help them address seemingly intractable problems in the face of mounting constraints on their time, money, and the other resources that always seem to be in short supply.

This book provides a practical approach for applying the principles and methods of improvement science to create meaningful and lasting change in the social sector. The book guides teams through an improvement journey (see figure I.1) to identify and understand key systems problems, leverage diverse expertise, and stimulate learning and discovery to achieve the desired outcomes. We target examples specifically from the social sector, especially health care and education, and anticipate the key moments and adaptations necessary to interrupt inequitable systems and practices.

IMPROVEMENT JOURNEY

An improvement science approach starts with a powerful inspiration and invests in collective learning as the main mechanism for getting results. Sometimes a network sets off on the journey together, sometimes a set of teams within an organization, and sometimes a single team. Regardless of the size or structure, the group's ability to tap into diverse forms of expertise, align their efforts, and learn together will determine how far they go.

Although the field of improvement science offers principles and methods for structuring collective learning, for teams setting out, it can be difficult to figure out when and how to pull on different methods and ideas to produce the kind of learning that sits at the heart of systems transformation. Figure I.1 is intended to provide teams with a broad overview of the phases of an improvement journey to guide their improvement efforts.

The journey begins with getting ready. Commissioning and launch require prioritizing what will be improved and who will be involved as well as cultivating the cultural and relational foundations needed for teams to lean into learning together. Leaders play a key role in setting up teams so that they can be successful. Their job is to set priorities, allocate resources, and empower teams to discover systems improvements.

As teams set out on their journey, a useful starting place is to develop a common understanding of the system that is producing the current or undesirable outcome. The work of this phase is to "see the system" anew by understanding the experience of end users (e.g., patients, students, families), observing current work practices, and digging into historically available data.

Through understanding the current system, teams discover or refine where they will focus their collective efforts. At this stage, teams set a clear destination and commit to heading in that direction together, despite not yet knowing how they will get there. Teams also identify measures that will serve as useful feedback about whether they are making progress toward their desired destination.

Along with a common direction, the team will need to generate ideas for change to help them achieve their intended results. Powerful ideas come from multiple sources: end users, the untapped ingenuity of people within the organization, other organizations that have solved a similar problem, and the research literature. Sometimes the changes that emerge are targeted, small, and powerful; sometimes they entail a significant redesign in the work of the team or the organization.

The learn-in-practice phase is the heart of the improvement journey. No matter how diligently teams engage in the initial phases, the dynamism and complexity of systems mean that the initial assumptions about what change is needed will often be wrong and always in-

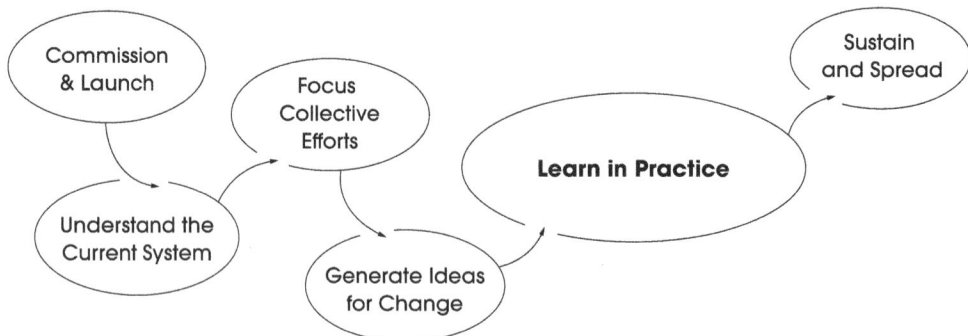

Figure I.1.   Improvement Journey

complete. Knowing this, teams go into the phase primed to learn, introducing changes using practical experiments to discover when, where, and for whom the initial ideas for change do and do not work. Unproductive ideas can be discarded quickly. Attention is paid not only to which ideas work to generate desired outcomes but also to how to get those ideas to work across a variety of different contexts.

Once teams discover changes that are an improvement, their attention turns toward how to sustain the newly discovered practices so that they become the default way in which work is done by the system. They may then think critically about how to spread the practices to other departments or organizations if they are commissioned to do so. Spreading change often results in beginning the improvement journey anew, with an expanded set of teams building on the initial learning and improvement, figuring out how to use that learning to produce meaningful change in their context.

Improvement as a Nonlinear Journey

Although the improvement journey is presented as a sequential set of phases, learning is rarely linear and often messy (see figure I.2). In reality, improvement teams shift back and forth between different phases and modalities as the learning demands. While teams are working to understand the current system, they often stumble upon ideas for change that they can put into action quickly. As teams are learning by introducing changes in practice, they may get stuck and realize that they need to rethink their focus or understand some part of the current system that is not yet quite clear.

Two of the most useful pieces of advice for those interested in taking on an improvement approach are:

1. get started before you are ready and
2. learn your way into improvement

Having said this, infinite flexibility and options are overwhelming and can be paralyzing. The improvement journey map is a scaffold to help teams get up, get going, and get on their way.

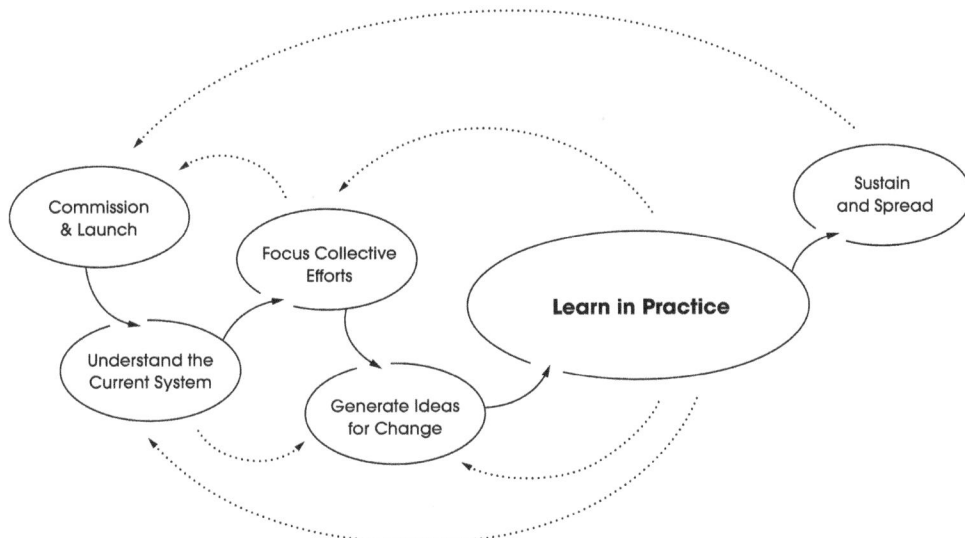

Figure I.2. The Sometimes Messy and Recursive Nature of an Improvement Journey

More often than not, the six phases describe how improvement efforts unfold. However, teams should avoid the tendency to treat the phases as a project plan or rigid set of steps to follow. With experience and coaching, improvers learn when to pull on which method to address the most important learning question at hand, and the need for a scaffold falls away. A good rule of thumb: if the team is not learning, something is wrong.

ORGANIZING IMPROVEMENT TEAMS

In this book, we will focus on how to activate and organize improvement teams to learn their way into improvement. Before we continue, it's worth coming back to the point that the social structure of improvement initiatives varies. Single teams (e.g., a team of math teachers or a surgical team in a hospital) use improvement science to enhance or reexamine their own work practices. Improvement initiatives within an organization often entail a coordinated set of improvement teams across departments or buildings looking to realign the system to better serve the needs of the user. More recently, improvement science has been used to structure the work of networks (Institute for Healthcare Improvement 2003; Bryk et al. 2015; Cincinnati Children's Hospital Medical Center n.d.). These improvement networks are made up of teams from different organizations and sometimes different sectors that have banded together around a commitment to a common aim.

At a high level, the phases of an improvement journey remain the same regardless of the size or structure of the improvement effort. Networks as much as teams have phases of understanding that transition to focusing and learning. The more people involved, the more contexts in play, the more time and coordination each phase will require. In addition to supporting the improvement journey of teams, leaders of large initiatives and networks also need to invest in the skills, infrastructure, and routines to manage, coordinate, and facilitate the efforts of multiple teams either within or across organizations. How they do this is the subject for another book.

Table I.1. Social Structures Using Improvement Science

Social Structure	Description
Improvement Team	Single team focused on improving its work practices.
Improvement Organization[5]	Multiple improvement teams within a single organization working in coordination to redesign the system to better meet the needs of its community.
Improvement Network	Multiple improvement teams from different organizations all focused on a common aim. Work of the teams often is coordinated by a central hub.

HOW TO READ THIS BOOK

The principal audience for this book is improvement teams and all of those who lead and support them. Teams are the common denominator in improvement efforts of all shapes and sizes. Teams are the building blocks of organizations that learn. Networks are made up of teams from different organizations. Investing in an improvement science approach means investing in team capability to solve problems. It means getting the right people, working on the right problems, and learning together.

This book is organized around the improvement journey, with parts for each phase. Chapter 1 addresses the foundations of an improvement science approach. An understanding of the theoretical underpinnings is important for improvers to adapt the key ideas and learning of the science of improvement effectively to new problems and contexts. If you read the book in order, you will experience the improvement journey as it typically unfolds. However, the individual parts and chapters are intentionally written to stand alone to guide the flexible application of the ideas. For example, if you find yourself needing to dig into how to spread a practice, jump to that part.

Make no mistake: for almost any organization or community, committing to an approach that puts collective learning at the center is a big shift from business as usual. It requires different relationships; the capacity for difficult conversations, new skills and mindsets; and a marked change in the rhythms of collaborative work. It's not about adding new tools to the current change strategy but, rather, fundamentally shifting how organizations go about making change.

1

Foundations

Every system is perfectly designed to deliver the results it produces.

—Central Law of Improvement (Langley et al. 2009, 79)

Consider an outcome we are all familiar with: turning on a hot-water tap, only to be confronted with a continual stream of cold water or worse yet, no water at all. How does this happen? The answer lies somewhere in the plumbing system, designed to make the magic of hot water possible by bringing the water from a source, running it through a water heater to a hot-water tap.

A *system* can be defined as a set of elements, organized around a common purpose[1] and interconnected in such a way that they produce their own pattern of behavior over time.[2] It is easy to see the design of the system as responsible for its outcomes when it comes to mechanical systems. We are also accustomed to recognizing the interdependent components of biological systems, which are notably more complex but still visible. Seeing systems becomes more difficult when we try to apply this concept to social systems. Social systems are also highly complex, and their components and interactions are less concrete and transparent. Take health care, for example. Numerous factors come together to affect the care people experience and their ultimate health outcomes: geography, income, beliefs, and cost; availability of medicines; access to nurses, physicians, pharmacists, and other caregivers; patients' age, gender, and ethnicity, as well as their trust in the health-care system itself. The list goes on.

Improvement science begins with the assertion that outcomes are the result of the design of the system. This seemingly simple assumption has a profound impact on how leaders, organizations, and teams pursue meaningful change. When faced with such complex interactions, many of which are hard to see and tease apart, most people default to reacting only to what is in front of them. For social systems, that often means responding to immediate events rather than examining fundamental causes that remain hidden in the complexity of the system. Another response is blaming people for producing unwanted outcomes (morbidity, mortality, and adverse events in health care, poor student achievement in education, etc.) instead of recognizing the ways in which the design of the system influences everyone's behaviors, even the behavior of those doing the blaming. In organizations, this missing the forest for the trees profoundly weakens our ability to create the outcomes we truly want.

This is not to deny that the visions for our systems are often grand, ambitious, and laudatory. The education system in the United States serves as an illustrative example. Although the purpose of education has evolved over time and remains contested terrain,[3] many would agree that Horace Mann's vision of schools as "the great equalizer" endures. However, even as we continue to uphold this vision, we also need to acknowledge the ways in which our education system falls short and the hard work that still lies ahead.

One of the inherent challenges that systems leaders face is that our social systems have been built over time and passed from generation to generation. The designs we observe today are an amalgamation of choices made in the past. Some actions, such as the common schools movement of the early 1800s led by Mann, the Brown versus Board of Education ruling in 1954, and the passage of the Elementary and Secondary Education Act (ESEA) in 1965, have moved us closer to our vision.

Other choices have been explicitly oppressive, leading directly to the disparities we currently experience. In 1779 Thomas Jefferson proposed a two-track educational system (for white, male children), with different tracks in his words for "the laboring and the learned." Scholarship would allow a very few of the laboring class to advance, Jefferson said, by "raking a few geniuses from the rubbish" (Mondale and Patton 2001). Prior to the Civil War, it was illegal in many states to educate enslaved people. After the war, black students in the South did not experience universal secondary schooling until 1968, more than one hundred years later. School segregation was strictly enforced for nearly ninety years, and de facto segregation occurs to this day (Fahle et al. 2020). Schools primarily attended by students of color have been and continue to be systematically under-resourced (Ladson-Billings 2006, 3; O'Day and Smith 2019). Within schools, students are tracked into different educational opportunities through a series of implicit practices and explicit policies (Oakes 2005; Diamond and Lewis 2015).

Some would also argue that widespread beliefs in meritocracy and education as the great equalizer help hold the blatantly inequitable systems in place. These belief systems are used perversely to justify inequality by attributing low performance to children and families— "parents just don't care," or "their families just don't value education," or "children need discipline and structure," or "these kids aren't motivated or don't have the right mindsets or the ability to succeed." Given this history, it is not surprising that today there is not a single school district in the United States where academic outcomes for black students are on equal footing with white students, or better (Reardon, Kalogrides, and Shores 2019), a reflection of design decisions baked into the system years ago that continue to manifest themselves today (Badger and Quealy 2017).

Thus, leaders who inherit these systems face the overwhelming task of excavation: unearthing the structures, practices, and beliefs that are producing our current outcomes so that they can be dismantled and redesigned to create healthier systems.

DEVELOPING A SYSTEMS LANGUAGE

In taking on this task of systems excavation, it can be helpful to have language to name and talk about the "set of elements" that come together to produce problematic outcomes.[4] The most tangible "layer" of the system includes the structures, policies, and organizational practices. In health care, these include, for example, the number of patient beds, pricing of treatments, operating equipment, hiring practices, staffing processes, and treatment protocols. Some of the practices, structures, and policies are specific to an organization (e.g., a hospital); others are shared by the larger industry or institution. They also range in size, from Medicare and Medicaid reimbursement policies to micro-practices such as how medications are stored. Policies and practices are the typical (and necessary) targets of reform when change is needed. But these efforts will be thwarted if leaders do not recognize how these practices are entwined with the other systems components that hold them in place.

A second layer of systems includes relationships and power dynamics among individuals. Social systems are made up of people, and how those people relate to one another impacts how decisions are made, who has access to information, and whose interests are considered. They influence both the historical and current policies and practices in any given place. In health care, power dynamics influence whether a nurse will speak up to a doctor when he or she spots a potential problem. These same power dynamics are at work when we consider who has access to the highest quality of care.

In the United States, for example, a person with a low income, no health-care insurance, little education, and who speaks English as a second language is very likely to experience a very different outcome from a person with a high income, top-tier insurance, high education, and who speaks English fluently. For the latter, these benefits afford them higher status and greater cultural capital, which gives them access to greater privilege and power within the system.

Finally, individual beliefs and mindsets are important components to understanding how systems produce what they do.[5] In education, biases frequently determine which students are suspended and expelled from schools (Skiba et al. 2016) as well as which students are referred into the tiered system of support known as special education (Skiba et al. 2008; Skiba et al. 2011). Beliefs about what students are capable of, what counts as learning, and how much parents care about their children's education shape the day-to-day practice in classrooms and schools. In a similar fashion, beliefs and mindsets influence pain management in our health-care systems with black patients being prescribed medications for pain management less often and in smaller doses because many physicians believe black people have a higher tolerance for pain compared with their white peers (Hoffman et al. 2016).

A systems approach requires recognizing the multitude of elements that come together to produce the unwanted outcome. Even from the relatively simple examples above, we can see the interdependencies between the different elements, and that optimization of one component does not necessarily lead to better overall system performance. Indeed, as Meadows notes, "A system is more than the sum of its parts" (Meadows 2008, 188). Many reform strategies myopically target one layer of the system while ignoring the others. For example, "implicit bias" training is often implemented with little attention to organizational or relational practices within the organization. In other instances, leaders attend to shifting policies and practices, ignoring how these practices fit or conflict with existing values, relationships, and beliefs.

The difficult balance in taking a systems approach is toggling between seeing the complexity inherent in all social systems and being able to take a step forward. It's the balance between seeing the forest and seeing the trees. Next, we will look at how systems thinking manifests in practice.

APPLYING THE SCIENCE OF IMPROVEMENT TO PRACTICE

Example: Cincinnati Children's Hospital and Medical Center

A passionate curiosity about shifting systems initially drew legendary improvement leader Dr. Uma Kotagal into improvement science. Dr. Kotagal became one of the key leaders responsible for transforming Cincinnati Children's Hospital into one of the very best and safest children's hospitals in the world (U.S. News and World Report 2023). Harnessing her seemingly relentless energy, she is a fierce, down-to-earth advocate for children. She began her career as a neonatologist, responsible for the care of newborn infants. When she joined Cincinnati Children's Hospital, it was known as a premier research center. This appealed to Dr. Kotagal, who sought to couple clinical practice with a research career. However, as she worked in the hospital, she found herself increasingly frustrated by the glaring gap between what was known in research and what was put into practice day to day. In her words:

> So if we know these things produce healthier children, then why don't we have a system in place to make sure we do it every time for every child? . . . For example, if we knew kids should get surfactant at four hours, why wouldn't they all get it at four hours? If we knew kids shouldn't get cold, why would they get cold anyway? It became really unbearable to know that there was this gap. Kids were getting hurt. (Kenney 2008)

As one of the early steps in Cincinnati Children's transformational journey, Dr. Kotagal and six of her colleagues pursued training in improvement science at Intermountain Healthcare. There, she found the missing piece of the puzzle she did not know she was looking for. In improvement science, learning how to put ideas into practice was treated with just as much rigor and discipline as the development of new clinical interventions through traditional research methods.

Over the next ten years, Dr. Kotagal and her colleagues would launch many improvement journeys: two that first year, ten more the second year, and many more in the years after. The first two projects launched during that initial course ended with impressive results: transforming care for children with cystic fibrosis[6] and reducing surgical site infections. This experience convinced Kotagal and her colleagues that investing in improvement capability and capacity[7] would enable the organization to transform the care they provided to children. "Being the best at getting better" was the succinct statement that board chair Lee Carter used to describe the organization's goal. Since that time the powerful combination of research excellence and improvement expertise has enabled Cincinnati Children's to provide some of the safest, high-quality care to children anywhere in the world.[8]

IMPROVEMENT KNOWLEDGE + SUBJECT MATTER KNOWLEDGE

Organizations often invest in what can be referred to broadly as "subject matter expertise." If an organization wants to provide exemplary care for cystic fibrosis, it needs research and professional expertise about the best treatment for cystic fibrosis along with patients' and families' lived experience of the disease. If better reading outcomes is the focus, then widespread knowledge of both the science and practice of reading development is critical. Subject matter knowledge deals with expertise in what is being improved. It pertains to the latest research on the topic and state-of-the-art practice by expert practitioners in partnership with users. When it comes to pursuing improvement in a particular outcome, this is predictably where leaders focus: more research, new programs, more training.

Subject matter knowledge is critical for improvement. At the same time, it is insufficient. Like Dr. Kotagal, most people who have tried to enact change know that what needs to happen is not the same as knowing how to get it to happen. This is particularly true in enacting change in complex social systems. We know quite a bit about how to teach kids to learn to read, for example, but less about how to build systems in which every child learns to read by the end of third grade. Along with subject matter knowledge, organizations need improvement knowledge—skills in how to take the "what" and put it into practice in a complex social system. In the words of Don Berwick, "The point is not just to know what makes things better or worse; it is to make things actually better" (Langley et al. 2009, xii).

The concept of improvement knowledge is a potentially game-changing development. Organizational leaders can be sure that whatever they are working to improve now, the focus and needs will change in the future. Typically, improvement is treated as an intention, not a skill. If teams and organizations can get really good at improving—that is, at enacting meaningful change—this is arguably one of the most valuable and durable skills that organizations can invest in. It is indispensable for leading in dynamic environments.

At the same time, here is the big idea: the intersection of improvement and subject matter knowledge is the sweet spot for transformative change (see figure 1.1). In the same way that good research knowledge about how children learn to read is not sufficient for developing systems in which every child learns to read, expert improvement knowledge will do little good for improving reading outcomes without reading expertise. We emphasize improvement expertise because it is the most frequently missing capability in most organizations. Ultimately, the power lies in the pairing of the two.

The main contribution of an improvement science approach is identifying the skills, capabilities, and capacities that fall under improvement knowledge so they can be purposefully developed. We turn next to describing these.

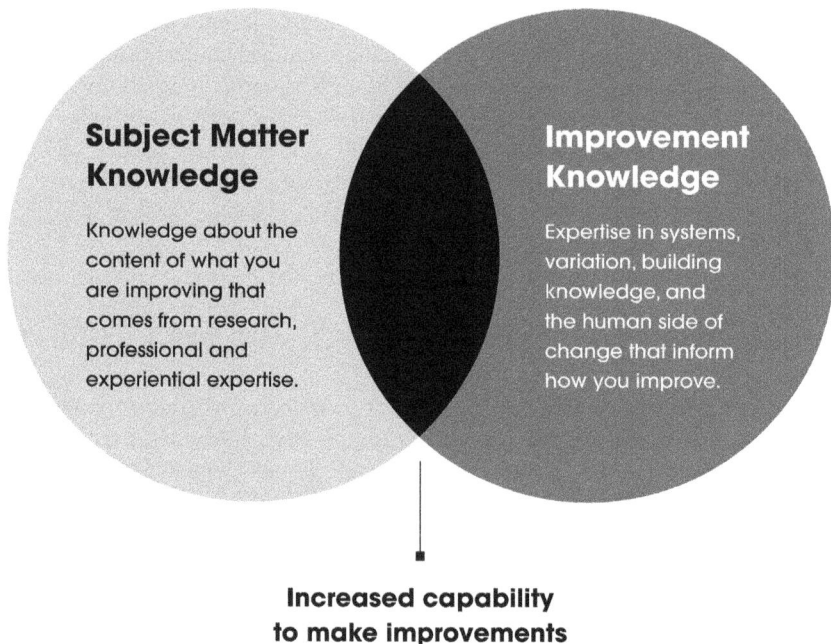

Subject Matter Knowledge

Knowledge about the content of what you are improving that comes from research, professional and experiential expertise.

Improvement Knowledge

Expertise in systems, variation, building knowledge, and the human side of change that inform how you improve.

Increased capability to make improvements

Figure 1.1.   Subject Matter and Improvement Knowledge
Source: Langley et al. 2009, 76

FOUR DOMAINS OF IMPROVEMENT KNOWLEDGE[9]

The circles in figure 1.2 describe the four domains of improvement knowledge. Starting at the top, the first domain is appreciation for a system, a fundamental capability that underlies all the rest. Leaders need to adopt a systems perspective as well as access to tools for seeing the components of their systems and how they interact to create the behaviors we all observe.

Connected to systems knowledge is the second domain of improvement knowledge: understanding variation. One of the most important windows into understanding the behavior of systems is data. Data comes in many forms, all of which can be used to describe the performance of the system. Data is also crucial to highlight the variation in what people experience as part of the system. Not every patient is healed in the same amount of time, let alone at all, even with the same diagnosis. Not every child succeeds in the same way academically. Variation exists. The questions we need to answer are for whom does it exist? Where in the system does it exist? Why does it exist? Is it intentional or unintentional? Answering these questions steers leaders to ideas about how to change their systems to achieve different outcomes.

People are a critical component of social systems. When we try to redesign the system, we are asking the people in the system to work and experience the system in different ways. This necessitates understanding the human side of change, a third type of improvement knowledge. Change can be jarring for some who might resist, refreshing and exciting for others who freely embrace it. Understanding what motivates people to work in a system, what assists in the

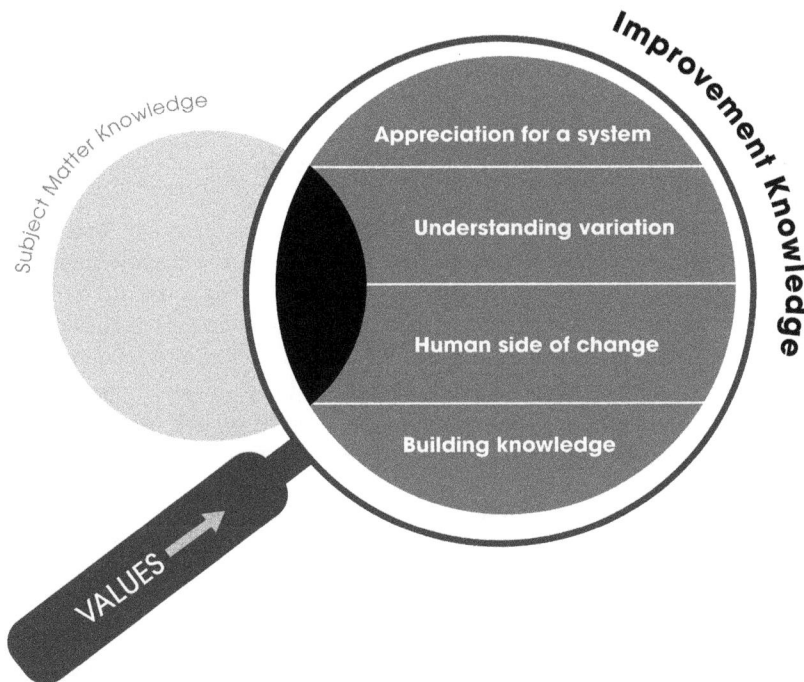

Figure 1.2. Four Domains of Improvement Knowledge[10]
Source: Langley et al. 2009, pg. 77

adoption of new practices and, more important, what gets in the way, is a big part of redesigning social systems. The fields of psychology, sociology, behavioral economics, and others have a great deal to teach us about how to engage people in changing their systems.

A final component of improvement knowledge is building knowledge. If we knew how to achieve better outcomes, we would have done it already. The truth is that we don't know how to heal everyone, we don't know how to educate everyone, we don't know how to achieve equity for everyone. Given this, we must learn what will work to produce better results. That means we need a way to learn in practice. Improvement practitioners frequently refer to this process as building a theory of knowledge. A philosophical term directly connected to Conceptual Pragmatism, a Theory of Knowledge[11] can be broken down into two components: 1) do we have a theory about what changes might work to achieve the outcomes we want and 2) do we have a method for learning if our theory produces results in practice? The answer to the second question is critical; without it, we don't have a disciplined way of trying things in real life and seeing if they yield the results we want.

The domains of improvement knowledge are often represented as a magnifying glass, as in figure 1.2, serving as a lens through which to see the system. Teams can use these domains to guide their work as well as determine why an improvement initiative is stalling. Does the team need to attend more to the human side of change, or tap into systems thinking, or understand variation, or build capability in collective learning? Or does it need better subject matter ideas?

As mentioned earlier, although most organizations contain at least some subject matter experts, most lack improvement knowledge and the expertise to apply it to their practices. As a result, if organizations want to achieve different results, they must invest in developing these capabilities within their organizations. Without it, organizations will struggle to redesign their systems in ways that create lasting change.

EQUITY AND VALUES

"Values" are located on the handle of the magnifying glass because they direct the concrete ways in which the four domains of improvement science are enacted when applied to a specific system or aim. They help organizations determine what constitutes a healthier system and which outcomes are worth pursuing. Improvement science is the science of how organizations redesign systems to produce better outcomes. But as a science, it is agnostic to what those outcomes might be. Corporate organizations can use improvement science to maximize profit as easily as social service organizations can use the science to improve outcomes for children and families. Values matter in defining the purpose of the system and which outcomes deserve attention.

For many social sector organizations, equity values drive the motivation to improve. It's worth pausing here to clearly define equity because we will come back to this word throughout the book.

> Equity is the state that would be achieved if how one fares in society no longer was predictable by race, ethnicity, linguistic background, economic class, religion, gender, sexual orientation, physical and cognitive ability, or any other sociopolitical identity marker.[12]

This definition articulates the vision and common purpose that we assume our social systems should seek to achieve. When looking at our current reality, however, we see a much different picture. Inequitable outcomes persist, reflecting the need for improvement or redesign of our systems.

It is important to note that inequity based on race is prevalent in the United States,[13] and at the same time, it is not the only type of inequity that exists. Inequities based on gender, class, language, disability, age, and other characteristics often come into play as well. People embody multiple identities, and the intersection of these identities influences the services and outcomes they experience from our systems.[14] For example, black LGBTQIA+ youth experience the child welfare system differently than black heterosexual youth or non-black LGBTQIA+ youth (Morton et al. 2018; Grooms 2020; Conron and Wilson 2019). Redesigning systems to be more equitable requires attending to the specific inequities in the local context targeted by the improvement work.

We have reason to be optimistic that improvement knowledge can be useful in disrupting inequities in the social sector.[15] Inequities are undoubtedly a system's problem, caused by a complex intertwining of policies, practices, relational dynamics, and pervasive beliefs. Data and stories can be useful for making the variation in experiences of different communities visible. Learning will undoubtedly be required. And the psychology of how people can come together to see, own, and discuss inequities is critical for the path forward.

At the same time, setting equitable systems as the destination also will require additional capacities. Systems of oppression play out in particular ways. The social psychology of dismantling inequities is not the same, for example, as the social psychology of improving timeliness of care. Each of the domains of improvement knowledge may be helpful, but understanding the unique nature of addressing long-standing social inequities will be required to apply them in useful ways.

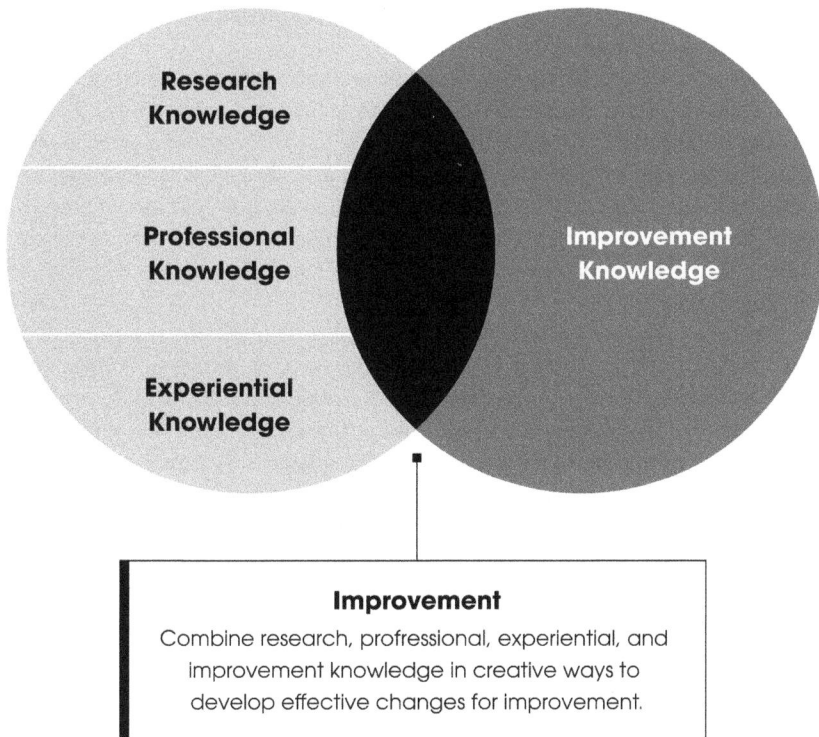

Research Knowledge

Professional Knowledge

Experiential Knowledge

Improvement Knowledge

Improvement
Combine research, profressional, experiential, and improvement knowledge in creative ways to develop effective changes for improvement.

Figure 1.3. Multiple Forms of Expertise[16]

One of the key shifts in an improvement science approach is broadening what is considered valuable expertise. Whereas traditionally in the social sector the word "expert" conjures up the image of a researcher or a surgeon or an organizational leader, improvement science has a broader conception of expertise that values knowledge of a context and experience in the day-to-day work. One indispensable kind of expertise is that of intended beneficiaries of the system, often referred to as the "end users." These people have important experiential knowledge of the systems that are the subject of transformation. Deeply understanding how students and families experience school and how patients experience care is essential for the improvement of these systems. Traditionally, experiential knowledge has been included underneath the umbrella of "subject matter knowledge" along with professional and research expertise. However, particularly when disrupting inequities is the focus of improvement, the authors find it useful to make the distinction between these kinds of expertise more explicit. Therefore, we often use figure 1.3 instead of figure 1.1 to describe the kinds of knowledge/expertise needed to consider for any given improvement aim.

FROM THEORY TO ACTION

> If you want to change how people think, give them a tool the use of which will lead them to think differently. —Buckminster Fuller, 1976

If the discussion about the foundations of improvement science seems conceptual so far, that is because we have been describing the underlying theory of improvement science. Figures 1.2 and 1.3, simple graphical representations of the foundational assumptions, can be used as a lens to guide improvement efforts.

What brings most people to improvement science is the pragmatic methods and practices that can be drawn upon to change the nature of systems in powerful ways. For the rest of this book, that is our focus. The main anchor we will use is the improvement journey (figure I.1); it takes the theory of improvement science and describes what it looks like in practice. At the same time, it is important to remember that methods and practices sit atop the theory, as a pragmatic way of enlivening a very different approach to change than is typical in most organizations. When methods become disconnected from the theory, they can lose their transformational power.

Ideally, there is a productive interplay among the theory, methods, and practice (see figure 1.4). Methods and tools are created to facilitate the ways of thinking, acting, and relating implied by the theory. With the right kinds of learning opportunities, these methods and tools can support the development of a new kind of practice in teams and organizations. The practice, in turn, informs the theory. Studying what happens as teams apply the science of improvement produces new learning to evolve the theory of improvement.

Numerous improvement methodologies have been developed over the past decades. Although there are aspects of different methodologies that arguably make them better suited to certain kinds of problems and contexts, overall, they are more similar than different.[17] What's most important is that an organization, network, or team has a common methodology for collective learning. The systems we are trying to improve are complex enough. Trying to make sense of what different teams are learning across different problem-solving approaches unnecessarily complicates an improvement effort.

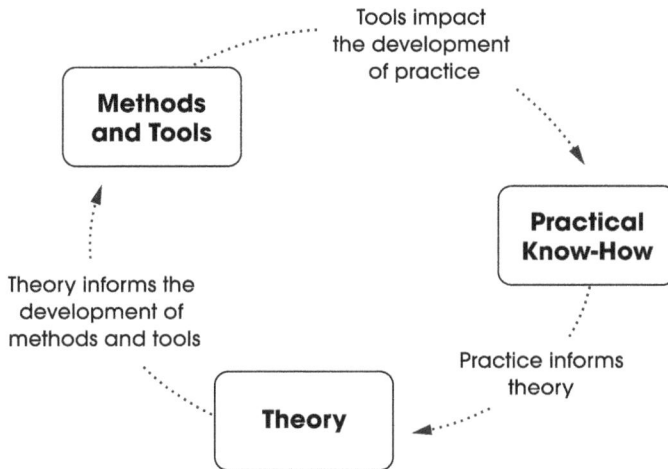

Figure 1.4. Interplay among Improvement Theory, Methods, and Practice

In this book, we build on a specific methodological approach first presented in *The Improvement Guide* (Langley et al. 2009). The methodologies it puts forth have been widely used in the social sector and beyond. They have been instrumental in the improvement revolution in health care and the more recent interest in improvement science in education. They are flexible and general enough to guide the pursuit of wide ranges of outcomes, and they are the ones in which the authors have the most expertise. The improvement journey map that we offer explicitly builds on these methods. Because these tactical methods build on the theories already discussed we next provide a brief overview of them.

THE MODEL FOR IMPROVEMENT

The Improvement Guide was first published in 1996, based on twenty years' experience supporting organizations to improve outcomes in agriculture, manufacturing, and health-care industries using the system of profound knowledge outlined in figure 1.2. The main contribution of the guide was an eloquently simple improvement methodology they called the Model for Improvement (see figure 1.5), which has since been used to make progress on problems big and small across multiple sectors.[18]

In motivating the need for the Model for Improvement, the authors put forth the all-too-true observation: "All improvement requires change, but not all change is an improvement" (Langley et al. 2009). They offer the Model for Improvement as a way of pursuing outcomes, sorting out the changes that are an improvement from those that are not.

The Model for Improvement begins with three questions:

1. What are *we* trying to accomplish?
2. How will *we* know that a change is an improvement?
3. What changes can *we* make that will result in an improvement?

What are **we** trying to accomplish?

How will **we** know that a
change is an improvement?

What changes can **we** make
that will result in improvement?

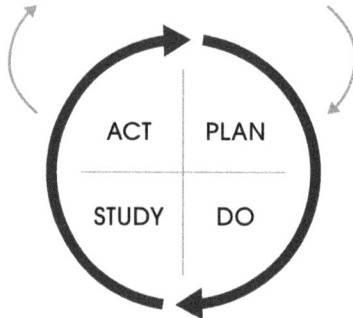

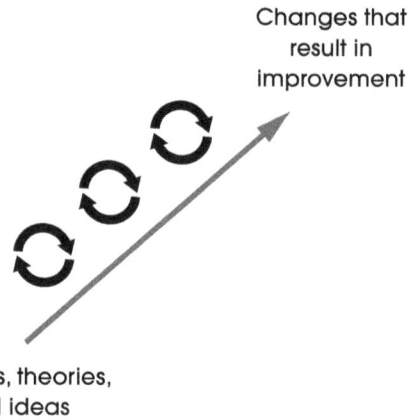

ACT | PLAN

STUDY | DO

Changes that
result in
improvement

Hunches, theories,
and ideas

Figure 1.5.   Model for Improvement[19]
Source: Langley et al. 2009, p. 24

Seemingly simple, these three questions provide an important disciplining function for improvement efforts. As teams and groups come together, answering these questions, they develop a common aim, common measures, and a common theory of improvement (see chapters 7, 10, and 12 for more on these topics).

Paired with the three questions is a Plan-Do-Study-Act cycle (PDSA cycle) to structure learning in practice. Systems are dynamic. It is much easier to learn which changes work and which do not by trying them rather than by sitting around and talking. The PDSA cycle structures the introduction of change as an experiment. Teams PLAN the change they intend to introduce, DO the change, STUDY the results, and based on their learning decide what to do next (ACT).

The final part of the Model for Improvement is a "PDSA ramp." In short, the PDSA ramp suggests trying new ideas on a small scale first and scaling up only those ideas that show promise. In the early stages, teams use PDSA cycles to sort out which change ideas work and which ones do not. Once promising ideas are discovered, the scale of the test is expanded, and the learning turns to how to get changes to work across contexts. Eventually, PDSAs are used to learn how to embed new practices into organizational routines so that results are sustained. This way of introducing change sits in stark contrast to ways many organizations "try out" new ideas. They think of it, buy it, or plan it, and then roll it out, everywhere, all at once.

IMPROVEMENT JOURNEYS

The beauty of the Model for Improvement is its simplicity and accessibility. Anyone anywhere can start asking the three questions and lean into iterative learning.[20] People with very different roles and in different contexts can use it to improve their own work. And you can go

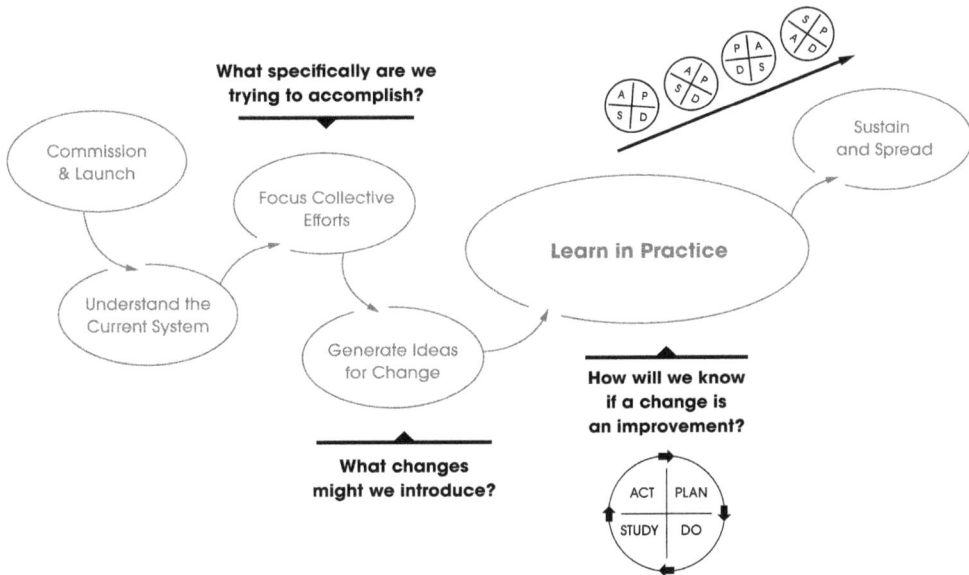

Figure 1.6. Mapping the Model for Improvement onto the Improvement Journey

to a conference in a completely different sector and have a window into what they are doing because you recognize the problem-solving methodology.

Of course, as soon as you start to try to improve something, even simple frameworks prove to be more complex. Improvement is fundamentally a social endeavor; it's a team sport. And although the Model for Improvement provides the technical backbone, it can be difficult to imagine what it looks like to bring a team together to improve something.

The improvement journey map intends to fill that gap. In it, we outline the typical phases that teams go through as they use improvement science methodologies to reach their improvement aim. The journey map explicitly builds on the Model for Improvement (see figure 1.6).[21] We add a beginning step "commission and launch" to draw attention to the work that needs to be done (often by leaders) to bring people together and support the development of high-functioning teams that can learn together. We also add a second step to emphasize a need to come to a deeper understanding of the current system before rushing into changing it.[22] For effective change, particularly in reengineering systems so that they work for a much broader community than those for whom they were originally designed, coming to better shared understandings of how those systems work is critical.

CHANGING PRACTICE

In the introduction we defined improvement science as "an evolving field of study focused on the theories, methods, and practices that facilitate or hinder organizational efforts to continuously improve performance." In this chapter we foregrounded the "theory" to set up the discussion of "how to" that will occupy the rest of the book.

Things go awry when the theory-method-and-practice become disconnected. Tools and methods are seductive in nature; they will always be the most visible and easily spreadable aspect of an improvement science approach. Indeed, for many of us who have spent the better part of our careers trying to improve, the idea that there are methods to guide improvement—ones that have succeeded in getting results—is an exciting discovery. However, new methods do not magically translate to skilled practice. And when methods become untethered from their foundations, they can easily reify old ways of working instead of supporting new ones.

Example: Math Instruction—When Theory, Method, and Practice Become Disconnected

As an example of how this happens, consider attempts to shift math instruction in education.[23] In the 1980s, math experts started describing a new vision for what new math learning should look like. In short, they described classrooms where students were actively engaged in problem solving and making sense of math, instead of memorizing math facts and completing drill-based worksheets. Compelling rationales and research about this form of math learning were produced. Curriculum designers created curriculum and instructional materials intended to enliven these kinds of classrooms. Districts bought up these new tools and methods, implemented them, and expected great results.

Yet, more often than not, these new tools and materials produced very little change in instructional practice. You could walk into classrooms where these new materials were being implemented and see nothing particularly new. Rich mathematical tasks intended to engage students in problem solving were turned into problems that teachers worked out at the front of the room as students watched and tried to copy. Well-intentioned, skilled teachers inadvertently adapted the materials to teach the way they always had. Changing practice—of all kinds—requires more than new theories and the addition of new tools.

The same is and will be true about improvement science. Improvement science involves changing organizational practice—namely, the practice of how organizations go about change. Underneath improvement science is a powerful theory, and along with it come pragmatic methods and tools. But whether those methods will produce better outcomes depends on what happens in practice.

CONCLUSION

We view improvement science as a powerful way to reengineer social systems to produce better outcomes. Combined with lived experience, subject matter, and professional knowledge, improvement knowledge (appreciation of the system, an understanding of variation, the human side of change, and building knowledge) provides us with a robust theory for how to enact change. Theory is brought to life through teams applying methods and tools to structure collective learning. In this book we will use the Model for Improvement as the main improvement method. We describe the phases of an improvement journey for teams to use as a road map as they apply the method in practice. The rest of this book is devoted to the journey; each part explores and describes a phase, offering pragmatic guidance to practitioners and highlighting important moments to consider as teams learn their way into better outcomes. So, let's get started and get to the learning.

I

WHO'S AT THE TABLE?

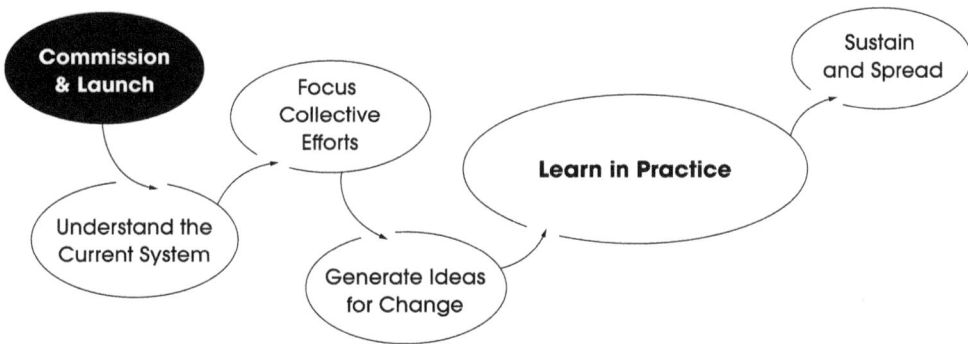

An improvement journey begins when the leaders of an organization officially commission a team to investigate and address an area aligned with its strategic priorities. In addition to identifying a focus for the improvement work, commissioning entails selecting and recruiting members to the team and providing them with the time, resources, and support they need to go on the journey. Once a team is recruited, then the process of team formation begins. Working as a high-performing improvement team takes time; establishing a strong foundation in a few key capabilities early on will serve the team well as they continue to move through the journey.

Leaders play a critical and important role in this phase of the journey. From an operational standpoint, they are responsible for determining the focus and scope of the improvement effort, keeping in mind the organization's strategic priorities, commitment to equity, and available resources. In addition, it is helpful for leaders to anticipate the type of improvement project needed given the circumstances. Some projects focus on design, creating a new process or subsystem that does not currently exist. Others imply a redesign of current processes to produce better results. A third type is organized around spreading practices from one part of the organization to another. These factors combined will influence the time frame and number of improvement teams needed for the effort as well as how much time teams will need to spend in different phases of the journey moving forward (see chapter 16).

From a cultural and equity standpoint, leaders are responsible for modeling the key principles and behaviors that exemplify the improvement science approach when commissioning and launching a team.[1] This is especially true when leaders decide who and how to invite people to the table. Leaders cannot mandate who is on the team and what they do. That top-down approach simply signals business as usual and reflects a power dynamic that runs counter to an improvement approach. Leaders must also recognize the power dynamics at play when engaging people who have been historically marginalized and excluded from the table. Leaders must share decision-making authority with everyone on the team, admitting that they do not have all the answers and recognizing the knowledge others bring to the table. They also need to create environments where team members feel safe sharing different opinions and trying ideas that might fail.

Although we highlight the role of the leader in this part of the book, we begin first in chapter 2 by articulating the characteristics of an improvement team, distinguishing it from other types of teams. We also describe the different team roles.

Chapter 3 focuses specifically on the role of leaders in setting the conditions necessary for improvement teams to thrive. We begin by articulating the characteristics of successful improvement projects to give leaders a picture of what they're striving for. Next, we offer guidance on how to select a focus area and team structure as well as information about the resources needed to support the team. We close the chapter with advice for leaders on how to invite people to the table and set it in a way that reflects the characteristics of a "lead learner": authentic vulnerability and curiosity, the ability to recognize the knowledge and expertise of everyone at the table, and a willingness to share decision-making authority with the team.

In chapter 4, we turn to team formation. Here we introduce the group capacities teams need to develop. First is building a shared sense of trust and purpose. Second is the ability to have meaningful, sometimes difficult conversations that come with collective learning, especially around topics related to equity. Finally, teams need to establish and maintain a set of routines and a cadence of learning that keeps the team's momentum going during the journey.

Getting teams off to a strong start is the primary goal of the commission and launch phase. If leaders act as gracious, welcoming hosts and invite and set the table well, then teams will have the confidence, support, and resources they need to make the most of the journey ahead.

2

Improvement Teams

> Complexity requires group success.
>
> —Atul Gawande, 2012

For many, the initial appeal of improvement science is the pragmatic methods and tools that help structure organizational change efforts. But methods don't produce change; people do. The transformative power of improvement science is its ability to support collective learning—to help teams broaden how they see the world, to integrate diverse voices, to surface and test tacit assumptions, to come to new shared understandings, and ultimately, to change systems for the better.

Although collective learning has a nice ring to it, instances of it are quite rare. Particularly in the United States, values of rugged individualism and images of lone heroes translate into organizational governance structures that rely on and reward individual contributions, not group success. In some organizations, this plays out as top-down leadership where leaders (or researchers, or coaches) are the knowers who tell the front line what to do. On the flip side, many organizations, especially the social sector, are governed by norms of professional autonomy. Professionals—whether social workers, doctors, or teachers—know best and have ultimate decision-making authority.[1] What these opposing approaches have in common is that they depend on individuals and individual knowledge as the path forward.

In contrast, given improvement science's roots in systems thinking, teams, not individuals, are the basic building blocks of organizational change.[2] People need to come together across typical boundaries of identity, role group, department, organizational position, or geography. Organizations need to shift who's at the table and whose voice is heard. With systems thinking comes the humility that no matter where a person sits, no one individual can "see the system" or understand its complexity, much less redesign the system to produce different outcomes.

Getting the right people to the table is one thing; learning together is quite another. Research on team learning has repeatedly demonstrated that collective insight is not simply the sum of individual insights; rather, thriving teams develop group capacities that enable the collective to be wiser than the sum of its parts (Katzenback and Smith 1993; Edmondson 2012). Part of what enables teams to thrive is personal: individual members need to show up as learners with humility, transparency, and curiosity, ready to roll up their sleeves and dig in. Another part is relational: people need to trust one another to offer their perspectives, explore those of others, and face what may not be working. And the final part of collective learning is technical: teams need routines and ways of working together that structure productive collaborations, turning intentions into collective actions. Thus, creating spaces where people can relate to and work with each other in new ways requires as much if not more attention as the introduction of new improvement methods and tools.

WHAT IS AN IMPROVEMENT TEAM?

There is no shortage of research and advice on effective collaboration in organizations. Much of this is motivated by the fact that although teaming is common in organizations, examples of high-functioning teams are quite rare (Edmondson 2012).[3]

For our work, we draw on Katzenbach and Smith's definition of a team in *The Wisdom of Teams* (1993, 41): "A team is a small number of people with complementary skills who are committed to a common purpose, performance goals, and approach for which they hold themselves mutually accountable." Katzenbach and Smith provide a useful classification system that differentiates their definition of a "real or high-performing" team from other ways small groups work together in organizations (see Table 2.1).

Reviewing this classification, it becomes clear that most group experiences do not count as "real" teams. For example, grade-level or department teams in schools usually come together to share ideas or complete managerial tasks but rarely to work toward a clearly defined goal for which they hold themselves mutually accountable.

The nature of work requires improvement teams to be at a minimum "real teams." Teams form around a commitment to a common and specific "purpose" or aim for which they hold themselves accountable (for more on aims, see chapter 7); the improvement methods and practices serve as the common "working approach" that helps the team learn their way into improvement.[4] Given this, it is important that leaders establish the organizational conditions necessary for real teams to form (see chapter 3).

Table 2.1. Differentiating Groups and Teams

Working Group	Pseudo Team	Potential Team	Real Team	High-Performing Team
Regularly interact to share information of perspectives, but its work remains individual	Has an opportunity to work collectively, but it has not focused and committed to collective performance	Is trying to improve its collective performance, but it lacks clarity about the purpose, goals, or common approach	Is equally committed to a common purpose, goals, and working approach for which they hold themselves mutually accountable	Outperforms expectations. Meets the conditions of real teams and has team members who are also deeply committed to one another's personal growth and success.

Source: Katzenbach and Smith 1993, 89.[5]

WHO'S ON THE TEAM?

Like other kinds of high-functioning teams, improvement teams work best if they stay relatively small, usually 4–6 persons.[6] This makes it easier for the team to develop a sense of mutual accountability, engage in meaningful dialogue, meet regularly, and move nimbly. The small size sits in tension with the kinds of expertise that improvement teams need to access to inform their work. To manage this tension, it is often useful to distinguish people who are on the improvement team from key supporting roles and additional resources.[7] A simple rule of thumb is that if you are on the team, you attend all the weekly or biweekly team meetings. Key supporting roles and additional supports, in contrast, come in and out of team meetings as needed, usually less frequently.

Table 2.2 displays the typical roles and responsibilities of improvement team members and key supporting roles. The improvement team takes the lead role in examining core work processes and testing changes to see if they lead to an improvement. As a result, there is usually a close connection between who's on the team and the focus of improvement. For example, if the improvement work is focused on improving ninth-grade math performance, ninth-grade math teachers will make up the heart of the team. They are, after all, the best situated to test new practices and discover improvements in processes and norms in their classrooms. For practical purposes, improvement teams should designate one member as the team lead. He or she is the point person for the team, organizes team meetings, and is the liaison with others supporting the team.[8] Usually the team lead is trained in improvement methods, facilitates many of the improvement activities, and sets the tone for the work.

People in key support roles establish the conditions and provide the resources necessary for the team to succeed. The sponsor is usually a formal organizational leader with the authority to create the space for the team to do the work. The sponsor does not attend all team meetings but checks in with the team or team lead at least once a month to stay connected to the work. The improvement coach supports the work of the team, especially the team lead, helping guide the team through the improvement journey and further building their improvement skills.

The team may also draw on additional resources as appropriate. These include content experts with research and professional knowledge about the area of focus, additional testers to try out different change ideas in their contexts, or a data analyst to help create measures, data collection instruments, and data visualizations. Table 2.3 provides examples of two different improvement teams.

The most critical but often overlooked voice needed in the work is that of the users—the individuals the improvement work is intended to benefit. The team needs to draw continually on the perspectives and experiences of those in the community to ensure that the work meets their needs. This could mean students and families, if working to improve educational outcomes; patients, if working to improve health outcomes; or community leaders and members, when focused on population-based outcomes. For improvement work to create more equitable systems, it must be done *with*—not to—the communities they are intended to serve. As an added benefit, evidence from the field of health care suggests that improvement teams incorporating users are 2.78 times more likely to achieve their aim than those that do not (Kostal and Shah 2021, 5).

So, having a user on the improvement team is ideal; however, if this is not possible, it is essential that the team find ways to connect with users at every phase of the journey and integrate their voice and perspective. Although changing complex systems requires the ideas and perspectives of a variety of stakeholders, the voice of the user must stay front and center. How are

Table 2.2.   Improvement Team Roles

		Description	Key Activities
Improvement Team	**Team Lead**	Point person for the team. Manages the team and communicates with key stakeholders.	• Organizes and facilitates team meetings. • Communicates regularly with improvement coach and team sponsor.
	Team Members	Individuals responsible for day-to-day work of the team.	• Meet weekly or biweekly. • Test changes. • Collect and reflect on data. • Consolidate and share learning.
Key Supports	**Sponsor**	Formal organizational leader who serves as a local champion for the improvement team.	• Authorizes the work of the team. • Protects time and space. • Removes barriers. • Helps spread learning to the rest of the organization.
	Improvement Coach	Experienced improver who supports the team in flexibly using improvement methods to guide learning. In some cases, may double as team lead or serve as team lead at the start of improvement work.	• Helps launch improvement team and create initial charter. • Guides team through journey; provides coaching and feedback. • Builds team's improvement skills.
Additional Resources	**Lead User(s)**	Individuals directly impacted by the area of focus (e.g., patients, students) who provide the team with regular feedback. If possible, having a lead user on the team is ideal.	• Develops or reacts to change ideas. • Shares perspectives and experiences. • Engages other users to capture their perspective.
	Content Expert(s)	Individual who provides research and/or professional knowledge to the team.	• Provides access to resources about areas of focus; shares evidence-based practices. • Develops or reacts to change ideas. • Helps team make sense of what is being learned.
	Tester(s)	Additional individuals outside the team who test changes in varied contexts.	• Tests changes, collects data, reports on learning.
	Data Analyst	Provides additional data support as necessary.	• Helps identify and/or develop measures and data collection instruments. • Produces or supports team in producing data visualizations.

Table 2.3. Examples of Improvement Teams

	TEAM 1 *Improving Quality of IEP (Individual Education Plan)[9] Goals In a School District*	**TEAM 2** *Improving Surgical Safety*
Team Lead	• District special education program specialist	• Attending physician/department head
Team Members	• Principal • School psychologist • Elementary special education teacher • Guardian of child receiving special education services	• Fellow • Chief resident • Anesthesiologist • Surgical nurse • Patient
Sponsor	• Director of district special education department	• Chief of surgery
Improvement Coach	• Improvement coach	• Improvement coach
Additional Resources	• *Testers*: 2–3 elementary special education teachers • *Data analyst*	• *Testers*: 2–3 surgeons depending on specialization • *Data analyst*

users involved in choosing organizational priorities more generally and improvement priorities specifically? How are users involved in efforts to understand the system and set a direction for the work? How are users involved in identifying changes to the system and, most important, deciding whether they are working? In the absence of an intention and explicit strategy, the users' voice is the one that improvement teams are most likely to leave out.

HOW ARE TEAMS INITIATED?

Improvement teams are initiated in a variety of ways. No matter how teams form, ideally, they focus on goals that benefit their own work as well as address the larger priorities of the organization. Below are two typical ways improvement teams are initiated.

Teams seeking to use an improvement approach to solve a problem in their immediate context. The team selects a focal area based on their priorities, values, and what is in the locus of their control. Here, the challenge for the team is to find a formal organizational leader to serve as the sponsor who can advocate for the work, provide the necessary resources, and connect it to the organization's strategic priorities. For example, a team of special education teachers was frustrated by the variation in quality of individual educational plans (IEPs) for special education students. They brought this issue to the attention of their principal and the special education director, who created time and space for them to engage in improvement work.

Formal organizational leaders (department heads, directors, senior leaders) wanting to enlist improvement teams to make progress on clearly defined organizational problems or goals. Here, the organizational leaders identify the focal area and invite appropriate individuals to join the team. For example, a hospital facing a high rate of surgical site infections may recruit or assign the chief of surgery to form a team and lead an initiative to bring down infection rates.

In the second scenario, one key challenge that leaders—especially senior leaders—face is taking a larger organizational goal and identifying a more appropriately scoped, high-leverage starting place from which progress can be made. To do this, leaders often convene a larger team of diverse stakeholders from the organization and engage in the "understanding the system" phase of the improvement journey (see part 2). This allows the organization to develop a clearer picture of the current system and illuminate key leverage points from which to start the organization's improvement work. From here, an appropriate team is recruited.

For example, to improve high-school graduation rates, the district senior leadership cabinet might bring together principals, counselors, teachers, parents, students, and representatives from college access programs in the community to "understand the system" (see chapters 5 and 6). After examining the data, conducting empathy interviews with students and families, and mapping out key student supports, the group may decide to target counseling services on campus. From there, the senior leadership cabinet decides to begin with an improvement team at one high school to focus on counseling services. This eventually may lead to a portfolio of improvement projects run by various teams, all focused on different areas related to graduation rates.

It is important to note that handing off the work from one team to another is tricky. As in the example above, shifts in teams happen most often between the "understanding the system" and "focus collective efforts" phases. As leverage points key to changing the system are discovered, the original team configuration may no longer be appropriate. When the "understanding the system" team identifies counseling services as a high-leverage area to target, then it must hand off the work to a team that includes a principal, counselors, students, and families at the site level, because they have the closest connection to the work processes that are the target of improvement.

Although a handoff or shift in teams most often happens early in the improvement journey, it can occur at any point in the work when what's learned or discovered necessitates a change in team membership. For example, as the high-school improvement team learns what works, then the senior leadership cabinet will likely need to initiate additional teams to help spread those practices to other high schools in the district. Anticipating and attending to potential shifts or launching additional teams is an important job for leaders of an organization.

CONCLUSION

For improvement work to succeed, groups of individuals need to become real or high-functioning teams focused on a common purpose, have a mutual sense of accountability, and use a shared approach. Identifying the right constellation of people with complementary expertise and experiences is also critical. Bringing these teams into existence falls on the shoulders of the leaders of the organization. In the next chapter, we discuss the organizational conditions leaders must establish to successfully launch an improvement team.

3

Leadership

Setting Up Teams for Success

> Transforming a system is really about transforming the relationships between people who make up the system.
>
> —Kania, Kramer, and Senge, 2018, 7

Although establishing specific criteria for effective teaming as well as clear team roles and responsibilities is important, successful improvement teams don't just come into their own. They require leaders who create the organizational conditions necessary for them to learn and improve; this includes choosing an appropriate focus area and team structure, providing ample time and resources, and offering access to the data they need. We refer to this as commissioning.

Equally important are the relational moves that leaders make as they initiate the work. They must invite team members to the table in a way that sets the tone and culture for the work moving forward. This means taking a learning stance: engaging in early conversations with the team with a sense of curiosity and recognition of the knowledge and experience each team member brings to the table, as well as letting the team own the work, connecting it to their priorities and values, and allowing them to make decisions that drive the work forward.

SUCCESSFUL IMPROVEMENT PROJECTS

Many of the decisions made in the commissioning phase will have implications for the project's success. Table 3.1 describes the characteristics of successful improvement projects.

Table 3.1. Characteristics of Successful Improvement Projects

1. Aligned to organizational priorities.
2. Collectively owned by the team.
3. Appropriately scoped.
4. Within the locus of control of the team.
5. Availability of data.
6. Protected time for weekly team meetings.

These characteristics highlight areas where teams typically struggle. Improvement rarely takes root when the focus is mandated, disconnected from organizational priorities, or mismatched with the resources at hand. Collective learning predictably stagnates when teams do not have access to data to track their progress or protected time for weekly team meetings. By attending to these characteristics up front—in how they choose a focus area, allocate resources, and invite teams into the work—leaders can take steps to establish the conditions for team success.

CHOOSING A FOCUS AREA AND TEAM STRUCTURE

One of the most important decisions a leader must make is determining the focus and scope of an improvement effort. First, it should reflect the organization's values and strategic priorities. For example, organizations driven by a commitment to equity should target their efforts on addressing pernicious equity gaps and meeting the needs of those the system currently doesn't serve. Second, the scope of the work should be matched with the appropriate resources. Improvement work is not free; it requires a substantial investment of time and attention. When leaders find themselves in a place where their improvement aspirations outweigh current resources available, their role is to find a useful, appropriately scoped starting point.

Figure 3.1 displays a continuum of educational improvement projects that range from less complex, more contained projects on the left-hand side, to more complex, longer-term projects on the right. What makes improvement priorities on the far left less complex is that they usually involve a single process and a single team; and improvement is more likely to be achieved within a short period of time, such as a single semester or calendar year. As you move to the right, the improvement priorities imply changes in multiple processes and require the coordination of more teams working across typical organizational boundaries. This entails the investment of more resources usually over a longer period, often multiple years.

Many, if not most of the aspirations that motivate organizations to invest in improvement will fall on the right-hand side of the complexity scale. The outcomes articulated in the organization's mission or strategic priorities, for example, tend to be more complex. Leaders usually pursue one of two common paths for more complex initiatives. One is launching or joining a collaborative or network in which multiple improvement teams work together on redesigning a significant part of the system.[1] Not surprisingly, this path requires a significant amount of time and resources. Alternatively, leaders can invest strategically in a cascading sequence of improvement projects that start by targeting one high-leverage area or process tied to a larger outcome and then moving onto another. For example, a team in Shasta County, California, began their journey to improve early-grade literacy by focusing on improving formative assessment with a handful of first-grade teams. They then moved to focusing on small-group

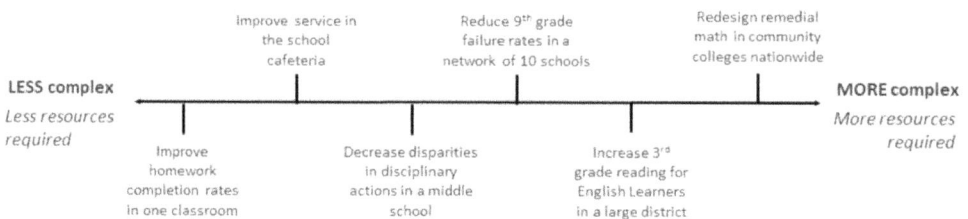

Figure 3.1. Complexity of Improvement Initiatives in Educational Settings

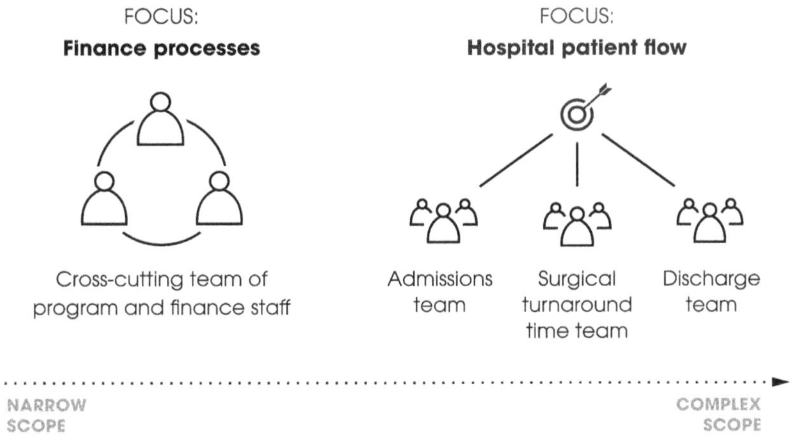

FOCUS:
Finance processes

FOCUS:
Hospital patient flow

Cross-cutting team of
program and finance staff

Admissions
team

Surgical
turnaround
time team

Discharge
team

NARROW
SCOPE

COMPLEX
SCOPE

Figure 3.2.   Examples of Teaming Structures

instruction followed by other literacy practices (for more on how Shasta County arrived at this starting point, see chapter 5).

Another choice leaders might make is to scope down their work by focusing on improving an outcome in one locality with a single improvement team (e.g., a grade level in one school or a single hospital department or ward/floor) and then spreading those learnings more broadly. For example, one high-school improvement team in a charter network in San Diego reduced chronic absenteeism rates in their school and then spread their learning to other schools in their network (Bryk et al. 2020).

Where leaders decide to start will shape how many improvement teams are needed and how their work is organized. More narrowly scoped projects might only require one team whereas larger initiatives will require coordinated action among multiple teams. For example, a small nonprofit organization seeking to improve a finance process will likely only need one improvement team with members from both the program and finance staff. On the other hand, a hospital trying to reduce the average length of stay for patients may launch several improvement teams focused on different aspects of patient flow in and out of the hospital. This may include one team working on reducing time to admission, another working on reducing turnaround time between surgeries for operating rooms, and a third focused on reducing variation in time of discharge (see figure 3.2). With more complex initiatives with multiple teams, it is important that leaders design and support a social structure that both enables individual team learning to thrive and provides intentionally designed spaces for learning to travel across improvement teams.

RESOURCING IMPROVEMENT

One of the most important responsibilities of organizational leaders is to allocate the appropriate resources for teams to engage in improvement work. In most organizations, 100 percent of resources are currently allocated to running or maintaining the system as it is. Leaders will have to strike a balance between running the current system and improving it. Deciding what percentage of resources to allocate to running the system versus improving it is a key decision (e.g., 90/10 split).

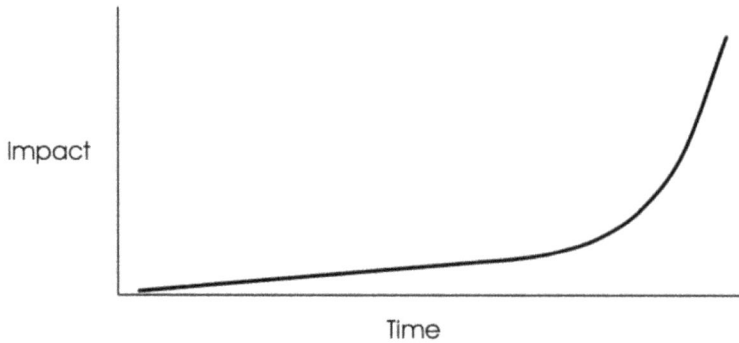

Figure 3.3. The Curve of Improvement

THE LONG GAME

One aspect of resourcing improvement is committing to focusing on a project or initiative for a reasonable amount of time. Sustained systems-based improvement on large organizational outcomes, such as improving safety for an entire hospital system, result from multiyear efforts (Tucker and Edmondson 2009, 1–23). Political pressures and a felt sense of urgency often push leaders to demand improvements in unrealistically short time frames. Expecting quick results, however, promotes investment in Band-Aid fixes and silver-bullet thinking that thwarts real systems change.[2]

Nowhere is balancing expectations with improvement more difficult than at the beginning of the journey, when teams are focused on understanding the current system or testing changes on a small scale. Until people experience how these early activities can result in significant, meaningful systems change, the tension between seemingly small actions and the magnitude of the problem is difficult to manage. The learning curve that characterizes typical improvement work is displayed in figure 3.3. Investments in systems investigations and small-scale testing lead to accelerated progress, approximating an exponential curve of impact. Keeping this curve in mind can help leaders invest the necessary resources up front, knowing that the payoff will come if they are willing to play the long game.

PROTECTING TIME AND SPACE FOR TEAMS

In addition to setting realistic time horizons for achieving outcomes, organizational leaders need to protect time and space for teams to engage in the work. Teams should generally meet weekly or biweekly and engage in activities in between, such as running plan-do-study-act (PDSA) cycles, collecting data, and identifying or developing change ideas. The make or break for many teams is their ability to establish a consistent, productive learning rhythm, which is often linked to the time and space provided by leadership. (For more on team-based improvement routines, see chapter 4).

It is important for leaders to remember that improvement isn't free. Two of the most straightforward strategies to create the necessary space for improvement are to take something off people's plates and/or repurpose existing time for improvement work. For example, social sector executive teams might allow repurposing a standing weekly check-in or huddle into an improvement team meeting—a common practice in health-care settings. For school teams, team leads can be given an extra prep period, teacher collaboration time can be repurposed for improvement meetings, or leaders can give teachers the choice to opt out of other district initiatives that take time. Generally, improvement team members need 1–2 hours per week for the improvement work; team leads should have 0.25–0.5 FTE. Allocating the necessary time allows teams to establish and maintain momentum for the improvement journey and communicates its importance to the organization.

Example: 20,000 Days Campaign—Resourcing Improvement

One example that highlights the importance of resource investment comes from a project in New Zealand. In 2011, the Counties Manukau District Health Board (CMDHB) launched an initiative to reduce the number of in-patient hospital days. This work was led by Ko Awatea, an internal improvement organization tasked with the continuous improvement of outcomes by the system. The community's health demands were outpacing the hospital system's capacity. It was estimated that CMDHB needed to reduce the number of in-patient hospital days by twenty thousand per year to meet the needs of their growing community.

Ko Awatea launched a two-year improvement initiative—the 20,000 Days Campaign—that engaged eighteen teams to take on an improvement project in their area, all focused on the initiative's goal of reducing in-person hospital days. Some of the teams were from inside the hospital, focused on reducing the length of stay in the hospital without compromising health outcomes. Other improvement teams worked in the primary care setting or community health environment and focused on preventing avoidable admissions to the hospital (Middleton, Dowdle, et al. 2019; Middleton, Mason, et al. 2014).

Teams applied to be part of the initiative. Ko Awatea provided each team with NZ$50,000 to support their improvement work. Most of the teams used the money to free up staff time (e.g., backfilling nurses' time so they could engage in the project during the workday). In other cases, the funds were used to purchase equipment and other resources. For one community health group working to reduce obesity, that meant buying two stationary bikes they could use as part of their hospital admission prevention program.

In addition to the direct financial support, teams received other important benefits and resources as members of the network. The network director and improvement adviser organized convenings where teams could learn improvement skills and share their learning with the rest of the community. The network also had a centralized measurement system that helped teams track their progress. Finally, each team had access to an experienced improvement coach that supported them through the journey.

The 20,000 Days Campaign was a wild success. Collectively, the teams saved twenty-six thousand in-patient days through the improvements they discovered (Middleton, Dowdle, et al. 2019; Middleton, Mason, et al. 2014). These improvements helped teams provide better care to their patients, and with the savings in hospital days across CMDHB, the health board could now meet the growing needs of their community. The investment in the improvement journey paid off.

MEASUREMENT INFRASTRUCTURE

The work of Ko Awatea highlights the final resource that is critical to the success of improvement projects: access to institutional data. Teams without access or a strategy to get real time feedback on their improvement work struggle; the work remains amorphous, and motivation wanes when they don't have the information they need to see if they're making progress. As Donella Meadows once wrote, "You can make a system work better with surprising ease if you can give it more timely, more accurate, more complete information" (Meadows 2008, 173).

As improvement priorities come into view, whether it be at the onset of an improvement journey or as the team engages in an understanding of the current system, improvement leaders should take stock of the existing measurement resources for the proposed project. Leaders should consider what measures are available and anticipate the measurement needs of the team as the work unfolds. Whenever possible, improvement work should leverage institutional data that is currently collected or available. New measurement development is technical work. When new measures are required, teams will need support scanning for and adapting measures to their purpose. Getting a jump start on gathering data and identifying measures that can be used in improvement work is a key way to accelerate the progress of improvement teams (see chapter 12).

INVITING PEOPLE TO THE TABLE

In addition to creating the organizational conditions necessary for success, leaders must pay careful attention to who and how people are invited to the improvement table. It's not enough to identify the right people; they need to be brought to the table in ways that make it clear that their perspectives and ideas are valued. As mentioned earlier, for many organizations, improvement work often means engaging people who have historically been excluded from the table, in particular marginalized communities most negatively impacted by the system. Improvement journeys also require bringing people across typical organizational boundaries to work together in new ways.

It is worth pausing to note that inviting people to the table often means confronting and grappling with power dynamics that persist within communities and organizations. Leaders would be well served to consider what dynamics are and have been at play in their environment, surfacing them in early conversations and noting how this initiative will recognize and mitigate them in an effort to achieve real and lasting improvement on the outcome of interest.

Thus, the tone and actions of senior leaders in inviting people into the journey is critically important. First impressions matter; how leaders set the table should signal how this work is different from business as usual. In early interactions with the team, leaders need to show up as "lead learners," demonstrating vulnerability by recognizing what's not working and curiosity by actively seeking out the perspectives of others. Doing so helps create environments where improvement teams feel psychologically safe and can engage in the "interpersonal risk taking" necessary to achieve the mutual accountability and personal commitments of a high-performing team (Edmondson 2012, 125–35).

So, how then do leaders introduce and frame the improvement work in ways that model the behaviors of a lead learner? First, leaders need to connect the improvement journey to both the organization's priorities and the team members' personal motivations. Often when leaders introduce a new initiative, they focus on justifying its importance to members of the team who were most likely mandated or "volun-told" to participate. However, as systems expert Peter Senge notes, this is a weak strategy for forging a shared vision and common direction: "The hardest lesson for many managers to face is that ultimately there is nothing you can do to get another person to enroll or commit. Enrollment and commitment require freedom of choice" (Senge 1990, 223). Compliance usually leads to lackluster team interactions as teams "go through the motions," overpowering the learning potential of even the most intentionally structured improvement activities.

Developing shared commitment to a common purpose and improvement journey results from finding common ground between organizational priorities and individual values and motivations. The work of leadership is to facilitate this process. One example illustrating this comes from a network focused on improving outcomes for students with special needs. At the first meeting, the two leaders of the hub shared the vision for the network and then asked the other members to reflect on how they personally connected to the work. Participants shared personal stories of family members and close friends with special needs who weren't adequately served by the system. This helped create a close bond and sense of shared purpose among participants. It's the collective "why" that provides the motivation and energy for the journey ahead. "Organizations do not empower people; people empower themselves once they see the opportunity and understand how their values and aspirations are aligned to the needs of the organization" (Langley et al. 2009, 189).

In addition, leaders need to send clear messages about the teams' and leaders' roles on the improvement journey. Many organizations are governed by top-down approaches to change in which leaders decide what to do and the front line "implements their ideas with fidelity." In this scenario, where the leader is perceived as the expert, a clear power imbalance exists.[3]

Systems improvement requires a different orientation. Leaders expect the team to make changes to the systems they are focused on, so they must give team members the power and authority to redesign the systems in which they work. The initial meetings with the team provide leaders with the opportunity to interrupt traditional relational dynamics, giving people permission to show up in new ways and take on new roles. Leaders should explicitly highlight the limits of their own knowledge and what they cannot see or learn given their distance from the day-to-day work on the ground. They should also make sure that individuals who have been invited to the team feel like they have been selected because of the knowledge, experience, and important perspectives they possess. In addition, teams need clear roles and a "line of sight" between the work they are taking on and how their discoveries will be used in the organization. Team members must feel safe when lifting up what's not working and suggesting improvements, even with those in the room who have real or perceived power.

Finally, leaders should clearly articulate the responsibilities of the team as well as the resources and support they will receive. As mentioned above, this means removing other projects and responsibilities from their plates to ensure that they have ample time in their work portfolios to participate in the journey, communicating the importance of the work to the larger organization, and scheduling regular check-ins to get updates on the learning and to listen for barriers that need to be removed.

Of course, these leadership moves do not guarantee wholehearted buy-in from the team. Leaders are looking for enough interest and willingness to get started and trust that the team momentum will build from there. Skepticism and pushback can be healthy signs of engagement, an indication that team members are actively wrestling with the project at hand. Silence, compliance, or resistance pose greater risks to the development of a learning culture within the team and require attention. Leaders might want to explore underlying factors or reconsider team membership.

Although a leader's initial actions matter for how teams engage in the journey, equally important is how the leader follows up these messages as the work unfolds. The clearest way to communicate the importance of the improvement priority to the organization is not just saying it but following it up with regular check-ins about how things are progressing. Again, it is important that the leader listens more than talks during these conversations, follows through on removing barriers raised, and elevates and spreads (where appropriate) what the team is learning throughout the organization. In doing so, leaders "walk the talk," reinforcing the learning stance and culture introduced when initiating the work.

CONCLUSION

Leaders play a significant role at the beginning of any improvement journey. They are responsible for commissioning the work, establishing a clear focus, allocating time and resources, and inviting team members to the table. Creating a safe space and modeling the mindsets and behaviors to do the work will go a long way in ensuring that teams start strong and achieve success.

4

Team Formation

If we want to build reliably effective teams we need to manage the human side of the enterprise with the same level of rigor and discipline with which we manage the technical.

—Weber 2013, 14

High-performing teams are not simply groups of high-performing individuals. Rather, these teams develop ways of working together that enable them to be smarter and more effective than the sum of their parts (Katzenbach and Smith 2015; Edmondson 2012; Senge 2006). That said, it's easy to say that improvement teams work differently; it is another to live it. Carefully crafted messages from a leader about the purpose of the project and need for collective learning can easily be overpowered by early experiences that feel like business as usual: conversations dominated by a handful of voices or meetings focused on working through a to-do list as opposed to learning.

Improvement teams are a microcosm of the larger systems they are trying to redesign. As a result, they need to apply the same foundational ideas of improvement to the formation and development of the team itself. Systems thinking can help team members illuminate the beliefs and mind-sets that shape their behavior, recognize and negotiate the relationships and power dynamics on the team, and see the necessity and value of drawing on the perspectives of everyone on the team. Recognizing the psychology or human side of change can support team members who are being asked to change how they work together. Finally, what are the team's assumptions about how to work as an improvement team? How will the team learn how to work more effectively together as the journey unfolds?

Improvement teams don't magically appear overnight; it takes time to develop the skills and culture necessary to work together effectively.[1] To set the tone for the work ahead, the team's initial meetings and activities should feel notably different than business as usual. They should foreground key foundational concepts of improvement science and highlight the personal, relational, and technical work they will need to do to grow into a high-performing team. These meetings should feel action oriented, like improvement work itself. Teams need to try new ways of working together and learn what works and what doesn't if they are going to discover what it takes to become a high-performing team (see chapter 2 for a definition of high-performing teams).

During the early stages of working together, teams should focus on three key areas. The first is building trust and a shared sense of purpose; it serves as the cornerstone of all effective teams, and without it, success is highly unlikely. The second is being able to have productive conversations without shying away from conflict. Finally, teams should establish robust routines for learning that will help build and maintain momentum around the work.

Team formation marks the start of a relationship that will evolve and deepen over time. How teams begin their journey will vary. Some may start with a half- or full-day meeting to kick off the work; other teams may prefer to hold a series of shorter meetings close together in time (e.g., one per day for a week). Ideally, the team lead, with the support of an improvement coach, will design these meetings intentionally, developing agendas that incorporate activities that keep the improvement principles and key skills in mind. This chapter will describe each skill in greater detail and highlight activities that can be used during early meetings as well as rituals that the team can use to build on the initiating activities.

1: BUILDING TRUST AND A SHARED SENSE OF PURPOSE

According to Charles Feltman, trust is "choosing to risk making something you value vulnerable to another person's actions" (Feltman 2021, 9). When there is trust, team members feel safe with each other; they are more open and curious, willing to reflect on one's own actions, and able to discuss and debate ideas. In contrast, distrust occurs when "what is important to me is not safe with this person in this situation (or any situation)" (Feltman 2021, 11). When this happens, people will engage in strategies to protect themselves—defending, blaming, avoiding, and withholding information and ideas—which makes it nearly impossible to work effectively with each other.

What trust looks like in action has been described by different researchers (Bryk and Schneider 2004; Brown 2021; Feltman 2021). Key characteristics of trust include a sense of personal regard, reliability, competence, and integrity. Personal regard is showing care and respect for each other as individuals. Reliability is doing what you say you're going to do. Competence refers to having the capacity, skills, and knowledge to do the work. Integrity is "choosing courage over comfort, what's right over what's fun, fast and easy" through your actions, not just your words (Brown 2021, 192).

Trust builds over time through "small moments" (Gottman 2011) and actions imbued with the characteristics just described—checking in to see how someone's day is going, owning up to a mistake you've made, following through on a task the team is relying on you to complete. Given this, it is important to create spaces and activities that encourage team members to behave in ways that build trust. For example, as described in chapter 3, inviting team members in a network focused on improving outcomes for special education students to share personal stories about how they connected to the work was a powerful way for the team to get to know each other better and to establish the team environment as a safe space.[2]

Initiating activities also provide an opportunity for the team to coalesce around a common purpose, a defining characteristic of an improvement team described in chapter 2. Having team members simply share why the aim is important to them is an easy way to identify commonalities across the team. In addition, activities that center the work on the needs of those they seek to impact are particularly powerful. For example, sharing stories of past successes and failures in meeting the needs of patients, students, or others helps team members build connections across their experiences and highlights the importance of grounding the improvement work in the voice of the user.

Visible curiosity and joy are telltale signs that the team is creating a climate where learning is likely to flourish. Learning requires curiosity, and collective learning experiences are punctuated by moments of laughter and joy. Curiosity and joy also require vulnerability (Brown 2018, 171), so their presence indicates that team members feel psychologically safe.

Activities for Building Trust and a Shared Sense of Purpose

Icebreakers or generic team-building activities are tempting but often do little to build an authentic space in which trust and a shared sense of purpose can grow (Aguilar 2016, 41). Further, these activities do not signal the difference in the type of work the team is about to embark on. As a result, it is critically important that the team lead and coach select activities specifically designed to build the key skills the team needs to succeed (see table 4.1 for activities that can build trust and a shared sense of purpose).

Table 4.1. Initiating Activities for Building Trust and a Shared Sense of Purpose

Activity	*Description*
Team Norms	Set of guidelines or expectations that inform team members' interactions. They can include both relational and operational norms.
Personal Story	Opportunity for team members to share experiences that have shaped their values and beliefs and interest/commitment to the work.
Identity Work	Ways for team members to reflect on and share how they see themselves and how others see them.
User Stories	Ways for team members to connect with the people with whom they seek to work to achieve impact.

Continuing to Build Trust and Shared Sense of Purpose

Beginnings are where patterns of interaction are consciously or unconsciously formed. However, initiating activities are only a starting point; relationships among team members require ongoing care and nurturing. Incorporating rituals into team meetings that build on early activities will help the team stay connected to its purpose and provide opportunities for members to deepen their personal relationships. Table 4.2 describes various rituals teams can use to reconnect with each other and the purpose of the work.

Table 4.2. Rituals for Deepening Trust and Shared Sense of Purpose

Rituals	*Description*
Human Check-In	Way for team members to connect personally and emotionally at the start of a meeting.
Celebrations	Opportunity for team members to recognize individual and team successes.
Team Check-In	Opportunity for teams to reflect on how they're working together and to request specific supports from other each other. Teams can use the team rubric (see chapter 16) and the improvement habits (see appendix C) to structure their check-in.

2. BUILDING CONVERSATIONAL CAPACITY

To be curious about how someone else interprets things, we have to be willing to admit that we're not capable of figuring things out alone. If our solutions don't work as well as we want them to, if our explanations of why something happened don't feel sufficient, it's time to begin asking others about what they see and think. When so many interpretations are available, I can't understand why we would be satisfied with superficial conversations where we pretend to agree with one another. (Wheatley 2009, 39)

One of the most important building blocks of collective learning is the ability to have open and honest conversations, even in the face of conflict (Edmondson 2012; Senge 2006; Weber 2013; Patterson et al. 2012). As systems thinkers, team members must recognize that their individual perspectives are just one of many and shaped by their specific experiences and identities. Differences of ideas are to be expected and, ideally, welcomed. However, although the value of open, honest conversations is easy to ascribe to, in practice they are hard and rare. It's more common to stay safe, leaving tough topics unsurfaced, which ultimately hampers team learning. "You want the kind of heat and disagreement in a meeting that sheds light and makes ideas better. Some of the most illuminating moments [in meetings] . . . come from differences of opinion, perspective, or ideas that people have been comfortable and courageous enough to share" (Boudett and City 2014, 108).

Individual and Team Skill

Engaging in productive conversations is, in part, an individual skill. Listening without a personal agenda takes intention and practice. The more we know ourselves and are in touch with our own thoughts and how they are shaped by our experiences, the more candidly we can share our perspectives. Sharing what we think and handling the discomfort that occurs when we are faced with perspectives that conflict with our own require courage and vulnerability.

Although individual skills matter, having candid, curious conversations is also a team skill. In his book *Conversational Capacity* (2013), Chris Weber describes conversational capacity as a team's "ability to have balanced, non-defensive dialogue about tough subjects in tough circumstances" (Weber 2013, 15). A team's ability to stay in dialogue even in the face of conflict does not happen right away; it grows over time, with explicit attention and practice. Small moments of candor and curiosity among team members eventually add up, creating an environment where the team can broach more challenging conversations. An improvement team's ability to tolerate conflict in conversation is a clear sign that the team has developed deep trust. It is also a sign that the team is continually learning (Senge 2006, 249). Conversely, conversations where one team member dominates, contributions are fragmented, or talk stays polite are telltale signs that something is off.

Conversational Capacity and Improvement Work

Developing strong conversational capacity is critical for improvement teams. First, the work of improving systems requires collaboration across boundaries—of location, expertise, occupation, or identity. That could include schools partnering with families, researchers working with practitioners, or hospitals engaging with patients. However, groups often develop ways of thinking, norms of relating, and a specific language that are unique to them.

This can make communication and collaboration difficult when different groups are asked to interact with each other.

This is usually further exacerbated by differences in status and power that are an inherent part of our systems. These differences stem from organizational hierarchy (principal versus teacher), perceived expertise (doctor versus nurse, researcher versus practitioner), and how voices are valued based on identity (white versus black parents, male versus female). Although formal hierarchy is one of the most predictable saboteurs of conversational capacity, any difference in status and power, perceived or implicit, can diminish a group's conversational capacity. Thus, although one of the most powerful accelerators of improvement is diversifying who's at the table, it can only happen if the team has the conversational capacity to successfully leverage different perspectives as part of the improvement journey.

Conversations about Race[3]

With equity-focused improvement, having strong conversational capacity means being able to have transparent discussions about race and systemic oppression, topics considered taboo or off-limits in many organizations. In the United States, conversations about race often are particularly charged and predictably lie outside many teams' and organizations' conversational capacity. These "undiscussables" can become the key limiting factor in improvement work.

Example: Race-Based Disproportionality in Discipline and Tracking in Schools

For example, one district launched an improvement effort with six of its schools. The two improvement coaches assigned to support the schools had assumed that the teams would dig into the racial disparities present in the schools. The teams' data clearly showed disproportionalities in discipline and tracking, which relegated students of color to less rigorous academic work. Yet every time these topics emerged, the conversation was either avoided, loaded with defensiveness, or stunted with notable silences. After six months of trying to spur a productive conversation by introducing different improvement tools, the coaches decided they needed a different approach.

Fortunately, the improvement coaches also had substantial expertise in facilitating conversations about race. They assumed the capacity to discuss racial inequities in these schools was further along because it had been a focus of previous professional development efforts. This seemed not to be the case. So, they paused the improvement work and used the allocated time and space to support the schools by strengthening the equity culture on their campuses. They started by creating race-based affinity groups to allow people to engage in personal reflection and share their experiences. They invited school leaders into the conversations to create or revisit equity visions for their schools. And they engaged in activities explicitly designed to build the school team's capacity to name and talk about the impact of race in their settings. With this foundation in place, they relaunched the improvement work and continued to deepen their conversations and collective understandings about race through the work.

Equity-focused improvement work, on one hand, can help organizations interrupt beliefs, practices, and policies that are producing inequitable outcomes; the conversational and relational capacity required to redesign systems can develop through the work itself, as new partnerships are formed and collective action is taken. However, an openness to having conversations about race as well as relational and organizational stability are prerequisites for embarking on an equity-focused improvement journey. Improvement work shouldn't be the first time that explicit conversations about race happen, and teams shouldn't be asked to center race in the work if leaders haven't already begun to build awareness. If teams are unable to engage in conversations about race productively, then leaders need to focus attention here first.

Activities for Building Team Conversational Capacity

As mentioned in chapter 3, leaders set the tone for future conversations during their initial meeting with the team. It is important that leaders not only share their ideas but also actively listen and create space for team members to safely express their own views as a way of modeling the type of conversations necessary for the work. During the early stages of their journey, teams should continue to engage in activities designed to build their collective conversational capacity.

Most teams benefit from having a coach, particularly in the early stages to help build the team's conversational capacity. The coach can model vulnerability, design and lead activities, and hold up a mirror to the conversational patterns of the team. In addition, the initiating activities described earlier in the chapter provide natural opportunities for teams to practice their conversational skills and build authentic team dialogue.

Table 4.3. Activities to Build Team Conversational Capacity

Activity	Description
Creation of conversational norms	Develop a shared definition of "productive conversations." Identify concrete behaviors that exemplify this definition. Provide opportunities for team members to share what they need to stay engaged in productive conversations.
Personal reflection on conversational tendencies	Ways for team members to reflect on how they think and how it shapes how they engage in conversation.
Conversational capacity facilitator	Identify person who observes conversation and takes note of team's conversational patterns.

Table 4.3 describes activities that can be used specifically to build a team's conversational capacity. The purpose of these activities is to help team members become self-aware of their conversational tendencies, to develop a common language for engaging in productive conversations, especially about equity and race, and normalizing conflict. Again, drawing on key improvement concepts such as systems thinking and the psychology of change can be helpful as teams build their conversational capacity. Understanding the importance of hearing different viewpoints (systems thinking), the ways in which our thoughts are shaped by cognitive biases (psychology), and the value of double-loop learning (theory of knowledge) can reinforce the importance and support the development of strong conversational capacity.

Continuing to Deepen Conversational Capacity

Developing good team conversational capacity is an ongoing process. Indeed, every meeting is an opportunity for every team member to practice and reflect on their conversational skills. It is also important that the team establish rituals or pause points that allow them to reflect as a team on their conversational capacity as they move through the improvement journey (see table 4.4). Empathy interviews, data conversations, generating change ideas, and deciding

Table 4.4. Conversational Capacity Rituals

Ritual	*Description*
Protocols	Structured guidance to support focused, productive conversations.
Conversational Check-Ins	Periodic opportunities for team members to reflect on how the team's conversational capacity is developing, revisit conversational code of conduct.

what's working and what isn't all require high conversational capacity. Missteps and disagreements will arise. Making sure that the team creates the space and deepens their conversational skills to effectively navigate these moments is critical.

3: SETTING UP A CADENCE AND ROUTINES FOR LEARNING

Another key practice the team should prioritize at the beginning of the journey is setting up robust routines that support team learning. Team learning has a particular cadence to it. Teams organize the work using iterative learning cycles: selecting a key learning question, engaging in activities to gather information during their day-to-day work, and coming back together to make sense of what they discovered. Although the questions and methods change and evolve during a team's improvement journey, the learning cycle rhythm remains the same. Establishing a cadence to the work allows teams to move agilely and learn quickly as the dynamism of systems demands. It also stands in contrast to more common meeting structures and change strategies that privilege talking and planning over action.

The trick, of course, is figuring out how to embed improvement team learning as part of one's day-to-day work so that it doesn't feel like an add-on. Although leaders are responsible for providing resources and space for teams to meet and do the work, teams also need to protect this time for learning, which requires ample headspace but rarely feels as urgent as one's daily responsibilities.

Team Meetings

Establishing a robust meeting routine helps teams stay focused. Team meetings serve multiple purposes. They provide a setting for the team to connect regularly, process what they're learning together, revise and align their theories based on what they've discovered, and then decide what to do next. In addition, the meeting routine helps the team maintain momentum around the work by creating a sense of accountability and continued urgency. In many organizations, this will feel much different than how work usually gets done. At the start of most projects, a team will hold long planning meetings before jumping into the actual work. Although some planning is necessary when starting an improvement project, we encourage teams to get going before they necessarily feel ready to ward against the tendency to over-plan.

Table 4.5 provides guidance for different kinds of team meetings. Many teams establish a regular cadence by interspersing short, frequent huddles with longer team meetings. Huddles help maintain a rhythm, providing a setting to quickly share learning, and troubleshoot issues that need to be addressed immediately. They are short check-ins with a predictable structure designed to easily fit into a regular workday. Longer team meetings provide time for the team to connect personally, to choose a new direction or learning question and/or consolidate learning since the last team meeting. Although the team's sponsor may drop in on team meetings

Table 4.5. Types of Meetings

Type of Meeting	Approximate Rhythm	Who	Purpose
Team Meeting	Usually every 3–4 weeks 60–90 minutes	All team members Coach	Make sense Consolidate learning Make decisions Share learning
Huddles[4]	Weekly 15–30 minutes	All team members	Share learning Make quick adjustments Remove barriers
Sponsor Check-Ins	Usually every 6–8 weeks 30–60 minutes	Team lead Sponsor Coach	Share learning Remove barriers
Learning Sessions	Quarterly 1–3 days	Team leads Team members Coaches Sponsors	Reenergize team(s) Learn new skills Cross-team learning Set up the next phase of learning

occasionally, it's helpful for the team to establish a separate check-in meeting with the sponsor to share wins and struggles and to highlight roadblocks that require the sponsor's help. Learning sessions usually occur when multiple improvement teams are working across an organization or network. They provide opportunities for cross-team learning and for team leads or the whole team to further develop their improvement knowledge and skills.

The combination and exact rhythm of meetings will depend on the context and nature of the improvement being pursued. Over time, the team may learn that certain parts of the year lend themselves to more activity for which more frequent huddles or longer team meetings are needed. For example, the school year has a particular rhythm to it that influences when and how frequently a team meets. What is being improved will also influence the meeting rhythm. If the processes that are the target of improvement happen daily, then teams likely will meet more frequently. For work that happens less frequently, a slower rhythm may be more appropriate. As a rule of thumb, teams should meet weekly or at the very least biweekly. Any less frequent creates disjointed conversations and stunted progress.

Example: Improving Special Education—Establishing a Rhythm of Team Meetings

A school district commissioned a team to improve outcomes for students with disabilities. The team of six included special education directors, case managers, and teachers. One of their first tasks was to create a regular meeting schedule.

The team decided to meet weekly for an hour on Friday mornings before the demands of the school day took over their attention. At first, some team members were skeptical of adding an extra early morning meeting, but soon they looked forward to this part of the week. It was a time to work on an aim that felt important, maintaining a consistent focus on improvement outcomes for a vulnerable student population. In these weekly team meetings, they met with their improvement coach, shared their latest learning, and decided what to do next. When needed, they would huddle briefly between team meetings. The sponsor periodically stopped by to get an update and see what kind of support she could lend to the work.

The team was part of a network with five other teams in California all working together toward a common aim. During the quarterly network learning sessions, the team had an opportunity to share their work with their peers, learn new skills, and plan collectively for their next wave of activity. The meeting structures provided the cadence needed for the team to maintain a good pace of learning and allowed them the time they needed to contribute to the learning of the network overall.

Failing to establish a productive meeting rhythm is a typical reason some teams flounder instead of flourish. Logistics matter. Thus, it is essential that teams design and establish a clear meeting rhythm at the start of an improvement journey to build momentum around the work. In addition, many teams find it helpful to add operational agreements to the team's norms to highlight the importance of attending meetings and ways to navigate meeting conflicts that might arise.

Teams also benefit from creating a common workspace where meeting notes and other shared documents can easily be located. If the work starts off quickly, the team will soon be inundated with insights, data, and learning artifacts. Setting up good knowledge and document management processes from the start will save time and frustration in the long run. Chapters 8 and 13 will provide more detail about necessary knowledge management routines for the team. In the beginning, it is enough to establish a shared space and to start using it.

CONCLUSION

Launching improvement work intentionally and purposefully can go a long way in signaling new ways of working and creating a team culture focused on learning. However, attending to the health of the team requires ongoing maintenance throughout the rest of the journey. The improvement practices outlined in the coming chapters will provide ample opportunity for improvement teams to deepen their collaboration and learn new ways of relating and thinking together. If team meetings start to feel flat or lack energy—a telltale sign that little learning is happening, then the team may want to revisit some practices described in this chapter to reground itself and jump-start the work.

II

WHAT ARE *OUR* CURRENT OUTCOMES, AND WHY ARE *WE* GETTING THEM?

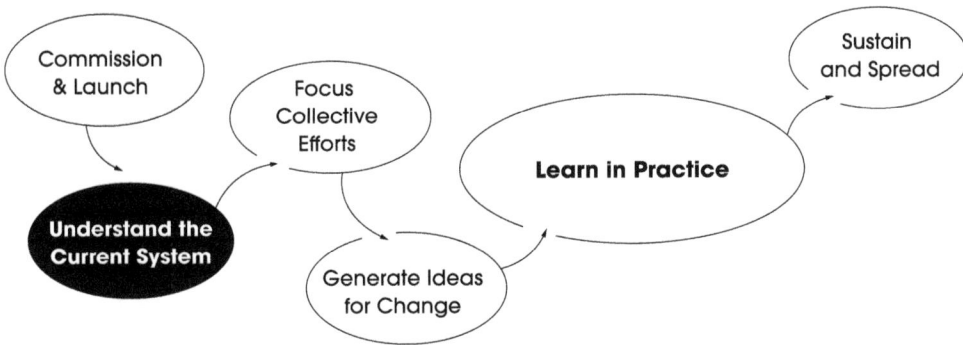

Commission & Launch → Understand the Current System → Focus Collective Efforts → Generate Ideas for Change → Learn in Practice → Sustain and Spread

Most organizations rarely take the time to ask the question, "Why are we getting the outcomes we are currently getting?" The pressure to improve performance as soon as possible often pushes leaders to reach for the most convenient solution, hoping that the latest program, technology, or innovation will produce the desired improvements. This tendency toward "solutionitis" not only fails to produce meaningful outcomes, but it also results in overburdened professionals and overloaded systems that become fatigued as one solution after another is layered on.

Dedicating a phase of work to understanding the system can help teams better see *how* the system is producing the current outcomes and highlight key issues to address.[1] Armed with this information, teams can strategically focus their improvement efforts, targeting changes to the root causes of the problem, thereby increasing the likelihood of success.

Teams start this phase by putting on their detective hats and investigating their system. They begin with the question, "What are our current outcomes?" Although some might be able to answer this question in broad terms, few know exactly how their systems are performing and, in particular, the variation that lies within. From here, teams ask the more challenging question, "Why are we getting the outcomes we are currently getting?" Answering this question requires teams to shine a light on the system, illuminating not just the policies, processes, and practices that constitute an organization's everyday work but also the relationships, power dynamics, and mental models that lie beneath. What teams often see is the aftermath of years and years of policies and initiatives piled on each other and wide intended and unintended variation in the services people receive. They also see people who are working hard but in silos, leading to disconnected and incoherent work. It is the team's job to untangle and make sense of what they see, just enough to identify a place where they can focus their improvement work and move forward on their journey.

Navigating this phase will require the team to oscillate between different ways of thinking and managing the inherent tensions that come with it. On the one hand, teams need to think expansively and explore their systems with an open mind, recognizing that their view of the system is inherently limited. However, teams need to balance this with periods of focused thinking where they come to shared understandings and agreements about next steps. During this phase, teams will seesaw between these ways of thinking as they home in on a place to start.

Although necessary, this back-and-forth isn't always easy. For some, especially those eager to move more quickly to changes, exploring the larger system can feel overwhelming, requiring a certain tolerance for uncertainty and ambiguity. For others, this way of thinking is endlessly fascinating, but team members can get stuck given that there's always something new to learn and uncover about complex systems. Further, the different experiences and backgrounds that team members bring to the table naturally will lead to differing opinions and interpretations of what they see. The make or break of coming to an insightful understanding will rest then on the willingness of team members to share their perspectives candidly without holding onto them too tightly and the ability of the team to appreciate the complexity of the system while being willing to take a step forward.

Establishing a learning routine that intentionally balances these ways of working will help the team manage the tensions that come with it. Teams start by asking a learning question, gathering multiple forms of data ranging from user perspectives to observations of practice to quantitative data, and then collectively making sense of it to answer the question. Doing so almost always raises a new learning question and another round of investigation, pushing the team to look deeper into their system until they find a place to start making change. Occasionally, there are situations in which teams can significantly shorten or bypass this phase. For example, if teams already know the problem they want to tackle and have been gifted a set of changes from another team from a similar context (see chapter 14 on change packages), then they can move to setting an aim and testing changes.

For those ready to dive into understanding their system, in chapter 5 we offer guidance on planning an investigation and describe different methods teams can use to gather data about their system. This includes using empathy methods to capture the user perspective; analyzing quantitative data to see patterns and variations in practice and performance across the system; and visualizing processes to see how work is currently organized and executed. Each provides a different window into the system that collectively gives teams a more holistic and nuanced picture of what's currently happening.

In chapter 6, we help teams home in on a starting point for their improvement work. As teams gather more information about their system, they can use tools such as cause-and-effect analyses and Pareto charts to help them organize and cull through their data to highlight places in need of redesign. Although these "technical" tools can help generate concrete evidence that ideally will identify a handful of places to start, getting to a final decision is, in large part, a social process. Here, it is important for team members to recognize how they interpret the evidence is largely a result of how our brains work when making sense of what we see.

Which data we focus on or attend to and how we interpret it is largely shaped not just by our specific backgrounds and experiences but also the cognitive biases we all carry. As a result, it is important that team members intentionally slow down their thinking, surface and challenge the assumptions and beliefs that shape each other's thinking, to come to a collective decision about where to start.

This phase can feel overwhelming and challenging, not just because of the complexity of the systems we are addressing, but also because it is the first time that teams are asked to learn and collectively make decisions together. Teams should take heart, though. The skills and trust they will develop from successfully navigating this phase will serve them well throughout the rest of the journey. In every phase, teams will make new discoveries, experience the need to come to shared understandings about what they've learned, and then decide what to do next. That is simply the nature of collective learning and decision-making, which is what the improvement journey is all about.

5

Learning to See Systems

Before you disturb the system in any way, watch how it behaves. . . . If it's a social system, watch it work. Learn its history. Ask people who've been around a long time to tell you what has happened. If possible, find or make a time graph of the actual data from the system—people's memories are not always reliable when it comes to timing.

—Meadows 2009, 170

In 2016, a team from the Shasta County Office of Education in Northern California came together to improve literacy outcomes in their region. In this rural area, where many school districts are composed of single schools, the county office provides key centralized resources such as coaching, professional development, and data support that most people associate with services provided by centralized school district offices. A strategic priority of the region was improving literacy.

Initially, the team planned to target students in middle school to take advantage of a grant from a large foundation that was supporting efforts in middle and high schools. However, the team had some disagreement about whether this was the right place to focus. To ground the conversation in a common understanding of the current reality, the team began by looking at their literacy outcomes. The most readily available data came from state tests for grades 3–8. They structured their initial analysis around the seemingly simple question, "What percent of our students are currently not reading on grade level?" They knew there were enough to be worried about, but they did not fully understand why so many students were struggling or how reading proficiency varied across grade levels.

One of the initial graphs the team produced is pictured in figure 5.1. As the team looked at this data, they recognized that they did indeed have a middle-school literacy problem: 43 percent of sixth graders, 39 percent of seventh graders, and 48 percent of eighth graders read below grade level. That was simply too many. At the same time, they noticed that 43 percent of students did not meet the literacy standards in third grade, the earliest data they had easy access to, and that there was little variation across grades 3–8. The "problem" they were seeing in middle school already existed in third grade. The data convinced the team that they needed to focus further upstream to address middle-grades literacy.[1]

Armed with the data, they went back to the foundation and said they wanted to focus on early-grade instead of middle-grade literacy. Persuaded by their argument, the foundation agreed.

Now the team turned to investigating why 43 percent of their students were not reading proficiently by third grade. They generated a starting list of questions that would entail look-

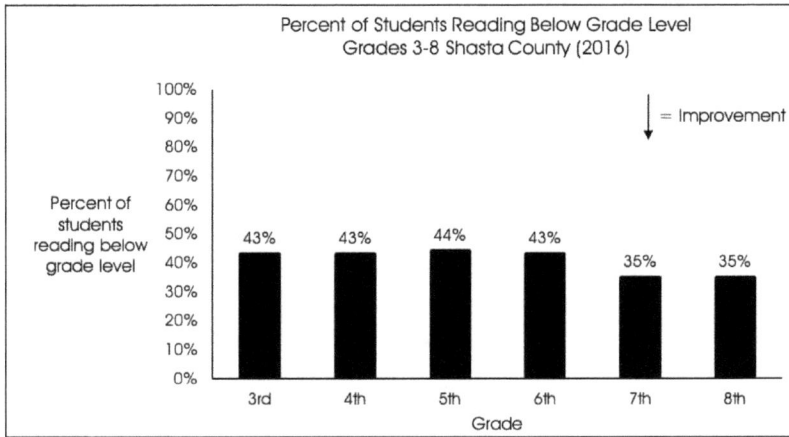

Figure 5.1. Shasta County Literacy Outcomes

ing at what was happening from the perspective of the children and families, the professionals working in the system, and the lens of literacy research:

- What are the literacy outcomes in kindergarten, first, and second grade?
- How do students feel about reading? Do they enjoy reading?
- Which students are struggling with reading?
- Which literacy practices are used in early grade classrooms?
- What kinds of literacy-related practices are happening at home?
- How are teachers supported to teach literacy?

Underneath each question were another handful of questions about the specific outcomes, practices, and factors to explore. To keep from getting overwhelmed, they structured their learning as a series of investigations: they would ask a question, identify a method useful for answering that question, collect relevant data, and come back together to make sense of the learning with the rest of the team. They took advantage of data they had or could collect opportunistically. They knew a complete understanding of the system would be elusive; they just needed to figure out a useful starting point for their improvement efforts; a place where targeted action had the potential to really pay off.

Some contributing factors the team uncovered were outside their current sphere of influence. For example, many teachers they talked to identified trauma in the home as a key factor. To confirm this, the team looked at the county's Adverse Childhood Experiences (ACE) data. ACE scores, as they are known, quantify traumatic experiences between the ages of zero through seventeen, with a score of four or more being highly predictive of poor long-term health outcomes.[2] In 2013–2014, approximately 40 percent of students in K–12 reported experiencing four or more ACEs in comparison to 17 percent across the state (Shasta Strengthening Families Collaborative n.d.). Although the team recognized this as an important factor, they also knew that addressing it would require the engagement of a much broader set of stakeholders, including the public health and health-care systems. They would raise this with a local community coalition as something to address over the long haul while continuing to figure out a starting point, something that was currently in their bounded sphere of influence.

Other factors rose to the surface; in this rural area, teachers often had limited access to support. They were often the only first-grade teacher in their school, and they were left to fend for themselves. Many teachers had not figured out classroom management strategies that allowed them to organize small groups in their classrooms—a key practice for meeting the divergent developmental needs of their students. Phonics instruction was hit or miss. The list went on.

Answering the question, "What are the literacy outcomes in kindergarten, first, and second grade?" proved to be less straightforward than the simplicity of the question might suggest. State testing didn't begin until third grade, and different schools had different ways of assessing early-grade literacy. In total, they found that first-grade teachers across the county were using twenty-eight different literacy assessments. They noted the need to create a more aligned early-grades assessment policy but decided not to focus their limited attention there now. The team took advantage of the fact that most districts in their county collected fluency[3] outcomes in grades 1 and 2. This allowed the team to look at early literacy across the region. Compiling the fluency data (a laborious task in and of itself) revealed that 54 percent of students were not meeting the fluency standard by the end of first grade (see figure 5.2).

The team knew that this was a problem. Although fluency is only one aspect of literacy, it is an important predictor of comprehension. If early readers stumble over every word, it gets in their way of being able to draw meaning from a text. If only half of students were reading fluently in first grade, it made sense that they were seeing problems down the line.

After a couple of months of investigating, a starting point came into view: working with teams of first-grade teachers and literacy coaches to improve first-grade reading fluency. Within first-grade fluency, they would start with formative assessment,[4] a key practice from instructional research (Black and William 1998). The intention was to assess students' fluency regularly and use this to form small groups to provide differentiated instruction that better met students' individual needs (Gerstein et al. 2009). In addition to being important,

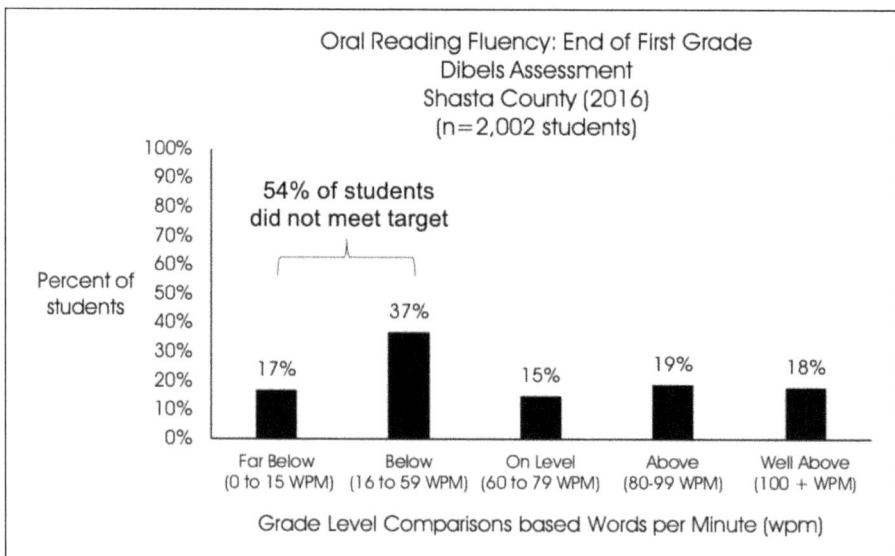

Oral Reading Fluency: End of First Grade
Dibels Assessment
Shasta County (2016)
(n=2,002 students)

54% of students did not meet target

Percent of students

Far Below (0 to 15 WPM) — 17%
Below (16 to 59 WPM) — 37%
On Level (60 to 79 WPM) — 15%
Above (80-99 WPM) — 19%
Well Above (100 + WPM) — 18%

Grade Level Comparisons based Words per Minute (wpm)

Figure 5.2. First-Grade Fluency Data

formative assessment processes were also a pain point for teachers and schools; they took a lot of time and did not consistently generate information that teachers knew how to use. As a bonus, collecting common assessment data would also serve as useful data to guide the overall improvement effort. On the one hand, the focus on first-grade fluency felt like a narrowed version of their overall vision of literacy for the county. At the same time, it was concrete and focused enough that teachers could wrap their arms around it, see some improvement within a couple years, and build momentum for literacy-related improvement work going forward.

TAKING TIME TO "SEE THE SYSTEM"

Improvement efforts are often driven by an impulsive reaction to an undesirable outcome, a convenient solution, or, in social sector settings, opportunities for external funding. The rush to action is often motivated by good intentions: the urgent need to do better now. The danger, of course, is that limited resources get expended in the wrong place.

Beginning the improvement journey by taking time to "see the system" can help teams and organizations strategically target their improvement efforts. The early stages of this phase often involve widening the aperture, inviting in new perspectives, and wading through the complex set of factors that come together to produce an outcome. This is precisely what the team in Shasta County did, expanding and pivoting from middle school to investigations of early literacy, guided by available data and experiential knowledge of their system.

In this chapter we will describe methods teams can use to see the system. Ultimately, the goal of the investigative phase is to identify specific outcomes, practices, and places as the target of improvement efforts. This necessitates narrowing the focus and cueing into "leverage points" where targeted action can have big payoffs. We will describe methods and considerations for narrowing a focus in chapter 6.

INVESTIGATING THE SYSTEM

> By the very nature of systems, each of us only sees a part of the system. The problem is, the part we see is very compelling. —Attributed to Peter Senge

Systems require investigation because they are notoriously difficult to see. The Sufi tale of the blind men and the elephant is often evoked to illustrate the inherent difficulty of the endeavor. In it, three blind men encounter an elephant. The man whose hand reaches an ear describes it as "a large and rough thing, wide and broad like a rug." Another man who feels the trunk says, "I have the real facts about it. It is like a straight and hollow pipe, awful and destructive." And the third, who feels its legs, says "it is mighty and firm, like a pillar" (Meadows 2009, 7; Senge 1990, 66). Perspective matters, and in the context of systems rarely can one or even a few people perceive all the interconnections within the system that lead to its current outcomes. Seeing the system then requires humility, remembering the inherent limitations in what any one person can see and organizing the work in a way that maximizes the diversity of perspectives that can be brought to bear to reveal the design of a system.

The scope of the problem and the complexity of the system under study will influence who needs to be involved and how long is required for teams to move through this process. In systems where teams have a great deal of autonomy over the management of day-to-day work, this process will move faster. An already activated improvement team can dedicate a phase of their work to understanding the system before they try to change it. A hospital-based team in the maternity ward, for example, wanting to improve their services may start by trying to understand how expectant mothers currently experience care to identify opportunities for improvement; the benefit of engaging these users is learning from people who have experienced the whole system.

For more complex problems, where connections exist across multiple departments or across levels in the organizational hierarchy, this will likely be a longer process involving more people. Particularly when an improvement effort is inspired by a general focus or broad organizational priority, a phase of work dedicated to understanding the system can help identify an appropriately scoped focus (for more on scoping, see chapters 3 and 7). In the Shasta case, for example, a multidisciplinary team dug into understanding literacy outcomes in the county. This work resulted in the identification of first-grade fluency as a place to focus, which in turn spurred the formation of improvement teams made up largely of first-grade teachers.

Finally, the available resources also influence how long teams should spend understanding the system. If a team has a three-year time horizon to dedicate to an improvement effort, it may make sense to spend 6–9 months getting a clearer, more expansive view of what is happening. Not only can this provide the team with more strategically focused improvement efforts, but it can have the added benefit of building will and relationships among stakeholders who have not engaged in improvement together before. At the same time, if the team has only a year, spending 6–9 months to end up with an insightful understanding but no real change to the system defeats the purpose of the effort (see chapter 16 for additional guidance on estimating the time frame of an improvement project).

Because our social systems are complex and defy complete understanding, it is hard for teams to feel like they are "done" with an investigation. There will always be more learning questions and more to uncover, so it is often useful to time bound this phase, setting a date when the team will shift to action. Importantly, teams will continue to learn about the design of their system as they try to change it.

STRUCTURING AN INVESTIGATION

The entry point for a systems investigation is a sense of the problem to be solved. A problem is simply the recognition of a gap between a vision of what might be accomplished and the current reality of the outcomes the system produces (see figure 5.3).[5]

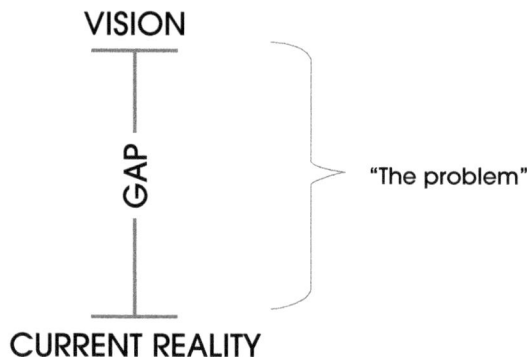

Figure 5.3.   Acknowledging the Gap between a Vision and the Current Reality

In the early stages of a systems investigation, the team works to come to a shared under-standing of the seemingly simple question, What is currently happening? Even after a problem or focus area has been identified, team members are often not readily aware of the specifics of the current outcomes, and they are often operating off different implicit assumptions about what already is (or is not) happening in practice. Through trying to see the system as it exists, conceptions of "the problem" often shift. From there the team moves to a second important question: Why are we getting the outcomes we are currently getting?

Some people find language about "problems" to be negative, unmotivating, or worse, deficit oriented. It is worth emphasizing that the problems and visions go hand in hand. The vision of all children learning to read by third grade entails problematizing the current reality. The opposite is also true: problematizing the current reality requires a belief in a vision of what could be. It is not easy, but it is possible to be both hopeful and critical at the same time. Fo-cusing on the vision will be useful for most of the improvement journey. It draws on the hope, optimism, and excitement that support a team to move forward. In this phase of the journey, when the team is trying to understand the system and eventually analyze it, it is often helpful to speak of problems. The language of problems prompts teams to name, acknowledge, and own the ways systems are not living up to their intended promise.[6]

The rhythm of understanding a system involves iterative rounds of asking questions, gath-ering data, and making sense of it [7] together as a team. In an early meeting, the team crafts an initial problem statement and comes to agreement on what they know about the current system and what they want to learn. Then the team prioritizes a question and a method for the first learning cycle. When the team gets together again, they discuss what they learned and determine what they need to learn next (see figure 5.4).

Teams almost always ask more questions than they have time to answer. A well-defined rhythm helps discipline this process. For example, a team may determine that they have time for three two-week rounds of learning cycles.[8] The short cycle rhythm and regular team huddles keep the team moving as they build from one cycle to the next. At the end of the three rounds, they come back together to consolidate what they have learned and decide what to do next (for more on consolidation and improvement routines, see chapter 13).

To support their investigation, the team will draw on a variety of improvement methods, each of which provides a different perspective on the system. The methods in this phase gener-ally fall into three buckets: empathy methods, analyzing quantitative data, and visualizing key processes. In the remaining part of the chapter, through a few examples we will describe each and show when and how they are used.

EMPATHY METHODS

Empathy methods provide a particularly insightful window into systems. They can help teams see past an intended design and into the actual experiences of those the system is supposed to serve. Any attempt to understand "what is currently happening" is incomplete without an understanding of the end users' experience.

According to researcher Brené Brown, empathy is connecting to the emotion another person is experiencing, even if you have not experienced the situation yourself (Brown 2018, 140). She goes on to describe:

> We need to dispel the myth that empathy is "walking in someone else's shoes." Rather than walking in your shoes, I need to learn how to listen to the story you tell about what it is like in your shoes and believe you even when it doesn't match my experiences. (Brown 2021, 122)

Team Meeting	ROUND 1 Learning Cycle(s)	Huddle/ Team Meeting	ROUND 2 Learning Cycle(s)	Huddle/ Team Meeting	ROUND 3 Learning Cycle(s)	Team Meeting
1 hour – 1 day Depending on size of the group	1–3 weeks	30–60 min	1–3 weeks	30–60 min	1–3 weeks	1 hour – 1 day Depending on size of the group
Define the problem Generate Learning Questions Prioritize 1–3 questions & select methods	Go learn Collect data Can pursue 1 question at a time or multiple concurrently	Make sense of the learning Determine next focus	Go learn Collect data Can follow up on previous question or work towards a new one	Make sense of the learning Determine next focus	Go learn Collect data Can follow up on previous question or work towards a new one	Consolidate learning Identify leverage points Ready to move on?

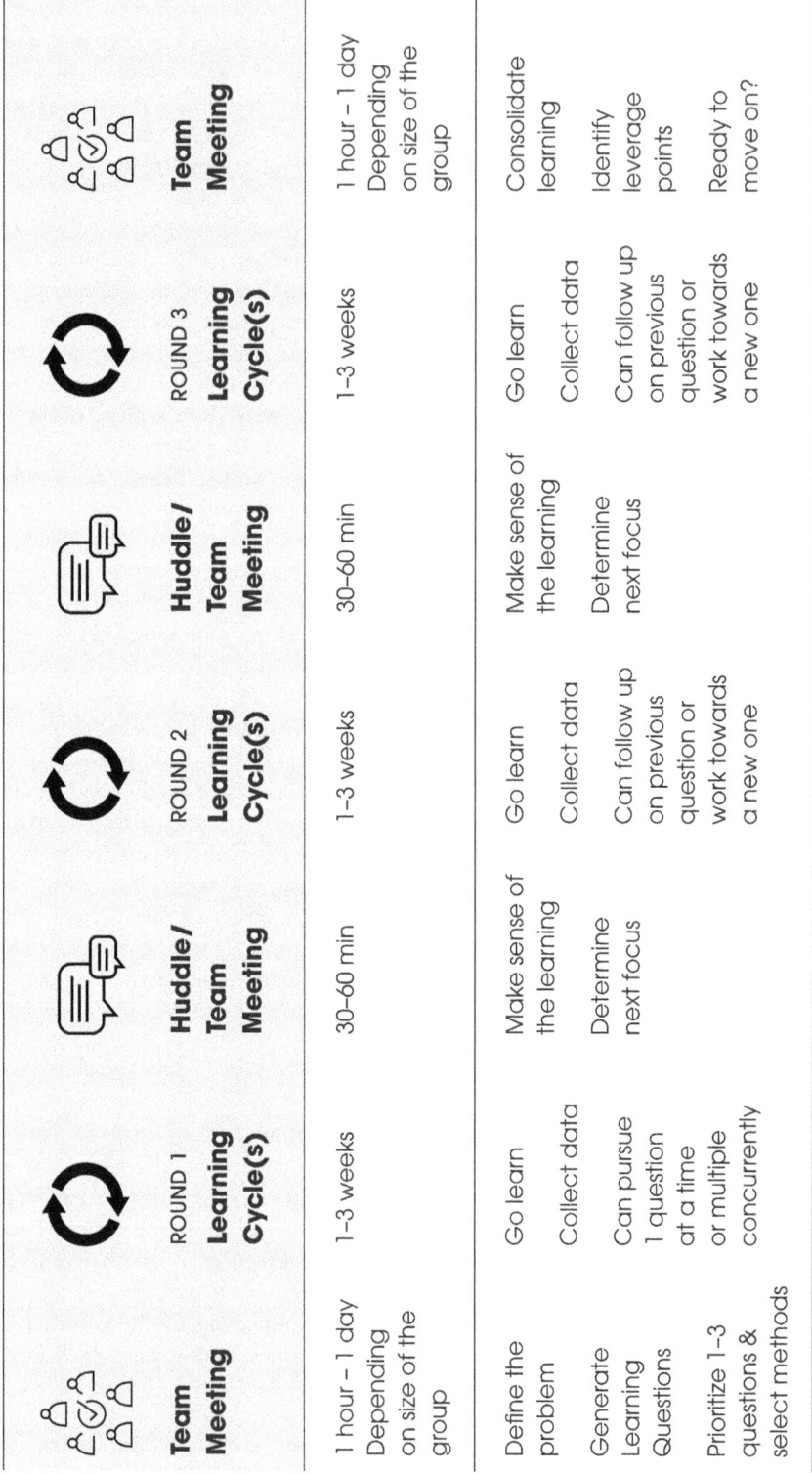

Figure 5.4. Applying Improvement Routines to Understand the System

Empathy interviews and empathy observations are two common methods to generate deeper understandings of the end users experience. When done well, these methods help build stronger, trusting relationships with those the team seeks to serve and authentically and meaningfully inform the work of the team.

Example: Empathy Interviews Provide Insights into Reasons for Chronic Absenteeism

A team from a midsize, high-poverty school district set out to address chronic absenteeism in their district. On average, 25 percent of the students in the district were chronically absent.[9] The district was particularly concerned about its most vulnerable student populations that included multilingual learners, students with disabilities, and African American students. Despite being part of statewide efforts focused on chronic absenteeism, the problem was persistent. They needed a different approach.

The district partnered with improvement coaches from Community Design Partners[10] and formed a multidisciplinary improvement team that included teachers, administrators, front office staff, transportation, food service staff, and community partners. One large district team included school-level teams from each school in the district.[11]

They began by trying to understand why students were chronically absent. They used empathy interviews to surface the perspectives of students and their families. Each team member agreed to conduct three empathy interviews. Teams were advised to interview students and families who had different attendance records, focusing primarily on students with multiple absences. The improvement coaches provided suggested questions for the interviews. The questions were open ended, designed to elicit feelings, stories, and experiences.

For Students

Tell me one great experience you had in school. What was it? Why was it great? How did you feel? Tell me more.

Tell me about a day you didn't want to come to school. What was going on? What did it feel like? Tell me more.

Tell me about a recent time you were absent from school. What was it like to return to school? Why? Tell me more.

What is something in your life—inside or outside of school—that makes you happy?

For Families

Tell me about a recent time you visited your child's school (for any reason). What was the visit like? Who did you talk to? How did you feel?

Tell me about a day your child was excited to go to school. What was going on? How did you know they were excited?

Tell me about a day your child didn't go to school. What was going on? How did you feel?

Tell me about a recent time your child was absent. What, if any, interaction did you have with the school? What was your experience when your child returned to school?

The coaches helped the team understand how empathy interviews were different from other kinds of interviews and provided guidance on how to listen deeply, take notes, identify potential power dynamics, and provide care for the interviewee. They practiced with each other during a preparatory meeting and worked out the logistics. In some cases, bilingual interviewers would be needed. They agreed to enter their notes in a common database to use at their next team meeting.

Across the district they conducted more than one hundred empathy interviews with parents and students.[12] When the team reconvened, they shared what they heard with each other. They used an analysis strategy called headlining[13] to capture the qualitative data they had gathered. The headlines included statements such as:

Some students want more friends at school.
Start time is too early, and some students oversleep.
Students feel overwhelmed when missing school.
Parent is overwhelmed with basic needs; school comes second.
"I feel invisible, and no one knows my name."

Centering the conversation around student stories helped build common ground among the group. The interactions with students also challenged some assumptions team members held about what was preventing students from coming to school. Many team members had come to the table with ideas for providing incentives for attendance or improving access to transportation. They were surprised to hear how many students didn't feel welcome at school and had not thought about how coming back to a pile of makeup work impacted returning to school after having missed a day. Although many team members had initially been impatient to start enacting what seemed like obvious solutions, they began to realize they had mistaken assumptions about what students thought and felt.

Listening to how end users experience the system often shifts the team's understanding of the current reality and the definition of the problem to be solved. With any empathy work, the most important step is adopting a beginner's mind-set. Team members should enter with a sense of openness and curiosity, avoid making assumptions, and listen and observe without judgment. Further, the team's job is not to control or fix the situation during this part of the journey but simply to understand what it is.

Guidance for Engaging in Empathy Interviews and Observations

Empathy interviews are distinct from other interviews in that they are designed to elicit stories from the interviewee that provide a window into the system and uncover potential root causes of a problem. As a result, empathy interview protocols are loosely structured; interviewers generate a short list of questions to guide the conversation but can also ask follow-up questions to probe more deeply based on what arises. In general, the questions should be open ended while also eliciting clear and specific information. For example, avoid asking interviewees what they "usually" do; instead ask them to "Tell me about a time when . . ." The greater level of specificity in this second prompt elicits experiences from the interviewee.

Empathy observations are another method for "seeing the system." Hospital teams, for example, can follow a patient's experience through the various steps of a hospital visit to better understand how they experience care (goShadow 2019). The Stanford d. School created the shadow a student challenge to provide guidance to school teams looking to understand students' experience (Stanford d. school n.d.). More specifically, school teams looking to better support students' oral language development can begin by shadowing students and noting the language opportunities they do (or do not) have throughout the day (Soto 2012).

Unlike traditional observations that are evaluative or used for teaching purposes, empathy observations are more open ended and help observers see how the system impacts an individual's actions and decisions. Team members may decide to conduct observations like a "fly on the wall" and simply watch and document what they see (LUMA Institute n.d.). They may also choose to ask questions during or after the observation to better understand what the individual is doing, thinking, and feeling.

Empathy observations and interviews generate data that can be used to guide improvement journeys. There are a variety of ways to capture this data in concrete artifacts that can be regularly returned to. As described in the example above, one option is headlining. Team members identify descriptive sentences or representative quotes that express what was observed or heard. These headlines are qualitatively analyzed to identify themes.[14]

Another effective method for summarizing empathy data is a journey map. A journey map is a visualization that tracks the key activities or actions an individual goes through to achieve an outcome. It may also include annotations that describe an individual's emotions or thoughts during the journey. A journey map could be used, for example, to summarize a patient's experience of care. Although hospitals are often organized by "departments," the journey map helps visualize the patient experience as they move through these departments. The same could be said of people moving through the social welfare system, navigating housing and financial support, child protective services, and various treatment programs.

Although empathy interviews are an invaluable source of data, how a team might act on that data will likely be mediated by the number of interviews conducted. One or two in-depth interviews will provide teams with deep, rich contextual knowledge that cannot be captured through quantitative methods. However, it is difficult to support definitive claims from a small sample size.[15] A larger sample will increase a team's confidence in any claims or conclusions made from the data that influence a team's decisions or actions. In general, team members should ward against conducting empathy interviews and observations perfunctorily or treating the data casually. Doing so can lead to misinterpretations of the data and potentially jeopardize relationships with those invited to the table.

It is worth noting here that engaging in empathy methods to understand what is currently happening is only a small part of what it means to ground improvement work in the user experience. Empathy methods provide important data that often challenge initial perceptions about the outcomes that the system is producing and the problems to be solved. However, this does not check the box on integrating user voice. Centering user voice requires attention throughout the improvement journey, not just in the beginning. One effective way of doing this is to have end users directly on the team.

PRACTICAL GUIDANCE FOR EMPATHY METHODS[16]

Empathy Interviews	Empathy Observations

• Create criteria to identify end users.
• Generate open-ended questions.
• Prepare.
  ◦ Practice deep listening and open questioning.
  ◦ Create a note-taking structure.
• Analyze and capture: Stay as descriptive as possible.
	• Identify a learning question.
	• Select an appropriate observational method.
	  ◦ Fly on the wall
	  ◦ Contextual
	• Prepare.
	  ◦ Create a note-taking structure.
	• Analyze and capture: Stay as descriptive as possible.

ANALYZING AND MAKING SENSE OF QUANTITATIVE DATA

Quantitative data provides another perspective on the question, What is currently happening? Although empathy methods provide a detailed, close-up view of a system, quantitative data can provide useful descriptions across the system, enabling the discovery of patterns. Quantitative data can help teams see the variation that their systems produce, which in turn can produce powerful conversations about where they should focus their improvement efforts.

Many people may approach improvement with justified reservations about the value of quantitative data. Often their view of quantitative data is shaped by an accumulation of experiences where data analyses are used primarily for the purpose of accountability and judgment, offering little actionable information. The challenges associated with quantitative data, however, arise from the contexts in which it is used rather than any inherent characteristics of the data. In improvement, data is used in the context of learning (see chapter 12 on distinguishing data for improvement from data for other purposes). It is used to understand the behavior of systems. The analyses are driven by the team's learning questions and designed to provide information that will spark valuable conversations for the team as opposed to providing definitive solutions for addressing the issue at hand. For many people, using data in this way will require them to shift their relationship with data. Creating an improvement culture that emphasizes data for the purposes of learning will help support this shift.

Understanding Baseline

As the Shasta example revealed, many teams often do not have a good or common understanding of the outcomes their systems are currently producing. If they have data, it is often presented in aggregate form or provides only a snapshot of performance during a given moment. These displays often mask or distort what is happening. Very rarely are the outcomes the same for everyone, in every part of the system, over an extended period. Failing to understand variation can lead to "one-size-fits-all" improvement efforts instead of strategically focused efforts that target change where and for whom it is most needed.

Analyzing quantitative data begins with identifying an outcome that matters to the organization. It can be a large consequential outcome, such as literacy proficiency or mother-to-child transmission of HIV; or more proximal outcomes, such as school attendance or daily discharge rates at a hospital (for more on outcome and process measures, see chapter 12). How the data is analyzed depends on the question to be answered. It is useful for improvement teams to start with learning questions focused on describing "what is currently happening" with particular attention to variation over time, across departments, and across different community populations.

For example, a district that wants to get a handle on student attendance might ask the following descriptive questions; each one uses the same data but in different ways:

What is the average attendance rate in our district?
How many students are chronically absent (missing ≥10 percent of school days)?
How has the chronic absenteeism rate changed over time?
How does the chronic absenteeism rate vary across grades? Across schools?
How does the chronic absenteeism rate vary across different student groups? (racial groups, students from various socioeconomic status groups, students with disabilities, and so forth).

The questions that are asked determine what is learned. A district could have a seemingly high average rate of daily attendance of 95 percent that hides the presence of a group of students that are chronically absent or a particular school where absenteeism rates are problematically high (Bruner, Discher, and Change 2011). An aggregate measure that displays improvement over time can hide the performance of a particular population moving in the opposite direction. Research, as well as professional and local knowledge, can help identify useful questions for generating insight into a particular outcome in a particular place. By exploring these questions and disaggregating their data in various ways, teams begin to see the variation their systems produce.

Example: Using Quantitative Data to Understand Hospital Discharges

An improvement team at a hospital in an urban center set out to increase the accessibility of hospital care. The hospital was in a growing city; as the leaders looked to the future, they recognized that the population was growing faster than their ability to meet the clinical demand. Constructing a new hospital or expanding the existing hospital center would be one strategy for meeting the growing demand. However, these solutions are capital and time intensive. In the meantime, the hospital could work to reduce the "average length of stay." Patients and hospitals alike prefer that stays be as short as possible—assuming, of course, that effective care has been provided.

The length of stay of individual patients is a function of many things: their illness, recovery time, the demand for hospital services (admissions), and importantly, the discharge processes of the hospital. As a result, hospitals track the number of discharges each day. If hospitals are maximizing safe discharges, then they are creating space for new patients to be admitted and may be reducing the length of stay for patients ready to return home safely.

The team decided to analyze their readily available daily discharge data to see what they could learn. They began with the most straightforward question, "How does our discharge rate vary over time?" They graphed the number of discharges per day over the past five months (see figure 5.5). The average number of discharges was 154.7 per day but varied wildly from 15.5 to 293.9 (centerline and calculated limits displayed on their initial Shewhart chart).

As the clinicians looked at the data, they noted that it looked "funny" to them, and they cued into the repeated oscillating pattern in the graph.[17] Using their professional knowledge, they suggested ways the data could be disaggregated that might explain the patterns and result in graphs that would be more useful for their improvement work. First, they needed to disaggregate between medical reasons for being in a hospital (i.e., treatments for an illness) and surgical reasons (i.e., requiring a surgical intervention to solve a health problem). These are two different hospital pathways that should be described separately. Second, the clinicians could see a temporal pattern in the data that in retrospect made sense to them. They knew from experience that discharges were harder to execute on weekends when fewer clinical staff were on duty.

Their second set of graphs looked at the weekend/weekday pattern for patients admitted for medical reasons (see figure 5.6). As they had suspected, the weekday discharge rate was higher than the weekend discharge rate (an average of 188.6 on weekdays versus an average of 72.7 on weekends). A number of days with unusually low discharge rates on the weekday day chart needed further investigation by the improvement team.[18] But in the weekend data they discovered a pattern that intrigued them. It appeared that Saturdays consistently had a higher rate of discharges than Sundays.

In their next cut at the data, the team created separate graphs for Saturdays and Sundays (see figure 5.7). On Saturdays, the team typically discharged 89.2 patients; on Sundays the average rate was 56.2. This disaggregation would be useful for their improvement journey. Overall, they worried that their system of discharges was based not on patient need but, rather,

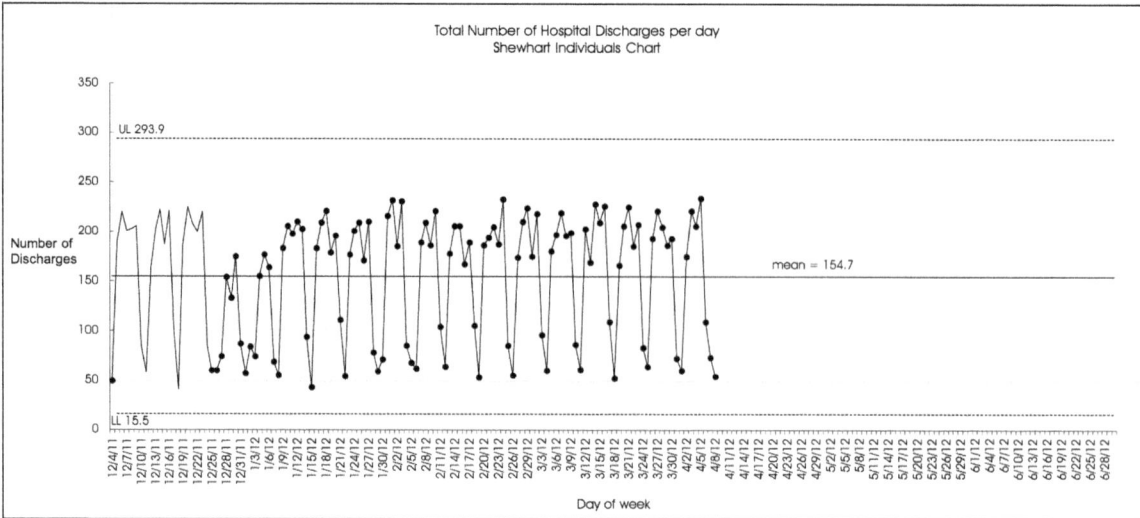

Figure 5.5. Hospital Discharges Per Day

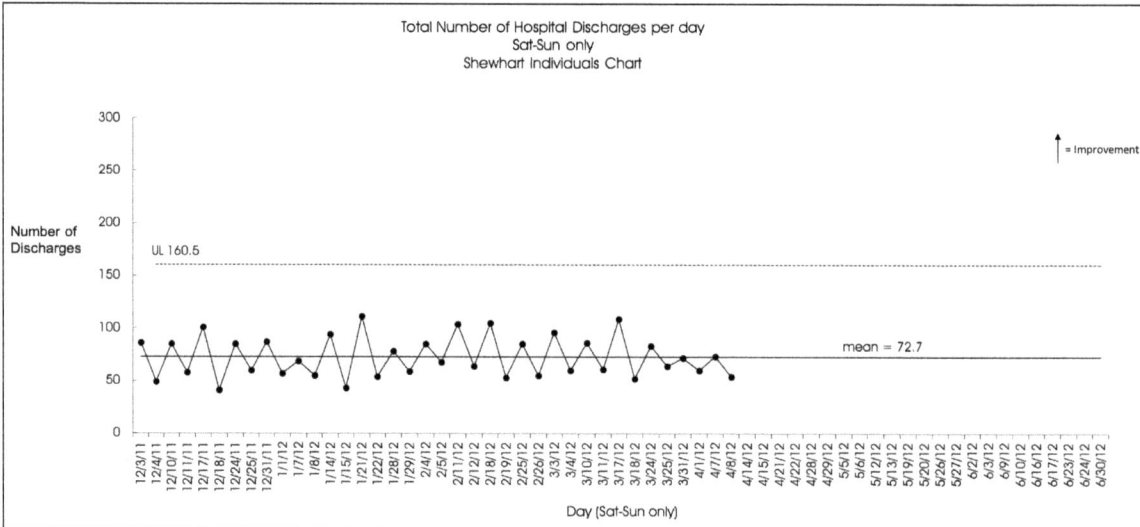

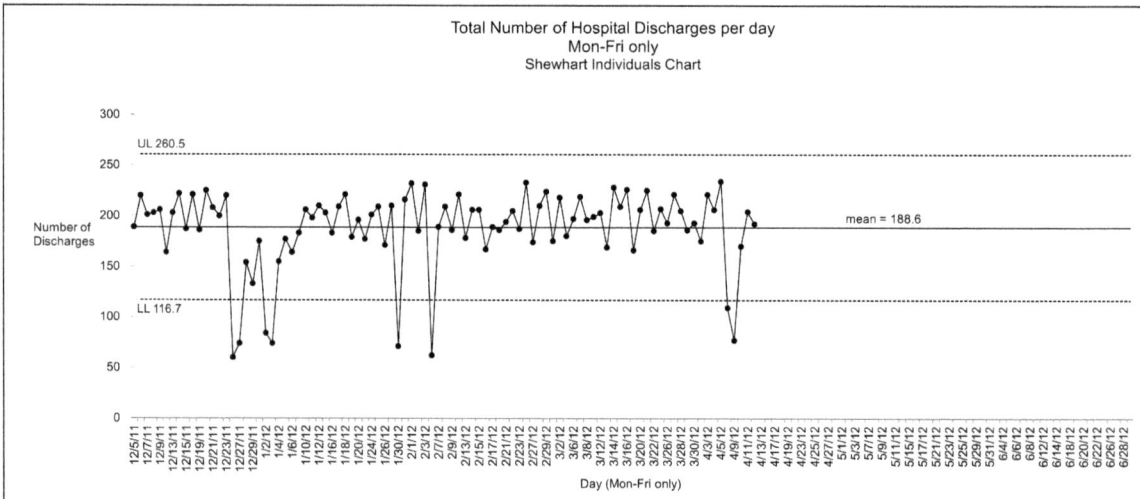

Figure 5.6 Hospital Discharges: Weekdays versus Weekends

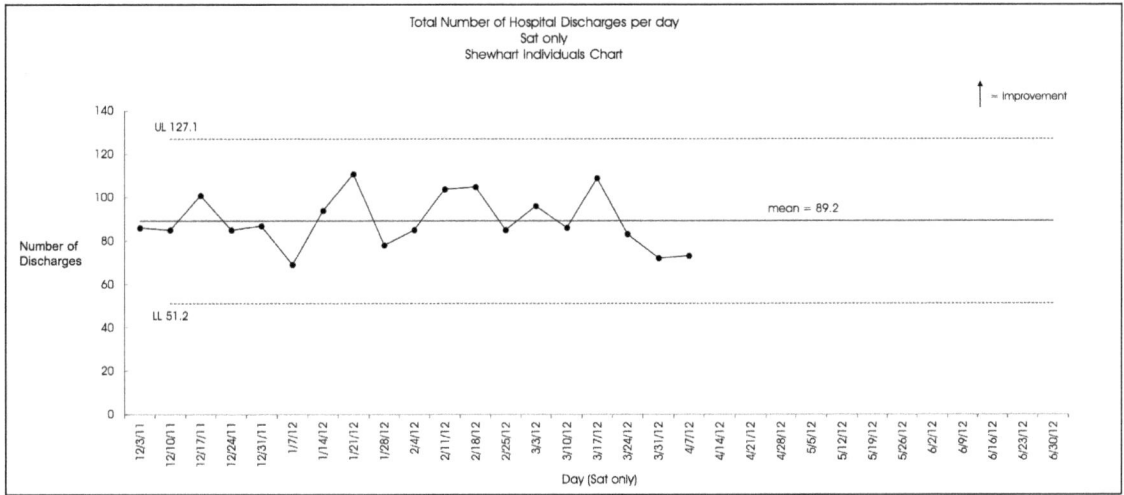

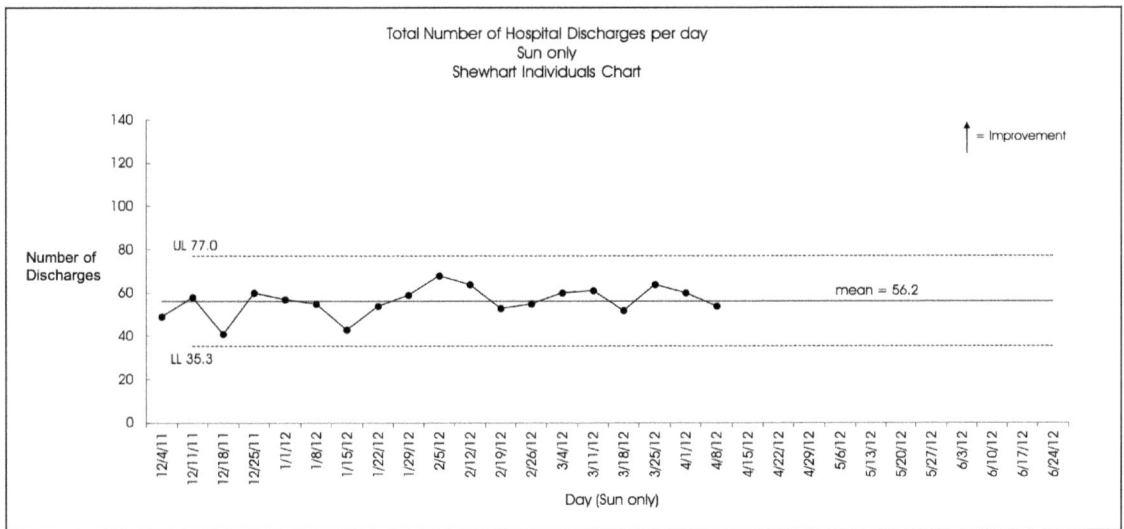

Figure 5.7.   Hospital Discharges Saturday versus Sunday

on the preferences of clinicians and entrenched staffing patterns. Through looking at their data, they realized that the hospital was operating as if it had different systems on weekdays, Saturdays, and Sundays. This led hospital leaders toward targeted improvement of the discharge process happening on Saturdays and Sundays. Reflecting on the data created the insight that changes made to increase weekend discharges would not be the same changes needed to increase discharges during weekdays.

Understanding Variation

Looking at the outcomes currently being produced can provide important insights into how the current system operates. Many problems that improvement teams will face are problems of variation. Some patients get the care they need whereas others do not. Some of the variation that systems produce is intended variation; patient's length of stay should vary based on their need. Other variation that systems produce is unintended variation; patients with the same need but that happen to get admitted on a different day of the week should not expect a different length of stay. Teams can disaggregate their data in different ways to help them see the variation that their current systems produce. They can then decide which sources of unwanted variation they may want to work to remove.

In an equitable system, there would be no unwanted variation in the health care, education, and social services that different populations receive. But we know that this is not the case. A critical component of understanding the current system is exploring who in the system is served well and who is not. The broad view that quantitative data affords is helpful in this regard, illuminating patterns that would be difficult to detect in a single classroom, practice, or caseload. Local subject matter expertise is used to anticipate which subpopulations might be underserved. Measures are disaggregated based on these subpopulations, grounding the team in a shared understanding of whether and where inequities exist.

For example, a charter school network with a strong commitment to equity decided to use data to take a closer look at which of their graduates went directly to a four-year college. Overall, their college-going rates were high; 65 percent of seniors went directly to college. To test whether they were serving their students equitably, they disaggregated their data in multiple ways. They looked at differences based on race/ethnicity, class, income, and gender. Through this process they discovered an equity gap: African American, Latino, and Native American males enrolled in four-year colleges at a rate 10 percent lower than their peers. As a result, they decided to focus there, starting by talking to their boys of color to understand how the organization was unintentionally creating this disparate experience.

Guidance for Analyzing and Making Sense of Quantitative Data

Getting a window into a system's performance using quantitative data often requires multiple rounds of asking questions, analyzing data, and making sense of the resulting graphs. Whenever possible, improvement teams should start by learning from existing data. Data collection is resource intensive, and organizations often collect scores of data that they have not yet leveraged for learning. As teams analyze data, they should be curious about variation over time, across units, and between different populations. Visualizing this variation and then trying to understand it can help teams figure out where to target their improvement work.

The same data can be analyzed in many ways to create useful insight into system performance. In the hospital-based example above, discharge data was disaggregated by day of week and analyzed for patterns unfolding over time. One question led to another as the team tried to make sense of graphs that were produced. The same data could have been treated differently: disaggregating between medical and surgical pathways, by age ranges of patients, by subpopulations of patients, and so forth. Each chart created from these disaggregations could produce important insights into where and for whom variation exists in the system. Disciplining the analysis using learning questions based on subject matter expertise can help prevent an improvement team from getting stuck in a rabbit hole of seemingly infinite permutations when analyzing quantitative data.

The real payoff in analyzing data in this way are the conversations that the analyses produce. Data do not produce insights; people looking at the data do. Data analysts can create the graphs, but it's important to engage people with subject matter expertise in generating learning questions, suggesting ways of disaggregating data and interpreting the data displays. The clinicians in the earlier example, for instance, could readily suggest explanations for what looked like highly variable discharge rates. Their on-the-ground knowledge was important in informing what analyses would be useful and making sense of what they saw.

Data conversations provide opportunities for teams to develop a system's view of their problem of practice. Time should be set aside to make sense of the analyses together. In these conversations, people who see the system from different angles can propose interpretations for the patterns they see. When data reveal unflattering interpretations of the system, the team's conversational capacity will often be put to the test. People will put up defensive barriers to deal with the discomfort, which can sometimes lead people to dismiss the data or engage in deficit-oriented conversations that blame individuals (e.g., "if the patients only complied, then we wouldn't have this problem"). Setting up strong norms, using conversation protocols, and cultivating strong conversational capacity can make data conversations more productive, creating space for team members to challenge each other's interpretations even in the face of defensiveness (for more on data conversation protocols, see chapter 12).

An important principle in using data for improvement is that those who produce the data participate in its interpretation. Pragmatically, this can happen within a team meeting or as an important next step coming out of an initial data conversation. This not only produces better conversations, but it is also an important way of disrupting power dynamics where data is collected from people for other people's use. This dynamic is common between researchers and practitioners, leaders and workers, and institutions and the people they serve. In the words of Brandi-Hinnant Crawford, "When you want to focus on a data point instead of the voice of the person who is the data point, that makes the whole process jaded and, in many ways, invalidates it" (Caillier 2022).

PRACTICAL GUIDANCE FOR ANALYZING AND MAKING SENSE OF QUANTITATIVE DATA

1. Identify a relevant outcome or measure. Use existing data whenever possible.
2. Specify a learning question to discipline the analysis.
3. Visualize variation

   a. across time,
   b. across populations,
   c. across "units" (departments in a hospital, grades in a school, schools in a district, etc.).

4. Make sense of the analysis with people who have the appropriate expertise.
5. Determine next steps.

VISUALIZING PROCESSES

Once we see the relationship between structure and behavior we can begin to understand how systems work, what makes them produce poor results, and how to shift them into better behavior patterns. —Meadows 2009, 1

Pictures work for this language {discussing systems} better than words, because you can see all the parts of a picture at once. —Meadows 2009, 5

Another angle into "seeing the system" is taking a closer look at organizational practices as they currently exist. Although it can be tempting to get right to the business of adding new practices or programs, rarely do change efforts occur on a blank canvas. As a result, before setting off to change the system, teams should develop a shared, grounded understanding of what already exists. Observing current practice, with a particular eye toward the user's experience, can reveal specific insights about where improvement is needed.

The language of processes can be helpful for examining organizational practice. From a technical sense, a process is defined as a "set of causes and conditions that repeatedly come together in a series of steps to transfer inputs into outcomes" (Langley et al. 2009, 36). Friendly synonyms for processes are "routines," "pathways," and "workflows." For any given outcome, multiple processes likely come together to produce the outcomes that are seen.

For example, the system that produces literacy outcomes is made up of multiple processes that interact in important ways to produce the outcomes observed, both quantitative and experiential. These include classroom processes such as formative assessment, small-group instruction, and independent reading time. They include routines at the school level such as scheduling, coaching, and intervention processes. District processes for providing professional development and purchasing instructional materials also come into play. Finally, literacy routines in the home also likely influence literacy outcomes. Understanding the details of how these routines occur and how they interact can generate useful insights for ensuring that more students become thriving readers.

Processes are the basic building blocks of systems.[19] They provide a concrete entry point to see and talk about the structure of the system. Once teams identify the processes related to the outcome at hand, it can be helpful to select the most consequential ones and examine them more closely. Seeing the details that make up these processes can reveal useful insights about what kind of change is needed.

Process mapping is a method for creating a visual representation of a workflow for an individual, group, or organization. The typical nomenclature for a process map is displayed in figure 5.8.

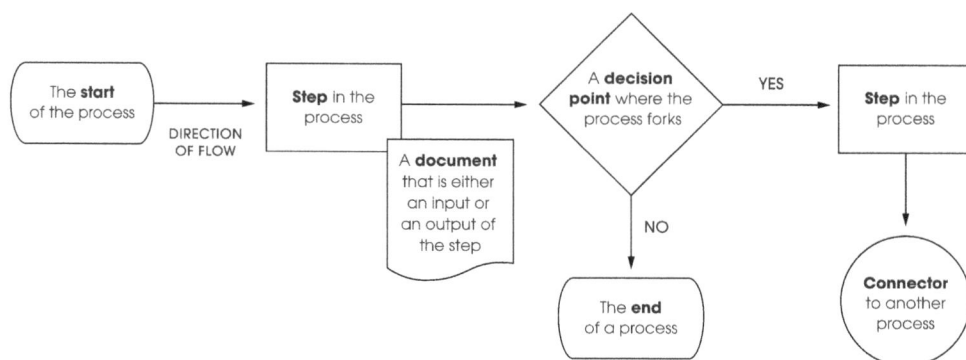

Figure 5.8. Symbols for Process Maps

The details of how work gets done often live in the minds of individuals. The act of visualizing together helps teams build a shared understanding of what their work entails—in what order things happen, where bottlenecks are located, how long things take, and who does what. It can highlight how people's work is interconnected and comes together to produce the user's experience. Oftentimes, this highlights specific places where breakdowns occur or unwanted variation is produced.

Example: Process Mapping Antenatal HIV Care in KwaZulu-Natal, South Africa

In 2007, a hospital team in the KwaZulu-Natal province of South Africa[20] set out to reduce the mother-to-child HIV transmission rate in the community they served.[21] The work had been spurred by a landmark study that estimated that twenty thousand children were born HIV positive every year just in this province (Rollins et al. 2007). As a point of comparison, at the same time only 115 children were born HIV positive in the entire United States despite it having thirty times the population (Centers for Disease Control and Prevention 2008, 11). Mother-to-child transmission of HIV was preventable with the right antenatal, delivery, and postnatal care. However, knowing how to prevent transmission was different from being able to create a system that reliably put that knowledge into practice.

When the hospital team looked at their data on antenatal visits, they saw that only 35 percent of expectant mothers were tested for HIV during their first visit. This was a problem. A positive test was what triggered the care that prevented mothers from passing on HIV to their babies (as well as receiving the care they needed to stay healthy). The clinicians on the team did not know what more they could do. Every woman who came in for antenatal care was referred to the HIV clinic in the same hospital for testing. But only 35 percent of the women followed that advice, no matter how they emphasized its importance. It seemed to the team members that the women must not want to get tested, perhaps because they did not care about being HIV positive, were scared of the results, or did not understand why it was important. The team was in danger of falling into deficit-oriented thinking.

With some prompting from their improvement coach, the team decided to map the mothers' experience of the antenatal care visit, during which the HIV test was supposed to occur. At first this did not seem like a useful exercise to the team. Of course, they knew what happened during a visit. After all, these visits were routine practice; they saw dozens of expectant mothers daily. However, visualizing the process was more difficult than they expected. Different people were responsible for registering the mothers, checking up on the pregnancy, and screening for HIV. Each person knew what they did but did not frequently see their work in relation to the other parts of the visit. After the team mapped it out, they realized that for the women the visit entailed quite a few steps (see figure 5.9).

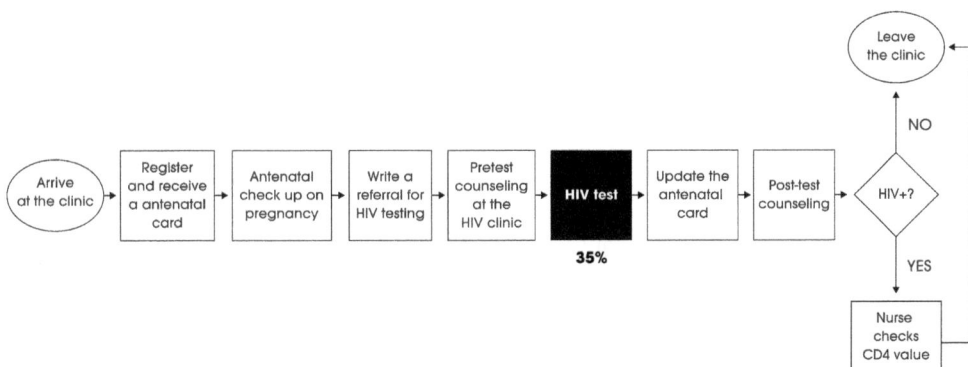

Figure 5.9. Antenatal Visit: Map of the Current Process

The team knew that only 35 percent of mothers completed the HIV test (the fifth step in the visit). They began to get curious about what happened to the 65 percent of mothers who skipped the HIV testing. Where did they lose them along the way? They decided to observe the process to figure out what went wrong (see figure 5.10).

As they watched mothers go through the process, a couple of things stood out to the team. They recorded their observations on the process map (see figure 5.10). First, when the mothers arrived at the clinic, it was not unusual for them to wait fifteen to thirty minutes. After finishing the antenatal visit, they were supposed to report to the HIV clinic where they could initiate testing. The HIV clinic was in the same hospital, but it was about two hundred meters away, requiring a seven-minute walk and several turns in a confusing, unmarked corridor. In contrast the exit, leading straight to the bus stop, was conveniently located just meters from where the check-up occurred. They suspected that this was where they lost many of the mothers who headed home instead of finding their way to the HIV clinic. What's more, as they talked to mothers, it became clear that the antenatal visit was the primary purpose and most important part of their visit. After suspecting they were pregnant, they were anxious to learn about the health of the pregnancy. The need to get an HIV test often came as a surprise. It was not the reason that they came to the hospital in the first place.

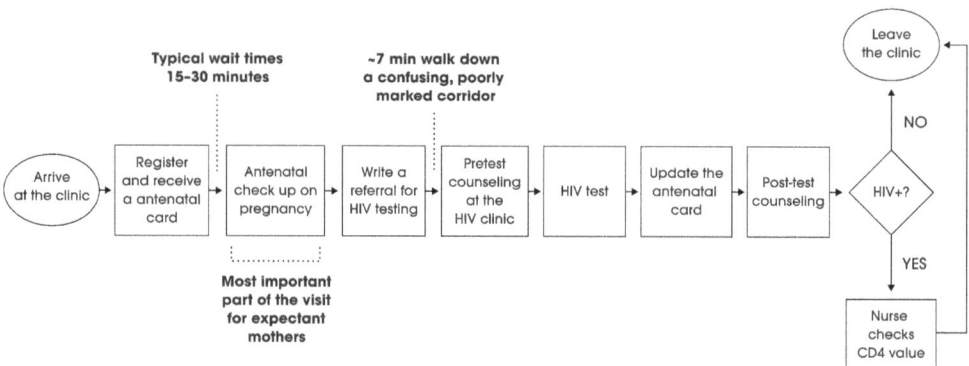

Figure 5.10. Antenatal Visit: Process Analysis

Observing the process in action gave the team some ideas about how to make HIV testing easier. They could embed a nurse from the HIV clinic in the antenatal clinic so the mothers could get all their care in one place. They moved the HIV testing to the early part of the visit, taking advantage of the time the women were waiting anyway, and putting the part of the visit they came for—the check-up—at the end. The team prototyped a new process, tried it out, and tweaked it until it eventually became the new process of care for expectant mothers (see chapter 11 for more on testing changes in practice). Through these changes, they increased the percentage of expectant mothers who accepted and received HIV testing from 35 to 95 percent (see figure 5.11).

Taking the time to observe current practice can produce insights to help teams productively target their change efforts. Had the hospital team operated off their original assumption that the women did not understand or want HIV testing, they might have wasted time and resources adding educational programs on the importance of knowing your HIV status. Instead, just rearranging the steps of care made the visit simpler, solving the problem without expending additional resources.

Looking more closely at processes can also provide insight into how inequities are built into the way the system operates. When people typically talk about processes in organizations, they tend to focus on their ideal form. Hiring processes are described with reference

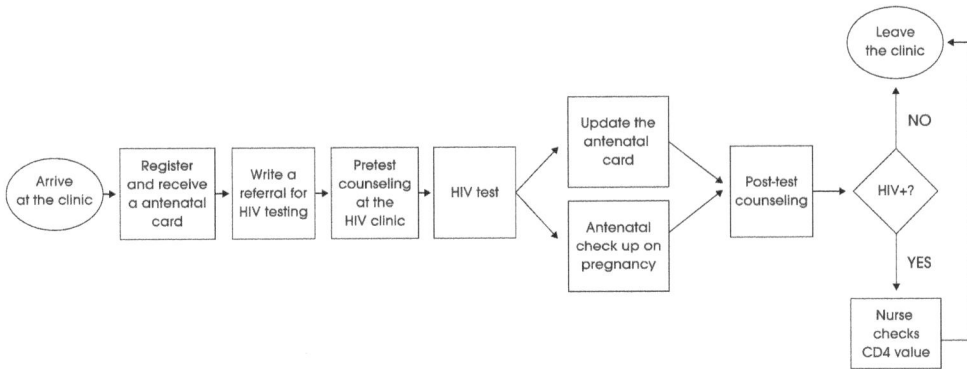

Figure 5.11. Antenatal Visit: Redesigned Process

to a recognizable set of steps. Schools create disciplinary processes that lay out what will happen in what order. In their ideal form, these processes appear to apply equally to everyone. Yet when they play out in practice, they produce differential outcomes. Although the organizational routines previously mentioned are presented officially as being race and gender neutral, black boys are disciplined at disproportionately higher rates (Lewis and Diamond 2015), and gender influences hiring decisions (Kline, Rose, and Walters 2021). Investigating how processes are carried out in practice can provide insights into how disproportionate outcomes are often unintentionally produced. This, in turn, can help teams redesign systems to make them more equitable.[22]

Guidance for Visualizing Key Processes

Teams looking to use process maps to visually represent current practices need to start by identifying processes related to the outcome of interest.[23] The team can then prioritize which processes to further explore. Content experts are often useful in helping point teams toward key processes. In the Shasta example, literacy expertise helped point the team to look at formative assessment practices (and eventually grouping and small-group instruction) as key processes to understand.

The map can be created by bringing together the various participants involved in the process and asking them to use their collective understanding to identify the key steps. Even in teams that work together regularly, attempting to create a common visualization can surface confusion and difference of opinion about the order in which steps occur or who is responsible for them. Process maps can also be created empirically—either by observing the process or having someone follow the steps of a process from start to finish in real time, mapping each step and decision point as the work unfolds.

Once an initial process map has been created it is useful for teams to analyze the process, reflecting on whether the process is serving its intended purpose. Details can be added to prompt reflections. Useful details include connections to other processes, who is responsible for each step (and any handoffs implied by the arrows), where each step occurs, when it happens, and how long it takes. The teams can analyze the process, noting where problematic delays, breakdowns, and unwanted variation occur (see table 5.1).[24] Analyzing the process often leads the team directly to change ideas focused either on particular steps in the process or the process as a whole.[25] Other times it leads to the realization that other related processes need to be better understood.

Table 5.1. Common Questions for Process Analysis

Details to Add to Your Process	Analyses of the Process
• Time: How long does each step take? • Space: Where does each step take place? • People: Who performs each step? Who owns each arrow?	• Are any of the steps unnecessary? • Are the steps in the right order? • Where do delays occur in the process? • Are there any problematic handoffs? • Are there bottlenecks? • Are there steps characterized by unwanted variation?

PRACTICAL GUIDANCE FOR MAPPING PROCESSES

1. Identify key processes related to the outcome of interest.
2. Prioritize a process to better understand.
3. Create an initial process map to

   a. facilitate people who engage in the process *or*
   b. observe the process and create an initial visualization.

4. Define quality for the process.
5. Add detail to the process map (time, who owns each step, timing, etc.).
6. Analyze the process.

INVESTIGATING THE SYSTEM: SELECTING A METHOD

As the examples throughout this chapter demonstrate, multiple methods can be drawn on as the team seeks to "see the system" producing the current outcomes. Empathy interviews surface the needs and insights of the intended beneficiaries of the improvement work. Analyzing quantitative data uncovers variation (or a lack of variation) and enables the discovery of patterns that go beyond what a single individual can see. Process mapping ground-checks people's assumptions about current practice and can illuminate important details about how work is organized. Each of these methods provides a different view into the system; all offer a different take on the question of what is currently happening. The appropriate method depends on the learning question, and the questions can build on each other over time.

Figure 5.12 shows an example of a learning agenda that a team working on understanding chronic absenteeism could use to guide the investigation.[26] The chart prompts the team to share what they think they know and, importantly, what they don't know. Different questions imply different methods. The questions should drive the methods, not the other way around.

Teams will rarely have the time and bandwidth to answer all the questions. Rather, they can keep the list of questions as a learning agenda. They can designate a particular rhythm for investigating, organizing the work in learning cycles, prioritizing a question (or two) for each round (see figure 5.4). Sometimes different team members take on a different question—one person takes the lead on analyzing the data, for example, while others map a process. Other times, the team takes on a question together, each person interviewing an

What we **KNOW**:

- 25 percent of our students are chronically absent.
- Students who are chronically absent experience lower levels of academic achievement.

What We *Want* to Learn	Method	What We *Learned* (artifact)
How do students and families decide whether to attend school each day?	Empathy interviews and headlining	
How have chronic absenteeism rates varied over time?	Analyzing quantitative data—Shewhart chart or run chart	
How do chronic absenteeism rates vary by different student groups?	Analyzing quantitative data using Shewhart charts	
What is the process for students to make up work?	Process map	
What are the current practices for tracking and following up on absences?	Process map	
What are the different reasons students are absent? Which ones are the most frequent?	Empathy interviews analyzing quantitative data Pareto chart	
Which factors influence absences?	Cause-and-effect diagram	

Figure 5.12. Learning Agenda to Guide an Investigation

end user, for example, and coming back together to share what they learned. Regular team meetings help establish a rhythm, creating a place to share learnings, coalesce around key artifacts, and determine what needs to be learned next. The rhythm and structure help team members stay curious and tolerate the ambiguity inherent in the often winding, nonlinear path of investigating systems.

PRACTICAL GUIDANCE FOR STRUCTURING AN INVESTIGATION

1. Define the problem to be investigated.
2. Gather the appropriate people.
3. Use a learning agenda chart to

   a. agree on what is "known."
   b. identify "learning questions."

4. Prioritize a question(s).
5. Select the appropriate method:

    a. empathy methods.
    b. quantitative data analysis.
    c. process mapping.

6. Create artifacts that represent the learning.
7. Make sense of the learning as a team.
8. Prioritize the next question (return to step 4).

CONCLUSION

Team members often enter systems investigations implicitly believing they know "what's currently happening." Looking at the system from different angles and different perspectives reveals gaps in the team's understanding that may, in turn, help explain why previous efforts have fallen short, pointing them in new directions. Investigating together also helps team members move from individually held viewpoints to a collective understanding.

The early stages of understanding the system are about divergence and discovery. Teams start by defining a problem, generating learning questions, and choosing methods to help them achieve important insights into the design and performance of their system. "Data" from the end users, quantitative analysis, and visualizations of processes are all useful in different ways. Through the investigation, people often realize that the system they are trying to improve is more complex than they originally assumed. "Seeing the system" can produce a curiosity, a need to learn and work together that energizes the entire improvement journey going forward.

At some point, however, the team needs to begin to focus. Improvement work requires resources, and not all the system components can be changed at once. In the next chapter, we describe methods that can help teams converge on a focus, identifying leverage points to work on in the system.

6

From Seeing to Selecting

For any complex problem to be solved, the individual players all need to recognize how they unwittingly contribute to it. Once they understand their own responsibility for a problem, they can begin by changing the part of the system over which they have the greatest control: themselves . . . the greatest opportunities for lasting change arise when all the players reflect on and shift their own intentions, assumptions, and behavior.

—Stroh 2015, 18

A good investigation looks at a situation from a variety of angles, connecting multiple forms of evidence that lead to important insights. In detective movies and television shows, the image of an evidence board captures the heart of the investigation process. The evidence board often covers a large wall; it is the place where teams pin clues and discuss theories based on their learning to date. In the early stages the clues are often disjointed, occupying random spaces on the wall. As the investigation unfolds, the team discovers connections between the clues, and the board gets rearranged, creating a more coherent picture. Eventually, the pieces of the puzzle converge to produce sometimes surprising explanations for the mystery at hand.

This chapter is designed to help teams answer the question, "Why are we getting the outcomes we are currently getting?" Systems investigations in improvement science proceed much the same way as the evidence boards described above. Teams first try to understand what is currently happening, looking at the problem from multiple perspectives. Different kinds of data offer different clues, which can be pinned on a metaphorical evidence board. As more clues accumulate and more of the system is revealed, teams naturally shift to diagnosing or theorizing why they are getting the current outcomes, ideally identifying parts of the system to redesign in hopes of moving it in a more productive direction.

To do this, teams can draw on a variety of methods to guide the analysis and illuminate potential starting points. However, settling on where to begin usually involves team negotiation. In most situations, multiple starting points exist, and team members may differ in where they think they should begin. As a result, having structures to navigate these discussions are critical so teams can come to consensus and get going.

LEVERAGE POINTS[1]

In a systems investigation, the "culprits" the team is looking for are the specific system components driving the current outcomes. As we described in chapter 1, these elements include policies, practices, structures, power dynamics, relationships, beliefs, and mindsets. Although many components are naturally involved in the interconnected nature of systems, the team is looking specifically for "leverage points" in the system—places where relatively small action can lead to comparatively big results (Forrester 1973; Senge 1990; Meadows 2008).

In the literacy example from chapter 5, the team identified formative assessment practices as one leverage point that impacted first-grade fluency (which, in turn, was hypothesized as having leverage in impacting literacy outcomes in later grades). The "leverage" in formative assessment practices comes from their interdependencies with other parts of reading instruction. Improving formative assessment gives teachers better knowledge of student reading behaviors, which, in turn, influences a host of instructional practices done one-on-one, in small groups, and as a whole class. It can influence how students are grouped and help teachers identify students in need of extra support. In other words, focusing on assessment practices has a ripple effect, impacting the system of reading as a whole. In addition, formative assessment practices were a notable pain point for teachers, who experienced them as time consuming and cumbersome, making these practices an excellent place to start.

Finding leverage points entails going beyond the symptoms of problems to discover the underlying causes, which is not always a simple task. Systems scholars have pointed out key systems principles that highlight why the identification of the causes of outcomes can be challenging:

> Cause and effect are not close in time and space. (Senge 1990, 63)

> Small changes can produce big results, but the areas of highest leverage are often the least obvious. (Senge 1990, 63)

> There is no single, legitimate boundary to draw around a system. We have to invent boundaries for clarity and sanity; and boundaries can produce problems when we forget that we've artificially created them. (Meadows 2008, 97)

At the beginning of a system's investigation, it is useful to stay broad, seeing across typical department boundaries and past presumed solutions. This allows teams to explore a broader terrain where leverage points may be hiding. However, it is easy to get stuck in "analysis paralysis," where teams strive for certainty and a complete understanding that complex systems defy. Instead, teams must purposefully shift from divergent to convergent thinking and zero in on a handful of leverage points where the team can act. The goal of improvement, after all, is not just to understand the system but to change it.

Teams will draw on a combination of evidence and subject matter expertise when pivoting from understanding the system to deciding where to act. We will highlight two methods that can help teams identify where to begin: 1) cause-and-effect analysis and 2) Pareto analysis.[2] More than tools, these methods exemplify ways of thinking that are helpful for deciding how to target improvement efforts. Then we turn to the question of why we need methods at all, why we can't simply think or talk our way into insightful understandings.

CAUSE-AND-EFFECT ANALYSIS

A cause-and-effect diagram (also called a fishbone diagram or Ishikawa diagram) is a visual method for summarizing a team's answer to the question "Why are we getting the outcomes we are currently getting?"

The "effect" or problem to be addressed is specified on the right-hand side (or the head of the fish). On the left-hand side, are the hypothesized causes. They are logically grouped into "cause categories" with the more specific causal factors located on the bones associated with each category (Ishikawa 1982; Tague 2015; Bennett, Grunow, and Park 2022).[3] The cause categories represent different leverage points where improvement work could be focused. A cause-and-effect diagram for a district wanting to address high rates of chronic absenteeism is displayed in figure 6.1.

The analysis represented in a cause-and-effect diagram is only as insightful as the perspectives and evidence used to generate it. Teams can use this document to summarize what they learn during their investigation. For example, a team may go through 2–3 rounds of asking questions and collecting data using the methods described in chapter 5. When it is time to decide where to focus, teams can review their data to identify themes that can serve as cause categories and create a diagram that consolidates key learnings from their investigation.

Some teams opt to start by creating a cause-and-effect diagram through brainstorming to surface assumptions about the causes of the problem. With larger groups of diverse stakeholders, this can be a useful way to initiate a collective conversation that gets beneath debating favored solutions.[4] One potential danger of this approach is that a nicely created diagram gets mistaken for an insightful analysis. When starting here, it is important to follow up the conversation by collecting actual evidence, putting the initial assumptions to the test.

Example: Cause-and-Effect Analysis for Chronic Absenteeism[5]

For example, the district team investigating chronic absenteeism from chapter 5 created an initial cause-and-effect diagram at their kickoff meeting. They brought a wide variety of stakeholders to the table and began by reviewing the districts' data on chronic absenteeism and coming to agreement on the problem. Then members of the group, based on their experience, individually identified key factors they believed contributed to the problem. Together, they grouped the causes into themes and created Version 1.0 of their cause-and-effect diagram. Hear-

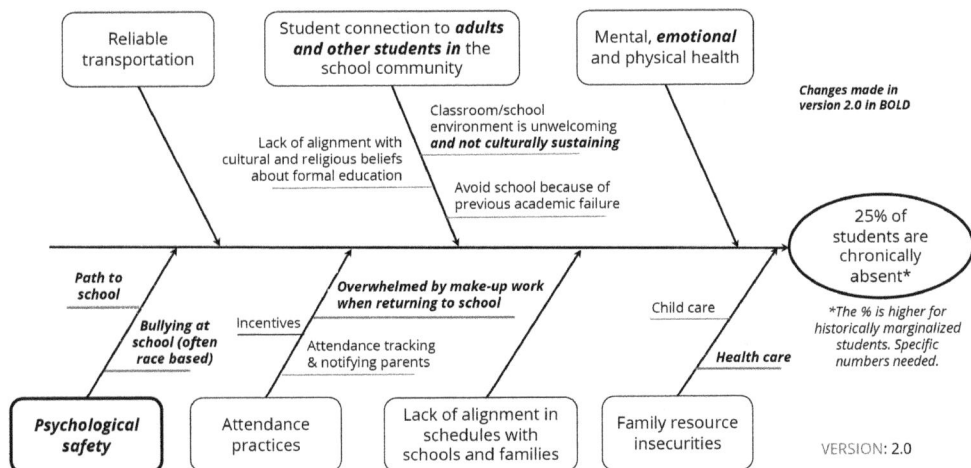

Figure 6.1. Cause-and-Effect Diagram for Chronic Absenteeism

ing how different stakeholders understood the problem was an important initial step in seeing the problem more expansively and helped build common ground for the work moving forward.

Although varying perspectives were in the room for the initial analysis of the problem, the voices of students and families were glaringly missing. The improvement coaches helped set up a process for conducting empathy interviews. As described in the section in chapter 5 about empathy interviews, the group conducted more than one hundred interviews with students and families in the following weeks. At the same time, the improvement coaches did a literature scan on chronic absenteeism. When they came back together for their second team meeting, they used what they learned through the interviews and scan to iterate on their cause-and-effect diagram, creating Version 2.0. First, they used the evidence from both methods to identify additional causes that did not come up during the initial meeting as well as add nuance to some of the causes they had initially hypothesized. They did this by capturing headlines or themes from the data and mapping them onto the initial diagram to see where there were gaps or potential discrepancies.

The literature scan, for example, noted that one reason why students often reported not coming to school was psychological safety, both in traveling to school and during the school day. This was added as a new cause category. In the empathy interviews, students talked about not coming back to school after legitimate absences to avoid the overwhelming feeling of needing to catch up when they returned. This highlighted a part of the student experience that hadn't occurred to the adults in the system. Teachers followed up by using process maps to better understand the "make-up work process" from the point of view of the students.

Second, the team used the empathy data to test the validity of causes initially identified as well as to prioritize potential focus areas. They quantified the data by adding a dot sticker to a cause category every time that cause came up in the interviews. They discovered that students and families talked most about a) connections to the school community and b) mental health. Prior to the empathy interviews, many people on the team felt confident that lack of incentives and barriers to transportation were the causes that needed to be addressed. But this turned out not to be the case. Although psychological safety had been highlighted in the research as important, this cause did not come up in their specific context. Instead, team members overwhelmingly heard stories of students and families feeling unwelcome in the school community. The team soon realized that building stronger ties between school and home was the leverage point that they needed to focus on.

The Pareto Principle

As seen in the chronic absenteeism example, creating a cause-and-effect analysis is helpful in breaking down a big problem to more specific, actionable places to work. When teams move to action, rarely will they take on all the causes identified; rather they will prioritize 1–2 leverage points as a starting point. For this, the Pareto principle can be useful for teams to consider.

In 1896, Italian economist Vilfredo Pareto found that 80 percent of the distribution of wealth in nineteenth-century England belonged to 20 percent of the people and that this pattern was repeated in other countries he examined where data was available (Koch 1998, 6). This 80:20 pattern, where 80 percent of the phenomena is the result of 20 percent of the causes, is known as the Pareto principle.[6]

In improvement science, the Pareto principle is typically used when analyzing outcomes and identifying the most frequently occurring cause categories.

Of course, the 80:20 "rule" is not literally true in all situations. However, what the Pareto principle suggests is that not all causes are created equal; some causes are more influential than others because of their frequency of occurrence.[7] If teams can identify the most influential causes, then they can direct their limited time, attention, and resources more strategically, assuring a greater return on investment.

Example: Pareto Analysis to Understand Where Community College Math Students Are Lost from the System[8]

In a formal Pareto analysis, teams look at each instance of a problem and categorize why and/or where it occurred. For example, a team from a community college math department sought to increase the number of students who completed their college-level math requirements. The team was particularly worried about the large number of students placed in remedial math. In the early stages of their investigation, they asked, "How many students who place into remedial math successfully complete college-level math?" One striking finding was that for many students who placed two levels below a college-level math course, only 10 percent completed the college math requirement they needed to earn their degree or transfer to a four-year college. This low completion rate was persistent across multiple cohorts of students. This was eye-opening for the math faculty who knew how their students fared in their specific classes but did not know how the system served these students as a whole.

As their investigation continued, the team next asked, "Where are we losing so many students within the math pathway?" They were particularly interested in whether some courses were more difficult than others for students to pass. Privately, some team members also wondered if some faculty were "just not as good" as others. To answer this question, they conducted a more detailed analysis of the cohort of incoming students from the two prior years. Of these students, 742 placed two levels below college-level math, which meant that completing college-level math would look like this:

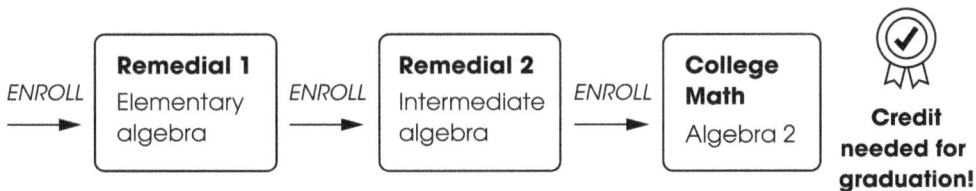

Figure 6.2. Traditional Pathway for Completing College-Level Math

However, fast-forwarding two years, only 79 of the 742 students completed college-level math. Where had they lost all the students? Logically, there were a limited number of moments students could fall through the cracks. They could a) fail (or withdraw from) a class or b) not enroll; with three required courses, this added up to six potential "failure points" in the system. They classified each of the 663 students who did not complete college-level math according to where the system lost them. The Pareto analysis is displayed in figure 6.3. The bars describe the number of non-completing students that fit into any given category, ordered from the most frequent cause to the least frequent. The line graph uses the axis on the right to display the cumulative percentage of the non-completing students attributable to a particular

Reasons Students do not Complete College Math

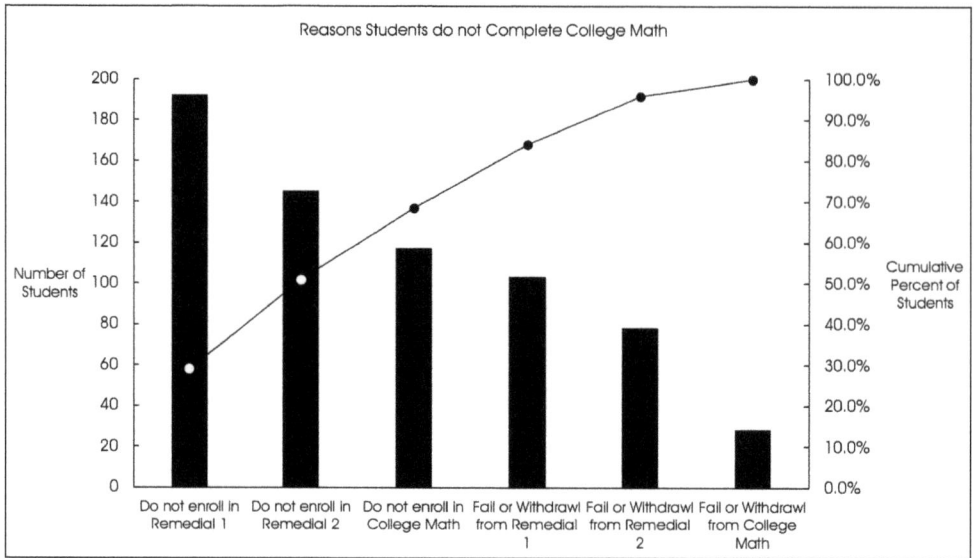

Figure 6.3. Pareto Chart: Where Students Exit the College Math Pathway

cause and the ones before it. The analysis shows, for example, that the first three cause categories account for 69 percent of the students who do not complete college-level math.[9]

The results were striking to the team: they lost way more students between classes than within. Their conversations to date had been about changes needed in classrooms, but after looking at the data, they realized that the more pressing problem was getting students to the classrooms in the first place.

Whether or not teams use a formal Pareto analysis, the ability to separate the "vital few" from the "useful many" is helpful. Pareto thinking has already been visible in the examples used in previous chapters. The school teams wanting to address chronic absenteeism used data from students and families as a way of seeing what was most important. The hospital team wanting to decrease the length of hospital stays realized through their analysis that focusing on weekend discharges would give them the biggest bang for their buck (see chapter 5). Pareto thinking is particularly helpful in making the transition from trying to understand the system to deciding where to start.

EXAMINING BELIEFS IN THE CONTEXT OF COLLECTIVE DECISION-MAKING

Different points of the improvement journey require different kinds of decision-making. It is fine, even productive, for team members to pursue divergent lines of inquiry when trying to understand the system or to test different change ideas to learn what works in practice. But when it comes time to decide where to focus, team members need to achieve consensus. They must collectively put a stake in the ground and head in the same direction together.

The methods described in the previous two chapters generate data that can inform decisions about where to focus, but coming together around a decision is fundamentally a social process. Team members will naturally come to the work with their own intentions, experiences, and beliefs. Even looking at the same evidence, people will have varied interpretations. If the team can productively surface differing interpretations and examine them together, they can leverage the diverse perspectives to make better decisions and come to new shared understandings. However, this can be hard to do. It requires team members to enter conversations expecting and interested in differing perspectives (for more on conversational capacity, see chapter 4). That in turn requires an intellectual humility; a willingness to reflect on our assumptions and reexamine our own beliefs. Learning more about the ways in which people think can help us be a little less attached to our first draft thinking and lean into the power of group decision-making.

How People Think

Most of us, when asked why we believe something we do, think we came to our conclusions through an orderly and systematic thought process. Cognitive psychologists, however, have demonstrated that most judgments we make are made automatically without conscious awareness.

In his book *Thinking, Fast and Slow*, Nobel laureate Daniel Kahneman highlights this phenomenon:

> You may not know that you are optimistic about a project because something about its leader reminds you of your beloved sister, or that you dislike a person who looks vaguely like your dentist. If asked for an explanation, however, you will search your memory for presentable reasons and will certainly find some. Moreover, you will believe the story you made up. (Kahneman 2011, 415)

For most everyday tasks, concluding quickly is helpful and productive; it helps us manage the vast amount of information coming at us at any moment of the day. To do this, however, our brains take shortcuts, which result in biases that predictably influence our judgments or decisions. Cognitive psychologists have identified and named numerous cognitive biases. Table 6.1 describes six common cognitive biases that are particularly relevant for decision-making in organizations.

When people experience conclusions that quickly and easily come to mind, they often assume this means that they are correct (Kahneman, Sibony, and Sunstein 2021, 31). Learning about cognitive biases can create a healthy skepticism about conclusions that arise with ease (see table 6.1). They describe how we selectively attend to and weigh some information more than others (availability and anchoring biases) and how our brains seem to prefer tidy, coherent stories over dissonance (confirmation, hindsight, and halo effect).

The human brain can, of course, slow down and make decisions more deliberately when it matters. Deciding where to focus improvement efforts is one of those deliberative moments. Applying the tools and methods described in this chapter can help. It is also useful to enter decision-making with an awareness of cognitive biases. If we falsely believe that we see the world objectively, we have no real reason to expect or explore interpretations that are different than our own. If we understand the limitations of our own thinking, the opposite is true—we need to expose our interpretations to see where they might be flawed.

Table 6.1.   Common Cognitive Biases That Impact Decision Making[10]

Confirmation Bias	Our underlying tendency to notice, focus on, and give greater credence to evidence that fits with our existing beliefs.
Hindsight Bias	Our tendency to look back at an unpredictable event and think it was easily predictable. It is also called the "knew-it-all-along" effect.
Halo Effect	When our positive impressions of people, brands, and products in one area lead us to have positive feelings in another area. This cognitive bias leads us often to cast judgment without having a reason.
Availability or Recency Bias	Our tendency to use recent events or information that comes to mind quickly and easily when making decisions about the future.
Anchoring Bias	Causes us to rely too heavily on the first piece of information we are given about a topic. When we are setting plans or making estimates about something, we interpret newer information from the reference point of our anchor instead of seeing it objectively. This can skew our judgment and prevent us from updating our plans or predictions as much as we should.
Fundamental Attribution Error	When making judgments about other people's behavior, we often overemphasize dispositional factors and downplay situational ones. In other words, we believe that people's personality traits have more influence on their actions than other factors they can't control.

Ladder of Inference

One tool that teams can use to explore their interpretations is the ladder of inference. Organizational learning scholar Chris Argyris posited that one of the key barriers to collective learning is the widespread tendency to avoid surfacing and reflecting on conflicting assumptions. The theory goes that people hold tacit (often unexamined) assumptions that guide their behavior. Groups learn together by surfacing assumptions and reflecting on them together in conversation. The trick is that conflicting assumptions can be perceived as threatening, particularly if you believe you see the world objectively, which leads to what he called "defensive reasoning" (Argyris 1999, 56). Socially and cognitively, people prefer coherent stories and harmony over dissonance. So tacit assumptions stay hidden to preserve the comfort of the team. Argyris created the ladder of inference to help teams access and share their tacit assumptions so that they could be reflected upon (Argyris, Putnam, and Smith 1985, 57; Argyris 1990, 88).[11]

As depicted in figure 6.4, the "ladder" sits in a pool, which represents the pool of data available in any given situation. This pool of data is larger than the human brain can process. Therefore, we select some of the data and interpret it, making meaning and adding our own assumptions to fill any gaps. We draw conclusions based on these interpretations, which then form into beliefs. These beliefs, in turn, inform our actions. All of this happens in a split second without our awareness. Emotions cause us to jump up the ladder more quickly. Moreover, the beliefs we form influence which data we pay attention to, creating a reflexive loop that strengthens both thought and behavioral patterns that further reinforce our beliefs.

The ladder of inference helps explain why people working to explore the same problem in the same organization can come to different explanations. People pull on different observations, filter them through their own lenses, and are primed to come to conclusions based on their past experiences. If the conversation stays high on the ladder—with people discussing their opinions—the likelihood of disagreement increases. Walking down the ladder—sharing the data being attended to and the interpretations being added—can be a productive way

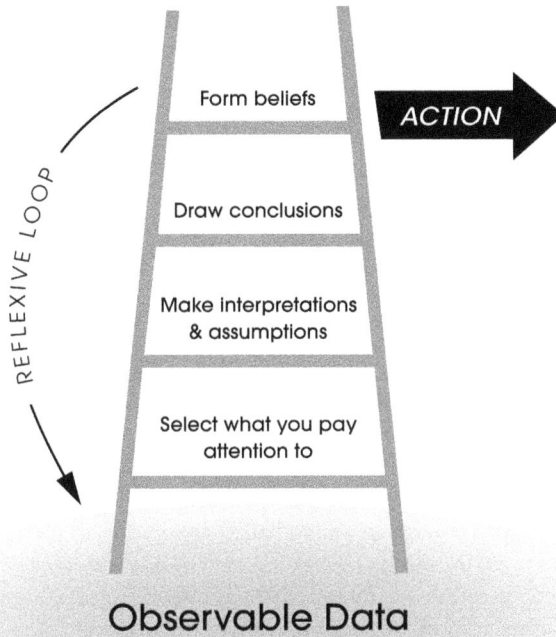

Figure 6.4. Ladder of Inference

for teams to get beneath different assessments of the situation. Teams can use the ladder of inference as a tool to discipline conversations, support team members to make their thinking public, lean into multiple interpretations, and see assumptions that may need to be tested. The tools and methods of improvement (including those in chapters 5 and 6) help guard against biases. The ladder of inference and strong conversational capacity support teams as they interpret what they find and make important decisions about what to do as a result.

Deficit Thinking

Multiple factors influence how each of us "jumps up the ladder." Our identities, roles, and experiences impact what we are primed to see. The cognitive biases in table 6.1 influence which information we selectively pay attention to and how we weigh some forms of incoming data more than others. The fundamental attribution error suggests interpretations that blame or credit individuals will be favored over those that highlight the role of context or systems. And as a final piece of the puzzle, common cultural narratives influence which explanations are most readily available to us as we seek to make sense of what we see.

In the United States, for example, we have justified inequitable education systems by blaming students and their families. These "cultural deficit ideologies" have roots in the scholarship of the 1950s and 1960s, which suggested that children of color were "victims of pathological lifestyles" (Ladson-Billings 2007, 316–23). Although this scholarship has largely been debunked, the beliefs still exist. And they are continually fed through the media and popular culture. So, when educators look at differential educational outcomes for students of color, it is not uncommon to hear explanations that have their roots in deficit thinking:

> The parents just don't care.
> These children don't have enough exposure/experiences.
> These children aren't ready for school.
> Their families don't value education.
> They are coming from a culture of poverty.
> This will be too hard for my students.
> Students aren't motivated. (Ladson-Billings 2007; Singleton 2015, xv)

These cultural narratives form well-worn grooves in our minds, influencing the explanations that quickly pop to mind when interpreting incoming data.

Deficit thinking will predictably emerge when "investigating the system." After all, beliefs and mindsets are key elements that hold the current system in place (see chapter 1), and the improvement team is part of the system they are trying to change. In investigating the system, it is important to create a context in which beliefs can be surfaced and examined collectively.

As team members in the district working on chronic absenteeism discussed previously brainstormed potential causes for their cause-and-effect diagram, some suggested "a lack of student and family motivation." Lack of motivation is a typical deficit orientation. It is a rationalization often used to defend current practice, blaming individuals instead of recognizing the influence of systems.

The coaches were not surprised that this assumption had surfaced. They had purposefully designed a phase of work to support the group to wrestle with these kinds of assumptions and unpack them. They invited a diverse set of stakeholders who were likely to see the problem differently. They used cause-and-effect analysis to structure a conversation that generated multiple hypotheses for consideration. They paired the brainstorm with the use of "five whys" in which teams had to ask why five times to dig beyond surface-level explanation. Most important, they engaged everyone in conducting empathy interviews with students and families, exposing people to new "pools of data" to consider. When the group reconvened, the coaches explicitly prompted a reflection about how the starting assumptions needed to be revised given that the empathy interviews did not generate any evidence that students or families did not want or care about school. However, they did surface specific reasons that made it difficult to come or return to school that were new to them. As a result, the focus moved from assuming they needed to motivate students through incentives to rethinking school practices that were inadvertently making students and families question whether they were welcome at school.

COMING TO A CONSENSUS ON A STARTING POINT

The problem is not that we have shortcuts in our thinking. The problem is that we forget that we do.[12] The speed with which the human mind can process information is remarkable, and this quick thinking serves us well much of the time. However, when seeing things in new ways or forging new directions is what we are after, we are better off slowing down, adding discipline, and working in teams with multiple perspectives.

Understanding the current system is an important part of slowing down to come to better decisions. Improvement methods structure ways to generate evidence and deliberately test assumptions. Integrating multiple perspectives guards against the limitations of any one view. When teams come together to make sense of the data they have collected, beliefs will surface, and interpretations will conflict. This is a natural part of collective sense making. If a team can productively debate, challenge, and reexamine their assumptions, these can be some of their most powerful learning moments. The personal and relational skills that get built here will be useful at multiple points along the improvement journey where there is a need to come to collective understandings and to make shared decisions.

The goal of engaging in a phase of work to understand the system is to coalesce around a high-leverage focus for the improvement work. This can be a hard pivot for teams to make. The human preference for certainty will make it tempting to continue to gather evidence in search of an elusive complete understanding. To guard against this, teams set a deadline up front and establish a rhythm consisting of prioritizing learning questions, running learning cycles, and coming together to make sense of the evidence they have gathered (see figure 5.4). As the time for understanding ends, they step back, consolidate their learning, and decide where they will focus their change efforts.

The decision of where to start will rarely be clear cut. The evidence they have gathered will inform the decision. The characteristics of successful projects can help identify the conditions in which improvement is more likely to take root (see table 3.1). Finally, tapping into places where there is will and motivation or where early wins are likely can provide the team with valuable momentum. In the end, it is important to remember that there is no one perfect place to begin but, rather, a moment when there is more to be learned by trying to change the system instead of studying it.

CONCLUSION

Teams begin a systems investigation asking the low inference question, "What is currently happening?" With a shared understanding in place, they move to analysis, asking the higher inference question, "Why are we getting the outcomes we are currently getting?" To close the investigation, they look for leverage points, places where they might focus their change effort to move the system in the direction of interest.

The purpose of dedicating a phase of work to understanding the system is to break down a larger problem into smaller actionable parts. Cause-and-effect diagrams help summarize a group's hypotheses about the causes of the current undesirable outcomes. The Pareto principle reminds us that some causes may have a bigger impact than others. Both can guide teams as they select among several potential options for where to start. Once teams decide where to start, they pivot to learning about the system by trying to change it. A first step is capturing their focus in a clear, compelling aim statement, the topic of chapter 7.

III

WHAT ARE *WE* TRYING TO ACCOMPLISH?

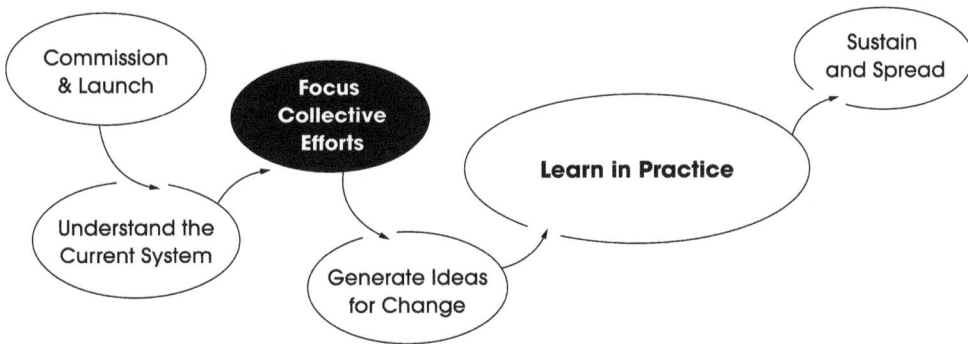

```
Commission          Focus                              Sustain
& Launch          Collective                         and Spread
                   Efforts

Understand the                              Learn in Practice
Current System

                  Generate Ideas
                  for Change
```

In answering the question "What are *we* trying to accomplish?," teams set the destination for the improvement journey, creating and committing to a common definition of success (Langley et al. 2009). The answer to the question is a seemingly simple *aim statement* that on the surface looks like an ordinary organizational goal with time frames, measures, and clear targets.

What distinguishes an aim, however, is its use within the context of systems thinking. In systems, a goal plays a crucial role. In the words of Donella Meadows,

> One of the most powerful ways to influence the behavior of a system is through its purpose or goal. That's because the goal is the direction-setter of the system, the definer of discrepancies that require action, the indicator of compliance, failure, or success . . . If the goal is defined badly, if it doesn't measure what it's supposed to measure, it doesn't reflect the real welfare of the system, then the system can't possibly produce a desirable result. Systems, like the three wishes in the traditional fairy tale, have a terrible tendency to produce exactly what and only what you ask them to produce. Be careful what you ask them to produce. (Meadows 2008, 138)

As a result, improvement aims must thoughtfully answer the question, "What are *we* trying to accomplish?" Setting an aim requires teams to draw boundaries around a part of the system they want to improve. It must be both high leverage, if it is to move the system as a whole in the right direction, and reasonably scoped given the resources at hand. What the team decides matters. The aim is a direction setter, influencing everything that follows. It broadens or constrains the imagination. It disciplines decisions about which changes to pursue, whether the changes made are sufficient, and if new ones are needed.

Arriving at a powerful aim is technically simple but socially complicated. The aim must be an improvement from the user's point of view and aligned with the organization's strategic priorities. As described in chapter 2, the aspiration that initiates improvement work comes from a variety of sources. Most often, it comes from leaders of an organization who select the focus area. On other occasions, a group of people in an organization come together to solve a pressing problem in their sphere of influence. In cases where the starting point is less clear, the focus comes through the discovery of a leverage point as part of understanding the current system.

Wherever the aspiration comes from, the improvement team must feel collective ownership of the aim. You can recognize quickly when teams are working out of compliance to an external mandate versus a shared commitment to an aim that they played a part in creating. Teams that rally around a common aim they value generate energy and momentum. Team members reference the aim regularly in discussions, are anxious to track progress toward the aim, and speak authentically and proudly about the importance of what they are trying to accomplish.

This sense of ownership is easily lost in transitions: when leaders hand responsibility to teams, when new people join, and in cases where the people involved in understanding the system decide on a focus that implies another team taking the lead on making improvements. As a result, the team that ultimately takes responsibility for the improvement work needs a chance to align visions, add their local expertise, and articulate the aim in a way that is valuable to them. At the same time, leadership must be on board with the direction the team chooses. Leaders play a key role in enabling the sustained attention that worthwhile improvement aims need.

In chapter 7 we provide guidance for getting to a clear and powerful aim statement. Crafting an aim requires specificity and agreement on measures, time frames, and specific targets. For some teams, getting to a shared aim will produce visible angst, surfacing differing visions, assumptions, and definitions of what matters that previously existed below the surface. Getting to a shared aim will require teams to put a collective stake in the ground, agreeing to align their energies in a common direction.

Along with the aim, teams identify outcome measures that let them know whether the system is changing in intended ways. Selecting measures requires courage and transparency, naming a specific destination they do not yet know how to reach. The outcome measures will only be one part of the measurement system used to guide their improvement efforts. Process measures, balancing measures, and qualitative data will provide invaluable feedback as they learn their way into improvement. After reading this chapter, some readers may choose to skip ahead to chapter 12 to get a fuller picture of the use of measures in determining whether changes are an improvement.

The aim lives in the team's charter—a document that holds the team's commitments to each other and the organization. Chapter 8 describes the key elements of a team's charter and how the charter is used. The aim and the compelling rationale are the centerpiece of the charter. It is endorsed by leadership and along with it, the permission and resources to carry out the work. In part IV we will describe how teams generate changes and articulate a theory of improvement. These, too, will be added to the team's charter as a provisional theory of how they might reach their aim.

7

Coming Together around a Shared Aim

> A shared vision is not an idea . . . It is, rather, a force in people's hearts, a force of impressive power . . . When people truly share a vision they are connected, bound together by a common aspiration . . . a common caring.
>
> —Senge 1990, 206

Imagine yourself in a room with 20–30 other people. The facilitator asks everyone to close their eyes and extend their arm out with their finger pointing straight ahead. The person then asks everyone to move their bodies so they're pointing north and finally, to open their eyes. As you look around the room, you see that everyone is pointing in a different direction. This is often what it feels like when working on a team or in an organization. We assume everyone is working toward the same goal, but in reality, people are directing their efforts toward different "norths."

Ensuring that everyone is facing the same direction is a critically important part of this phase of the improvement journey. Teams do this by crafting a shared aim, which serves as the team's anchor and north star as they navigate the inevitable twists and turns they'll face during the rest of the journey. In this chapter we will provide guidance on how teams coalesce around a collective aim that is at once strategic, appropriately scoped, and collectively owned by the team.

WHAT IS AN AIM?

Simply put, an aim is the team's collective answer to "What are we trying to accomplish?" The purpose of the aim, as this phase of the journey implies, is to focus the team's efforts strategically. It articulates a clear, common definition of success, a criterion for any high-performing team (see chapter 2 for a definition of high-performing teams). Equally important, it inspires and motivates collective action. Striking the right balance between specificity and inspiration can be tricky, but when done well that balance is powerful in moving a team forward.

Defining Success: "Some Is Not a Number; Soon Is Not a Time"

Although the question "What are we trying to accomplish?" seems simple and straightforward, embedded in it are multiple questions the team needs to answer to define success clearly:

- What will be improved? (clear, operational definitions of all key terms are needed)
- By how much? (measurable, specific numerical goals define the nature of improvement)
- By when? (provides an expected time frame for the journey)
- For whom and where? (specifies the target population for whom improvement is sought)

Agreeing on the answers to these questions requires teams to hash out conflicting, often implicit assumptions about what "improving" or "getting better" mean. For example, say a team's initial aim is to "increase the number of students who graduate college ready." First, what will be improved? The phrase "graduate college ready" hints to students attending college upon graduation from high school, but this is still vague. Second, it's unclear how much of an "increase" counts as improvement given that baseline performance is not specified nor how much of an increase the team would consider to be a win. Third, when does the team expect results? In one year? Or three? Fourth, who is the target population? Will the work focus on all high-school students, or will it specifically focus on improving the experience of specific groups of students? Are there different assumptions about which students are outside the scope of the aim (i.e., special education students or continuing education students)? Finally, where are these students? In a single high school? Across five high schools in a district? Across an entire state? A clearer definition of success for the team might look like this:

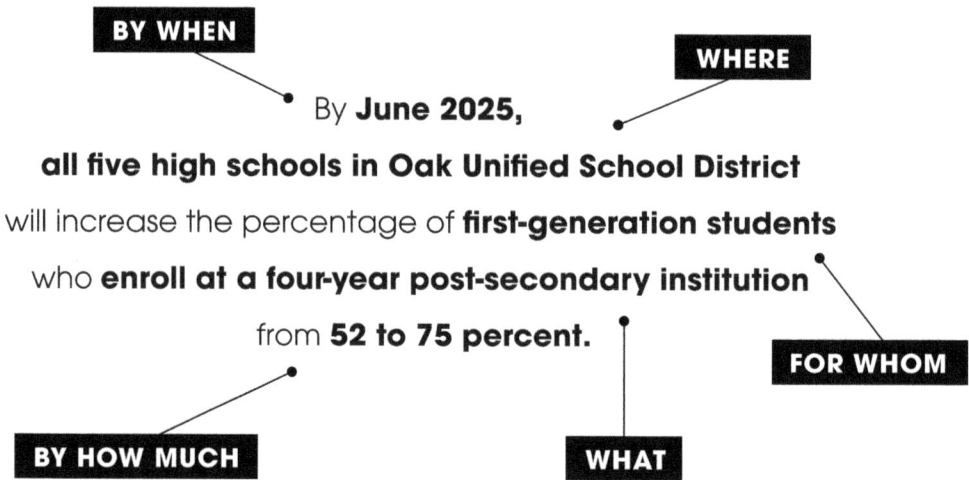

Figure 7.1.   Example Aim Statement

Although getting specific may feel like a technical exercise, the answers to these questions intersect with what inspires and motivates people to action. Some people may be more motivated by bigger, more impactful aims that tap into why they joined the profession in the first place. For example, in the aim statement in figure 7.1, achieving improvement in four-year post-secondary enrollment across all high schools in the district in a couple of years may be inspiring and motivating to some. Others may find this aim unrealistic and overwhelming and, thus, demoralizing. They may prefer an aim that is smaller and more contained—either achieving the aim in just one high school or scoping down the aim to focus on improving one key process linked to four-year post-secondary enrollment, such as completion of the Free Application for Federal Student Aid (FAFSA) or summer melt[1] across the schools.

BALANCING SPECIFICITY AND INSPIRATION

Getting to a clear, specific aim statement that also inspires and motivates collective action is not always an easy task. Teams often begin with a purpose statement or general focus area such as "improving college readiness." They iterate on their statement as they learn more about the current performance and work together to answer the questions just articulated. As they do so, they will want to keep a few things in mind to balance the tension between specificity and motivation.

Setting Boundaries and Scoping

Bounding the improvement effort is an inherent part of setting an aim. In chapter 3, we described the importance of scoping—ensuring that the ambitions for an improvement project match the resources allocated. As teams get specific about what they will improve, the choices they make have implications for the scope of the effort. In working on college readiness, for example, improving four-year college enrollment is more complex than aiming to improve FAFSA rates (see figure 3.1 for a complexity continuum for improvement projects). As Donella Meadows describes, setting boundaries is hard but necessary:

> The lesson of boundaries is hard even for systems thinkers. There is no single, legitimate boundary to draw around a system. We must invent boundaries for clarity and sanity; and boundaries can produce problems when we forget that we've artificially created them. (Meadows 2008, 97)

Many improvement initiatives are motivated by aspirations that are larger and more complex than one team could achieve. In these cases, improvement is organized as a network of teams or a cascading set of improvement projects to achieve the larger goal. For example, as described in chapter 3, the leadership at Ko Awatea in conjunction with the Counties Manukau District Health Board in New Zealand set a strategic goal to dramatically decrease the days that community members were unnecessarily spending in the hospital. They estimated a need to reduce the in-patient hospital days by twenty thousand per year to be able to serve their growing community. Achieving this aim would require helping patients, served by different departments with a wide range of conditions and health needs, get healthier faster. As a way forward, the leadership launched a network with eighteen improvement teams, both within the local hospital and the larger community. The network joined together around the aim of returning twenty thousand well and healthy days to the community. Each team had its own aim statement, tied to the specific part of the system most aligned to their work.

Authentically answering the question "What are we trying to accomplish?" while simultaneously setting boundaries is hard. This can lead to scope creep when crafting an aim. As a result, many improvement teams find it useful to articulate multiple aim statements: one that represents the long-term aspirational or "big-dot" goal at the heart of their overall purpose and another proximal aim statement that anchors the current improvement effort (see figure 7.2). Another example from the work of Ko Awatea illustrates this point; Ko Awatea, working with seven early childhood education centers in Auckland set a "big-dot" goal to improve oral language acquisition in students ages 0–5. Redesigning the system to achieve this aim would be a multistage endeavor. They decided to start by focusing on access to early childhood education, setting a proximal aim of increasing enrollment and attendance at the centers.[2]

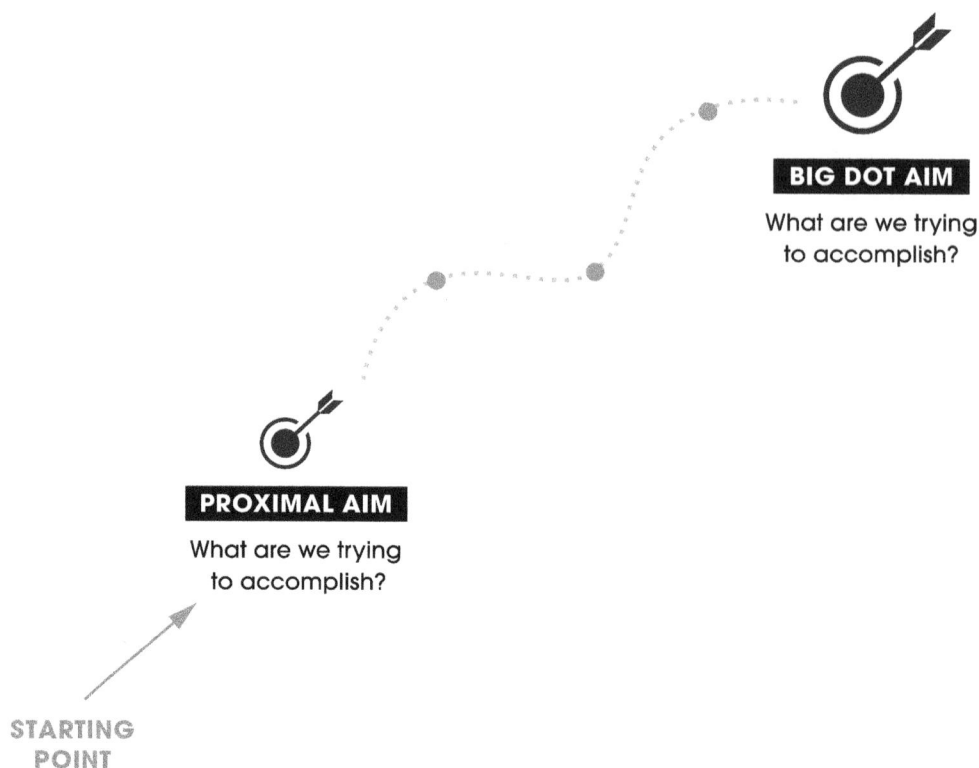

BIG DOT AIM

What are we trying
to accomplish?

PROXIMAL AIM

What are we trying
to accomplish?

STARTING
POINT

Figure 7.2.   Setting Proximal and Big-Dot Aims

Creating a big-dot aim and proximal aim statements can help teams stay focused on an appropriate scope of work while not losing sight of the organization's bigger strategic priorities or the larger vision for the system. It also helps alleviate tensions some teams may experience in mediating the aspirational desires of some members and the need for more bounded and "realistic" goals of others.

When teams find themselves in a place of needing to "scope down" their current aim to an appropriate size, they have multiple strategies at their disposal. They can focus their proximal aim on a high-leverage process tied to the big-dot aim. Chapters 5 and 6 provide teams with investigative methods to uncover "leverage points" within the system that they can target. Another scoping strategy is to reduce the size of the improvement effort. A hospital team, for example, might set an initial aim to improve outcomes for a subset of patients or within a single department while maintaining a commitment to improved outcomes across the organization. One proximal aim leads to the next as the team or organization learns their way into achieving their big-dot aims.

Connecting the Aim to Purpose

Although a "big-dot" aim can be motivating, the technical language of a well-specified aim statement can sometimes feel disconnected from the deeper purpose it represents. As Heath and Starr note in their book *Making Numbers Count,*

We lose information when we don't translate numbers into instinctive human experience. We do hard, often painstaking work to generate the right numbers to help make a good decision—but all that work is wasted if those numbers never take root in the minds of the decision-makers . . . The work that is being done to understand the most meaningful things in the world—ending poverty, fighting disease, conveying the scale of the universe, telling a heartbroken teen how many other times they will fall in love—is being lost because of the lack of translation. (Heath and Starr 2022, xii)

As teams work through the technical components of crafting an aim statement, they need to keep the connection to the motivation that energizes the work.

To address the human side of change while also maintaining specificity, teams can craft an aim that foregrounds the real purpose of the work while keeping the more technical details present but in the background. For example, the Carnegie Math Pathways network changed the way they communicated their aim statement in their second phase of the effort, making it easier to communicate and more inspiring for spurring collective action.

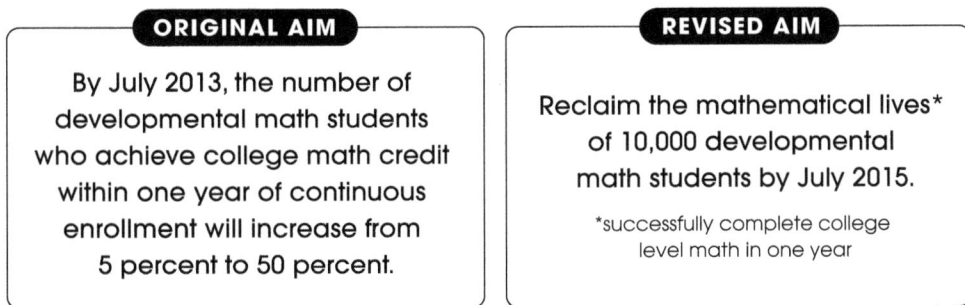

ORIGINAL AIM

By July 2013, the number of developmental math students who achieve college math credit within one year of continuous enrollment will increase from 5 percent to 50 percent.

REVISED AIM

Reclaim the mathematical lives* of 10,000 developmental math students by July 2015.

*successfully complete college level math in one year

Figure 7.3. Composing Aims That Inspire

Improvement teams can also use stories, key research findings, user quotes, and taglines in conjunction with their aim to stay grounded in the "why" that motivates their improvement work. For example, one network focused on new teacher retention used a quote from one of the network leaders as a way to introduce the aim: "We are eating our young, and nobody seems to care." The quote highlights the way in which the system churns through new teachers with little concern for their well-being or long-term development as professionals. Finding ways to connect the aim to the "human experience" is important in motivating and inspiring teams in their work.

AIMS AND EQUITY

Amid the numerous choices involved in crafting an aim, it is important for teams to reflect on how their equity values inform these choices. There is no one-size-fits-all relationship between equity and aims. Teams can pursue more equitable systems by a) directly working on a disparity, b) strategically deciding where and what to focus on, and c) centering the voices of the intended beneficiaries in determining what will be accomplished.

In some cases, improvement work is initiated with the explicit purpose of addressing an equity gap. One question that frequently comes up in these cases is whether the aim should explicitly highlight the inequity in the system. For example, imagine a health system that discovered during the investigative phase of the improvement journey a clear, persistent equity gap in maternal mortality across its five hospitals. When creating their aim, they could: 1) directly address the equity gap and center their aim on improving outcomes for Black and

> **AIM**
>
> By June 2027, decrease the maternal mortality rate for Black and American Indian & Alaskan Native women at Forest Grove hospitals from 40 to 15 deaths per 100,000 live births.

> **AIM**
>
> By June 2027, decrease the maternal mortality rate at Forest Grove hospitals from 30 to 20 deaths per 100,000 live births.

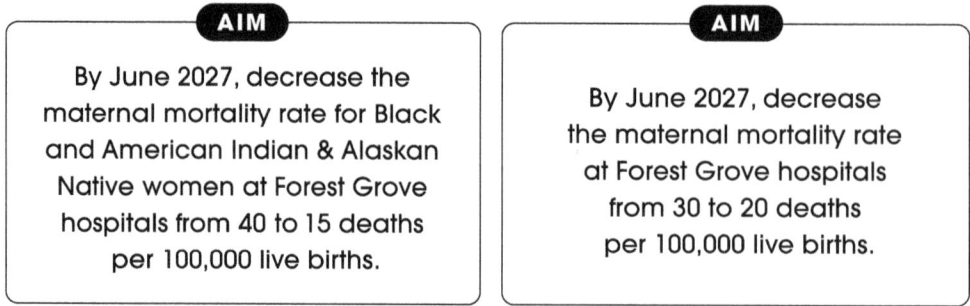

Figure 7.4. Addressing Equity in an Aim Statement

American Indian and Alaska Native (AIAN) mothers or 2) set an aim of decreasing the overall maternal mortality rate for all mothers knowing that moving the needle of this larger population would require redesigning care for black and AIAN mothers (see figure 7.4). Or 3) the team could set two aims, pursuing both at once.

For improvement work focused on closing disparities, it is generally useful to call out the inequities in the aim statement. It's too easy for broader aim statements, such as the one on the right in figure 7.4, to lose sight of those most marginalized by the system. In the words of Donella Meadows, "One of the most powerful ways to influence the behavior of a system is through its purpose or goal" (Meadows 2008, 138). However, there are contexts—political and otherwise—in which the more general aim serves as a better rallying cry for improvement work, garnering the energy for change that is needed.[3] The team should still disaggregate their data, tracking both their overall outcome and the outcome for specific populations they serve less well. In both cases, an important next step is to identify changes that specifically focus and disproportionately impact those who are currently underserved.

A second way that equity values play out in aim statements is on the decision of what and where to focus. Along with an aim statement come resources in the form of time and attention. Allocating those resources toward improving outcomes and addressing problems that affect populations that have been historically marginalized is a way to pursue more equitable systems. For example, the System to Achieve Food Equity Learning Network (SAFE) was launched in 2020 with the big-dot aim of eliminating childhood food insecurity in Cincinnati, Ohio (All Children Thrive Learning Network Team 2022). To understand the current system, they used a measure called a "meal gap" to look at the variation in childhood food insecurity across the city and over time (Feeding America 2022). Based on this analysis, they decided to focus their first efforts in three neighborhoods with the greatest food insecurity: Avondale, East Price Hill, and Lower Price Hill. Not surprisingly, these neighborhoods had experienced decades of underinvestment, beginning with redlining practices in the 1930s. Their set their initial aim as:

Improve food security in three neighborhoods by 10 percent by September 30, 2022.

Their choice of both what to work on and where to start was informed by their explicit commitment to pursuing equitable outcomes in the community. Equity-focused improvement teams can make similar choices—dedicating their time and attention to people and places that have been historically underserved.

A third way that equity values play out in setting an aim is by directly involving the intended beneficiaries in determining where to focus. In chapter 12, we will describe a partnership in Cincinnati that had the global aim of reducing child abuse and neglect. One early aim focused on improving families' experience when they called Jobs and Family Services seeking support. Their initial aim was:

> By May 1, 2023, reduce the call abandonment rates from 38 to 15 percent.

The aim was selected by community members who identified the calls as a point of frustration. Working together to achieve the aim built trust and momentum for the future stages of work. It matters how aims are selected and whose voices are included. Aims that on the surface look somewhat mundane—such as reducing dropped calls—can take on a different meaning when their origin story is told. Equity values should inform both where the team decides to focus and how the decision is made.

Finally, improvement aims are not always focused on redesigning systems to make them more equitable. Organizations may aim at other improvements such as decreasing the number of days it takes to pay a vendor, reducing monthly energy consumption, or other issues related to operational efficiency. Equity issues may arise in the pursuit of these outcomes, but the primary focus is not to address an inequitable outcome.

IDENTIFYING OUTCOME MEASURES

Coming to a collective aim often requires teams to hash out conflicting, often implicit assumptions about what "improving" or "getting better" mean. One move that helps teams shift from a general focus to a specific aim is to choose the outcome measures they will use to track their progress.

In an improvement context, outcome measures are one part of a family of measures that teams use to answer the question, "How will we know that a change is an improvement?" The outcome measures play an important role: they define success for the redesigned system. Teams will need other, more proximal data and measures along the way to guide their learning. We will provide a more complete treatment of the team's measures in chapter 12. For now, it is important to note that teams must identify 1–3 outcome measures to clearly define "what will be improved" in their collective aim.

Selecting outcome measures requires teams to put a stake in the ground about the change they intend to create. It requires moving from more general aspirations that brought the team together—to shared definitions of what constitutes progress. Table 7.1 provides examples of outcome measures that could be used to translate a general focus into a specific aim. For each example, many others are available. What teams select will depend on what data is practically available and what they intend to achieve.

Outcome measures must be both meaningful and practical. They should capture worthwhile improvement from the point of view of the intended beneficiaries. The measures must provide useful feedback to the team, helping them assess whether the system is moving in a positive direction. Teams should take advantage of existing data whenever possible and select just enough measures to provide the feedback they need.

Table 7.1. Examples of Outcome Measures

Focus	Example Outcome Measure(s)
Increase the number of students who graduate college ready	Percentage of students who enroll in a four-year college directly after high school stratified by percent overall, percent of first-generation students, and so forth
Improve special education	Percentage of students completing goals in their individualized education plan (IEP), reported monthly Average IEP goal quality, reported monthly
Eliminate childhood food insecurity	Percentage of meals covered by neighborhood (also known as the "meal gap"), reported monthly
Increase patient safety	Rate of adverse drug events, reported monthly Rate of surgical site infection, reported monthly Rate of maternal mortality, reported monthly
Increase quality of care in nursing home	Falls per thousand bed days, reported monthly Pressure injury rate per patient, reported monthly

For many projects in health care, education, and social welfare, assessing the health of the system will require teams to disaggregate their data, tracking outcomes for different subsets of the population. An aim on improving college access, for example, may track overall college-going rates and those for first-generation students. Tracking two outcome measures lets teams know if the improvement work is living up to its intended promise—redesigning the system to reliably provide the support that different students need.

One strategy that often helps teams get concrete is collaboratively sketching the graphs of the outcomes they want to see (see figure 7.5). Sketching the graph requires talking through the labels on the x-axis and y-axis as well as the data points that will be plotted. They can imagine what they want it to look like when their aim is achieved. The conversation often naturally will raise questions about the operational definitions of key terms in their aim statement. For example, a hospital team may aim to increase safety by reducing the number of falls in the in-patient unit. Underneath the seemingly simple concept of a "fall" are a few decisions. Does this include assisted falls—when a patient begins to fall and is assisted to the ground by another person or object? What about unassisted falls? Is it considered a fall only when it results in injury, or do noninjurious falls also count? Further, in an assisted fall, do we only count an injury to the patient, or do we also include possible injuries to the person assisting? In defining their measures, teams make important decisions about what they will improve and for whom.

By How Much?

Once a team's outcome measures are defined, they should create graphs displaying their baseline data. The benefit of using existing measures is that it makes it easier for teams to define baseline performance for the given population and, subsequently, a target for improvement. It is useful to think about the target—the answer to the question "by how much?"—as a prediction of what the redesigned system would achieve. Achieving the aim should also feel like a significant accomplishment as opposed to tinkering around the edges.[4]

Some team members will want to set aims, especially big-dot aims, at perfection or 100 percent. After all, that is often what we want: no child should be hungry, all students should

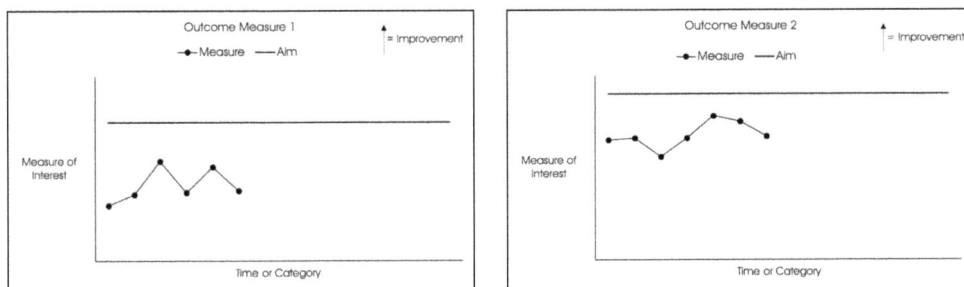

Figure 7.5.   Sketching Outcome Measure Graphs

reason mathematically, and no patient should experience avoidable harm in a hospital. Team members may know that they will likely not achieve perfection, but the aspiration is a source of continued motivation and a forcing function to attend to every "error" the system produces. Others, however, might find setting an aim at 100 percent overwhelming. It is hard to maintain hope toward an aim that feels beyond reach. It is, as Joe McCannon, founder of the Billions Institute, described, the tension between setting a bold aim that "electrifies" a team into action versus an overly ambitious aim that "electrocutes" or burns out a team.

In addition, achieving perfection might require a redesign of the entire system. Realistically, teams usually start by focusing on a key leverage point or a subsystem of the larger system. Their aim should reflect their prediction about how much the outcome will move if they improve the part of the system that they intend to change. Once the first leverage point is improved, then the team can move on to another. As a result, the team can increase the target in chunks as they address more parts of the system. If we use Shasta's literacy work described in chapter 5 as an example, the team has two choices in setting their big-dot aim. One is to set the aim of perfection with a long time horizon for reaching it; for example,100 percent of students reading at grade level by third grade in ten years. The second is to set a less ambitious aim to be achieved in a shorter time frame—60 percent of third-grade students reading at grade level in three years—with 60 percent representing a prediction of how much improvement would result from focusing on classroom practices in the first phase of the effort. As they get closer to achieving the first aim and move on to address other important parts of the system—for example, reading intervention services—the team can then increase the ambitiousness of their aim as more of the system is redesigned. Again, what inspires or motivates team members to action will vary and will likely need to be negotiated.

If perfection is really the aim, the "half-life method" for setting targets can be useful for a team. Teams set their first proximal aim halfway between current performance and perfection, striking the balance between an electrifying and electrocuting aim. As they work toward this aim, they will learn valuable lessons about what it will take to get the rest of the way to perfection, which can inform the setting of their next aim (Schneiderman 1988).

The way improvement teams set targets is one key way that aim statements are different from other organizational goals. Teams answer "how much" in the context of "what are we trying to accomplish?" The answer must go past the "safe" and incremental targets that are incentivized when targets are set for the purpose of accountability. The answer must be enough of a reach to inspire rethinking about how the system is organized and important enough to hang on a banner as a sign of a journey well spent. And then, of course, teams will need to find change ideas strong enough to get them there.

CONCLUSION

Successful improvement teams are bound together by a commitment to a common aim. Although an aim statement may look simple and straightforward, the process of creating one usually is not. To drive collective learning, the aim statement must be clear and specific; the team needs to put a stake in the ground about what will be improved, by how much, by when, and for whom. It should align with the priorities of the organization and reflect the needs of the people it serves. At the same time, it also needs to motivate and inspire the team to act; as a result, the team must feel a sense of ownership and personal connection to the aim.

Along with the aim, the team identifies outcome measures and begins to work out the details of how they will be defined. These will be an important disciplining force for the team, helping them decide which change ideas to pursue and providing important feedback about whether the system is changing as intended. They will build out the rest of their measures once they have a better sense of the changes they want to test. We will return here in chapter 12.

An improvement team's collective aim statement and outcome measures form the heart of the team's charter. The charter holds the team's agreements to each other that they can regularly revisit. In chapter 8, we describe team charters and how they are used in an improvement journey.

8

Chartering an Improvement Journey

> Put a stake in the ground.
>
> —English idiom

When you decide to take a journey with others you may spend time exploring options for where to go. You price tickets, imagine the experiences you might have, and negotiate with prospective travelers. Then there comes a time to commit, to put a stake in the ground, to declare you're in for the adventure, and to begin charting a course.

Improvement teams record their travel destination along with their initial travel plans in a project charter. The term "charter" is borrowed from other contexts where it refers to a document that formally communicates specific agreements, responsibilities, and allocation of resources. Chartering a flight or a ship entails borrowing a vessel for a particular voyage. A municipal charter is a legal document that defines the structure, powers, and responsibilities of a city or municipality. Businesses and some schools need to be granted a charter to operate. An improvement team's charter is a less formal document that serves the same purpose, articulating the intention to pursue an improvement journey toward a particular aim. Leadership signs on, agreeing to provide the provisions that are needed.

Charters play an important role in establishing improvement as a legitimate line of work. In most organizations continuous improvement is rarely considered a line item in budgets. It is new work layered on top of the day-to-day work of an organization as persistent gaps in performance are identified by leadership or the front line. The charter raises the visibility and highlights the importance of the improvement work so it is not overlooked amid the organization's daily operations.

WHAT IS A CHARTER?

A charter is a public document that the improvement team creates to communicate the aim, resources, and people necessary to execute the work moving forward. Once leadership approves the charter, highlighting it as an organizational priority, the team can begin to change the system in service of the aim.

Charters are organized around the three questions of the Model for Improvement (Langley et al. 2009; see chapter 1 for a description of the model):

1. What are we trying to accomplish?
2. How will we know that a change is an improvement?
3. What change can we make that will result in improvement?

These questions are the charter's anchor points, bounding the work and ensuring that the effort stays true to task. A charter may also include other elements that "enable everyone touching the issue to see through the same lens" (Shook 2008, 7). What is included and the degree of elaboration likely will vary given the level of complexity of the work. Table 8.1 describes the elements that make up a team charter. Its cornerstone is always the improvement aim, along with the associated outcome measure(s) and time frame for the work. The items in bold—the compelling rationale, aim statement, team members, sponsoring leader, and resources allocation—should be part of all improvement charters. These elements contain the minimum information neces-

Table 8.1. Elements of a Charter

Element	Description	Chapter
Background	Short section that contextualizes the improvement work, providing information that is helpful for explaining the project to diverse audiences.	
*Compelling Rationale	Statement that highlights why the improvement work is important for the organization and how it aligns with the organization's strategic priorities. Can include compelling data or quotes that capture the motivation for the work.	3, 7
Understanding of the Current State	Summary of a more complete analysis that describes what is happening and the possible causes behind the current outcomes. At minimum, baseline data for the outcome measure(s) should be included.	5, 6, 7
*Aim Statement	Statement that answers the question, "What are we trying to accomplish?" Strategically focuses the team's efforts by providing a clear, common definition of success and motivation for collective action. Includes clear definitions of what will be improved, by when, and for whom.	7
Initial Theory of Improvement	The team's provisional answer to the question, "What changes can we make that will result in an improvement?" The hypothesized changes can be captured as preliminary concepts, a list, or an initial driver diagram.	9, 10
Measures	A list of the measures the team will use to answer the question, "How will we know the change is an improvement?"	12
*Team Members/ Leadership Sponsor	Roster of who is on the team. Designation of a team sponsor: the leader(s) responsible for empowering the team and removing organizational barriers.	2
Team Norms/ Routines	Description of norms that will guide how the team will interact, communicate, and resolve conflicts with each other; agreed-upon team routines.	4, 13
*Resource Allocation	Articulation of budget allocation, each member's FTE allocation, and any other resources necessary to support the improvement effort.	3

*Must be included

sary for leaders to officially authorize the work. The rest of the charter elements can be added as they are developed and when they are needed.

The main goal of the charter is to communicate the priority and direction of the work. It is useful to begin with a clear, compelling case for improvement, motivating why time and resources should focus on this aim. The charter should be as succinct as possible, ideally no more than 1–2 pages in length (or 5–8 slides).

Exhibit 8.1 shows a sample improvement charter for a school district team focused on improving outcomes for students with disabilities. Their long-term aim focused on ensuring that students with disabilities met the goals created uniquely for them. This charter is centered on the aim for the first phase of work that focuses on one of the drivers: improving the process of writing educational goals. The team was part of a larger network that shared the same long-term aim. As part of the network, the team had access to a provisional theory and set of measures the team could use to understand if and when they were making progress. Even though they were part of a network, the team still needed a charter to ensure that local leadership was on board with the direction of the work.

EXHIBIT 8.1. IMPROVING THE PERCENTAGE OF IEP GOALS MET BY STUDENTS WITH DISABILITIES

EXAMPLE CHARTER

Team Name: Exemplar Unified—Special Education Services   Date: August 2021

Background: Exemplar Unified School District serves more than four thousand students with disabilities. Approximately 40 percent do not graduate from high school, and less than 20 percent graduate career and college ready. Each student with a disability has an individualized education program (IEP) designed to address the needs related to their disability. The goals articulated in the IEP inform which services the student receives.

Rationale: IEP goals are the heart of the educational program for students with disabilities. We believe that we can improve Exemplar's system design so that 100 percent of IEP goals can be achieved, setting up students for a lifetime of access and success.

Assessment of Current Conditions:

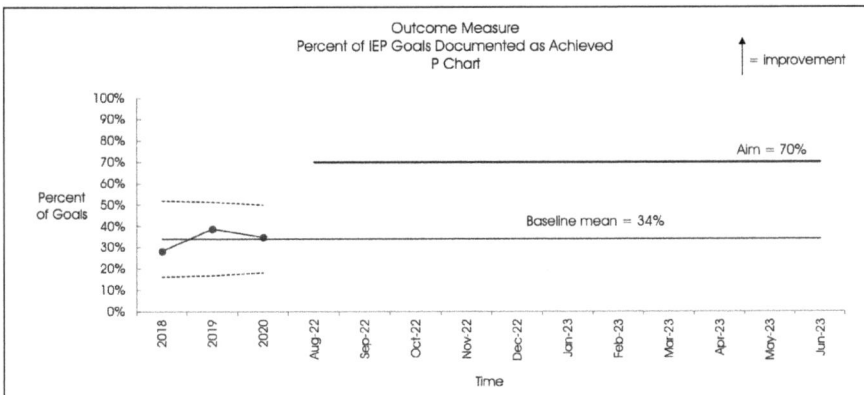

(continued)

EXHIBIT 8.1.   *Continued*

Assessment of Current Conditions (*continued*):

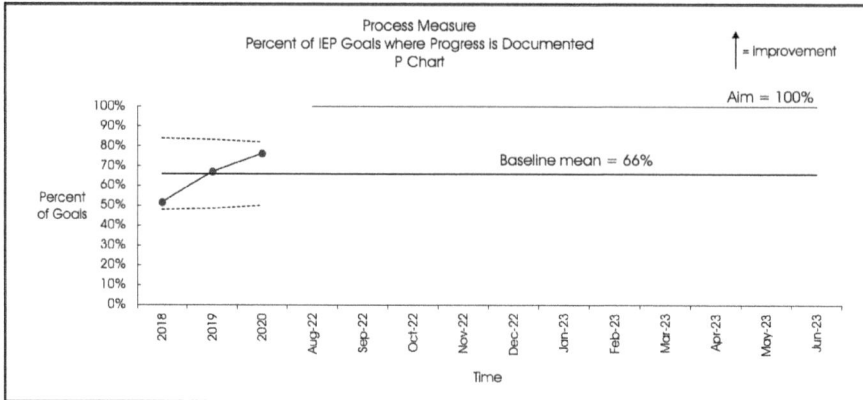

Aim Statement: Exemplar Unified will increase the percentage of IEP goals achieved from 34 to 70 percent by June 2023.

Theory of Improvement:

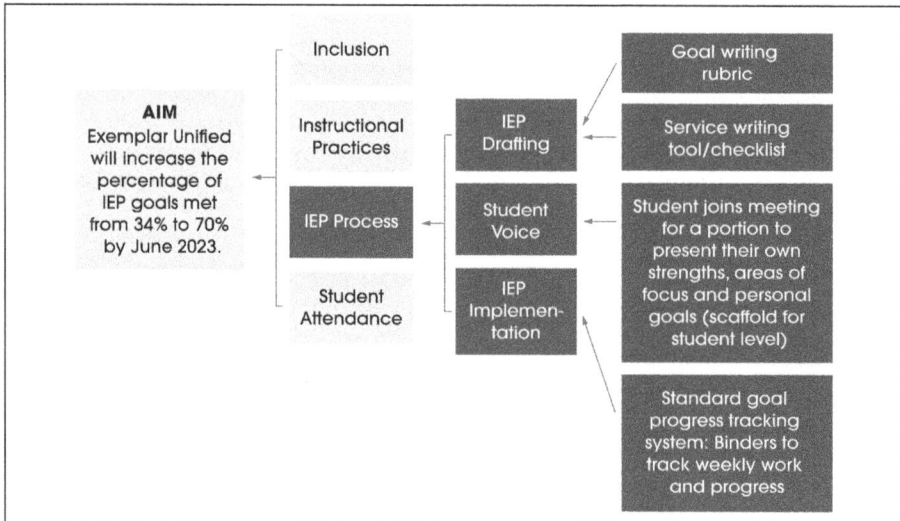

Measures:

Name	Measure Type	Definition	Frequency	Suggested Data Display
Percentage of IEP goals documented as completed	Outcome	Number of students with disabilities completing goals identified in IEP (individualized education program)	Annual	Shewhart Chart or Run Chart
Average IEP goal quality score	Process	Each month, ten IEPs are randomly selected. For each IEP, all goals are assessed using a standard rubric. The average goal quality score is then calculated for all goals assessed in the month.	Monthly	Shewhart Chart or Run Chart
Percentage of goals where progress toward goal is documented	Process	Number of goals in IEP with met/not met documented	Monthly	Shewhart Chart or Run Chart

Team Members/Leadership Sponsor:

Theresa: Sponsor (administrator, SELPA & legal compliance)
Anne: Team lead (assistant director, special education)
Rose: Team member (special education teacher)
Jaimie: Team member (special education teacher)
Carrie: Team member (director, special education)
Kristen: Team member (assistant director, special education)

Team Norms and Routines:

Norms	Routines
Embrace the path of uncertainty. Stay relentlessly present and curious. Be transparent. All teach; all learn. Give and receive feedback. Be clear about who is doing what. Provide opportunities for reflection: self and whole group.	Weekly improvement team meetings Quarterly meetings with network At least one PDSA per week Monthly data collection

Resource Allocation:

We expect a commitment of 2–3 hours per week (5 percent of FTE per team member). Other resources will be used as needed (office space, copier facilities, etc.) at the discretion of the team sponsor.

HOW ARE CHARTERS CREATED?

The genesis of the charter occurs during the commission and launch phase of the journey. The improvement work is launched with at least a general focus in mind; and during this time a sponsor is identified, a team is recruited, and resources are allocated to begin the journey (see chapters 2 and 3).

The team is ready to create a charter when they have a collective aim, clearly specifying what will be improved, for whom, and by when. Although the sponsor often leads the commissioning of the work, it is the improvement team that drives the creation of the charter. Improvement coaches often help the team craft an aim, identify outcome measures, and divide the work into phases. When the initiating focus is vague or large in scope, the team can go through a phase of work focused on understanding the current system to choose a high-leverage starting place (see chapters 5 and 6). With a clear aim, time frame, and estimate of the resources that will be required, the team returns to the sponsor with a more specific proposal in the form of a charter. If the sponsor agrees with the direction, they authorize the work, agreeing to protect time and remove the barriers the team might face.

The charter is a living document that grows and holds the team's shared artifacts. When the team identifies change ideas they want to try and develops a shared theory of improvement, they are added to the charter (see chapters 9 and 10). When the team builds out a more complete set of measures to provide feedback as they test changes in practice, these also are added (see chapter 12). Sometimes the measures and initial theory are included in the charter document that gets approved; other times they are added later. Regardless, the charter is a core document for the team, declaring its commitment to achieving a specific aim and holding their agreements to each other.

TELLING AN IMPROVEMENT STORY: CHARTERS TO STORYBOARDS

Once the work has begun, the charter evolves into a storyboard that captures the "learning in practice." Storyboards are often used in film, television, and books to describe the overall arc of the story being told. Similarly, improvement teams can use a storyboard to communicate the story of their improvement journey both internally and with external audiences. There is no clear moment when the charter becomes a storyboard but, rather, a smooth transition as teams add to the document that captures both their agreements and the key moments of their journey.

Teams benefit from having regular opportunities to share their unfolding improvement story over the course of the journey. Presenting their work can renew momentum, supporting the team to build a shared narrative and occasion to celebrate their work. It also provides avenues to communicate with a variety of stakeholders connected to the system they are trying to improve. Finally, opportunities to invite in "outside eyes" help the team identify blind spots, alternative paths forward, and conclusions that might need to be reexamined.

Like any genre, improvement stories have a recognizable narrative structure. They begin with a clear, compelling "why," a description of the team, and any other background information that the audience might need. The "why" is followed by the aim statement, contextualized with a graph of baseline performance, making it clear how much improvement is expected. The main part of the story focuses on the learning. Teams describe their initial theory, display updated graphs of all their measures, and include the main insights from the latest learning cycles. Examples of theories and assumptions that have changed take center stage. The story closes with what the team believes now considering the evidence and where they intend to focus their learning next. Figure 8.1 describes the arc of the improvement story and artifacts in the storyboard that support its telling.

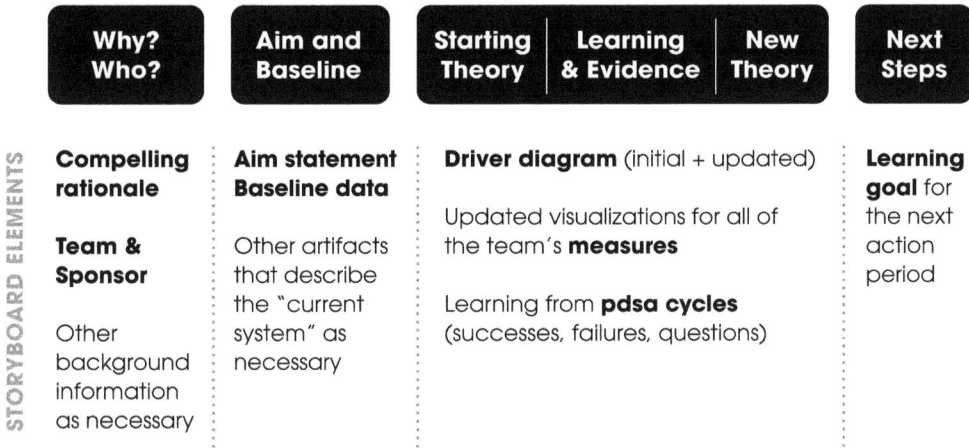

Why? Who?	Aim and Baseline	Starting Theory	Learning & Evidence	New Theory	Next Steps

STORYBOARD ELEMENTS					
Compelling rationale **Team & Sponsor** Other background information as necessary	**Aim statement** **Baseline data** Other artifacts that describe the "current system" as necessary	**Driver diagram** (initial + updated) Updated visualizations for all of the team's **measures** Learning from **pdsa cycles** (successes, failures, questions)			**Learning goal** for the next action period

Figure 8.1. Telling the Story of an Improvement Journey

The common language that comes with adopting a shared improvement approach facilitates communication between teams and among stakeholders. The audience comes to expect succinct answers to three improvement questions and can devote all their attention to the content of the team's learning. Improvement stories are told visually. The team's storyboard should be dominated by key artifacts, such as user quotes, aim statements, annotated graphs, driver diagrams, and Pareto charts. When used well in the arc of the story, these artifacts can capture clearer insights rather than wordy explanations.

The storyboard is only useful as a communication tool if it is regularly updated as part of the team's improvement routines. Teams should designate moments to periodically step back, consolidate their learning, and update their storyboard. These "consolidation" moments can be scheduled at regular intervals and can take advantage of natural opportunities to share the learning with the team's sponsor, other improvement teams, or external audiences (for more on consolidation, see chapter 13).

CONCLUSION

Charters focus the work of an improvement team. They communicate the rationale for the work, who is involved, resources allocated, and the outcome being pursued. When done well, charters are an effective tool for garnering support for the work across the organization. They become part of the team's storyboard, which will support the team to share the story of their improvement journey as it unfolds.

To achieve their aim, teams need to discover how to change the system in the direction they seek. The team adds their initial change ideas in their charter as a starting hypothesis. We turn there next.

IV

WHAT CHANGES CAN *WE* MAKE THAT WILL RESULT IN IMPROVEMENT?

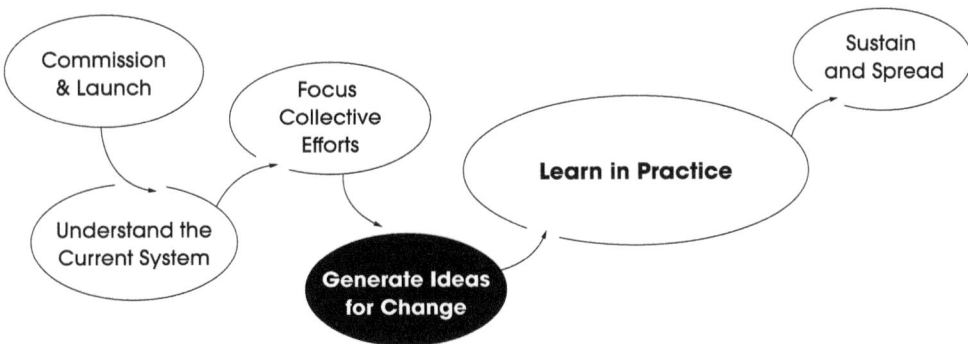

Commission
& Launch

Understand the
Current System

Focus
Collective
Efforts

Generate Ideas
for Change

Learn in Practice

Sustain
and Spread

Of all the questions in the Model for Improvement, "What changes can *we* make that will result in improvement?" is likely the one that organizations ask most frequently (Langley et al. 2009, 5). The problem is that the question is often answered implicitly, leaving little opportunity to uncover potential flaws in the rationale behind the changes being made. Or the changes represent a reaction to the status quo that may temper the impact of the problem but only temporarily. In both situations, there is change but not much improvement.

Imagine the CEO of a hospital who is worried about its rate of patient hospital-acquired infections. The CEO recently learned that the hospital's infection rate is higher than the state average. The CEO, a former practitioner, regularly participates in hospital rounds, which is when a medical team visits patients under their care to review their status and care plans. One day while rounding, with the high infection rate weighing heavily on the CEO's mind, the CEO notices a group of nurses at their station, chatting and drinking coffee. In that moment the CEO runs up the ladder of inference (see chapter 6), reacting to this sliver of data, and filling in the story of what's happening based on presumptions. The CEO concludes that the high rate of infections is due, in part, to inattentive nurses taking too many breaks. The CEO takes action, instituting fewer breaks for nurses and removing the coffee from their station, believing that these actions will reduce nurse inattentiveness and reduce infections. Will they? Of course not. But this anecdote isn't about wrongheadedness in reducing infections. It is about how we often approach change in organizations.

Changes are predicated on beliefs. Whether they are implicit or explicit, when people try to change their systems, they act on them. In the worst case, beliefs are misguided, misinformed, and do not reflect reality, evidence, or experience. They lead to people blaming others instead of taking a systems view. However, even in the best-case scenario, when changes are well intentioned, they are still based on beliefs, shaped by inherent biases and specific experiences, about what *might* work in practice. Until local evidence is gathered, we can't know for sure about the validity of our beliefs or the theories we hold.

In the day-to-day work of organizations, the assumptions and beliefs underlying the changes people make tend to stay implicit and unexamined.[1] As a result, organizational learning requires us to pause and make our often-flawed assumptions public and explicit so they can be tested and revised. Improvement teams "learn their way into improvements" by a) articulating their theories and b) testing them in practice. This process helps teams build practical knowledge based on empirical evidence, one of the core capacities of improvement (see chapter 1).

Using if-then statements to articulate a theory when someone wants to make a specific change is one way to surface their assumptions. *If* nurses took fewer breaks, *then* they'd engage in more preventative actions, which *in turn* would reduce hospital-acquired infections. Sometimes simply slowing down and publicly sharing the hypothesis behind a change is enough to see a flawed assumption in your thinking. Even when warranted changes are proposed, articulating the hypothesis behind the change is a critical first step in setting up the learning to determine whether the change really is an improvement (see part V).

As teams generate changes, they should ward themselves against typical behaviors— responding reactively to a fire that doesn't address the origin of the problem or choosing convenient off-the-shelf solutions (i.e., new tools, new programs, or the latest technologies) being touted as the next great cutting-edge innovation. Instead, teams should take a step back and develop changes that target the specific problems at hand and alter how the system operates in fundamental ways. In chapter 9, we describe several methods for generating *change ideas* that take teams beyond reactionary, off-the-cuff solutions. These methods involve drawing on research, pulling in multiple forms of expertise, taking a closer look at current practices and activities, and foraging for ideas outside the team's local context.

Given the complexity of the social sector ecosystem, improving outcomes will require multiple change ideas and coordinated action on different parts of the system at the same time. In chapter 10, we introduce the *driver diagram* as a way of documenting and organizing the changes into a coherent theory of action that helps guide the team's work. As the change ideas are tested in practice, the driver diagram also serves as a knowledge management tool, capturing the evolving theory of the team.

Chapters 9 and 10 can be read in either order. Some may prefer to read them in sequence, starting with ways to identify concrete changes and then exploring how to represent them in an overall theory of improvement. Others may prefer starting with driver diagrams, which provide a holistic picture of a theory of improvement, before turning to the methods for getting to specific changes.

Getting to the point where teams are generating changes represents an important pivot in the improvement journey. Until now the team has been investing in building the foundation for systems change: forming as a team, understanding the current system, and committing to a common aim. Now they begin to create something new.

9

Change Ideas

All improvement requires change, but not every change is an improvement.

—Langley et al. 2009, 109

In 2006, Peter Skillman created a design experiment to learn how groups of people collaborate.[1] Teams were given twenty pieces of uncooked spaghetti, one yard of transparent tape, one yard of string, and a marshmallow. The goal was to build the tallest possible structure with the marshmallow on top. He ran the experiment with different groups of people, comparing the heights of the resulting structures and noting the differences in how groups approached the task. Recent business school graduates were among the worst. They spent their time talking, strategizing, negotiating status, coming up with a singular plan and executing it, often only to find at the last minute that the structure collapsed. Teams of kindergartners created one prototype after another, developing taller, more interesting structures with each iterative design. The secret was in how they collaborated. They got right to work designing structures, trying them out, standing shoulder to shoulder, noticing what happened, and incorporating lessons into the next design (Skillman n.d.).

The talk-talk-talk-implement process that the business school students used is representative of how many teams decide what to do. Contrast this with what happens on an improvement journey, where teams, like the kindergarteners, treat "generating ideas for change" as acts of design. They move quickly from concepts to ideas to creating concrete prototypes that can be tested and iterated on in practice.

This chapter focuses on methods for generating ideas for change. Insightful ideas come from multiple sources. Teams can discover them by looking more closely at current practice, invoking new modes of thinking, and drawing on multiple perspectives. At first, teams usually will flare, identifying a multitude of possibilities. Eventually they will have to focus, using decision criteria to prioritize a manageable set of change ideas. Finally, they will need to create concrete prototypes that can be tried in practice. After all, the best way to learn about a system is to try to change it.

WHAT IS A CHANGE IDEA?

Teams generate change ideas to answer the question "What changes can we make that will result in improvement?" Change ideas are specific alterations to how work gets done in a system.

They come in the form of practices, processes, structures, tools, or norms hypothesized to shift the system in the direction of the aim. Altering the system entails adding to, redesigning parts of, or eliminating elements from what currently exists. The language of change ideas helps teams remain humble about the provisional nature of their initial hunches before they are tested in practice.

Change ideas that transform system performance come in a variety of shapes and sizes. Sometimes the changes are large and resource intensive; at other times, they are small but powerful. What matters is whether they result in a fundamental change to how the system operates. In developing and identifying changes, it is useful for teams to understand the distinction between fundamental and reactive changes.

When the system isn't producing the results expected, most people's response is to fix the situation immediately. For example, a counseling team adds a Saturday college application event or works extra hours to follow up with students when they notice a couple of weeks before the deadline that fewer students than usual have completed an application. Or a children's hospital adds staffing to handle an increase in the number of children showing up at the emergency room. These are examples of reactive changes; they address immediate challenges or special circumstances perceived as problematic (Langley et al. 2009, 112–13). Reactive changes are often necessary to maintain existing conditions. However, they leave the current system intact and do little to help the system reach new levels of performance. They do not address the reasons why students do not apply to college or why there is increased demand in emergency rooms. Engaging only in reactive change leaves the organization stuck in an endless loop of workarounds that help maintain the status quo but never actually make the system better.

Fundamental changes, on the other hand, push a system to an improved level of performance by altering or redesigning the system (Langley et al. 2009, 113–16). Fundamental changes often address the underlying causes behind the current outcomes. For example, a team that wants to increase college application rates could look upstream to prevent the downstream problem of seniors not meeting the application deadline. They could have students in their junior year develop wish lists of colleges they want to apply to or embed specific college application requirements, such as the essay, in senior English classes. When Cincinnati Children's Hospital noticed that children with asthma were returning repeatedly to the emergency department, they targeted a key underlying cause of these admissions and readmissions: environmental triggers. They worked with the local housing agency to ensure that landlords in neighborhoods where most cases were occurring reduced tenant exposure to these triggers (Beck et al. 2022). Improvement teams want to discover and develop fundamental changes such as these. Big or small, these changes alter the end users' experience of the system in meaningful, sustained ways.

We use the concept of "fundamental changes" in a similar way some people use the word "innovation," with one notable difference. Innovation is simply defined as "a new idea, method, or device" (*Merriam-Webster* 2023). However, in most settings, the word "innovation" conjures up images of big—sometimes drastic—change in contrast to small-scale incremental change. Although big changes at times are best to achieve impact, in improvement, small changes when targeted strategically to high-leverage areas (see chapter 10) can also make a significant difference. It is not the size or flashiness of the change that matters; rather, it is whether the change fundamentally alters the design of the system to push it to a higher level of performance.

METHODS FOR GENERATING CHANGE IDEAS

Teams often start by brainstorming changes that they believe will lead to an improvement. This may be an appropriate first step in building will and illuminating current theories team members' hold about what it will take to achieve better outcomes. It is a particularly useful starting point when end users are at the table or when frontline workers on the team historically have not had the autonomy or opportunity to contribute their expertise.

That said, for most improvement problems, teams will need to go beyond brainstorming.[2] After all, if the changes needed were easily known, they would likely have been discovered already. Cognitive biases, such as recency bias (see chapter 6), combined with the difficulty of seeing systems, make it likely that brainstormed changes will tend to be reactive, not fundamental. New, fundamental changes tend to come from doing a closer analysis of the current system (see chapters 5 and 6), looking for ideas that have worked elsewhere, or provoking new ways of thinking about how the system might be redesigned.

As mentioned earlier, change ideas can come from multiple sources. In chapter 1, we described the importance of drawing on experiential, professional, research, and improvement expertise (see figure 1.3) to inform the improvement journey. This is particularly true in this phase of the journey, as different forms of expertise can provide different insights into the changes needed to improve performance. Teams can use a variety of methods to develop and identify change ideas, each of which taps into different forms of expertise and sources of knowledge. In this chapter we will focus on learning from and with end users, logical thinking, bright spotting, scanning, creative thinking, and applying change concepts (see table 9.1).

Table 9.1. Methods for Developing Change Ideas[3]

Method	Description
Learning From and With End Users	Engage in empathy interviews, observations, or immersions in the user experience to discover needed changes to the system. Directly engage with end users to codevelop change ideas. Learn from lead users.
Logical Thinking	Analyze the current system using methods such as process mapping and qualitative analysis to uncover how a process or the system is working and not working. Apply logic to these discoveries. Does the process make sense? Are the steps happening in the best or most efficient order? Are current solutions targeting the most important or most frequently occurring barriers?
Bright Spotting	Identify and learn from bright spots, positive deviants, or special causes: people or places that have unusually high performance as indicated by Shewhart analysis (see appendix A).
Scanning	Review what already is known about a particular topic. Scanning can include reviews of the research literature, identification of change packages developed by others (see chapter 14), interviews with professional experts, and learning from other sectors.
Creativity Methods	Use creativity exercises to provoke divergent thinking around a specific problem.
Change Concepts	Use one or more change concepts: general approaches to change applicable in a wide range of contexts that are used to generate multiple specific, concrete change ideas related to a particular problem or opportunity within the system (e.g., use reminders, move steps into process closer together).

Learning From and With Users

Regardless of the source of the ideas, developing change ideas should always focus on better meeting the needs of those served by the system. One obvious way to do this is to tap directly into the experiential knowledge of the end users. In chapter 5, we described several empathy methods for understanding the daily lives, needs, and values of the end users, including empathy interviews, observations, and immersions into key experiences. Change ideas can emerge directly from engaging in these methods.

For example, the hospital team in KwaZulu-Natal, South Africa, generated some of their most powerful ideas for reducing mother-to-child transmission of HIV by trying to understand expectant mothers' experiences with the health-care system (see chapter 5). When the team walked through the antenatal visit with the mothers, they saw how the design of the appointment created barriers to getting the mothers tested for HIV. This gave the team immediate ideas about how to rearrange the visit to increase HIV testing while simultaneously improving the women's overall experience.

Ideally, users themselves also have opportunities to develop change ideas. These can emerge through learning from "lead users" (see bright spotting section below) or elicited directly from users in facilitated sessions. In 2020, the System to Achieve Food Equity Learning Network (SAFE) in Cincinnati, Ohio, was launched in response to a dramatic increase in food insecurity resulting from the COVID-19 pandemic. To tackle this issue, the network invited community individuals and organizations to submit proposals seeking funding for their ideas through a local foundation. Neighborhood leadership councils, composed of 5–7 members from the participating neighborhoods, reviewed and selected nine community-designed interventions, such as a community garden, mobile food pantry, and meal kit delivery service, to receive funding. In addition to financial support, the network provided coaching and other resources to help community members bring their ideas to life and test them in their neighborhoods.

In the ImproveCareNow (ICN) network, which seeks to improve health outcomes for children and adolescents living with inflammatory bowel disease, patients and families also play an active role in developing change ideas. For instance, a young patient (Ella, age twelve) with Crohn's disease, who requires regular intravenous infusions of medication, designed a comfortable piece of clothing for children to wear when they undergo specific treatments. She was solving a problem the medical community had not—how to receive care comfortably—while still allowing her arms to be accessible by her clinical team. Her product, the IV sweatshirt, has been widely praised and adopted and is now available for both children and adults who could benefit from it (Shamash 2020).

Logical Thinking

Developing a clearer understanding of the system will often reveal obvious problems with logical solutions. The redesign of the antenatal visit described above is an example of changes developed by learning from users and applying logical thinking. No creativity was needed, simply a closer look at the system and how people were experiencing it led team members to conclude which changes were needed. A team from New Visions for Public Schools[4] in New York City set out to improve graduation rates in its network of high schools. When they dug into their data to better understand why students weren't graduating, they discovered that the course coding system was so confusing that it resulted in students not being placed in courses they needed to graduate. Years of layered reforms in New York City had resulted in a proliferation of course titles and offerings and with them more than 40,000 different course codes. The team could logically see that this was a barrier to getting students in the right courses and worked to simplify the coding system, ensuring that students were placed in courses that qualified them for graduation.

The changes that arise from logical thinking are not always flashy but can be high leverage. Chasing shiny new innovations can lead teams to overlook the importance of fundamental details that make systems work. Logical thinking is particularly good for identifying wasteful and unneeded practices. As in the New Visions example above, the change needed was paring down and streamlining the system. This flips our normal thinking about change ideas. They do not always need to be new or additive. Change ideas that remove or clear away practices and processes to simplify the system can also improve performance.

The constraint of logical thinking is that it involves focusing on what already exists. Sometimes the current system doesn't reveal what's needed or illuminate new possibilities. In these moments, looking for change ideas outside the system can help.

Bright Spotting

Bright spotting is a method that draws on the success of others. It entails 1) identifying a place that has already made progress on a similar aim and 2) harvesting the change ideas that worked there. For example, a network in Arizona was working to increase the number of high school seniors who received federal financial aid to increase college access. School teams began by testing change ideas they brainstormed to increase the number of students who completed the financial aid form (FAFSA).[5] After a couple of rounds of testing, they did not see increases in FAFSA completion and were running out of ideas about what to do. The network leaders examined the variation in FAFSA completion across the schools using Shewhart Charts (see appendix A) to identify any schools with unusually high performance in FAFSA completion. The analysis revealed that three schools were getting notably higher rates of FAFSA completion than the others. Through a series of interviews with the teams at these schools, the network leaders discovered that the counselors at all three had developed a routine for tracking which seniors had not completed the FAFSA, regularly reviewing the data, and divvying up responsibility for following up with students who had not yet completed the application.[6] The network leaders documented the routine, gathered some of the tools used that the bright-spot schools used, and shared these with new schools to try.

A first step in bright spotting is to identify people or places with unusually high levels of performance, often referred to as positive deviants. A quantitative measure, such as the number of students completing a FAFSA, facilitates this process.[7] Once the bright spots have been identified, the next step is to pinpoint the specific practices that may be producing the remarkable outcomes. Identifying the key practices can be difficult as people and teams may not be aware of what they are doing that is different from other places. When possible, it is useful to visit and see practices firsthand. Alternatively, interviews can be used to pull out key practices. When multiple bright spots are identified, it can be helpful to listen for which practices these places have in common that differ from current or common practice.

Bright spotting can also be used as a method to learn from users. For example, humanitarian aid workers John and Monique Sternin uncovered powerful change ideas to combat child malnutrition in Vietnam by talking to families with children who appeared more well nourished than their peers living in similar socioeconomic circumstances. They learned that these families fed their children more meals per day and supplemented them with shrimp and crabs found in the rice paddies and sweet potato greens found alongside the road (Pascale, Stemin, and Stemin 2010, 19–52). In many systems, end users figure out how to reach the outcome of interest despite the current design of the system.[8] The ingenuity of their "workarounds" can be used to redesign how the system operates for everyone.

Scanning

Teams can also use literature reviews and interviews with experts to identify evidence-based practices that can be used as change ideas. A team working to reduce maternal mortality, for example, could start by reviewing the literature on the leading causes of maternal mortality and practices to prevent them. When the research literature is diffuse, the team can read a couple of seminal articles and then interview research experts who can help highlight the key ideas and practices. For topics where previous improvement work has been successful, teams can also turn to change packages, which articulate the salient changes that led to the desired outcome (see chapter 14 for more on change packages). The work of the team then becomes figuring out how to reliably embed these practices in the day-to-day work of the organization.

Teams can also scan for professional expertise. For example, a team at Evergreen High School in Portland, Oregon, sought to improve ninth-grade success of Pacific Islander students at their school. This subgroup of students experienced more failures in ninth grade than the rest of their peers; the team knew that regular attendance and passing core classes in ninth grade were key predictors of students graduating from high school (Allensworth and Easton 2007, 3–14; Pileggi, Liu, and Turner 2020, ii). Teachers and students on the team started by brainstorming change ideas themselves, but when they ran out of ideas, they began to look externally. During their search, they found Wesley Hingano, a long-standing case manager for Pacific Islander students in Oakland Unified School District. Hingano shared change ideas that addressed the specific needs of the Evergreen students. These included ideas for how to engage local churches in supporting students and question cards he gave parents to help facilitate their interactions with their children's teachers.

Professionals from organizations in other fields can also be a source of inspiration. Out-of-field experts are individuals who have solved the same or an analogous problem in a different sector. For example, a team focused on improving the feedback process for new teachers interviewed attending physicians responsible for training medical residents. A team from Cincinnati Children's Hospital looked to the airline industry, known for its effective safety routines, to learn about how to improve the safety of patients in their hospital. Looking out-of-field can help teams see beyond the taken-for-granted ways work is organized in their own context and expose themselves to new and novel ideas.

When scanning the literature and engaging in expert interviews, it is often advantageous to gather and synthesize information across research, professional, and out-of-field expertise. For example, the team looking for ideas about how to support new teachers talked to researchers who study teacher development, interviewed professional experts known to have strong new teacher programs, and looked outside education to learn how other organizations supported new employee learning.[9] They used a 2:2:1 methodology,[10] reading two research articles, and interviewing two professional experts and one out-of-industry expert; synthesizing what they learned, and then deciding on the next wave of articles to read and experts to interview. After a few cycles of this routine, the team identified a handful of change ideas to test.

Creativity Methods

Applying creativity methods can help turn ordinary brainstorming sessions into ones that spark innovative ideas. Creativity methods are particularly helpful when the problem the team is trying to solve is well defined, and they need to generate new thinking about how to solve it.

These methods rest on the assumption that creative thinking is not an innate talent but can be taught. They use specific techniques, or lateral thinking methods, to help provoke divergent, generative thinking.[11] Teams can draw on numerous creativity methods (see, e.g., de Bono's lateral thinking methods [de Bono 1992] and IDEO [IDEO n.d.]). One example is a provocation method called random entry. In this method, teams a) define a specific issue, b) select a random word from a word list, and c) use this word as inspiration for generating new change ideas. Multiple change ideas are generated in rapid succession without judgment as to their use in practice (see section below on "selecting change ideas"). "The purpose of the provocation is to force our minds out of the usual groove and to increase the chance of getting across to a new idea" (de Bono 1991, rev. 2018, 6).

For example, a team in rural South Africa focusing on the low uptake of HIV testing used the random entry method when struggling to come up with new change ideas. They engaged in several rounds of provocation using different randomly selected words from a list and generating a variety of possible change ideas to increase the uptake of HIV testing. One idea was to put a mobile HIV testing site at the local market. This idea alone doubled the number of HIV tests conducted each week in this remote village.

Change Concepts

Change concepts are also a method for generating new change ideas. A change concept is "a general notion or approach found to be useful in developing specific ideas for change that result in improvement" (Langley et al. 2009, 131). Change concepts were developed by the Associates in Process Improvement, a group of improvement advisers who work across multiple sectors. They noticed that many organizations were working on solving problems that were similar conceptually; for example, processes with too many steps or handoffs. They created a list of seventy-two general change concepts that could be used by teams as a starting point to generate specific ideas for change. For instance, they include the use of reminders and constraints as concepts to solve problems related to "eliminating mistakes."[12]

Teams first choose a change concept related to the problem, then use it to brainstorm multiple specific change ideas.[13] For example, a team working on patient satisfaction at a hospital needed new thinking about how to reduce the anxiety families felt when their loved ones were in surgery. In looking at the list of change concepts, they identified, "give people access to information" as one that might help. This led to the generation of multiple change ideas. Two they tried included an electronic whiteboard that kept families aware of the patient's progress and assigning a nurse liaison to update families at critical moments.

GETTING TO CHANGE IDEAS THAT CAN BE TESTED IN PRACTICE

Learning from users, logical thinking, bright spotting, scanning, creativity methods, and change concepts are all ways to discover and develop changes for improving system performance. Teams can use them at the beginning of an improvement journey to develop an initial set of change ideas and can return to them when they're stuck and recognize the need for more or different ideas.

Selecting Change Ideas to Test

If used effectively, the methods just highlighted will almost always produce more ideas than are necessary or practical to pursue. The task of the team then is to select which changes to try first. In selecting change ideas, teams are looking for those that target the crux of the problem, have the potential for impact, are within the team's locus of control, and can build momentum for change. They are looking for ideas that go past tinkering around the edges and fundamentally change the way the system operates.

In some cases, teams can prioritize change ideas to test through voting or discussion. For a more structured approach, teams can use the impact-effort matrix depicted in figure 9.1.[14] Each change idea is written on a Post-it or in a text box (when working virtually). The changes are assessed by the team for their ease in enacting and potential benefit for the system and then placed accordingly on the chart. Changes in the lower left-hand corner (hard to carry out and without much benefit) can easily be discarded. Changes in the top right-hand corner (easy to carry out with potential for high benefit) are good places to start.

As teams select change ideas, they begin to articulate a theory of what it will take to solve a particular problem or reach a particular aim. As part of the process, it is helpful if teams make the hypotheses behind the change ideas explicit to ensure that they are addressing the aim. For most improvement projects, multiple changes will ultimately be needed to achieve the intended outcome. Often these changes are directed at different parts of the system, each being an important driver of the aim. In these cases, teams may find visualizing the overall theory of improvement using a driver diagram helpful (see chapter 10).

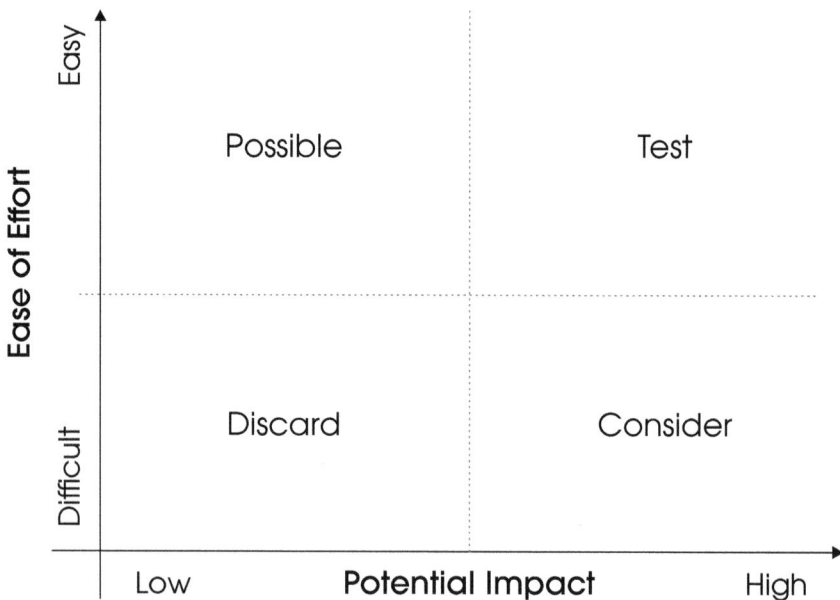

Figure 9.1.   Impact Effort Matrix for Prioritizing Change Ideas

Imagining new ways to redesign the system is important, but the real test comes in seeing what happens when the ideas are put into practice. Some changes will work in some places and not in others; some will be worth the effort to implement, and others can be discarded quickly. To maximize the power of learning by doing, teams need to move quickly, like the kindergarteners in the opening example, to create actual artifacts that can be tried in practice.

Creating Prototypes

To be tested, change ideas need to be specific, concrete, and actionable. As teams generate change ideas, it is not uncommon for the first versions to be vague. One way to make them more specific and concrete is by creating prototypes that can be used in practice. Prototypes are "anything that gets the idea in your head into an artifact people can experience and offer feedback on" (IDEO 2019). For example, in search of change ideas to improve outcomes for students with disabilities, one team scanned the literature, which suggested "providing opportunities for active student participation in the Individualized Education Program (IEP) process" to help students take greater ownership of their own learning. Although this felt like a promising recommendation for the team, it was not clear what it would look like in practice. Figure 9.2 shows one way that the team turned this vague concept into a concrete change that could be tested in practice.

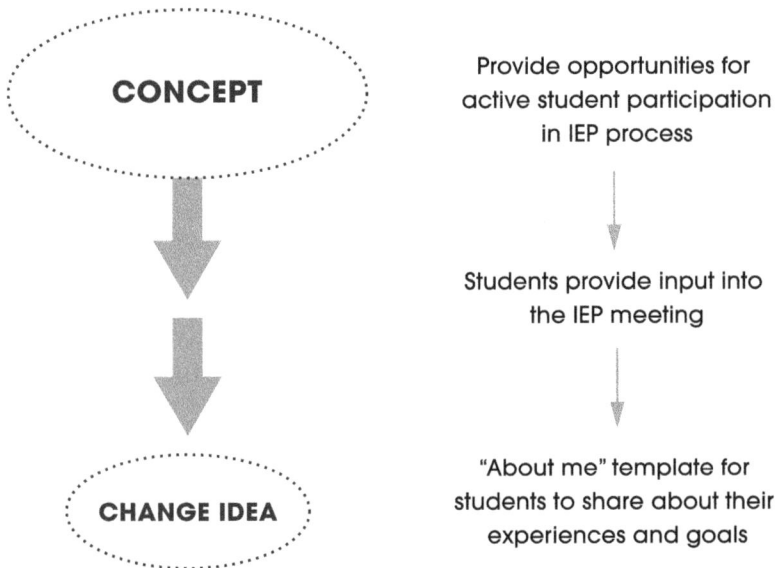

Figure 9.2. Translating a Concept to Tangible Change Idea

Prototypes come in various manifestations. Protocols, checklists, and process maps are typical forms of prototypes in improvement work. Table 9.2 contains examples of prototypes for changes mentioned in this chapter.

As the vignette at the opening of this chapter illustrates, prototyping helps keep teams from overthinking and move more quickly into creating concrete artifacts to test. Working out the details of what a change idea would look like in the day-to-day life of an organization surfaces assumptions and enables others to react to the idea in more meaningful ways. It is a critical step in unleashing the power of learning by doing (see chapter 11).

Table 9.2.   Potential Prototypes for Example Change Ideas

Change Ideas	Potential Prototypes
Working with local housing agencies to reduce asthma triggers in children's homes	Process map
Routine for tracking FAFSA completion	Process map Protocol for team check-ins to review the data
College tour for first-generation students	Flyer and/or agenda for the tour
Supplementing meals with crabs and shrimp	Photographs or pictures of meals to bring to other parents
Mobile HIV testing site	Mockup of the site Checklist of needed items
Nurse liaison to keep family members informed during surgeries	Sample role description Process for assigning liaisons
New structure of courses for community college math	Course catalog description
Feedback conversation between the principal and new teacher	Protocol for the feedback conversation

Translating Research into Change Ideas

Before asking teams to generate change ideas, it is worth reemphasizing the importance of tapping into existing research to figure out how to move forward. As described in chapter 1, better outcomes often come from the use of both improvement and subject matter expertise (see figure 1.1). Often, the inclination is toward starting from scratch rather than building on an existing knowledge base. Building on what is already known rather than relying exclusively on their own ideas can greatly accelerate a team's progress.

Teams will encounter challenges in leveraging research to identify useful practices. In some cases, the clinical knowledge base may be weak or nonexistent. In these instances, teams need to rely on other methods for generating change ideas. Through the improvement process, however, teams can build or strengthen the clinical knowledge base by testing and developing practices that work. Educators, for example, have discovered, codified, and spread practices for addressing chronic absenteeism in schools; health-care providers have figured out ways to reduce the number of falls with injuries in nursing homes (Schoberer et al. 2021, 86–93).

In other cases, although research can highlight powerful concepts or ideas that can be used to redesign systems, they tend to be broad or abstract and come with little guidance on how to apply them concretely in practice. For example, in 2006, social psychologist Carol Dweck published the book *Mindset: The New Psychology of Success*, which explored the relationship between individuals' beliefs about intelligence and their learning behaviors. In particular, she demonstrated that students with a "growth mindset," a belief that intelligence is malleable and can be developed through effort, showed higher levels of achievement than students with a "fixed mindset," a belief that intelligence is fixed and cannot be changed. What's more, Dweck's research showed that teaching students about the malleability of intelligence could shift students from a fixed to a growth mindset (Dweck 2006).

The work on mindsets offers important insights into helping educators support students to persist in learning complex topics. It offers an alternative explanation for what could easily be chalked up to lack of motivation on the part of students. However, to be useful, the concept of developing growth mindsets must be integrated into the day-to-day practice of classrooms and schools. To this end, improvement teams might first investigate ways in which the system currently promotes fixed mindsets. For example, not providing opportunities for students to make corrections on an assignment to develop knowledge or greater mastery of a skill over time. Or common teacher-student exchanges where fixed mindsets are unconsciously being reinforced—identifying a student as being "a math person" after the student does well on a math exam or counseling a struggling student to take an easier class. In addition, there may be certain moments during a student's schooling, such as the transition to ninth grade in high school, when having a fixed mindset has more consequential effects. With this understanding, the team can redesign or develop new practices that promote growth mindsets instead of fixed mindsets. These could include beginning-of-the-year lesson plans that teach students about mindsets, protocols for providing feedback to students on assignments that emphasize the value and importance of learning from mistakes, or short scripts that teachers can use to prime or reinforce a growth mindset before students take an exam. These change ideas are built on important research findings and are specific and concrete enough to be tested in practice.[15]

Even in instances when research articulates key evidence-based practices, there is still a need to learn how to embed these practices into the workflow of a system. For example, in 2000, Balas and Boren looked at various clinical procedures established through research and their rate of use in hospitals decades later (see table 9.3). They estimated that on average it takes 15.6 years to achieve a 50 percent implementation rate of clinically known best practices in hospitals (Balas and Boren 2000, 66).[16] Where evidence-based practices exist, the change ideas of the improvement team will focus on how to ensure that these practices happen reliably in their organizations (see the work on central line infections in chapter 12).

Table 9.3. The Knowing Doing Gap Exemplified in Medicine

Clinical Procedure	Landmark Trial (year)	Rate of Use in 2000 (percentage)
Flu vaccination	1968	55%
Thrombolytic therapy	1971	20%
Pneumococcal therapy	1977	35.6%
Diabetic eye exam	1981	38.4%
Beta blockers after MI	1982	61.9%
Cholesterol screening	1984	65%
Fecal occult blood	1986	17%
Diabetic foot care	1993	20%

Source: Reproduced from Balas and Boren 2000, 65–70.

The nature of the research base varies across sectors and across improvement problems. Health care, for example, has a much stronger commitment to (and funding for) evidence-based practice than education or social welfare, and along with it comes a stronger clinical knowledge base (Bryk et al. 2015, 240). Nonetheless, across the social sector a gap still exists between what is known in research and what is put into daily practice in organizations. By drawing on research, translating key findings into concrete practices that can be tried and tested in organizations to generate evidence, improvement work can help reduce that gap.[17]

COMMON PITFALLS

Table 9.4 describes common pitfalls that teams can expect to encounter when generating change ideas. Many of these pitfalls result from traditional beliefs about and ways of approaching change.

The first two pitfalls—more of the same and change the people, not the system—come from a lack of systems thinking. They arise from reactive modes of making change or when the changes that are produced are reactive, not fundamental. The second two pitfalls arise from traditional modes of thinking about change. The "not-invented-here" syndrome describes the

Table 9.4.   Common Pitfalls in Generating Change Ideas[18]

More of the same. A common first response to a problem is to add more: more money, more people, more training. Sometimes more is needed; however, the tendency to add usually results from not understanding the root causes of a particular outcome and/or the lack of ability to imagine alternatives. Doubling down on what has always been done often fails to produce a system capable of reaching new outcomes. This is an example of a reactive rather than a fundamental change to practice.
Change the people, not the system. Change ideas that focus on motivation or having people work harder or exert more self-discipline imply that the effort and will of individuals primarily is responsible for the outcomes we see. Using incentives, inspection, and other accountability mechanisms are examples of changes built on the notion that individuals, rather than systems, produce outcomes. Further, these approaches create unsafe spaces to learn from mistakes and failures, an important precondition necessary for improvement.
Utopia trap. A close cousin of "analysis paralysis," utopia syndrome involves getting stuck designing the perfect changes before moving forward. Teams experiencing this pitfall continue to talk about all interconnected aspects of the problem, focus on uncertainties, or wait to figure out the design of entire programs instead of moving to prototyping and testing changes. It can come from a fear of being wrong and be mitigated through leaning into small-scale testing.
Not invented here syndrome. People and teams tend to rely on their own ideas rather than exploring what others have tried. In its most extreme form, changes developed elsewhere are rejected defensively. The not-invented-here syndrome comes in part from assuming that each problem and context is unique. To be sure, changes developed elsewhere will need to be adapted to local communities and contexts. At the same time, failing to build on existing practices can seriously impoverish the ideas available to any improvement team.
Concepts, not changes. Change ideas are *specific alterations to how work gets done in a system*. They come in the form of practices, processes, structures, tools, or norms. As teams forage for changes, they often find ideas in the form of concepts. These concepts then need to be turned into concrete designs (prototypes) that can be tested in practice. Sometimes teams need to try various ways of enlivening the concept before settling on a specific practice that is useful in their context.
Tasks, not changes. It can be difficult for improvement teams to differentiate between "tasks" they just need to do and "change ideas" they need to test. Tasks are either precursor steps an improvement team simply needs to do to test a change idea (e.g., schedule a meeting, gather supplies, select data to collect) or a solution to a problem that is obvious and simple to execute (e.g., hanging a clock in response to patient feedback). Confusing tasks with change ideas bogs down an improvement effort.

tendency to see one's context as unique and thus to rely heavily on one's own ideas as opposed to looking to other places for new ideas. The utopia trap describes a hesitancy to move to testing ideas in practice. Teams in the utopia trap end up like the team of business school students at the beginning of the chapter; waiting to put the marshmallow on top until the last minute and only then learning that some of their core assumptions were wrong. The final two pitfalls most often arise when teams begin to test their ideas. Having a clearly designed change that someone can put into practice is a prerequisite for planning a test of change. However, it is not uncommon for teams to go into testing with concepts, not changes, skipping the important step of "designing the change." Finally, as teams learn to integrate plan-do-study-act (PDFSA) cycles in their work, some can overapply the tool; everything the team does becomes fodder for a PDSA cycle. Being able to distinguish tasks from changes can help teams know when the extra discipline of PDSAs is needed (for more on PDSA cycles, see chapter 11).

CONCLUSION

Starting with a strong set of change ideas is one key to accelerate a team's progress. These change ideas do not arrive magically and rarely through brainstorming alone. Instead, they are identified or developed purposefully using specific methods (see table 9.1). Even when these methods are applied, teams should expect their initial answers to the question, "What changes can we make that will result in an improvement?" to be wrong or at least incomplete. That is simply the nature of improving complex systems. Hopefully, recognizing this will encourage teams to move quickly from ideas to prototypes to testing in practice (see chapter 11). If a team's ideas don't pan out in practice and the team gets stuck, they can always come back to these methods to generate more ideas.

Generating change ideas, however, is only a piece of the learning puzzle. Through testing, teams want to move from hunches about what needs to change to a strong theory of improvement bolstered by evidence. With that in mind, we turn next to driver diagrams, which teams can use to explicate their initial theory and capture how it evolves as the improvement journey unfolds.

10

Shared Theory of Improvement

Without theory, experience has no meaning. Without theory, one has no questions to ask. Hence, without theory, there is no learning.

—Deming 2000, 103

In 2006, Fundacion Oportunidad, in partnership with Universidad de Diego Portales, Harvard Graduate School of Education, and Harvard Medical School, launched an effort to improve the quality of preschool and kindergarten education in Chile. The Chilean government had made large investments in expanding access to early childhood education. The leaders at Fundacion Oportunidad wanted to ensure the quality of these educational experiences, particularly those of children from vulnerable families, as a mechanism to counteract growing inequalities in Chile. To this end, they launched a project called Un Buen Comienzo (A Good Start) (Treviño, Aguirre, and Varela et al. 2018; "Un Buen Comienzo—Fundación Educacional Oportunidad," n.d.).[1]

In the first phase of work, the Un Buen Comienzo (UBC) leaders worked together to design, pilot, implement, and evaluate a strategy for improving early childhood education. The design team, made up of people with relevant research, and local, professional, and policy expertise, came together around a shared vision and theory to promote a) oral language development, b) health, c) socio-emotional development, and d) parent involvement. They designed an intensive professional development program for early child educators that included half-day workshops focused on learning strategies in each of the areas just listed. This was followed by biweekly coaching visits where experienced facilitators modeled specific strategies and observed teachers using them in the classroom. Teaching teams participated in six rounds of workshops and coaching visits each year.

Between 2008 and 2011, the program was implemented in the region surrounding Santiago along with a rigorous evaluation.[2] Perhaps the most surprising—and disappointing—finding of the study was that despite the intensive effort, the program showed no improvement in children's oral language development. Students in comparison classrooms made the same gains in oral language as those students in the classrooms participating in the program (Yoshikawa et al. 2015). But the data they collected also provided important insights into why students' oral language was not improving as they had hoped:

- Teaching teams implemented the strategies they learned in their classrooms. However, after two years of professional development and coaching, students were only experiencing an average of 12.5 minutes of oral language instruction per day.
- On average, students were absent 23 percent of school days; 65 percent of students were chronically absent, meaning they missed more than 10 percent of all school days (Treviño, Aguirre, and Varela 2018, 76).
- Students who attended more regularly saw higher than average gains in oral language, specifically in the domains of letter and word identification and emergent writing (Arbour et al. 2016).
- The evaluation used an observation instrument called CLASS to assess shifts in the instructional practice in the classroom. The professional development provided by Un Buen Comienzo improved the classroom organization and emotional support that students received. However, assessments of instructional support, the ability of teachers to facilitate instruction, remained low.
- School leaders were not actively engaged, and as a result, the program competed with other school initiatives.

With these insights, UBC leadership decided they needed a new theory for how to achieve improved early childhood outcomes and shifted to an improvement science approach. The original program had been thoughtfully designed by leading experts in the field, yet it hadn't yielded the intended results in practice. The schools perceived the program as being imposed from the outside, and as a result, their engagement was sporadic. Most important, the approach to learning what worked and what didn't was simply too slow. They needed to be able to pivot, adjust, and redesign along the way instead of waiting for years to see how their starting assumptions played out, as dictated by their initial experimental design using a traditional randomized control method.

In determining an aim, the UBC leadership decided to focus on the most important outcome, supporting early language development. Their aim read: Increase the percentage of children who achieve oral language proficiency by the end of kindergarten from 50 to 90 percent. The outcome measures were the percentage of students proficient in three dimensions of language development: vocabulary, oral comprehension, and emergent writing. In this phase, they would work with thirty-one schools in the province of Cachapoal. Each school improvement team crafted an aim that aligned with the aim for all schools using their individual baseline data.[3]

The design team then facilitated a process to get to a new theory, including a few change ideas that attempted to address the challenges raised in the evaluation of their initial phase of work. Consistent with an improvement science approach, they depicted their theory of how to improve early language development using a driver diagram—a visual representation of a group's current theory about which specific changes might improve the outcome of a process or system (Bennett and Provost 2015, 39).[4] The driver diagram begins with the aim, highlights the specific parts of the system where change is needed (drivers), and includes specific change ideas hypothesized to produce the desired result (see table 10.1 for a more detailed description of the elements of a driver diagram).

Hypothesizing that achieving the aim would require coordinated action across many players in the system, the team codesigned a theory with the larger community this time around.[5] Ev-

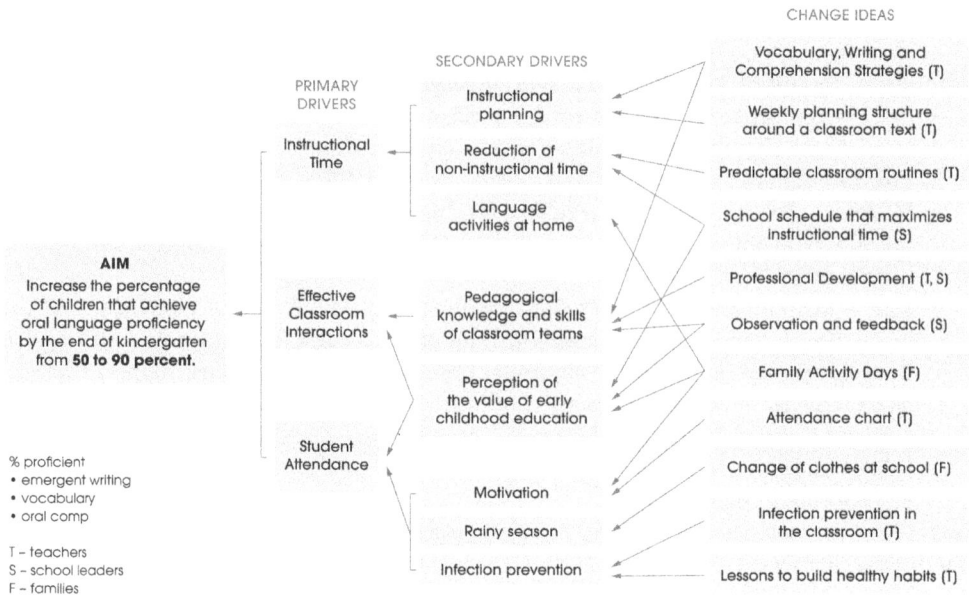

Figure 10.1.   A Theory for Improving Oral Language Development[6]

eryone involved in the effort engaged actively as *protagonistas* (protagonists), instead of some groups, teachers in particular, serving as passive players in a program developed by external providers. Each group tested change ideas in their spheres of influence and contributed to the overall theory of how to support students to achieve advanced language proficiency. The driver diagram helped align their efforts, visualizing how the changes that different people in the system were making were linked to the overall aim (see figure 10.1).

From 2011 to 2015, many school teams used the driver diagram as the starting point for their work. They tested the changes they deemed most relevant in their context, learned what worked and what didn't, and used these insights to update the theory (see chapter 11 on disciplined inquiry and chapter 13 on improvement routines for more on how to do this). They also collected measures to see if their efforts were leading to an increase in attendance, instructional time, the quality of interactions, and ultimately oral language development (see chapter 12 for more on measuring for improvement). Each year the UBC team revised the theory based on the ongoing learning from the sites. It took multiple iterations of testing and revisions to their theory to home in on what changes impacted each of the drivers in practice. But once they did, they achieved their aim: 92 percent of kindergarten children reached advanced proficiency in oral language (Treviño, Aguirre, and Varela 2018, 257–78).[7]

This chapter provides guidance about how to develop and use a theory of improvement as part of the improvement journey. Here, we focus specifically on the driver diagram as a way to capture a team's theory and its evolution over time. Creating a driver diagram during the chartering process (see chapter 8) helps the team articulate their initial theory and identify a prioritized set of change ideas. As the team learns in practice, their theory will naturally change and evolve as hypothesized causes and effects are put to the test in the real world. Through this process, the drivers of the system will come into clearer view, failed change ideas will fall by the wayside, and new ones that work will emerge. Ultimately, the goal of the team is to move from a provisional theory to a stronger one, by building practical knowledge and evidence about which changes achieve the outcome. Team members capture this knowledge and the evolution of their theory through their storyboard (see chapter 8). Ideally, at the end of the journey, teams will scroll through multiple versions of their driver diagram in their storyboard, marveling at what they "used to think" and celebrating their new insights.

WHY USE THEORY TO PURSUE IMPROVEMENT?

A theory is a map for how to get the desired outcomes. Theory is defined as "an idea used to account for a situation or to justify a course of action" (*Oxford Languages Dictionary* 2023). It comes from Greek, *theōria*, meaning contemplation and speculation. It is both thoughtful and a guess. It can be (and often is) wrong, requiring revision as new information or learning becomes available. We emphasize the use of theory for exactly this reason. In the context of our systems, we simply don't know what will work to produce the outcomes we desire. If we did know, we would already have done it.

The change ideas teams put forward are considered and speculative. It is important to emphasize both points. Teams will produce change ideas they strongly believe in, even before any evidence of effectiveness has been collected. For many teams in typical organizations, these beliefs lead directly to full-scale implementation of an idea based on little or no evidence. These investments are usually costly and lead to all sorts of variation in performance and frustration for workers within the system. Improvement science seeks to avoid this by emphasizing the speculative nature of ideas and the need for testing and evidence prior to investing in implementation (for more on testing, gathering evidence, and implementation, see chapter 11).

As the team sets out to learn their way into improved outcomes, the driver diagram serves a few key purposes (adapted from Bennett, Grunow, and Park 2022, 118):

- Capture a shared theory of improvement and its evolution across an improvement journey.
- Focus the work on changes to high-leverage areas of the system.
- Demonstrate the hypothesized links between the changes and the aim, so they can be tested.
- Coordinate action across groups working concurrently to improve the system.
- Inspire and inform measures designed to indicate if, when, and where improvement is occurring in the system.

To see how it fulfills these purposes, it is important to understand each element, how teams can generate one, and how it is used in practice.

ELEMENTS OF A DRIVER DIAGRAM

The elements of a driver diagram are described in table 10.1. On the left-hand side of a driver diagram is the aim, which answers the question "What are we trying to accomplish?" The middle of the diagram is made up of drivers that articulate which parts of the system need to change (primary drivers) and where in the system change is required (secondary drivers). The change ideas on the right-hand side answer the question "What changes can we make that will result in an improvement?," specifying how change will be pursued.

Table 10.1.   Elements of a Driver Diagram

Element	*Description*
Aim	The destination of the improvement journey. It defines what will be improved, by when, and for whom. The aim is directly connected to the outcome measure(s) and specifies the expected magnitude of improvement (for more on aims, see chapter 7).
Drivers	Drivers are high-leverage points in the system that represent the team's best thinking about which areas need to be targeted to achieve improvement. They tend to be of three types: *processes, structures,* and *organizational norms.* **Primary drivers** are high-level system elements that can be thought of as "what" needs to change and should have a direct impact on the aim. **Secondary drivers** are nested within primary drivers. They represent the specific, actionable places in the system where a change idea can be introduced and indirectly impact the aim. Secondary drivers should be included as necessary.[8]
Change Ideas	Specific practices the team can put into place that cause the system to function in fundamentally different ways. They can be new practices, processes, structures, tools, or norms. Over the course of the improvement journey, the changes that are included evolve from *change ideas* to *evidence-based changes resulting in improvement.* It is worth noting that the driver diagram simply names the change idea. The more specific design of any given change idea (i.e., its prototype) lives elsewhere (see chapter 9 on designing change ideas).

Source: Adapted from Bennett, Grunow, and Park 2022, 119–20.

What Is a Driver?

All improvement projects need an aim and change ideas—a clear direction and a proposed way to get there. Not all projects need a driver diagram.[9] Driver diagrams are useful when the aim requires coordinated action across multiple parts of a system, whether that system is big or small. The drivers capture the different leverage points in the system that are hypothesized as both necessary and sufficient to achieve the aim. Where there are multiple leverage points, the driver diagram helps organize the hypothesized change ideas needed to move each driver.

Articulating drivers requires speaking the language of systems. In chapter 1 we outlined the different kinds of systems components. The most tangible are the structures, policies, and organizational practices or processes that make up the day-to-day work. These are connected to less visible but often more deeply entrenched relationships, power dynamics, beliefs, and mindsets.

Improvement teams can articulate the key leverage points, or drivers, using three categorical types related to the system components previously outlined:

Processes: The workflow of the system—how things are accomplished, which steps are taken, and in which order. In some organizations, processes are named, and employees can identify the processes that are part of their work and for which steps they are responsible. In other organizations, processes are tacit and vague and must be mapped or visualized to improve them.

Structures and Policies: These include the physical design of a space, equipment, and materials, and/or how the workers are organized (e.g., departments, grades, etc.), as well as the guidelines and rules that govern how the system operates. They often articulate the boundaries that define the system and the hierarchies and relationships that lie within.

Norms: The written and unwritten standards that govern the behavior of members of the system. Norms include shared (often tacit) assumptions, beliefs, mindsets, and relational dynamics. Norms, which reflect the organizational psychology of the system, are therefore critical elements to consider when introducing change that will disrupt the status quo.

A team's driver diagram often will include all three categories of drivers. For example, the driver diagram that opened this chapter (figure 10.1) included processes such as instructional planning and language activities at home. Change ideas introduced to address the dip in attendance specifically targeted a structure, the rainy season. An important norm in the theory was the perception of the academic value of early childhood education. At the time UBC was launched, early education was still new to Chile and was primarily considered a way to prepare and socialize children for school as opposed to contributing to their academic development. This perception impacted how often parents sent their children to school, how much attention school administrators paid to early childhood education, and how teachers used classroom time with students.

How to Read a Driver Diagram

The driver diagram can be read from left to right or from right to left (see figure 10.2).[10] Read from left to right, it helps translate improvement aims into specific actions needed to achieve those aims. This counteracts the tendency in some organizations to focus only on "miracle goals" in the absence of "methods" needed to accomplish those goals.[11] The sentence frame below exemplifies how to follow the logic of a driver diagram from left to right using one primary driver from the UBC example above.

SENTENCE STEM FOR READING A
DRIVER DIAGRAM FROM LEFT TO RIGHT

If I want to _____ *aim* _____ then I need to focus on _____ *primary driver* _____ by _____ *secondary driver* _____ and one way to do that is to _____ *change idea* _____.

If I want to _____ *increase oral language development* _____ then I need to focus on _____ *attendance* _____ by _____ *addressing increased absences during the rainy season* _____ and one way to do that is to _____ *store a change of clothes at school*[12] _____.

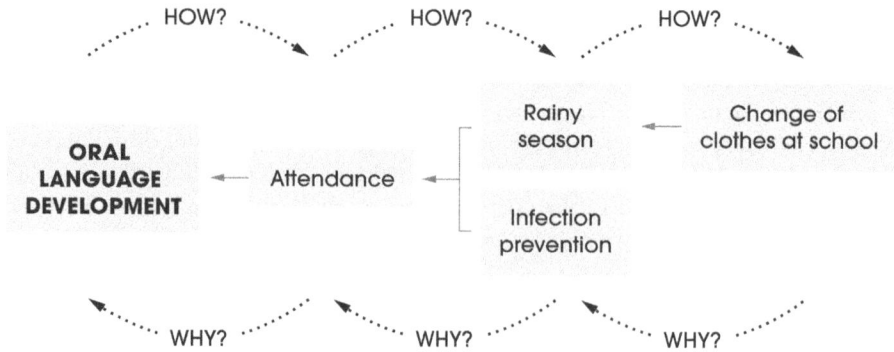

Figure 10.2.   Visualizing the Links between Aims and Change Ideas

Read from right to left, the driver diagram articulates the hypothesized causal links between the change idea and the aim. For example, storing a change of clothes at school is hypothesized to address absences during the rainy season, a key barrier to student attendance that, in turn, impacts students' oral language development. When team members have a new change idea, connecting it to the drivers and aim in these ways helps teams articulate the rationale for why it should be pursued. It also counteracts the tendency toward "solutionitis" by forcing the team or organization to clearly connect the change idea to the aim of the work.

The theory can break down at any part of the causal chain no matter how confident we might be. For instance, using the example above, storing a change of clothes at school might not sufficiently address parents' concerns about sending their young children to school during the rainy season. Or absences during the rainy season might not be the main (or only) factor leading to poor attendance. Or increasing attendance could be irrelevant to oral language development. At regular points during the journey, the team will revisit their driver diagram, assess which parts of the theory are playing out as expected and which are not. In these moments of consolidation (see chapter 13), they will need to decide where and how to evolve their theory based on what they've learned and update the driver diagram in their storyboard accordingly.

DEVELOPING A SHARED THEORY OF IMPROVEMENT

Creating a shared theory is both a technical and a social process. From a technical standpoint, the task is to create a strong theory of improvement: one that draws on subject matter knowledge (experiential, professional, and research) and systems thinking, allows for distributed learning, and shows the logical connection between the aim and the proposed changes. Important steps in creating a strong theory necessarily will happen before the team gathers to put one on "paper." For example, the team already should have agreed on the aim and outcome measures (see chapter 7). In addition, during the "understanding the system" phase, the team may have uncovered key system components that are missing or that need improvement through a data dive or process-mapping activity (see chapters 5 and 6). The components then become drivers in their theory. Teams also may have identified a starting set of change ideas that they are excited to pursue (see chapter 9) through an empathy interview or scan of the literature. Figure 10.3 provides an example of how previous learnings and activities connect to creating a driver diagram.

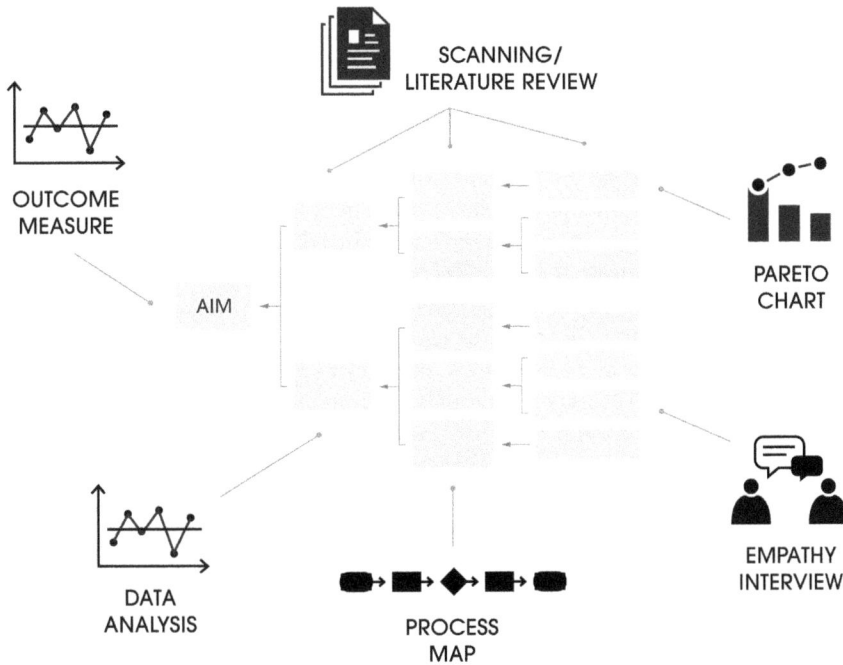

Figure 10.3. Using Tools and Methods to Build a Theory

Still, translating these learnings into a clear, concise theory can be tricky. It is important to start with the aim and outcome measures. The aim is the "direction setter" for the system. In naming what's being improved and for whom, the aim sets boundaries around which drivers are included and disciplines decisions about which change ideas to prioritize. From here, teams can follow one of two paths to visualize their theory. Similar to reading a driver diagram, teams can start in either direction. Some teams will work from left to right, first articulating key drivers based on the literature and their understanding of the current system and then identifying change ideas they theorize will impact individual drivers. Alternatively, some teams will find working from right to left more natural. Keeping the aim in mind, they will first prioritize change ideas based on their hypotheses of how to achieve the aim and then organize them using drivers.

Once teams have a first draft of their driver diagram, it is helpful to step back and view their theory as a whole. Seeing change ideas linked to aims in the context of a theory often will prompt reflection on where assumptions are weak or where prioritization is needed. A team can start by asking, "Do we believe these changes are adequate to achieve the outcomes we desire?" This pause is important as teams may realize that the changes are not sufficient to move the aim. One frequent mishap when creating a driver diagram is an equity trap known as "boomerang equity" (Safir and Dugan 2021). This happens when a team chooses an aim explicitly focused on closing a disparity, but then pairs it with change ideas that hold up the status quo.

A second important question is, "Do we believe all of these changes are necessary to achieve the outcomes we desire?" The goal is to create a theory that is as parsimonious as possible. When reflecting on their initial draft, it is not uncommon for teams to realize that they have overcomplicated their theory by including too many ideas, and they need to simplify or streamline their driver diagram. In this situation, they may start with the change ideas or drivers deemed most important and return later to determine whether the other changes are necessary.[13] Returning to the impact-effort matrix (see chapter 9) may be helpful in this scenario.

Regardless of which path a team chooses, getting to a visual representation of a theory is rarely linear. Teams will rearrange their theory multiple times, experience moments of both clarity and confusion, and toggle between zooming in on parts and stepping back to see the whole before getting to a good enough representation to test.

The social process for developing a driver diagram is as important as the technical one. After all, a driver diagram is meant to represent a shared theory. People naturally will have differences of opinion about what is high leverage and what should be excluded. Suggestions may be made that represent a deficit orientation and/or lack a systems view (see chapter 6 for more on deficit thinking and chapter 1 for more on a systems view). Cognitive biases might cause people to overemphasize or overlook a driver, or to prioritize a change idea that reflects a recency bias rather than the important causes of variation or failure in the system (see table 6.1). Here, it is particularly important that teams have the necessary conversational capacity to challenge each other's thinking, debate what to include and exclude, and find a common language to represent how they believe the system needs to change to produce better outcomes (for more on conversational capacity, see chapter 4).

Throughout these conversations, it is important for the team to stay grounded in the main purposes of the driver diagram: to focus efforts and guide team learning. An overly complicated visualization that is difficult to read or fails to provide clarity for a team is a sign that something is amiss.[14] Perhaps the team is not yet ready (or willing) to prioritize change ideas, or the complexity of the tool and its creation may be getting in the way of the team's ability to represent its thinking. What matters most is not adherence to the technical conventions but rather creating a picture that is jointly owned, captures current assumptions, and can help organize the team's learning journey.

Above all, it is important for the team to remain humble about their theory. It should be treated as a sketch on the back of a napkin, thoughtful yet speculative, that will change multiple times along the way. Adding the label "probably wrong and definitely incomplete" can help teams avoid theory lock: the tendency to become attached to a theory and, as a result, resistant to changing it. In the words of physicist Richard Feynman, "It doesn't matter how beautiful your guess is, it doesn't matter how smart you are. If it disagrees with the experiment, it's wrong" (Feynman, Leighton, and Sands 1963/2011).

UPDATING THE THEORY

Once a team has developed an initial theory, the real learning begins. Putting your theory to the test is hard: things don't happen as expected; assumptions and beliefs are challenged. But it's also when you learn the most. It is inevitable that the team's initial theory will need to evolve as they run learning cycles to discover what works, what doesn't, and what needs to be adapted, using the associated set of measures the team has identified as feedback (see chapter 12).

As mentioned earlier, teams often develop a first version of their theory as part of their charter (see chapter 8). At this stage, the theory only needs to be a good enough starting point to guide team learning in a reasonably strategic and focused way. As teams learn by enacting their theory in practice, they periodically pause to "consolidate" that learning, reflecting on the evidence they have gathered and using it to interrogate and revise their theory (see chapter 13).[15] Throughout the "learn-in-practice" phase, the driver diagram is a key knowledge management tool that anchors the team's storyboard and is updated regularly as the theory evolves. Finally, when the team discovers a theory that succeeds in producing the intended outcomes, the driver diagram is the basis of a "change package" that others can use as a starting point to improve outcomes in their context (see chapter 14).

Returning to the example of Un Buen Comienzo, one driver the team focused on was language instruction, with the goal of increasing the time spent on it to sixty minutes per day. They began by introducing teachers to new strategies through professional development sessions. Teachers used these strategies in their classrooms, and they were helpful, but they only spent twelve minutes of the five-hour school day focused on developing language skills. Based on this learning, they added a weekly planning process to help teachers select activities that could increase this language instruction time. This raised the average instructional time to sixteen minutes per day, a slight improvement but still well below the sixty-minute goal.

In the process of trying these change ideas with different teachers across several schools, they began to uncover the barriers getting in the way. Classroom routines were inconsistent, resulting in large amounts of *tiempos muertos* (dead time). Teachers struggled to keep students' attention during lessons, leading them to shorten lessons and favor other activities. Prekindergarten and kindergarten were considered separate from primary school learning, and as such, arrival times and lunch schedules were not coordinated with the rest of the primary school. It was not unheard of for eating to take up to two hours of the day.

To address these barriers, teachers, school leaders, and the UBC program team invented, tested, and adapted changes to their daily work. Teachers tested student engagement strategies, such as "turn-and-talks" and "buddy reading," and adjusted their classroom routines. Observations and feedback targeted specific instructional moves that teachers struggled with, and teachers were given opportunities to visit each other's classrooms to see the engagement strategies in action. At the same time, school leaders tested changes to the school schedule to enable more consistent classroom routines. Each year they updated their theory,[16] until the UBC team learned their way into a suite of changes that increased language instruction time to sixty minutes each day (Treviño, Aguirre, and Varela 2018).

CONCLUSION

In improvement science, teams learn their way into better outcomes through a continual process of articulating theories and testing them in practice. The driver diagram is a map, albeit an incomplete one, capturing the team's theory of how they will reach their destination. The long-term goal is to complete the map. Teams that successfully achieve their outcomes will have moved from a weak theory resting primarily on belief at the start of the journey to a strong, evidenced-based theory at the end that can be spread to others interested in achieving the same aim in their own contexts (see chapters 14 and 15).

Teams iterate their theory through collective learning. They work to create a common language to describe a shared theory that they evolve together over time. The next chapter describes how teams engage in disciplined inquiry to test change ideas in practice. Having a common method for inquiry enables all team members to participate in testing the theory and generates evidence that helps the team move from a weak theory to a strong one.

V

HOW WILL *WE* KNOW THAT A CHANGE IS AN IMPROVEMENT?

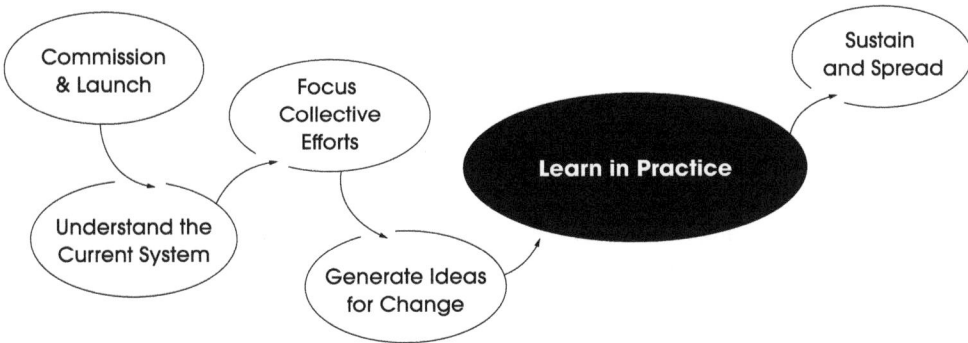

The learn-in-practice phase is the heart of the improvement journey. This is where the team will spend the bulk of their time[1] engaging in activities designed to help them answer the question, "How will *we* know that a change is an improvement" (Langley et al. 2009, 24)? Simply asking this question requires humility and a learning orientation. Some of the team's initial change ideas will play out as intended. Others will not. Systems thinking reminds us that it will be difficult to tell which is which up front. By following the learning, teams can move from initial theories to discovering a set of changes that move the system in the direction of the aim.

The earlier phases set the stage for what happens here: building relational capacity, grounding the work in a common understanding of the current system, clearly specifying an aim, and developing an initial theory and set of change ideas to test. Although the team undoubtedly has gained important insights along the way, there is no substitute for the learning that occurs when they finally put their ideas into action and observe how the system responds.

This part of the book has three chapters, each focused on one cornerstone of learn in practice: testing, measurement, and improvement routines. We start with testing because learning cycles are the central activity of this phase around which measures and routines are organized. Chapter 11 describes how changes are introduced in ways that optimize learning. Teams use iterative testing to identify which changes work, how to adapt them to different contexts, and ultimately, how to implement them so they become part of an organization's daily practice. Plan-do-study-act (PDSA) cycles help teams structure their tests of change, prompting them to identify clear learning questions, articulate their assumptions, and reflect on insights gained.

Chapter 12 describes how teams use measures to guide their learning. Teams identify outcome measures as part of their aim-setting process (see chapter 7). Now, with an initial theory in place, they identify a more complete family of measures that includes process measures tied to the parts of the system they are actively trying to change. For this data to be useful, it must be accessible at the right time and visualized in ways that reveal insights into their systems.

Finally, chapter 13 describes the improvement routines that enable team learning. Team huddles and meetings set the cadence for improvement work, establishing a place for teams to share and reflect on what's being learned and determine where to focus next. In between these gatherings, team members are testing changes and collecting data. Integrating these routines into daily work enables teams to maintain a shared focus while allowing them to act, adapt, and make decisions quickly.

Although we present testing, measures, and routines as separate chapters, these distinctions are arbitrary. In reality, they are intricately interconnected in both their design and execution. If any is absent or weak, the entire learning process will stall. As a result, it's important for teams to weave these strands together thoughtfully to maximize their learning.

Getting the technical details right will help facilitate team learning. Clear learning objectives and specific predictions help teams get the most out of testing changes. Selecting the appropriate data visualizations helps teams examine the variation that systems produce and determine whether they are moving in the right direction. That said, the relational and personal aspects of collective learning are equally important. The real power of running PDSA cycles and using data comes from the collaborative conversations that they produce. Sharing, challenging, and debating what is surfaced through PDSA cycles and data analyses is how new insights and knowledge are generated. The collaborative learning process also helps people see and shift the underlying beliefs that guide their behavior. Because team members and others engaged in the improvement journey are part of the system they are trying to change, they naturally have internalized ways of thinking that hold up the status quo and keep the current system in place. It is hard to see our habitual thoughts and even harder to revise them on our own. However, through conversation, we expose our beliefs to scrutiny in the face of differing perspectives and subsequently are forced to reevaluate them.

In the words of Margaret Wheatley,

> Noticing what surprises and disturbs me has been a very useful way to see invisible beliefs. If what you say surprises me, I must have been assuming something else was true. If what you say disturbs me, I must believe something contrary to you. My shock at your position exposes my own position. When I hear myself saying, "How could anyone believe something like that?" a light comes on for me to see my own beliefs. These moments are great gifts. If I can see my beliefs and assumptions, I can decide whether I still value them. (Wheatley 2009, 39)

The premise of this book rests on the belief in the transformative power of improvement science to foster collective learning. It depends on the ability of groups of people with diverse expertise to come together, surface and test tacit assumptions, and generate new shared understandings about how to make systems better. Nowhere is this truer than in the learn-in-practice phase of the journey. Robust collective learning will require interrupting hierarchical ways of working in which leaders, researchers, and external evaluators decide what the front line should do and what constitutes success, replacing them with distributed governance structures that integrate a wider range of voices in the knowledge-generation process. It will also require a different cadence. As seen in the Un Buen Comienzo example from chapter 10, using the traditional "implement and evaluate" approach, the team had to wait four years to learn whether the changes were an improvement. However, when they pivoted to using an improvement science approach, they ran shorter, iterative learning cycles that allowed them to learn and make adaptations based on context much more quickly. Finally, collective learning requires structured, safe settings where teams can collectively make sense of what is being learned. Thus, the learning in practice described in the next three chapters is not simply about adding tools and routines but, rather, about taking a fundamentally different approach to introducing change.

11

Testing Changes in Practice

Getting models out into the light of day, making them as rigorous as possible, testing them against the evidence, and being willing to scuttle them if they are no longer supported is nothing more than practicing the scientific method—something that is done too seldom even in science, and is done hardly at all in social science or management or government or everyday life.

—Meadows 2008, 172

FROM SMALL-SCALE TESTS TO IMPLEMENTATION

In 2014, a team of educators was commissioned by the Ministry of Education of New Zealand to improve enrollment and attendance, especially of their underrepresented groups, in early childhood education centers in South Auckland (for more on the setting of their aim, see chapter 7). To address this issue, the New Zealand government had recently rolled out an initiative that provided twenty free hours per week for all students enrolled in early childhood centers. Despite their efforts, an equity gap persisted; children from Māori- and Pacific Islander–identifying families were enrolling at a rate of 76 percent while children from Pakeha (European-descending) families were enrolling at a rate of 97.9 percent. A group of early childhood education centers were recruited to work together to learn how to better provide access to the primarily Māori and Pacific Islander families in their community (Tyler, Davies, and Bennett 2018).

At one early learning center, "C," the improvement team decided to focus first on increasing attendance of students already enrolled. An assumption the team made early in their work was that working-class families from the area were struggling to get their children to school each day. As a result, one of the improvement team's initial change ideas was to provide transportation to students. The idea made sense to the team, and they moved quickly to figure out how they could buy a van and hire a driver. Their improvement coach interrupted to ask if there was a way to confirm their assumption about the need for transportation before buying the van. Responding to their coach, the team decided to test their hypothesis by renting or borrowing a van and providing transportation for a few days. They thought this would confirm their suspicions about the need for transportation, allowing them to go ahead and purchase the van. This shifted the conversation from planning to action. One team member had access to a van they could use for a week. Jon, a Samoan staff member who lived in the community, said he would be happy to pick up and drop off students for a few days. Two days later, Jon began testing the idea, stopping by the homes of four students the team believed could benefit from access to transportation.

Although families thought providing transportation was a nice gesture, to the team's surprise, they discovered that it was neither necessary nor the main reason why their children sometimes stayed home from school. This small test of a change dampened the improvement team's enthusiasm for buying a van and hiring a full-time driver for their center.[1] As they debriefed their mini-experiment, Jon offered an insight he had while running the test. As part of the experiment, Jon had casual conversations with the students' parents and caregivers. Jon knew many of them personally and spoke the primary language (Samoan) of many of the families who lived in the area the center served. During the student drop-offs, two different parents shared with him the reason why they sometimes kept their children home: they were ashamed to send them to school on days when they didn't have food to send for lunch.

This insight was a powerful one for the team. Rather than continuing to test the idea of providing transportation, the team pivoted to exploring the specific need the families raised: free lunches. This is a core function of disciplined inquiry—to test assumptions prior to implementing changes in a system. Even with this powerful insight, the team still had much to learn: Could the center afford to provide lunch? Who would create and cook the food? How would it work? They structured their learning through a series of plan-do-study-act cycles (PDSAs), practical experiments that would answer these questions. Their first cycle focused on modeling the cost of providing lunch. When they were convinced that they could afford to provide free lunch to students, the team moved on to questions of logistics. They provided lunch for a couple of days a week to see what worked and what didn't—everything from purchasing food, to recipes, to service and clean up—before eventually implementing the idea for all students enrolled at the center. The use of several PDSA cycles, each focused on different questions, helped the team learn how to change the system in sustainable ways.

Providing lunch, in combination with other changes, ultimately did increase the center's attendance rates substantially (see figure 11.1). Notably, it was by trying an idea that "failed"—providing transportation—that the team uncovered a much more critical barrier to attendance—families not being able to provide lunch. From there, they were able to systematically figure out how to overcome this barrier and integrate a new practice into their system.

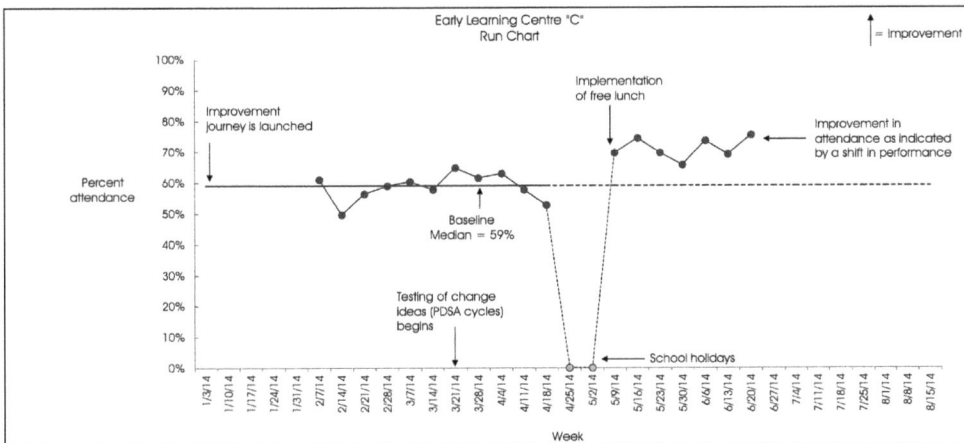

Figure 11.1.   Increasing Student Attendance at an Early Learning Center

This run chart shows the weekly attendance rate for children enrolled at early learning center "C" (for more on the use of run charts, see chapter 12). The solid line is the median attendance rate calculated for the baseline period before any changes were made. It represents a prediction of future performance for this center should no change in performance occur. The school holiday weeks were excluded from the calculation of the median based on the local assessment that they did not represent typical system performance. However, they were left in the graph to highlight the school closure, providing continuity for the story unfolding in the data. The seven consecutive data points above the median baseline performance after the school holidays represent a statistical signal (nonrandom variation) of improvement in attendance consistent with when changes to practice (provision of free to lunch to all students) were implemented by early learning center "C" (Tyler, Davies, and Bennett 2018, 109).

TESTING CHANGES

Observing how systems react when changes are introduced is one of the most powerful ways to learn how they are structured and which changes are needed to alter their performance. Although investigating the current system (chapter 5) and identifying powerful change ideas (chapter 9) can accelerate progress by establishing a strong starting point for teams, there is no substitute for trying changes in the real world. In the words of social and organizational psychologist Kurt Lewin, "if you want to truly understand something, try to change it" (Tolman et al. 1996, 31). Having a method for articulating hypotheses and then testing them in practice helps facilitate learning. Testing and learning also require a community, one in which different assumptions are shared, agreed upon, challenged, and discarded when no longer needed.

In this chapter we describe a way to introduce change that privileges learning by doing and testing changes before investing in full-scale implementation. At this point in the journey, teams have a set of change ideas that hold the potential for improvement based on their hypotheses. Teams then set up a sequence of iterative experiments to learn whether and how they work in their local context. This approach will help them quickly discard ineffective ideas and systematically learn their way into changes that lead to sustained improvement.

PLAN-DO-STUDY-ACT CYCLE (PDSA)

In improvement science, inquiry is disciplined by the three improvement questions depicted in the Model for Improvement (see chapter 1, figure 1.5). Answering the question "What are we trying to accomplish?" provides a clear, common destination for the winding path of improvement (see chapter 7). Teams identify useful measures to guide the path, allowing them to see whether their changes represent improvements (see chapter 12). In answering "What changes can we make?," they find an initial set of change ideas that might lead to an improvement (see chapters 9 and 10) (Langley et al. 2009).

When the team has initial answers to these questions, it is time to learn by doing: introducing changes into practice and discovering what it takes to achieve the aim. In this book, we use the plan-do-study-act cycle (PDSA cycle) to structure the team's iterative experiments. The PDSA cycle takes the scientific method and applies it to organizational practice to generate the pragmatic knowledge needed for systems improvement (Deming 2000; Langley et al. 2009; Moen and Norman 2010). Figure 11.2 describes the basic steps of the PDSA cycle and provides a PDSA example from the early childhood education work discussed at the start of this chapter.

Top Diagram

ACT
Next steps: Adapt, adopt, abandon, expand

PLAN
- What's your change?
- **What's your prediction?**
- Plan to conduct test

Making your theories and assumptions explicit

STUDY
- **Compare results to prediction**
- What did you learn?

DO
- Execute test
- Collect data, document observations

Revealing gaps in your understanding

Bottom Diagram

ABANDON van idea (for now)
TEST providing lunch on a small scale

CHANGE IDEA:
Provide transportation

ACT | PLAN
STUDY | DO

PREDICTION:
3/4 students will take the van

Our assumption that transportation was the main barrier may be wrong

1 out of 4 students take the van. Parents share that they are embarrassed to send their children to school without a lunch

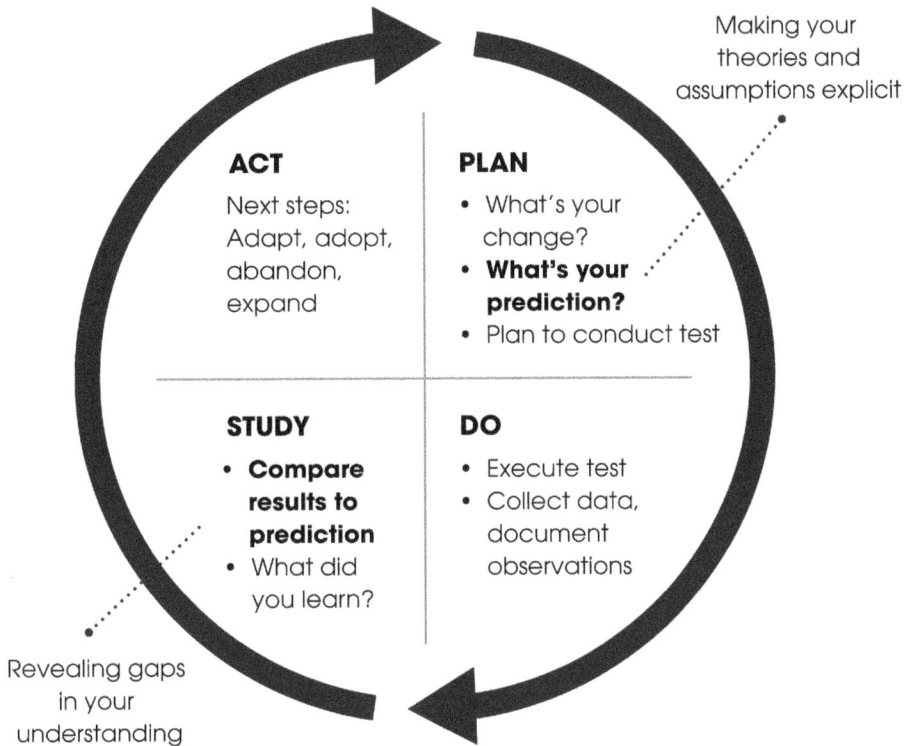

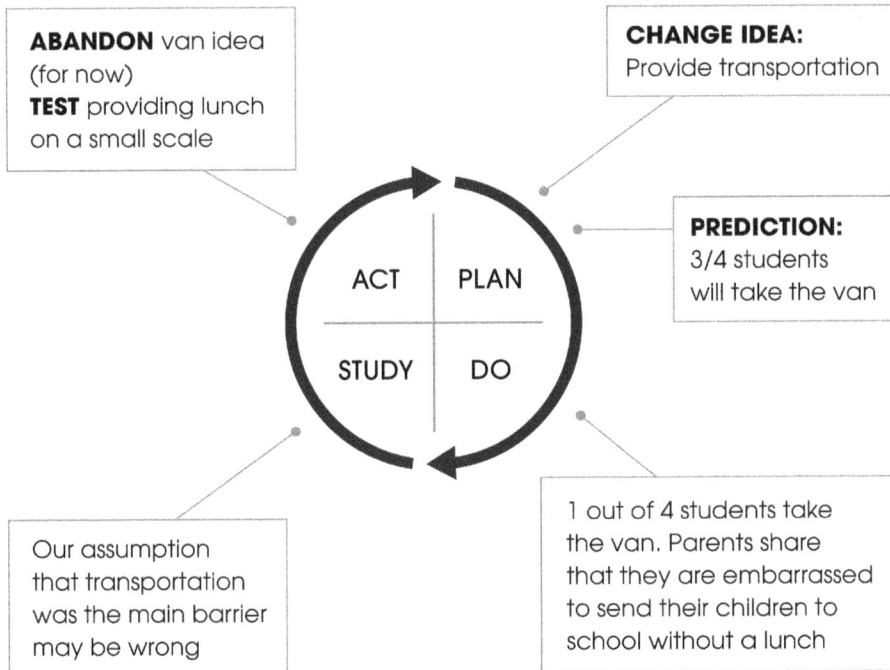

Figure 11.2. The Plan-Do-Study-Act Cycle

Table 11.1.   Key Elements in the PLAN of a PDSA Cycle to Test a Change[2]

- Strong, well-specified change idea (*with clear hypothesis*).
- Clear learning objective (see table 11.5).
- Appropriate scale of the test given the learning objective.
- Specific predictions linked to questions about how the change will work in practice.
- Data collection plan to answer questions.
- Plan for logistics.

Before engaging in a PDSA cycle, teams have identified and designed a change they want to test (see chapter 9 on prototypes).[3] To plan the cycle, teams articulate the hypothesis that lies behind their change idea ("If x, then y will result"). The hypothesis is often connected directly to the theory of improvement (see chapter 10). Teams then design an experiment. They identify what they want to learn, and find a place to test their hypothesis at an appropriate scale for the learning desired. Essential to the plan section is making clear predictions about what will happen when the change is tried and identifying data that can be collected to assess these predictions. Teams typically make multiple predictions for a single PDSA cycle. It can be helpful to use specific learning questions related to the learning objective to guide making predictions: a) How will the change play out (i.e., how long will it take, are all the steps complete?)? b) Will the change have the intended impact?, and c) Does the change unintentionally affect something else in a negative way? (i.e., it works but people hate it, or it takes a lot of time.) Table 11.1 outlines the key elements in planning a PDSA.

Then teams do the experiment. Usually this involves trying the change in practice during daily work and paying close attention to what happens. As the change is tested, data is collected and observations are noted.

After the change is tried, individual testers or teams step back to make sense of what happened. In the study portion of the PDSA, the team compares what happened to what they predicted, noting specifically where their predictions were incorrect. As exemplified in the van PDSA described above, unexpected observations captured during the test are often equally as powerful as the data intentionally collected, generating insight that informs the path forward.

After the team evaluates their original hypothesis, they determine how to build on their learning during the act portion of the PDSA cycle. In some cases, the team may conclude that the change idea should be abandoned; it just didn't work.[4] In other cases, the learning leads to an adaptation of the change idea or the support necessary to execute it. When the cycle goes well, teams may choose to adopt the change idea into daily practice and/or expand the scale of their next PDSA cycle, testing the change idea in a new setting or at a larger scale (i.e., for a longer time or for more end users).[5] The learning from any one PDSA cycle is necessarily limited. The power comes from running a series of iterative cycles with the learning from one cycle building to the next. W. E. Deming wrote about the value of the PDSA cycle: "This cycle is a flow diagram for learning, and for improvement" (Deming 2000, 131). Table 11.2 outlines the key elements in carrying out a PDSA.

Table 11.2.   Key Elements for Carrying Out a PDSA Cycle

- Carry out the plan.
- Record data and observations.
- Document unexpected events.
- Compare what happened to the predictions.
- Reflect on the original hypothesis.
- Identify next steps.

Predictions are one of the distinguishing features of the PDSA cycle and are essential for learning. In predicting how a change idea will play out and who it will work for, team members surface their current (often implicit assumptions) about how the system works. Deviations between predictions about what they think will happen and what actually happens illuminate a gap in understanding, which is a powerful opportunity for learning. It takes some work and discipline to see where our assumptions are wrong. Confirmation bias leads us selectively to take in and attend to information that fits with our existing beliefs. Hindsight bias makes whatever happened seem obvious after the fact, robbing us of seeing how our thinking has changed (see chapter 6 for more on biases). Clearly articulating predictions in advance, writing them down, and identifying data to assess them helps our brains to more easily see the learning opportunities that occur when we are wrong.

The greatest learning comes from what happens when changes do not go as predicted. Intuitively, we know that failed attempts are an inevitable part of a learning process. A child falls multiple times as he learns to walk; incorrect answers to math problems are recognized as powerful moments to develop mathematics skills; repeated failures are a prized part of the stories of innovations and scientific discoveries. However, learning from failures[6] is easier said than done, especially in a team setting. It requires vulnerability and psychological safety—"an environment where you don't fear rejection for being wrong . . . [that helps teams] do and say the things that allow [them] to learn and make progress in our changing, uncertain world" (Edmonson 2023, 38).

INQUIRY AND EQUITY

As discussed previously, although the technical aspects of running a PDSA as described above are important, it is the conversation about what the PDSA surfaced that generates the most learning. This is the powerful moment when our beliefs and mental models are brought "out into the light of day," tested against evidence, and scrutinized by others. These can be difficult conversations that require strong conversational capacity and psychological safety. However, they are critical conversations necessary for shifting mental models that lie beneath current organizational practices.

This is particularly true for equity-focused improvement. Oppressive systems are held up by powerful mental models that justify their existence and keep them in place. They do not manifest themselves only as explicitly racist or oppressive ways of thinking but also as subtle, deeply embedded forms of deficit thinking and behavior. It takes vulnerability, ongoing personal reflection, and a community to undo these narratives. Collaborative learning can be a powerful way to unearth implicit beliefs, blind spots, and deficit orientations so they can be challenged.

Example: Challenging Mindsets Using PDSA Cycles

A team of fifth-grade teachers, focused on supporting students to engage in rigorous math learning, worked with their coach to identify research-based instructional practices they could try in their classrooms. One practice involved posing a mathematical problem and having students work in small groups to explore multiple ways to solve it. One teacher was particularly hesitant about trying the new practice. It was a pretty big change in how she usually taught, and she worried that her students were not capable of this kind of problem solving. The coach offered to co-teach the lesson with her, ready to step in if the teacher needed help. Before the lesson, the coach and teacher sat down to make predictions for her PDSA. In talking through the lesson, the teacher anticipated that many students would be off task; she predicted that ten of her twenty-four students would be disengaged.

To the teacher's surprise, the lesson went much better than she anticipated. One student, Ricky, stood out to her. She recognized that he was one of the ten students she assumed would be disengaged, yet the opposite happened. Ricky genuinely seemed interested in the math problem and actively worked with the other students at his table, revealing a side of him that the teacher had not noticed before. The experience prompted the teacher to reflect on her assumptions about her students' math abilities in general and in her deficit orientation toward Ricky in particular. It also led to a willingness to try other new practices.[7]

With PDSAs, predictions (in the plan section) and inferences (in the study section) are two key places where deficit thinking predictably emerges. Students, patients, families, or colleagues can all, at times, be erroneously perceived as incapable (prospectively) or blamed (retrospectively) for the perceived failure of a new practice. When these moments are acknowledged and take place in social settings where they can be openly discussed, respectfully questioned, and thoughtfully reconsidered, they can initiate the process of dismantling the belief structures upholding our current system.

Who's at the Table?

Who is involved in the inquiry matters. Nothing safeguards the scientific method from being used to reify and reinforce oppressive ways of thinking and acting, except people. Leading up to World War II, a community of white (predominantly male) scientists used science to "generate evidence" of white people's superiority over black people. The movement within the scientific community, referred to as eugenics, is just one disturbing example of how science has been misused to perpetuate white supremacy (Wilkerson 2020, 78–82; National Institutes of Health 2022). Evidence is defined, interpreted, and adjudicated by people. Therefore, who has a seat at the table and the power to interpret experiences and data will have a significant influence on what is concluded.

Improvement science represents an important move away from the traditional model where leaders (or researchers) are the sole holders of knowledge and decisions to a more inclusive approach that capitalizes on and values the expertise of everyone in the organization. Having a common, shared, public method of inquiry provides a mechanism for democratizing knowledge creation, enabling everyone to participate. Chapter 10 describes the shift in Un Buen Comienzo's approach to learning from evaluation to improvement science. When they started using an evaluation approach, UBC team's theories, designs, and learning took center stage. In shifting to improvement science, teachers, school leaders, and support staff were equally involved in the learning, knowledge generation, and evolution of UBC's theory.

Improvement science goes a step further pushing for the inclusion of end users: students, patients, children, families, caregivers, and community members. These individuals bring valuable experiential insights that serve as critical sources of knowledge, enhancing the learning journey (Samuel et al. 2016; Bergerum et al. 2020). In the ImproveCareNow (ICN) network, which seeks to improve health outcomes for children and adolescents living with inflammatory bowel disease, patients and families play an active role in the improvement journey. Leveraging their experiential knowledge of the system, they serve as an invaluable source of change ideas for improving their health-care experiences as well as their overall quality of life. The network teaches them how to run PDSA cycles to discover what works for both them and others with their condition. In one notable example, patient leaders participating in the ICN Patient Advisory Council used a series of PDSA cycles to create a pediatric ostomy[8] toolkit (ImproveCareNow network 2015). Their understanding of what it's like to live with an ostomy led them to address aspects of life (e.g., clothing choice, the playing of sports, travel) that the medical community had not covered in the research or patient literature (David et al. 2018, 1–7).

When end users are not running the PDSAs, they still can and should be involved in the cycle when possible. For example, as we saw in chapter 8, end users can identify and design change ideas to test. In addition, teams should integrate end user feedback into PDSAs as data, critical for assessing whether a change is an improvement. End users can also be invited to the table when reviewing PDSAs to add interpretations that might otherwise be missed. As noted in chapter 2, "evidence from the field of healthcare suggests that improvement teams incorporating users are 2.78 times more likely to achieve their aim than those that do not" (Gwen and Shah 2021, 5). Like all parts of the improvement journey, methods can be helpful to structure a collective conversation, but what really matters is whose voice and perspective is heard.

SEQUENCING THE LEARNING

The purpose of collective, disciplined inquiry is to learn how to redesign systems capable of achieving better outcomes. Teams may start by testing changes on a small scale, such as providing transportation to four students, but they do so while keeping the larger aim in mind. Changing complex systems is a rigorous task that necessitates varied kinds of learning. The team must learn which changes are needed, how these changes work across varied contexts, and how to integrate them seamlessly into their daily workflow. Instead of trying to figure out everything at once, the learning is broken down into a series of iterative experiments that build on each other, enabling the team to move quickly and thoughtfully toward meaningful, sustainable change.

Example: Increasing Access to HIV Care—Learning How to Down Refer

By 2007, the staff of a rural South African regional government hospital had been working for two years to improve access to antiretroviral medications (ARVs)[9] for the local HIV-positive population. After two years of placing people into treatment, their HIV clinic was now overwhelmed with patients who required regular monthly check-ups. In any given week, up to fifteen hundred patients were visiting the HIV clinic for ongoing chronic care. These follow-up appointments were used to both monitor the effective management of their illness and the suppression of the virus in their bodies, as well as to distribute medications. The HIV clinic located in the regional hospital struggled to meet their patients' ongoing needs, and the volume of chronic care patients prevented the clinic from taking on newly diagnosed patients who needed access to life-saving ARV treatment.

The leader of the HIV clinic launched a multidisciplinary improvement team to address this issue. The team's initial change ideas required substantial resources the hospital-based clinic did not have: hiring more staff, extending clinic hours to evenings and weekends, and building a new exam space. One nurse on the team came up with a different idea: to "down refer" the care of their stable chronic care patients to the fourteen primary health centers (PHCs) that served the surrounding community. Community members accessed primary care at their local PHCs but traveled to the regional hospital for more advanced treatments, such as HIV care. The nurse's idea involved rearranging this system of care with the PHCs, not the hospital-based HIV clinic, as a way to provide ongoing HIV treatment.

The team members had mixed levels of enthusiasm for the change idea. However, instead of debating its merits and drawbacks, they decided to try it out with a couple of patients and see what happened. The team engaged in a design session to outline the specifics of preparing patients and care teams for treatment at a local PHC. They captured the change idea as a seven-step process for down referral (see table 11.3).

Table 11.3.   A Change Idea: Seven Steps to Down Referral

Seven Steps to Down Referral
1. Training the nursing staff at primary health centers (PHCs) on HIV care. 2. Orienting patients to what they could expect once down referred. 3. Prepackaging medications for each patient by name for distribution by PHC nursing staff. 4. Transferring patient record information to ensure continuity of care between facilities. 5. Transporting prepackaged medications from the regional hospital pharmacy to the PHC. 6. Sending a letter of introduction from the regional hospital HIV clinic staff to the PHC staff for each patient down referred. 7. Providing chronic care treatment for each down-referred patient at the PHC.

The team grew more excited as they developed a clearer picture of what "down referral" might look like. Still, they proceeded with caution, deciding to test the idea with just two patients in the PHC closest to the hospital. By starting small, they could learn about the change quickly and mitigate any unforeseen risks if the down referral did not go as planned so no patient would be harmed. The seven-step process worked perfectly for one of the patients, a young mother with three children at home. She received the treatment she needed and told her nurse she preferred being seen at her local PHC. She could walk there and didn't have to endure long wait times she had experienced at the hospital-based HIV clinic, saving both time and money. The other patient arrived at the same PHC only to find no medication waiting for him. The improvement team quickly hand-delivered the medication to the patient's home that same day.

For the improvement team, this first test "failed" in that it only worked for one of the two patients. However, the failure led to a key adaptation to the design of the idea. The team learned that the breakdown happened due to a gap in communication between the PHC and the regional hospital pharmacy where the ARV medications are prepackaged. To avoid future miscommunication, the team added an eighth step to the process—having the PHCs send a "pink card" to the regional hospital a week before the scheduled appointment with the patient's name and prescription. This "pink card" ensured that the medication would be there when the patient showed up for her monthly appointment at the PHC. The idea of the "pink card" was inspired by the use of Kanban cards in manufacturing, software development, and other customer service industries. They decided to test this new eight-step process with five patients at the same PHC. This time it worked! All five patients successfully received their treatment.

Over the next few months, the team continued to expand the down-referral process systematically to more PHCs. With each expansion, the team used PDSA cycles to learn what it would take for more PHCs to successfully execute the process (see table 11.4 for a summary of their learning).

Table 11.4. Summary of Learning from a PDSA Ramp Testing a Down-Referral Process

Cycle	Learning Objective	Size of the Test	Key Learning	Action
1	Test a new seven-step process for down referral	Two patients, one primary care center (PHC)	The idea of transferring care to primary care centers is potentially promising Current seven-step process is missing a critical step around medications	Adapt
2	Test a new (adapted) eight-step process for down referral	Five patients, one PHC	Additional step (pink card) solved the problem of missed medications	Expand
3	Test the eight-step process in a new context	Ten patients in first PHC Five patients in a new PHC	Replicated positive results Sufficient capacity in the second PHC to see patients	Adopt in two clinics Expand to remaining PHCs
4–12	Embed the eight-step process for down referral in two PHCs as the new normal Test the process in the remaining twelve PHCs	All patients who qualify to be seen in first two PHCs Small number of patients in twelve new PHCs	Replicated results in new PHCs Patients preferred treatment locally without travel to the regional hospital Clinical burden for chronic ongoing care was reduced at the HIV clinic at the regional hospital, creating space to initiate care for newly diagnosed HIV-positive patients Local PHCs varied in the total number of chronically stable patients they could see based on staffing levels and other patient demands	Implement the down-referral process system-wide (all fourteen PHCs in region)
13	Make the eight-step process the default care model for chronically stable HIV patients	All fourteen PHCs in partnership with the HIV clinic at the regional hospital	Systems change creating space for the initiation and ongoing treatment of HIV-positive patients in the district	Monitor for sustainability. Write up learning for spread to other hospital-based HIV clinics that could benefit from a down-referral process

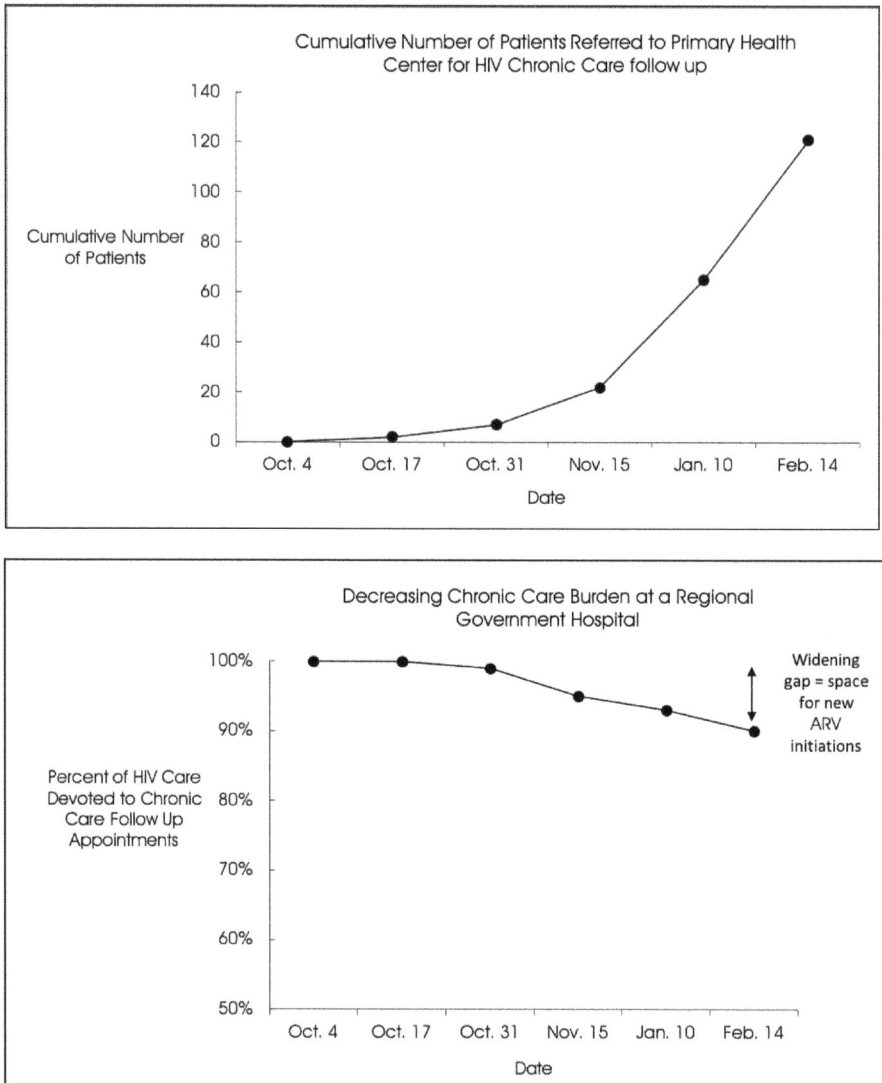

Figure 11.3. Impact of the Down-Referral Process on the Outcome of Interest

In the early stages of testing, the team's PDSA cycles were driven by questions related to the change idea's design, assessing its feasibility and functionality. As the team grew more confident in the design and viability of the change idea, their learning objective shifted to if and how the process would work in other contexts (cycle 3 and following). In particular, the team sought to understand the potential adjustments required by rural PHCs, where they hypothesized that medication delivery might be more difficult. With each new context, they tested the change idea first as a small-scale PDSA, down-referring only a handful of patients, to learn what modifications different local settings might require. However, at the same time, they accelerated the pace of change as they were able to successfully replicate results in more PHCs, moving from one PHC to two and eventually all fourteen in the district.

Over the course of five months, the team learned their way into successfully down-referring 120 patients. This represented a 10 percent reduction in chronic care demand at the regional hospital each week, which increased the hospital's capacity to initiate patients waiting for treatment (see figure 11.3).[10]

PDSA RAMPS: FROM SMALL TESTS TO IMPLEMENTATION

In typical change efforts, change is introduced across an entire organization all at once. Ideally, organizations will evaluate the outcomes of these efforts, but most often, they don't. As a result, they never learn what worked and didn't work for whom, under which conditions. The South African team took a decidedly different approach. They held the same goal in mind: results across the system. However, instead of using the traditional "planning to full-scale implementation" approach, they organized a series of learning cycles, systematically building the practical knowledge they needed to redesign the system to achieve better results.

The series of learning cycles form a "PDSA ramp" (see figure 11.4), with each cycle guiding the team's learning as they move toward implementation of the change (Langley et al. 2009, 103; Bryk et al. 2015, 131–33; Provost and Murray 2022, 10–12). Not all changes make it up the entire ramp. Some are abandoned during the early stages of design, such as the van idea described in chapter 9. The team may also discover that some ideas only work in certain contexts and not others. For those that do make it up the ramp, it's likely because the team has learned which adaptations and supports are needed to integrate a change into a wider set of contexts. A common rule of thumb in moving up the ramp is to expand the scale of testing from one to five to twenty-five to all (Langley et al. 2009, 259–60).[11]

The learning questions the improvement team needs to answer will change as they move up the ramp. In the beginning, the team will usually ask "What changes are needed?" Frequent, small-scale cycles are particularly useful here to sort out ideas that will work and those that won't. Once the team can demonstrate that a change can work somewhere, then the team needs to apply the change to an expanding range of conditions, and ask "What adaptations are needed for different contexts and/or users?" Here, it is useful for the team to test changes in conditions where the new practice might fail. This allows a team to learn the boundaries of a change idea's efficacy before implementing it at scale. With replicated success across contexts, the learning question shifts to "What supports are needed to sustain the change?"

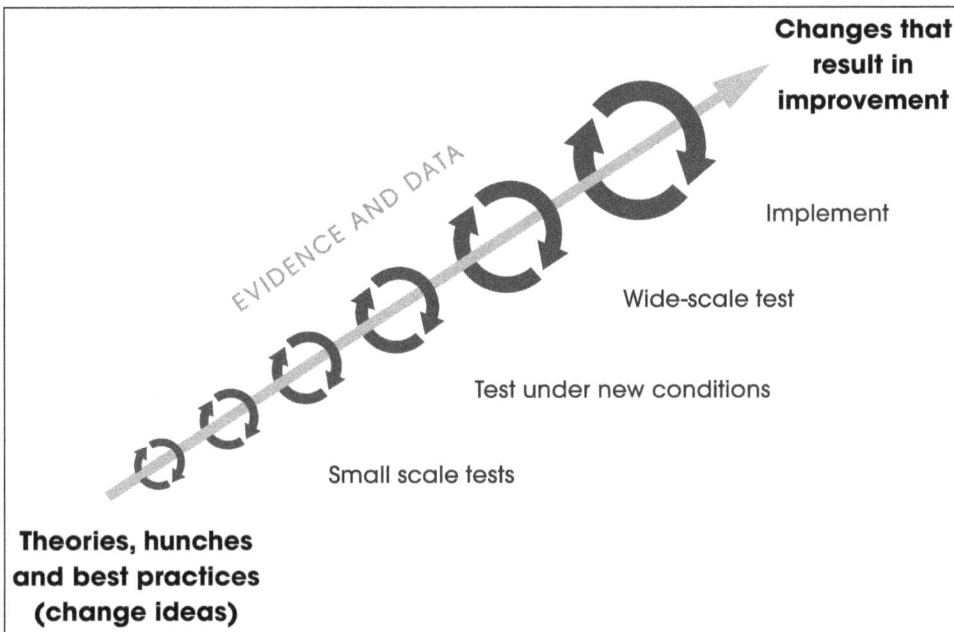

Figure 11.4.   PDSA Ramp

Table 11.5.   Common Learning Objectives for PDSA Cycles to Test Changes

- Test a change idea on a small scale to see whether it is worthwhile from the end users' point of view and/or feasible for the individuals responsible for doing it.
- Test a change idea to see whether it works in a new context.
- Determine the conditions under which the change idea works and under which it does not.
- Test whether the change idea (or combination of change ideas) has the desired effect.
- Give individuals an opportunity to try a change in practice before adopting it as the new status quo.
- Determine what other supports are required to embed a change in practice, making it the new day-to-day work of the system.
- Understand the potential unintended consequences of adopting a change.

When a team reaches this stage, they shift their focus toward understanding the organizational conditions necessary for sustaining the change in everyday practice (see the following section on implementation).

PDSA cycles guide the learning up the entire ramp. The scale, duration, and structure of the cycle will vary as the learning questions shift, but the steps and basic logic of the cycle are the same. Table 11.5 is a list of common learning objectives for PDSA cycles. Having a clear learning objective is an important precursor to structuring a useful inquiry cycle.

The data and evidence needed vary based on the primary learning objective of the PDSA. For example, in the early stages of testing the South African team's seven-step down-referral process, the team wanted to learn whether transferring care could work; as a result, the data relevant for their learning was largely qualitative and observational, designed to capture the patients' experience of the process and whether they received the care they needed. When the team moved up the ramp, they needed to collect data that highlighted potential variations in the execution and outcomes of the process in different contexts. Further, they sought to understand how specific contextual factors (e.g., the comfort of PHC nurses in providing HIV care, weekly patient loads, and medication transport times) in the different sites contributed to the variation to determine which adaptations were needed for the process to happen reliably across the district. Not until the process was up and running in multiple PHCs did the team ask if their change was an improvement based on their outcome measure—to decrease the number of chronic-care HIV patients served at the hospital to increase initiation of new patients. The improvement team never lost sight of its goal but sequenced their learning, collecting the most relevant data given the learning objective of each PDSA cycle.

Some changes are difficult to test with this iterative, sequential approach. In education, certain activities (e.g., hiring teachers, enrolling students in classes, or teaching a unit on fractions) only happen once per year. In health care, iterative tests are difficult for changes that target important but rare events, such as falls, central line infections, and rarely occurring diseases. Teams need to act strategically in these situations given their limited opportunities to learn. For example, teams may consider testing ideas through simulations or computer modeling to assess their viability and impact. As mentioned earlier, the team from New Zealand tested different cost models to determine the affordability of providing free lunch to students. They can also engage in more complex PDSA testing strategies that address multiple learning objectives at once to maximize the learning opportunities they have (Moen, Nolan, and Provost 2012).[12]

To achieve their project aims, most teams will need to move multiple change ideas up separate PDSA ramps. Each change or group of changes on a team's driver diagram will require its own learning journey (see figure 11.5).

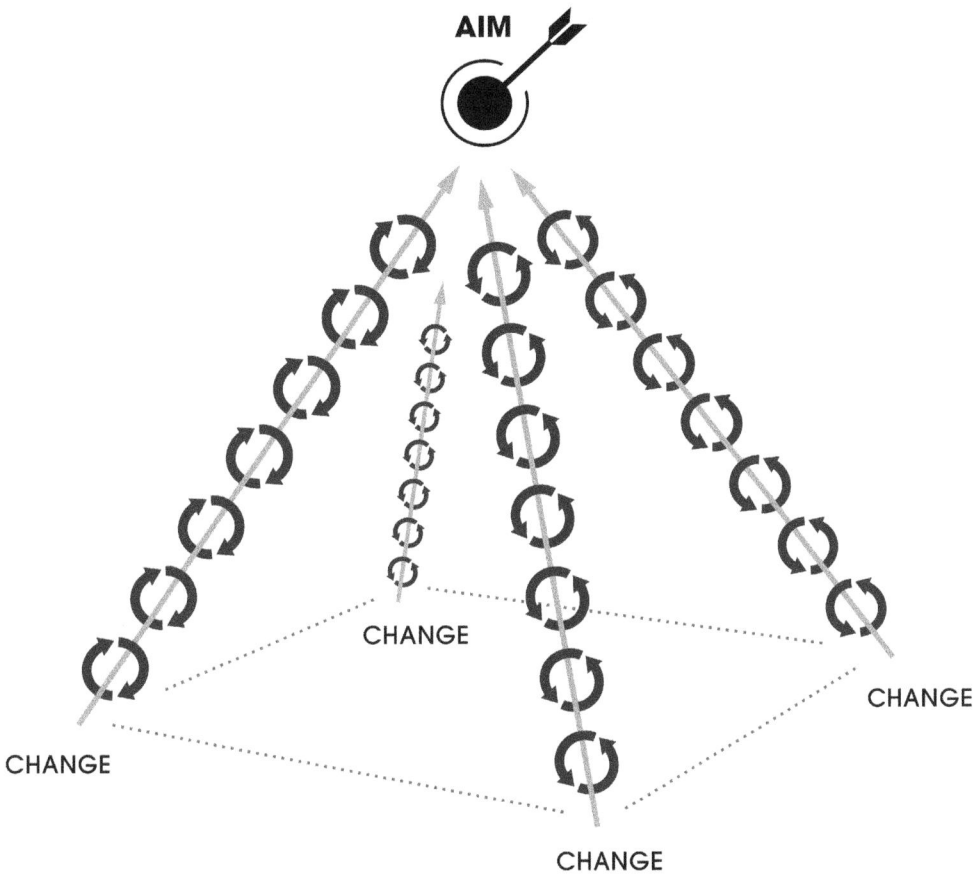

Figure 11.5. Pursuing Multiple PDSA Ramps to Reach an Aim

As will be described next, the excitement, confidence, and nature of the change will influence the pace and structure such learning will take. Regularly revisiting what needs to be learned about a particular change, proactively managing ramps, and knowing when it is time to move on helps teams focus their inquiry efforts on the most strategic learning objectives for the improvement they seek.

KNOWING WHEN TO IMPLEMENT

We commonly use the word "implementation" whenever we execute a change. In improvement science, the term "implementation" is defined more narrowly, referring to the actions needed to make a change permanent to the system at the designated scale so that it can be sustained after the team's improvement journey ends (Langley et al. 2009, 173).

What is considered "at scale" depends on the organizational structure where the change occurs and is usually reflected in the team's aim statement. For example, the South Africa team focused on one regional hospital's capacity to provide HIV care (initiation and ongoing chronic care) for the entire district, which included the fourteen PHCs. As a result, implementation meant down referring patients to all fourteen PHCs. The New Zealand team, described earlier in the chapter, aimed to improve attendance in one early education center, "C." Here, implementation meant instituting a permanent change, providing free lunches, in that one center. This can be contrasted with the concept of spread (see chapter 15) when early learning center "C" moved quickly to spread the idea of providing free lunches to the other six centers participating in their improvement network. Each of these centers went through their own PDSA cycles to implement the idea at their learning centers.[13]

On the path to implementation, teams vary the size and/or duration of their PDSA cycles to generate the learning needed to achieve change at the intended scale. The framework in table 11.6 provides teams with decision rules for determining the appropriate scale of a particular test (Langley et al. 2009, 146; Bryk et al. 2015, 120). In the bottom right-hand corner is the end goal: implementation. To justify the decision to implement a change or set of changes, the team should consider three factors.

1. First, the team must have a strong belief that the change will lead to an improvement (see the left-most column of table 11.6). A team's degree of belief relates to the confidence they have that the change will work in their local context.[14]
2. Second, the cost of failure should be small—introducing the change would not harm anyone or likely waste significant resources in the form of time, money, or will of the people impacted by the change.
3. Finally, those most affected by the change need to be ready; they need to be motivated, excited, and willing to make the change. With traditional approaches to implementation, organizations rarely consider these factors, which is why they often fail to produce the intended outcomes.[15]

The good news is that teams can learn their way into how to create the conditions necessary to achieve implementation. Teams can use the framework to develop a sequence of PDSA cycles that will help them build their degree of belief, decrease the cost of failure, and/or improve the readiness for implementing a change. For example, as noted in the learning objectives, teams can use PDSA cycles to give people in the organization an opportunity to try out the change on a small scale and offer feedback if they are somewhat resistant or indifferent about it. They may discover they like the change and feel more "ready" to implement it.[16]

Taken together, the PDSA ramp and the framework can help improvement teams keep their inquiry strategic and focused. A team's learning gets off track when the size and pace of testing is

Table 11.6.   Determining the Appropriate Scale for a Test of Change

		Readiness to Make the Change		
		Resistant	**Indifferent**	**Ready**
Low Degree of Belief that the change will lead to improvement	**Large Cost of Failure**	Very small-scale test	Very small-scale test	Very small-scale test
	Small Cost of Failure	Very small-scale test	Small-scale test	Moderate-scale test
High Degree of Belief that the change will lead to improvement	**Large Cost of Failure**	Very small-scale test	Small-scale test	Large-scale test
	Small Cost of Failure	Moderate-scale test	Large-scale test	Implementation

Source: Adapted from Langley et al. 2009, 146; and Bryk et al. 2015, 120.

not managed effectively. In general, PDSAs should stay small until the team's degree of belief is high enough to move up the ramp to larger and/or more diverse tests. When a team moves too quickly up the ramp, they bypass important learning opportunities that could hamper the team's ability to implement the change down the line or lead to temporary improvement because the team didn't fully learn what system supports were needed to sustain the change. Indeed, investing greater time and effort in the early stages of testing often generates learning that accelerates the team's movement up the ramp as they get closer to implementation.

That said, testing doesn't always need to start small. When the conditions are right—the team has a high degree of belief in the change, the cost of failure is deemed low, and people in the organization and those it serves are ready for change—teams can move quickly to implementation. For example, in the community college math case described in chapter 6, the network decided to change the traditional path out of remedial math by offering one year-long course that would replace the three courses needed to complete college-level math. This change was not tested using a PDSA ramp. In addition to being difficult to test on a small scale, the participating community colleges' will, skill, and confidence in the change, all of which were high, warranted going straight to implementation. This also allowed the network to allocate valuable resources to other changes that needed further development and testing. In addition, in the medical field, when basic science research demonstrates the value of a new technique or the efficacy of a new drug, teams may choose to focus PDSA cycles directly on implementing the change rather than reconfirming its efficacy. In these cases, the goal is the reliable application of a validated best practice. Testing requires resources, so it's important for the team to allocate them strategically to address the most important or difficult learning questions at hand.

IMPLEMENTATION

When the team reaches implementation, the main learning objective is to identify and put in place the key system supports needed to sustain the new practice, tool, or technique. Prior to this, the team has focused on designing a change and making it work in a variety of contexts. As they shift to thinking about sustainability of the change, the team's attention turns to the policies, practices, and infrastructure needed to make it a permanent part of the organization's fabric.

For example, once the South African team was confident that down referring was indeed an improvement, they turned their attention to cementing this process as the standard way of doing business. They documented the process as a standard operating procedure and distributed it to all fourteen PHCs in the district. They designated a senior leader at the regional hospital as the owner of the process, responsible for maintaining and updating it and fielding questions or concerns from medical personnel and/or patients impacted by the change. This person was also responsible for ensuring that patient data flowed from the PHCs to the HIV clinic at the regional hospital so they could monitor the quality of care being received at the PHCs. In addition, the team needed to make sure that various procedural documents, job descriptions, and onboarding training were updated at the hospital and local PHCs to ensure that all local clinicians were prepared for their new responsibilities. Table 11.7 provides a starting list of typical organizational areas that require change when making new practices permanent in an organization.[17]

PDSA cycles at implementation often involve a different set of people, specifically those responsible for work related to the areas listed in table 11.7. These cycles generally occur over

Table 11.7. Common Systems Components Implicated in Implementation

- Policies and Procedures
- Hiring Procedures
- Job Descriptions
- Staff Education and Training
- Measurement and Data Routines
- Resourcing

longer periods of time: a month, six months, even a year. Longer time periods are necessary to learn whether the changes have become the default way of working in the organization.

Improvement teams can anticipate increased resistance when they reach this stage, particularly when the implementation of a change idea has implications for many people in the organization. As Langley et al. write, "it is with implementation that the impending impacts of change become more real" (Langley et al. 2009, 189). Some changes, particularly those with a widely recognized benefit, may be picked up easily and with little effort. Others, particularly those that conflict with existing belief systems or require other notable organizational shifts, will take significantly more time and attention to implement. Leadership involvement is critical in mitigating resistance. Leaders can communicate relentlessly why the change is needed while also providing clarity on the time frame and expectations for adoption. This might mean giving people the chance to observe or try the change themselves before full adoption or to review evidence of the change's efficacy (for more on this topic, see chapter 15). People affected by changes in practice (e.g., end users and staff members) hold mental models that can and often do reinforce existing practices. Providing settings where people can surface and explore these existing beliefs is key to real, sustained systems change.

CONCLUSION

Improvement teams learn their way into systems improvement through testing changes in practice. The questions that guide the learning evolve over time, enabling the team to build the will and practical knowledge necessary to sustain changes to the system. They move from "What changes are needed?" to "How do these changes need to be adapted to local contexts?" to "How do we permanently integrate the changes that work into the system's daily operations?" The answers to these questions will not be straightforward and will require making sense collectively. The best learning opportunities will likely come when the team's hypotheses are wrong, and their change ideas do not produce the outcome intended. If the team has created the conditions to face these failures productively, they become important moments when theories evolve, and long-standing mental models shift. Through collective inquiry, the team can challenge biases and beliefs, produce stronger shared theories, and generate evidence and knowledge about how to improve system performance.

This chapter focused on testing and the underlying strategy for achieving meaningful change. Equally important are the measures that facilitate the inquiry process, keeping a pulse on the system's behavior and signaling when the team's theories need to be revised. This is the subject of the next chapter.

12

Measurement for Improvement

> The purpose of measurement for improvement is to speed learning, not slow it down.
>
> —Provost and Murray 2022, 53

Organizations always use data to guide their work, whether they know it or not. Individuals and teams are constantly taking in data, turning it into information, and acting on it (see chapter 6 on how people think). Measurement for improvement seeks to make the process of data selection, information creation, and strategic action more explicit, transparent, and inclusive. When used well, measurement for improvement provides valuable information throughout the improvement journey. It gives teams a window into their system, helps inform where they should focus their efforts, and highlights which changes are needed. In the learn-in-practice phase, teams use measurement to guide their learning as changes are introduced into the system.

The characteristics that define measurement for improvement stem from two central premises: a) systems produce outcomes, and b) improving systems requires collective learning. These tenets inform which measures are selected, how data are collected and with what frequency, which visualizations are needed to initiate conversations that drive learning, and who needs to be engaged.

This chapter describes how teams identify measures and use data to guide the learn-in-practice phase of an improvement journey. The measures that teams identify connect their theory to their aim, providing insights into what works for whom under what conditions. They serve as a critical feedback loop for the team and generate the necessary evidence warranting changes to the system.

WHAT IS MEASUREMENT FOR IMPROVEMENT?

Before going any further, it is helpful to define a few key terms. *Data* refers to "documented observations or the results of performing a measurement process. The concept of data refers to strings or patterns of characters that describe some aspect of the world" (Provost and Murray 2022, 28).[1] Data can be numeric (quantitative) or non-numeric (qualitative). Individuals take in data continuously as they interact with the environment; data can also be collected systematically. In addition, data analysis can be deliberate and methodical or happen automatically and unconsciously (see ladder of inference in chapter 6). *Measures* represent data generated through a formal measurement process. They, too, can be quantitative or qualitative. Blood type, levels of proficiency, wait times, college-going rates, and students' sense of belonging are all examples of measures that can be formally collected. Creating a measure involves identifying which snippet of data deserves attention. Operational definitions of measures are created to ensure that data are collected in the same way, adhering to a consistent process or use of consistent tools. Finally, neither data nor measures carry meaning on their own. *Information* is the result of giving context, structure, and significance to data, making it useful and actionable. Humans (or other intelligence) transform data into information by articulating the decision, action, or question the data is intended to inform.

To guide the learn-in-practice phase of the improvement journey, teams use data and measures to inform their answer to the question, "How will we know that a change is an improvement?" This question, at the heart of the Model for Improvement, connects the theory to the aim (Langley et al. 2009, 24). Because most theories require teams to work on various parts of the system (drivers), they need a set of measures to assess whether improvement in these areas produces the intended outcome. Teams will supplement these measures with other data needed to answer additional learning questions that arise as part of the learning journey (e.g., data related to specific plan-do-study-act [PDSA] cycles).

Measurement for Improvement Versus Accountability and Research

The use of data for improvement stands in stark contrast to other ways that organizations use data. Indeed, some people new to improvement start off wary of measurement, especially the use of quantitative measures, having experienced it as something done to them, rather than as a useful resource to guide learning. For this reason, it can be helpful to contrast measurement for improvement from other more traditional uses of measurement in organizations.

Solberg, Mosser, and McDonald, in their paper "The Three Faces of Performance Measurement," distinguish measurement for improvement from measurement for accountability and measurement for research (1997, 135–47). Accountability systems draw on "satellite data"[2]—data that, as the term implies, sits far away from daily practice. Accountability measures, designed for policy makers and system leaders, are available infrequently and after the fact. These measures can signal an unwanted gap in performance and direct the focus of potential improvement work, but they can't illuminate a path forward for the team when learning in practice. Measurement for research often entails collecting mounds of data at once to generate new generalizable knowledge. Those who provide the data are typically not involved in interpreting the results. If the findings eventually are shared, it's usually after a delay of months or even years. In general, measurement for research is usually too slow, too expensive, and too elaborate to be useful in improvement.

Measurement for improvement is notably different in its purpose, audience, and time cycle. Its purpose is to inform the collective learning of those engaged in the improvement journey and to ensure that the needs, as articulated by those being served, are being met. Teams start with what they want to improve and an initial theory for how to get there. With this as an anchor, they then anticipate which data they'll need and when, building out their measurement strategy and data routines from there. However, as their learning journey unfolds, the team should stay flexible and adjust the data needed according to what they're learning.

Most accountability and research measures are often insufficient for this purpose—they aren't granular or specific enough to answer the types of questions improvement teams ask and aren't available frequently enough to inform the interactive learning cycles described in chapter 11. Further, these measures sometimes have been used against individuals or organizations in ways that have led to suspicion and skepticism of their usage. So, although we encourage teams to draw on existing data whenever possible as developing new measures is resource intensive and time consuming, teams should not assume that all existing measures, especially those used primarily for accountability and research purposes, will be appropriate for improvement. As a result, teams must always be clear about how the data is being used and for whom.

Finally, for measures to serve as tools for learning, they must be collectively interpreted with the people who generated the data. This should be done in settings that foster open, inquisitive, and reflective discussions about the data shared.

IDENTIFYING USEFUL MEASURES

As mentioned earlier, teams use a small set of measures to assess whether improvement in specific parts of the system produces the intended outcome. These measures are often referred to as a family of measures, emphasizing the relationship of each measure to each other (Langley et al. 2009, 319; Provost and Murray 2022, 43). The family of measures stems from the team's theory of improvement and are typically collected for the duration of the project. It includes the outcome measure articulated in the aim (see chapter 7), as well as measures connected to specific drivers of the theory. The team also needs data beyond the family of measures to inform their PDSA cycles. This data tends to be more granular and varies based on the specific learning questions of the PDSAs. It helps teams learn which changes are needed, how to adapt them to local contexts, and how to sustain them in practice.

Example: Connecting Measures to Un Buen Comienzo's Theory

In chapter 10, we introduced the work of Un Buen Comienzo, an effort to improve early language development for children in rural Chile. The teams used a variety of data and measures to guide their learning. First, the team collected data related to their overall theory, including the amount of language instruction students received, observations of the classroom environment, attendance data, and data on students' oral language development. Any one measure was limited in scope, but taken together, they began to tell a useful story about the changes people were making and the impact they were having on students. Periodically, the team would review their suite of measures, seeking to discern insights from the data about their system, theories, and where to work next.

These measures were useful, but they functioned more like satellite data and did not inform a teacher's daily work. As a result, teachers collected their own data based on their specific learning questions when introducing new classroom practices. As part of each PDSA cycle, they recorded qualitative data and observations relevant to their questions. When appropriate, they identified measures that were directly related to what they were testing, giving them a broader view of change over time. Figure 12.1 shows data displays from two different teachers, one who was testing ideas on vocabulary instruction and another focused on student engagement using "read-alouds." A coach helped the teachers identify them and develop data collection strategies that could be carried out while teaching. In this case, the strategy was a sheet of

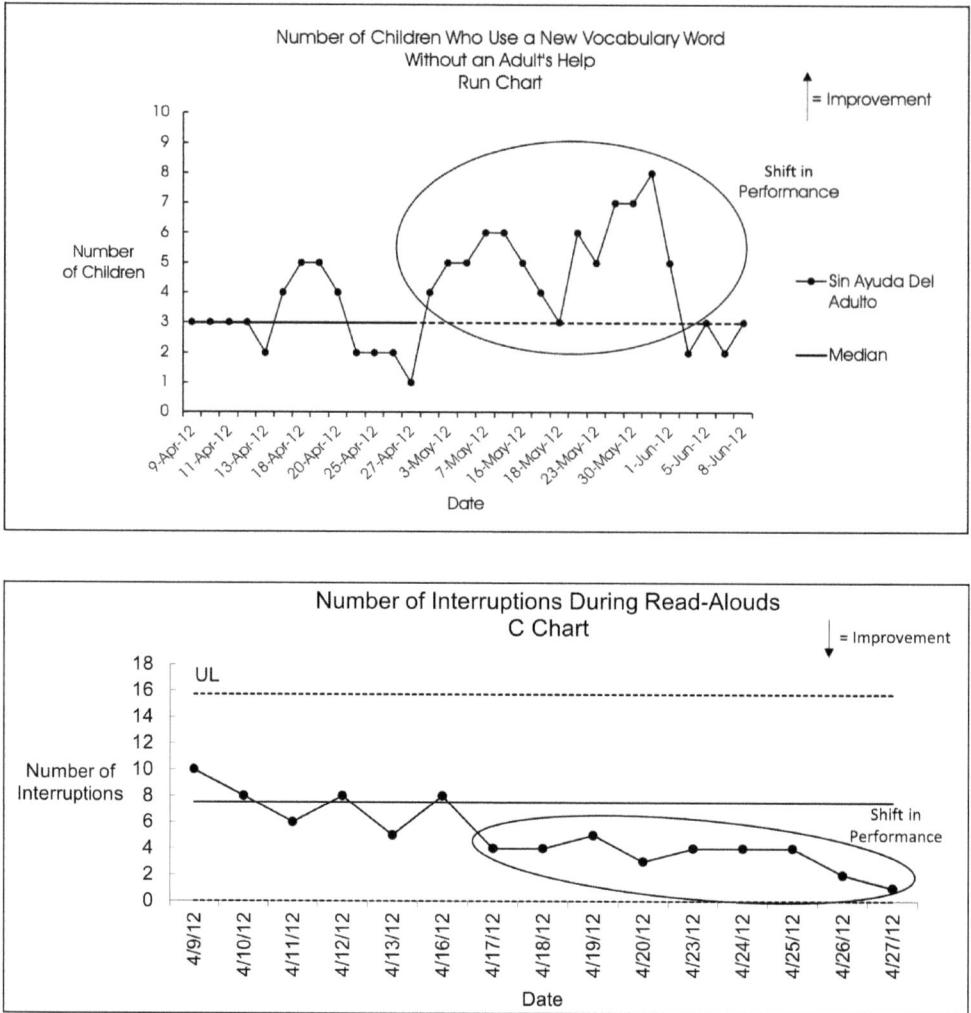

Figure 12.1. Example of PDSA Level Measures for Improvement—Un Buen Comienzo

paper conveniently located on the teacher's desk. When the teachers filled in their sheets, the coach helped turn the data into graphs to discuss at weekly team meetings. When the focus of their PDSA cycles changed, so did these measures.

FAMILY OF MEASURES

Teams enter the learn-in-practice phase, knowing that their initial theory probably is wrong and definitely is incomplete (see chapter 10). They engage in disciplined inquiry to evolve their theory of improvement and use a family of measures to highlight what's working and what's not. Having the right data at the right time provides teams the information they need to choose a path forward.

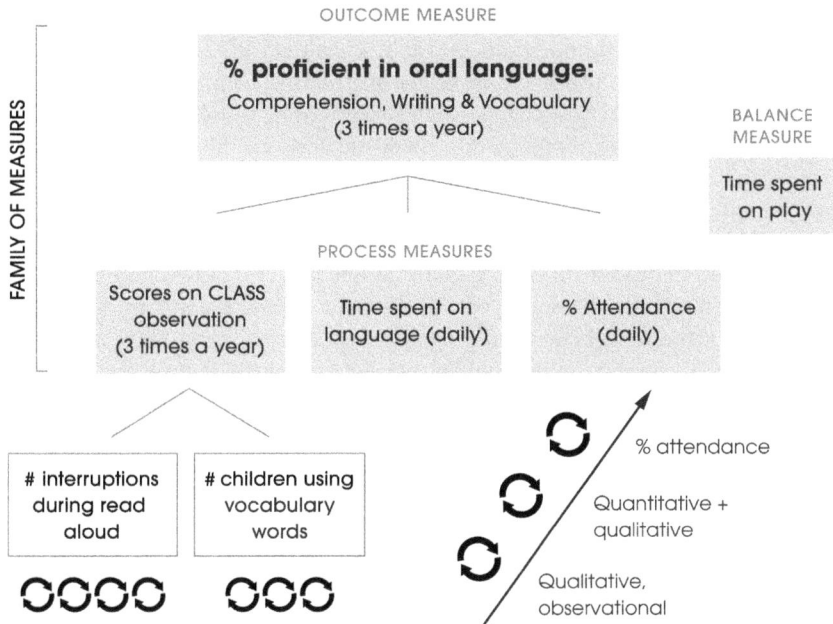

Figure 12.2. Measurement Tree for Un Buen Comienzo[3]

Figure 12.2 visualizes Un Buen Comienzo's family of measures using a measurement tree (Bennett 2018, 18–23; Bennett, Grunow, and Park 2022, 150–56). A measurement tree simply traces the logical connections among a team's measures. Teams will have to choose what to measure out of the large array of data that systems generate. The measurement tree can help identify potential measures and distinguish between measures that need to be collected consistently and ones that can be used for a shorter time.

A team's family of measures typically includes outcome, process, and balance measures. These are shaded in gray in figure 12.2 and are described in detail below. The measures and other data that are useful for PDSA cycles will be determined by the learning questions of each cycle. Identifying appropriate data and data collection mechanisms is part of planning a PDSA (see chapter 11).

Measure Types

Outcome measure(s): At the highest level of the "tree," the outcome measure(s) represent the primary motivation for the improvement work. Named in the aim statement (see chapter 7), this measure(s) defines success for the redesigned system. Any outcome measure should hold significance and relevance to the intended beneficiaries of the system. Outcome measure(s) are tracked for the duration of the improvement project.[4]

Process measures: One level below outcomes, process measures are selected, collected, and analyzed for two reasons: a) they represent the system's work deemed to have a direct impact on the outcome and b) they can be collected and analyzed more frequently, as often as the process occurs. Process measures provide teams with information about how the system is behaving long before results are observed in most outcome measures. Process measures are tracked for the duration of the improvement journey.[5]

PDSA measures and observational data: Nested below process measures are measures designed to answer the learning questions posed in individual PDSA cycles. PDSA measures draw on observational data, which can be either quantitative or qualitative. PDSA level data may include anecdotes about how changes are experienced by those affected by the process or system. Depending on the learning question, these measures can be tracked over time, or they may be one-time measures collected and analyzed as part of a single cycle.

Balance measures: The three cascading measures described above illuminate the measurement logic connected to the team's theory, but they are weak in one important area. Systems are complex; as a result, improvement work focused on one part of a system may have unintended consequences, good or bad, on another part of the same system. Balance measures track other areas of the system the team believes may be adversely affected by changes made to the primary area of focus. Common examples of balance measures include time spent on competing activities, the financial costs associated with redesigning a process or trade-offs evident in other process measures that assess the performance of processes tangential to those being improved. When identified, balance measures usually are tracked for the duration of the project.

SELECTING A FAMILY OF MEASURES

Team members should be actively involved in selecting the measures to guide their learning around their theory of improvement. Identifying a common family of measures facilitates the team to agree on the evidence used to determine whether changes made are an improvement.[6] Whenever possible, the data selected should be data that can be collected frequently enough to provide timely feedback to the team.[7]

Teams often will have access to outcome measures. In chapter 7 we suggest selecting outcome measures that the organization already collects due to the difficulty of developing new measures at this level. In some cases, improvement will target an aspect of the user's experience for which the organization does not collect any data. School teams, for example, may be interested in students' sense of belonging, something not usually collected in schools. Developing measures that provide useful information for areas such as "sense of belonging" requires time and technical expertise. Teams would be well advised to use already existing measurement instruments whenever possible, with an eye toward ensuring that they are practical for guiding improvement.[8]

Process measures are easier to come by in the sense that any regular routine or process generates data if the team wants to collect it. Selecting process measures requires identifying key processes and deciding which attribute of the process would provide useful, timely feedback for the team. Examples include how long the process takes, whether the process as a whole or one of the steps happens reliably, or whether the process produces a particular result. Ideally, teams are also collecting data on how the students, patients, and/or families are experiencing the process.

The measurement tree can help inspire a holistic set of measures, enabling the team to see the various processes that they intend to impact to get to their ultimate goal. However, the tree can also be overly comprehensive, identifying more possible measures than a team could realistically use in practice. There is a limit to the number of measures that a team can track and use well. Usually a set of 3–6 measures (i.e., a mixture of outcome, process, and balance measures) provides the team with a broad enough view to guide the learning without data collection and analysis being overly burdensome.

While working on the development of a family of measures for an improvement project focused on reducing mother-to-child transmission of HIV, one of the authors[9] created a measurement tree with more than thirty measures. Collecting, analyzing, and acting on that many measures was impractical given the team's resource constraints. Nonetheless, building the tree enabled the team to collaborate with subject matter experts in selecting six measures from the tree that provided enough insight into the system without imposing an excessive measurement burden on the team engaged in reducing HIV transmission (see figure 12.6 for an example of this family of measures).

Developing a family of measures requires careful selection by the team. Many teams find it helpful to first create a driver diagram (see chapter 10); they can then crosswalk their theory onto a measurement tree before selecting their final family of measures. Figure 12.3 demonstrates how the driver diagram's aim and drivers can assist a team in selecting measures for their measurement tree. Although there is not a one-to-one relationship between the driver diagram and the measurement tree, the theory informs and inspires which measures could provide deep insight into the improvement journey.

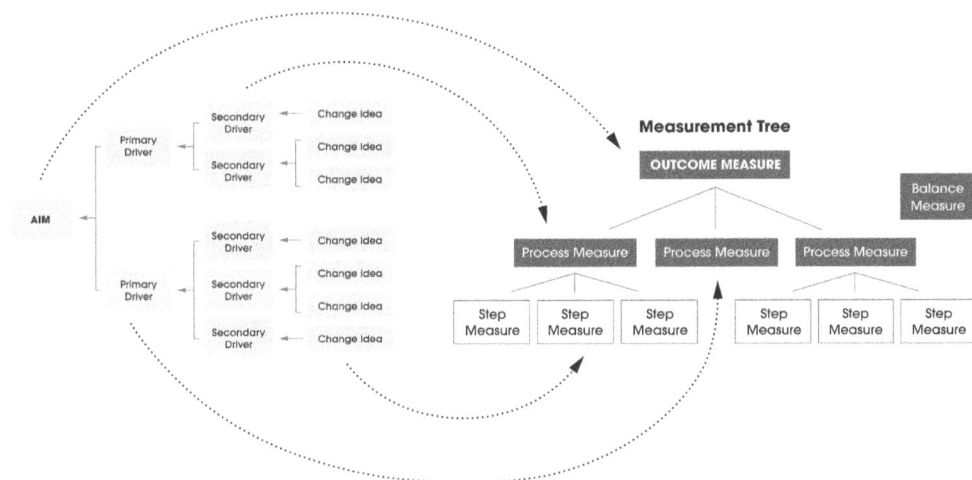

Figure 12.3. Relationship between Driver Diagrams and Measurement Trees

Selecting Data and Measures to Guide PDSA Cycles

The family of measures provides the team with a holistic view of the system they are trying to improve. They also need more specific and granular data to inform their learning cycles. This data will vary based on the learning objective of each cycle.

In the New Zealand early childhood education case, the team hypothesized that providing transportation would increase student attendance (see chapter 11). They decided to test the idea on a small scale by renting a van and picking up four students. The learning questions and data sources for their first PDSA are described in table 12.1.

Table 12.1.   Example Learning Questions and Measures for a Small-Scale PDSA Cycle

PDSA 1	
Change Idea: Pick up students in a van.	
Learning Objective: Assess the value to families of providing transportation to increase attendance.	
Learning Question	*Data Type*
How many students will take the ride?	Observational counts of the number of students who take the ride.
How will families respond to having transportation for their children?	Anecdotal: perceptual data gathered by the driver each day through conversations with families.
What are the other barriers to students' attendance?	Anecdotal: reports from conversations with families each week.

For small-scale PDSA cycles, the measures are typically different from the family of measures. As mentioned earlier, the family of measures provides a more holistic and distant view of the system. Not until changes reach the top of a PDSA ramp and are implemented will a team likely see movement in the family of measures. In figure 12.4, it is easy to see that the outcome measure (attendance), collected and analyzed weekly, didn't show any progress until the change idea (provision of free lunch) was applied to all students. Prior to implementation, the team relied on other specific measures to assess the value of the changes they were testing through their PDSA cycles. For the New Zealand team's PDSA on the van rental, the primary learning came from anecdotal data gained through conversation with the families. For the PDSA simulating the cost of providing free lunches, the team needed specific quantitative data on the estimated cost of lunch for all children offset by the increase in revenue associated with more children attending each day. In both PDSAs, the measures were specific to the cycle and, therefore, temporary. However, they were extremely valuable in generating the learning needed to keep the team moving forward toward their outcome.

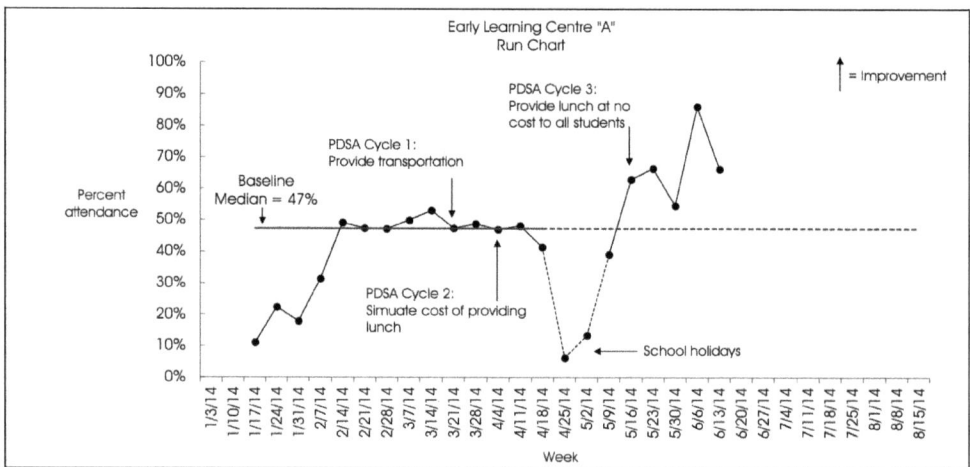

Figure 12.4.   Increased Attendance Once Changes Are Implemented

OPERATIONAL DEFINITIONS

Once teams have identified a family of measures, they will need to work through the details of how those measures will be defined, collected, stored, and analyzed. Underneath a seemingly simple measure such as "attendance" lie questions critical for generating useful information. What if students arrive late or leave early on a given day? Where is the data located? How is it accessed? Should we graph attendance rates or the number of students who are absent? Are daily, weekly, or monthly metrics more useful for the team to see? Answering these questions helps teams pull the right data and glean useful information from the measures they collect.

Teams come to shared operational definitions of each of their measures to create transparency and consistency in the collection and treatment of data. The operational definition includes details on how the measurement will be executed (i.e., which data will be collected, when and how) and establishes criteria for judgment (e.g., who is included and what counts as being "on time," "on track," or "attending") (Provost and Murray 2022, 47). Teams may find it beneficial to first sketch the graph they think will steer their data conversations (see section below) and then work backwards to articulate how they will get the required data to plot the points on the graph.

Example: Measuring Improvement; Reducing Central Line–Associated Bloodstream Infections

A group of teams commissioned by the Ministry of Health in New Zealand set out to work together to reduce central line–associated bloodstream infections (CLABSIs) in intensive care units (ICUs) across the country. According to research, these hospital-acquired infections occur commonly in ICUs around the world, but they could be virtually eliminated using prescribed changes in practice. Soon after initiating this countrywide effort, the coordinating team realized that most hospitals were not collecting data on the frequency of central-line infections, and those that were defined infections differently. This made it difficult to tell whether variation across sites was due to the way sites measured infections or to a more notable difference in their practices that might hold important clues for improvement. To learn collaboratively, all ICUs participating in the initiative needed to agree on a common definition for the diagnosis and counting of CLABSIs (see table 12.2).

Many details and judgments go into defining a measure. These details often remain hidden when we are not actively involved in defining the measures and are passive recipients of the data reports. Identifying and defining the family of measures is one place where teams may find it helpful to lean on the expertise of an improvement coach or data specialist, provided they are skilled specifically in the use of measurement for improvement. These specialists typically possess a deep understanding of the questions and answers needed to produce even a simple graph. At the same time, the team's subject matter expertise is also important. They will have critical knowledge (or know where to find it) that should influence how the numerator and denominator are defined to best inform their improvement work. They will also know how to disaggregate data in important ways to uncover potential sources of variation, such as those experienced by individuals coming from different subgroups (e.g., race category, socioeconomic status, geography). In the CLABSI case described, microbiologists were instrumental in crafting a definition all clinicians in New Zealand were willing to rally around (Health Quality & Safety Commission New Zealand and Ko Awatea 2014).

Table 12.2.   Example Operational Definition of Central Line–Associated Bloodstream Infections[10]

Measure of Central Line–Associated Bloodstream Infections
Description: The rate of central line–associated bloodstream infections for every thousand central-line days. Calculated by dividing the number of CLAB infections by the number of central-line days and multiplying the result by 1,000.
Type of Measure: Outcome
Definition of CLAB (*numerator*): Patients in the intensive care unit who had a central line at the time of infection or within forty-eight hours before developing the infection. <ul><li>**Exclusion criteria:** Cases where the infection is related to any other infection the patient has and must not have been present or incubating when the patient was admitted to the facility.</li><li>**Diagnosis:** CLAB—Attribution of CLAB is determined by someone external to the unit where the CLAB occurred (e.g., microbiologist, infectious diseases physician, infection prevention, or control nurse).</li></ul>
Definition of central venous line days (*denominator*): Daily count of the number of patients within the intensive care unit with one or more central lines of any type. <ul><li>**Inclusion criteria:** Central line is any intravascular access device or catheter that terminates at or close to the heart or in any one of the great vessels and that is used for infusion, withdrawal of blood, or hemodynamic monitoring.[11]</li><li>**Data collection:** The number of central venous line days—each ICU tallied this number and entered it monthly into a central database, which was then used to calculate the rate of infection for a site and for the country as a whole.</li></ul>

DATA COLLECTION

Once measures have been selected and defined, data collection begins. When possible, it is helpful if the selected measures draw on data already collected by the system (e.g., enrollment, attendance, minutes out of the classroom, frequency of disciplinary actions, infection rates, prescription errors, cost metrics). Anytime new measures are collected, the team should consider the context and feasibility of data collection. For example, as noted earlier, when a process is enacted, it automatically generates data; as a result, teams will need to collect the data in the course of enacting the process. User-friendly data collection forms kept in convenient locations will increase the likelihood that data will be collected. For example, the Un Buen Comienzo teachers used simple calendar printouts on their desks to jot down the number of minutes of language instruction each day. A photo of the calendar was sent to an improvement coach who added the data to a spreadsheet used to create the graphs for data conversations.

Another common strategy for easing the burden of data collection is sampling. A properly selected sample can provide a valid estimate of what is occurring in a population or system. Rather than counting each instance individually, the team can sample occurrences, analyze the resulting data, and make inferences about the performance of the system they are targeting for improvement. In chapter 8, readers were introduced to a team focused on improving individualized education program (IEP) goals for students with a disability. One measure identified in the charter as part of the team's family of measures was the average goal quality score. This team used sampling to reduce the measurement burden while maintaining a window into the performance of their IEP goal-writing process. Each month, case managers would look at the IEP goals of ten student plans, starting randomly and then pulling every fifth student record thereafter from the larger pool of students being served by the group of people working to improve the IEP process.[12] They would use a goal quality rubric to score the quality of these goals, calculate an average goal quality estimate for all goals written for students in that month, and plot that data point on a run chart (see section on run charts below). Using this sampling strategy, the team was able to learn about the pattern of IEP goal quality in their school district without having to spend the time to review every single student record every month.

Data collection does require resources, usually time. It is a routine improvement teams need to both design for and engage in. Who will collect which data, and when will they do so? What tools will they use? These are common questions every improvement team will need to answer as a part of their operational definitions.

DATA ANALYSIS

Data analysis is about making sense of the data collected. Data do not, on their own, carry meaning. Analysis and interpretation are required to give numbers context and significance. One advantage of quantitative data is that it can be turned into visual displays to reveal patterns and trends across time and place.[13] However, for the analysis to be effective, it must first answer a question that the team has posed related to the performance and variability of a specific measure tied to the improvement journey. To complete the analysis, the team must also choose a useful way to display the data, format the data to produce the graph, and present the graph in a way that facilitates interpretation. Data visualizations should always be created with the audience interpreting the data in mind.[14] When done well, these visualizations can spur powerful conversations, much more so than a spreadsheet of data. "A few carefully chosen graphs are often more instructive than great piles of numbers" (Moore 2007, xxiii).

Run Charts

Systems produce variation; no two days in an organization are exactly alike. As a result, it is important that teams visualize outcome or process data over time to distinguish expected variation from variation that signals impact of the changes made to the system.

The default graphical representation recommended for a family of measures is the run chart (Ott 1975, 39–44; Perla, Provost, and Murray 2011; Provost and Murray 2022, 77–122; Bennett, Grunow, and Park 2022, 183–97). A run chart is a line graph, usually displaying data over time. One of its distinguishing features is the inclusion of a median. The median is a prediction of how the system will perform in the future if the system's design goes unchanged. A second distinguishing feature of run charts (and all good data visualizations) is the use of annotations. Annotations are qualitative information added to the graph to help convey the story the data is trying to tell.

Figure 12.5 displays the run chart used to guide the New Zealand team working to improve attendance at early childhood education centers (Tyler, Davies, and Bennett 2018, 107). The graph shows the percentage of children who attended each week.[15] The team collected baseline

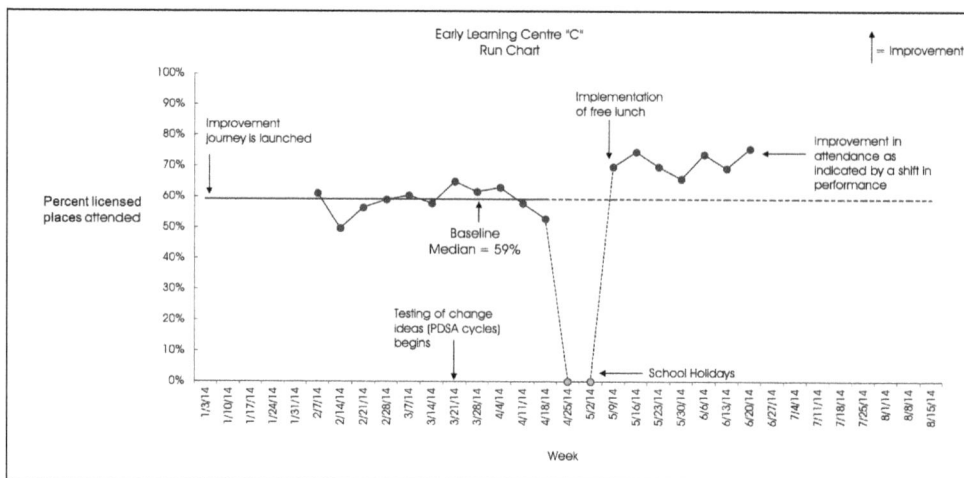

Figure 12.5.   Increasing Student Attendance at an Early Learning Center

data in the weeks leading up to the start of their PDSA cycles and used it to calculate their baseline median, 59 percent. Using this median as a prediction of future performance, they anticipated that if they did nothing, they could expect attendance to vary randomly around 59 percent. As the team worked to improve attendance, the run chart helped them both reflect on their progress and tell their improvement story. They annotated the graph with the change ideas they tried. They also labeled key events, such as school holidays, when attendance dropped to zero. Doing so, provided a clear explanation for the dramatic drop in performance; without it, the team may have reacted and intervened in the system in unproductive and unnecessary ways, wasting valuable time and resources. The annotations highlighted the impact of providing school lunch on attendance. After the change idea was implemented, attendance improved and stayed well above 59 percent for seven weeks in a row. This positive shift in performance increased the team's degree of belief that the change was indeed an improvement. For more on creating and interpreting run charts, see appendix B.

When using data for improvement it is important for teams to understand the variation that is present in their systems. Too often data is reported using aggregate averages, which hide variation contained within. It is also difficult to interpret variation when data is presented in tables or spreadsheets. This makes it difficult for people to use the data to answer important questions. For example, in the early childhood education work, should the team react when attendance increases or decreases by 5 percent week to week? Or are 5 percent fluctuations part of the variation that the system regularly experiences? Reacting to random variation leads to wasted time and energy changing a system that may not need improvement, but underreacting to nonrandom variation can cause teams to miss helpful clues about when a system's performance is changing in important ways. Using run charts that show all the data can help teams avoid such missteps, assisting them to discern what is random variation and what it is not and providing perspective on the ebbs and flows of a system over a longer period.

Most improvement teams find it helpful to display their family of measures all together, on a single page (Provost and Murray 2022, 46) (see figure 12.6). Figure 12.6 shows the family of measures for a hospital-based team in South Africa working to reduce mother-to-child

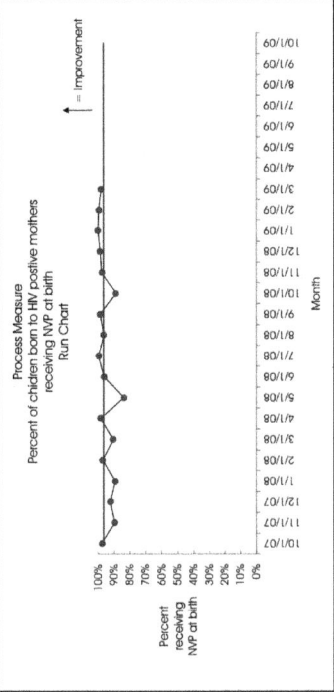

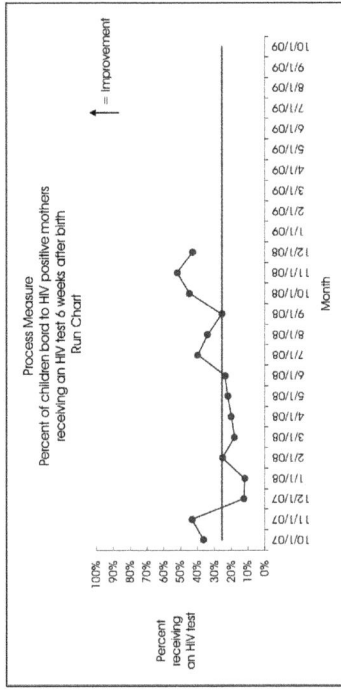

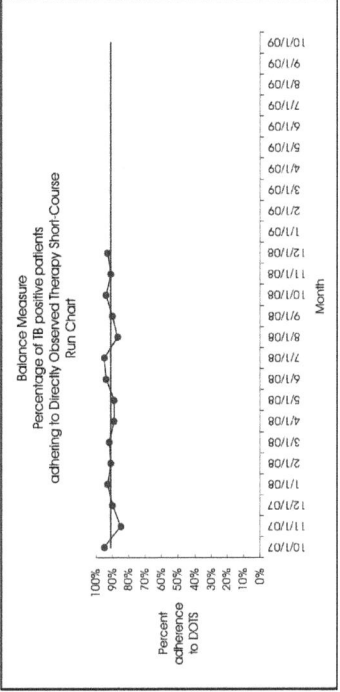

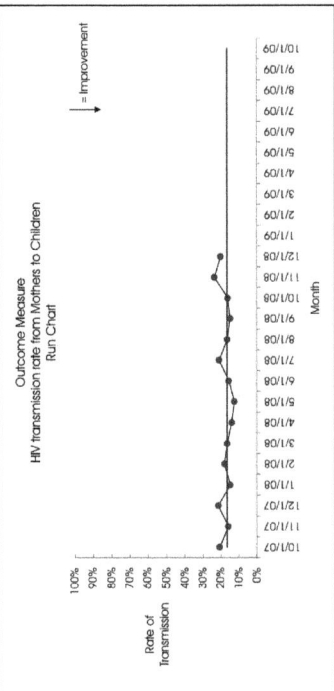

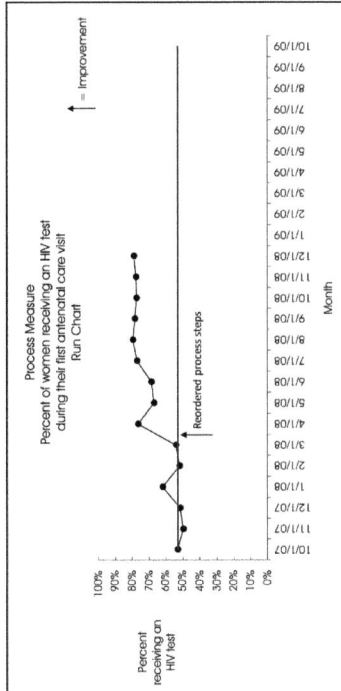

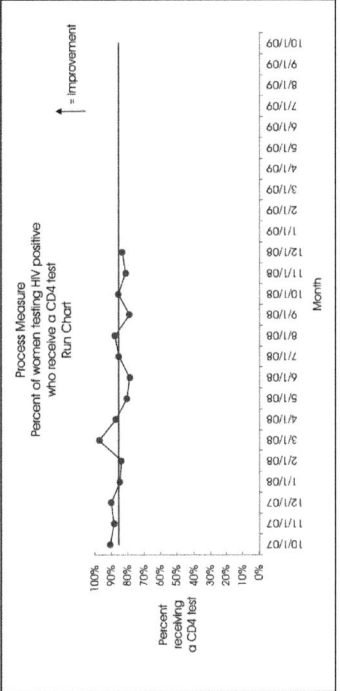

Figure 12.6.   Example Family of Measures Displayed Together

transmission of HIV. Putting the displays together helps teams see a holistic view of their system or project. They can see at a glance which processes are improving, if there are trade-offs in which improving one process results in another process moving in the wrong direction, and if movement in their process measures is leading to improvements in their outcomes of interest. Teams can produce these displays in preparation for their consolidation meetings, and use them to step back, make sense of the big picture, and decide what to do next.

DATA CONVERSATIONS

Although the team may have captured a few initial notes on their interpretation of the data during data analysis, more extensive conversations often are needed to make sense of any patterns, odd occurrences, and notable variations in the data. Individual team members—for example, the Un Buen Comienzo teachers—may use data displays while testing changes, while the entire team should collectively make sense of their overall family measures, usually as part of their consolidation routine (see chapter 13).

Setting aside moments for conversation is particularly important when one person, either on or external to the team, is primarily responsible for creating and updating the displays. Analyzing the data can illuminate patterns, but understanding them requires the knowledge of those closest to the processes being improved. As John Tukey, a pioneer in data analysis, noted, "leave most interpretations of results to those who are experts in the subject-matter field involved" (Tukey 1977, vi).

Productive data conversations require strong conversational capacity (see chapter 4). Team members need to be transparent about the assumptions behind the inferences they are making in interpreting the data. Table 12.3 describes a protocol that can be helpful in guiding teams through a data conversation (Bennett, Grunow, and Park 2022, 47).

It is important to begin these conversations by ensuring that everyone involved understands the data being displayed. Given the history of how data has been taught and used, it is not uncommon for people to feel anxiety around data and lack confidence in their ability to interpret what's presented. Care should be taken to make sure that everyone present feels comfortable participating in the conversation. For example, team members often will have clarifying questions when first seeing the data. They are usually related to the operational definition of certain measures; for instance, "Remind me again which patients or students are included here." Answering these questions or having a sheet with data definitions can help put people at ease about what they are looking at.

Table 12.3. **Data Conversation Protocol**

Set the Stage	• Review norms and objectives. • Orient to the data being shared.
Describe the Data	• What do you see and notice?
Interpret the Data	• What hypotheses or explanations do you have about what you see? • What alternative hypotheses may exist? • What additional questions do the data raise for you?
Next Steps	• Where do we focus our learning next? • What additional analyses are needed?

Next, it helps to describe the data using descriptive, low-inference statements before moving on to interpretations. Teams can do this as a go-around, giving everyone a chance to name what they see when they look at the data. With a shared understanding of the data, the team can move productively up the ladder of inference, generating as many potential explanations as possible for the patterns they see. It is not uncommon for biases or misinterpretations to arise here; team members should call these out or directly address them with each other. When the team agrees on an explanation, they can add it to the graph as an annotation.

Data conversations can serve as pivotal moments when the team's learning culture is put to the test. Feelings of disappointment or defensiveness can arise, particularly when the measures are not moving in the desired direction despite concerted effort by the team. This can be especially true when teams look at comparative data across classrooms, hospitals, or units. Although such data can produce conversations generative for learning, they can also become judgmental, exposing individual rather than systemic explanations for the observed patterns in the data. Deficit-oriented comments about patients, students, and families might also arise. Leaders can play a key role in these discussions, creating a psychologically safe space where team members can openly discuss what is not going well and explore explanations of variation with curiosity rather than judgment (Deming 2000, 23).

Ultimately, the goal of a data conversation is to help determine what to do next. Are there changes that seem to be working that imply turning attention to sustainability or spread? Is there evidence that what the team is focused on has the potential for moving the outcome of interest? Do we need new change ideas? Are there different ways to disaggregate or analyze the data that may provide insight? The data displays will not provide definitive answers to any of these questions, but they can serve as a launching pad to strengthen assessments and inform collective decisions about where to turn next.

PUTTING IT ALL TOGETHER

Example: All Families Thrive

At the opening of this chapter, we described how measurement for improvement differs in audience, purpose, and time cycle from measurement for accountability or measurement for research. In many organizations, the traditional use of measures has not been for frontline teams actively engaged in learning to improve. To make the shift to measurement for improvement, teams need to be actively involved in selecting, analyzing, and interpreting the measures that guide their work. An even better scenario occurs when the team works collaboratively with the intended beneficiaries of the system to carry out the data routines, ensuring that the data used for improvement is specific to their needs.

In 2022, a community-based partnership in Hamilton County, Ohio, set out to reduce the rates of child abuse and neglect within their population. The improvement initiative is a joint effort of the All Families Thrive partners—Cincinnati Children's Hospital and Medical Center (CCHMC) and Hamilton County Job & Family Services (HCJFS), with funding from a local foundation. The strategy was to work upstream on issues linked to community and family well-being to prevent downstream child abuse and neglect. The theory was that if policy and systems change could support families in moving from struggling and suffering to thriving, children would be less exposed to the risk factors that ultimately result in child abuse and neglect.

From the beginning, the improvement journey was community driven, with family and community partners, including parents, sitting at the center of the design table. Representatives from CCHMC, HCJFS, and the local community came together in quarterly learning and design sessions to discuss what kinds of changes families might need, deciding together where to focus. Many of the early conversations centered on access to resources, specifically those that address hunger and other basic needs (e.g., housing, safety, employment, quality child care).

A key moment in one of the early conversations came when a community member raised her hand and said something like, "You know what would be great? If you could fix what happens when we call Job & Family Services to access resources." Other parents in the room vehemently supported this idea; many became animated, and some acted out the experience of being on a call. This pantomime reflected the reality: calls were long, starting with legalese and layer on layer of prompts. Choose the wrong prompt or experience a dropped call, and you were forced to start over. Or you finally connected with someone at the exact moment you had to go back to work or manage the arrival of children; out of necessity, you had to hang up and try again later. When the call did get picked up, the person on the other end of the line was often grumpy, not very helpful, and may or may not have been able to address your problem. "If you could fix that," community members said, "that would be an excellent starting place."

Having heard their stories and felt their frustrations, the staff from HCJFS immediately embraced the challenge to make things better. They invited family partners to present to their assistant director for economic sustainability and her managers within the next week. These leaders, hearing these stories, were also compelled to action, realizing that these calls represented a crucial relational moment that marked the start of their engagement with families who were seeking their assistance. They launched an improvement team in one of their call centers to work with family partners to improve the experience of calling HCJFS.

As a starting outcome measure, they chose the call abandonment rate, understanding that this was a proxy for the experiences individuals were having. The call abandonment rate—the percentage of queued calls that were *not* answered by a call center representative, equaled a

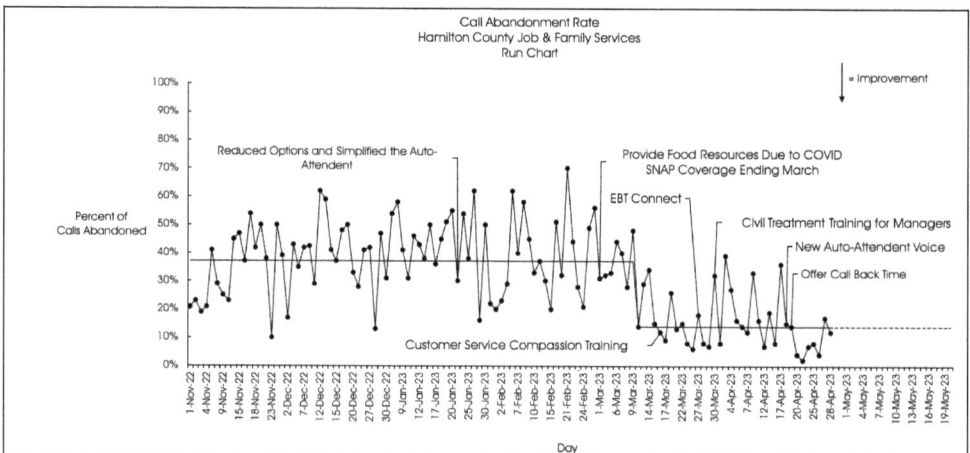

Figure 12.7.   Run Chart of Call Abandonment Rate at Hamilton County Job and Family Services

failure to help and likely frustration for those calling. They aimed to cut the abandonment rate from nearly 40 percent to 15 percent in six months. The team could think of a host of relational measures they wished they had, but they also wanted to start right away. They created an operational definition of dropped calls, worked with their data analyst to pull baseline data, and started figuring out how to improve families' experiences.

At one of the next quarterly meetings, the call center team came to talk about their improvement work. They shared their run chart (see figure 12.7) and their learning from the change ideas they had been testing. They also shared their struggles about what wasn't going well from their perspective. The call volume was high, and recently they had lost a staff member; that meant the remaining customer service representatives sometimes had to field more than sixty calls a day, a difficult if not impossible task, and incredibly demoralizing.

The conversations around this seemingly simple measure resulted in empathic understanding from both call center staff and community members. The call center staff could see the frustrated faces reflecting wasted time in each call that was dropped. The community members could hear the unending ringing of phones on the other side. One community member stood up and publicly apologized for the disparaging remarks she had made about staff from Job & Family Services, committing to repair any reputational damage she had done.

The team was able to improve the call abandonment rate in less time than they had allocated in their aim. Change ideas they tested and implemented included reducing the legal preamble to the bare minimum, making the language more commonplace, and limiting the number of prompts callers needed to navigate. They proactively identified additional resources to provide callers, knowing that upcoming policy changes would prompt higher call volumes and longer wait times. They also changed the automated voice to one that reflected the community and embodied a warm, welcoming tone. External to the team's efforts, an option was added statewide to receive a call back for individuals who could not wait the time needed to complete the call then, which further reduced the abandonment rate. In addition, the team invested in empathy training for all call center employees to hone their listening and communication skills. These changes successfully reduced the number of dropped calls from a median 38 to 13 percent, translating to 186 fewer abandoned calls per day. Excited by these results, Job & Family Services decided to share these change ideas with other call centers to see if they could replicate the results. If they could, they would then develop a change package reflecting their learning and successes (see chapter 14).

In an improvement effort, teams use measures to assess whether the effort is moving in the desired direction. As in Cincinnati, the measures will never fully capture the purpose (i.e., the rich, multilayered, intersectional experiences, interactions, and contributions) connected to the improvement work. But they can play a key supporting role when they are chosen carefully, shared transparently, and used to jointly reflect on whether the system is performing as intended.

When using data for improvement, a useful guiding principle is to, at a minimum, share the data with those who contributed it and incorporate their perspectives in the interpretation process. A hallmark of a strong team is the transparency with which they share data. Openly sharing data requires courage and safe spaces where people trust the data will be used for learning. As is true across the improvement journey, actively engaging users on the team is a surefire way to supercharge improvement efforts. Engaging in collaborative work not only accelerates the team's progress, but it can also transform relationships, a pivotal component of systems change.

CONCLUSION

Measurement for improvement provides teams with the information they need to understand where changes are needed in their system, focus their work, and illuminate when their theory of improvement has produced the desired outcomes. A family of quantitative measures connected to outcome(s) and processes in addition to qualitative data that captures the experiential impact of the work can provide deep, holistic insight for the team during their improvement journey. Data collection, analysis, and conversation should follow a regular rhythm connected to the pace the team anticipates change occurring. For many teams, this will mean analyzing and discussing their family of measures monthly at minimum. For others, these routines may happen even more regularly if their process data is available more frequently. In the case of PDSAs, data selection, collection, analysis, and discussion should occur at the start and end of every learning cycle.

As we've mentioned throughout the book, the pace of learning rests largely on a team's ability to establish robust and reliable testing, data, and team meeting routines. In the next chapter, we provide guidance on how to put them all together to propel the team forward in their journey.

13

Improvement Routines

You need to have momentum before you can start to steer.

—Ahlström 2014, 76

Improvement requires creativity. Our systems are complex, and unfortunately, silver bullet solutions are rare for the problems we face, to say nothing of innovating for the futures we imagine. When thinking about creativity, we often associate it with spontaneity, free spiritedness, and the flexibility of an unconstrained environment. But when we look closely at "creatives" (e.g., artists, writers, inventors, designers), what we see is discipline. Picasso produced about 147,800 works during his lifetime, averaging just over four per day, while Stephen King spends an average of four hours per day writing after his morning walk (pablopicasso.org n.d.; Greene and Parada 2014). As comedian Jon Stewart revealed in an interview during his tenure at *The Daily Show*,

> You'd be incredibly surprised at how regimented our day is and just how the infrastructure of the show is very much mechanized. People always think, "*The Daily Show*, you guys probably just sit around and make jokes," and we've instituted—to be able to sort of ween through all of this material and synthesize it and try to come up with things to do—we have a very strict day that we have to adhere to. And by doing that, that allows us to process everything and gives us the freedom to sort of improvise. I'm a real believer in that creativity comes from limits, not freedom. Freedom, I think, you don't know what to do with yourself. But when you have a structure then you can improvise off it and feel confident enough to kind of come back to that. (Stewart 2015)

Although seemingly counterintuitive, predictable routines and processes like these, help reduce cognitive load, reducing the mental energy spent tracking what needs to happen next, allowing individuals to focus on what's most important.

Successful improvement projects require the same sort of discipline and structure. Reliable routines help anchor a team and keep it focused on the learning journey. As we've emphasized throughout the book, the improvement journey is rarely linear. As a result, the team must stay open and flexible to the different turns the journey takes without losing sight of its purpose. The routines presented here provide a structure teams can improvise within. They also support teams in developing a common language, a shared sense of purpose, and joint accountability, all characteristics of high-performing teams (see chapter 2).

Integrating routines and rhythms for collective learning is one of the trickiest parts of doing improvement. Typical organizational norms for making change involve long periods of planning followed by full-scale implementation (remember Skillman's marshmallow exercise from chapter 9). The learning-by-doing approach described in chapters 11 and 12 requires a different rhythm, one that privileges more frequent feedback loops and opportunities to share learning in real time. Monthly or quarterly meetings are much too slow. Teams are more likely to make headway on their aim if they are able to embed consistent, reliable learning rhythms into their daily work from the get-go.

IMPROVEMENT ROUTINES

The rhythm that drives team learning is relatively straightforward—try something in practice, reflect together on what was learned, decide what you want to learn next . . . repeat. The improvement routines in table 13.1 help provide additional discipline and focus, bringing the improvement methods together in a way that informs the collective learning of the team (Bennett, Grunow, and Park 2022, 44).

The learning cycle and data routines relate to how teams apply the tools and methods of improvement. In chapters 11 and 12, we described the ways teams use learning cycles and data

Table 13.1. Improvement Routines

	Routine	Purpose	Timing and Frequency
	Huddles and Team Meetings	Huddles: Maintain learning momentum—share learning from PDSAs, articulate next steps, troubleshoot issues that arise during testing, and so forth.	Huddles: Weekly
		Team meetings: Reflect on progress—review data, consolidate learning from action period.	Team meetings: Usually 3–4 weeks
	Sponsor Check-Ins	Provide updates to senior leaders on progress of the work. Enlist support to remove roadblocks.	Every 6–8 weeks
	Learning Cycles	See the system. Test changes in practice.	Daily, weekly
	Data Routines	See the system. Get valuable feedback to help guide change efforts.	Daily, weekly, monthly
	Consolidation of Learning	Build a collective understanding of what is learned. Create knowledge artifacts for others. Update theory.	Usually every 4–8 weeks

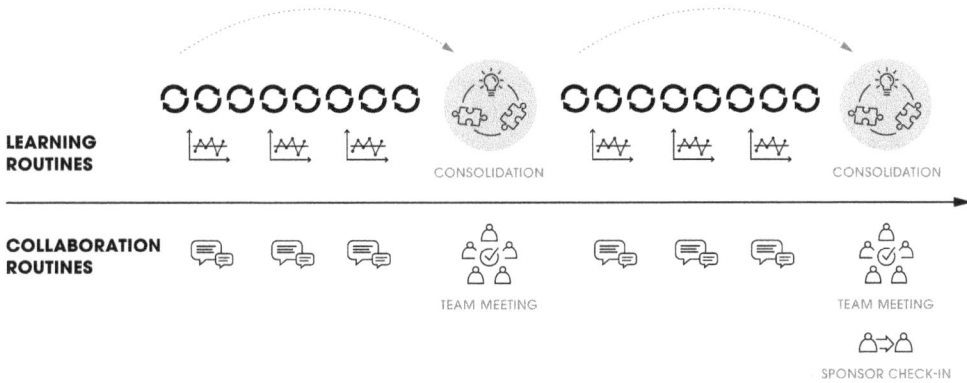

Figure 13.1. Creating a Rhythm Using Improvement Routines

to learn from trying changes in practice. In this chapter, we focus on how to build a rhythm around each. Clunky learning cycles that hobble along like a flat tire and measurement systems that do not provide timely feedback stymie team learning.

Equally important are the team's collaboration routines that support collective meaning-making. Short huddles help teams move quickly. Longer meetings provide space for teams to consolidate what they have learned, generate new ideas, and decide what direction to head next. The team lead should also check in regularly with the leadership sponsor to make sure the work stays an organizational priority and to help leadership anticipate longer-term implications of key learnings.

Although each routine itself is important, it is the synergy created when the routines are woven together that really drives the momentum and learning of an improvement team. Figure 13.1 provides a picture of how the routines fit together to support team learning. Because each routine plays a unique and helpful role in driving the success of improvement teams, it is critical that they be established as quickly as possible, becoming a team's standard practice.

Example: A Hospital Team's Improvement Routines

When a hospital clinic in South Africa decided to join a network focused on reducing mother-to-child HIV transmission, one of their first tasks was to clarify team membership and set up regular team meetings. As a member of the network, they would gain access to centralized data support and an improvement coach, but more importantly, they would need to prioritize the redesign of care for expectant mothers at the hospital. The chief medical officer was named the sponsor and played an active role in commissioning the project, helping to identify the team members, allocate time in their work portfolios, and ensure that the team and the improvement coach had access to the district health information system (DHIS) that housed the data the team needed. A physician from the HIV clinic served as team lead and was joined by the head nurse, two other nurses, and a pharmacist. The team already saw each other daily, but they would still need protected time and space to work together on this new line of work. They decided to hold hour-long weekly team meetings; their improvement coach would meet with them onsite. They also integrated a short standing huddle into their schedules between team meetings to review and plan learning cycles as needed. The physician updated the chief medical officer about their progress as an agenda item during their preexisting check-in meetings.

The improvement coach updated the team's measures monthly, extracting data from the DHIS and creating data displays for each measure in the team's family of measures. The coach brought the data visualizations, like those seen in figure 12.6, to the team meeting for a data conversation. In the early stages of the project, these conversations revealed data quality issues. Even though the coach was pulling the officially reported data, it was clear to the team that there were inconsistencies and errors in what was being collected and how data was being entered. The team would dedicate time in their team meetings to problem solve these issues until they built more reliable routines that produced data that accurately reflected what was occurring in their clinic.

The team also debriefed their latest plan-do-study-act (PDSA) cycles during team meetings. The team documented their PDSAs on paper and pinned them on a centrally located board in the clinic. They shared their learning from each cycle and discussed what else they needed to test. As they shared, the coach wrote down a short summary that was later added to an electronic PDSA tracker they used to see the progression of their team's learning over time. On a quarterly basis the team traveled to a network learning session to meet with other hospital teams across the region working toward the same aim. Before each session, the team consolidated their learning from the past quarter to share with other teams in the network. At the session, they generated new ideas that would inform their learning cycles going forward.

Having predictable routines made it possible for the team to embed the core activities of improvement into their daily work. Like developing a new habit, the routines required some attention at first, but once established, they served as a flywheel, propelling the team forward toward their aim.

In this chapter we will dive more deeply into each of the five improvement routines, focusing primarily on how they apply to the learn-in-practice phase. It is worth noting that the same learning rhythm can be applied whether the team is engaged in learning in practice or investigating the system. The difference is simply in the questions driving the learning cycles between the huddles and team meetings (for a diagram specific to the routines as they apply to understanding the current system, see figure 5.4). Either way, establishing reliable rhythms enables the team to learn and adapt quickly, moving from initial understandings to evidence-based improvements.

COLLABORATION ROUTINES

The collaboration routines—huddles, team meetings, and sponsor check-ins—are the backbone of the improvement work. They establish a cadence for learning and create spaces for the team to make sense of what they're learning together. Learning often will not feel as urgent as other professional tasks and demands that are a part of the daily work in organizations. Establishing a regular meeting routine incentivizes improvement activity; team members are more likely to complete a learning cycle if they know they need to share what they learned with the team. As described in chapter 4, once a team launches, they should immediately institute regular and frequent check-ins. This should be protected time, embedded into daily work, replacing, not merely adding on to, other responsibilities team members have in the organization. If a team can't reliably meet at least every week, if not every other week, it is likely that their learning will stall.

Teams can use a combination of shorter huddles and longer team meetings to establish a productive rhythm. Huddles are simply shorter team meetings, sometimes done while standing and often focused on a single objective (Provost et al. 2015). Teams often use them to provide quick updates on their learning from PDSA cycles or other improvement activities between longer team meetings. Meeting more frequently for shorter bursts of time moves the work forward faster than overplanning and holding longer meetings spaced further apart. A faster cadence helps teams hold each other accountable and supports teams to adaptively pivot, responding to what they are learning in practice. Teams will determine the combination of huddles and meetings that works best in their workflow. Weekly huddles with longer team meetings every 3–4 weeks are a good place to start.

Huddles and team meetings should model the ethos of improvement, providing a safe space for everyone to learn together. Because they focus on what the team is learning, they should feel qualitatively different from other operational meetings. Developing meeting rituals that start with opportunities to check in with each other personally, celebrate wins, and review conversational norms, helps team members transition into a learning mode (see chapter 4 for more details). The conversations should center on concrete artifacts from the improvement work—data displays of the team's family of measures, learning cycle results, process maps, headlines from empathy interviews, and so forth. Grounding the conversation around a common artifact allows team members to surface their varied perspectives and ideally arrive at shared understandings. Meeting agendas and shared protocols help keep meetings focused and efficient.

Knowledge Management

The team's common artifacts are organized in their storyboard. As described in chapter 8, the storyboard holds the team's aim, updated family of measures, and latest version of their theory. As the team's improvement journey unfolds, they add key learnings to the storyboard, documenting the twists and turns along the way. Teams also need spreadsheets to store their data and document learning from their PDSAs. The team will generate many other artifacts and resources over the course of doing the work. Ensuring that the team's artifacts are organized and stored so they are accessible when needed is not a trivial task. Teams usually create a shared online space and file structure to house important documents. Establishing clear processes and norms for how documents are named, where they are stored, and how they are updated is important. Although this may seem somewhat obvious or mundane, investing time upfront will save the team time down the line. Having an effective knowledge management system will help keep meetings focused on the current learning, reducing the amount of wasted time spent finding documents or trying to remember what was learned and decided during earlier phases of the work.

Sponsor Check-ins

In addition to meeting together, teams need to routinely touch base with their sponsor. Ideally, the team lead will update the sponsor on the team's progress every 6–8 weeks; this helps keep the work on the sponsor's radar, maintaining its status as an organizational priority. Further, the team likely will experience roadblocks during the improvement journey that will require senior leadership support (see chapter 3 for more on the role of sponsors). Flagging them sooner rather than later will help keep the team on track. Finally, as the team thinks ahead to the spread and scale part of the journey (see chapter 15), the sponsor will need to secure additional resources and engage others beyond the original improvement team. Keeping senior leadership up to speed on the team's journey will make it easier for them to smooth the path as the work evolves and spreads. Given the limited amount of time most team leads have with their senior leaders, an updated storyboard (see chapter 8) is an effective tool for sharing the key highlights and learnings from the journey thus far.

Improvement coaches, leadership sponsors, and team leads share the responsibility for creating productive collaboration routines. Table 13.2 describes common challenges in establishing routines along with strategies for addressing each.

Table 13.2. Common Challenges in Establishing Collaboration Routines

Challenges	Potential Causes	Ways to Address
Infrequent Team Meetings	Time has not been allocated	Teaming across departments and geographic locations can make finding a common time difficult. A lack of protected time is a leadership issue. Along with approval of the charter should come an agreement from the sponsor to adjust work portfolios and release team members from other responsibilities to make time for the work. Improvement work should not be launched if leadership is not willing to protect the necessary time.
	Misconceptions about the cadence of improvement	The iterative rhythm of improvement can come as a surprise to new improvement teams. After launch, teams may realize that regular meeting times are difficult to find, so they may need to consider dividing up responsibilities or integrating huddles to build the necessary learning rhythm. Long term, the sponsor may need to revisit the team membership, organizational barriers, and allocated resources to better match the cadence of improvement.
Lackluster Team Meetings	No agenda for the meeting	All meetings should have an agenda with a clear purpose.[1] The team lead usually is responsible for creating the agenda. Protocols and standard meeting formats can facilitate the process of creating an agenda.
	Taking up time on operational planning instead of learning	Whenever possible, project planning, scheduling, and other logistics should happen outside of team meetings or be limited to a small portion of the meeting agenda. This will help maximize the time for team learning by containing the logistical conversations.
	Unclear norms and expectations	Teams benefit from developing norms around participation, decision making, documentation, and communication. These norms often are established at the launch but should be revisited periodically.
	No new learning to discuss	The key learning activities (e.g., PDSAs, data collection and analysis, empathy interviews) happen between team meetings. When these activities don't happen, the team has little to discuss. See below for more details about building reliable learning cycles and data routines.
Shared Documents Are Difficult to Find	No centralized location to store documents	Create an online shared space that everyone can access. Some teams also find it helpful to have physical boards in a centralized location to make core learning artifacts (i.e., driver diagram) highly visible and easy to refer to.
	Disorganized files	Develop naming conventions and a file structure for online work. Create and agree to routines for updating and archiving key documents.
	Unclear or inconsistent documentation routines	Establish norms and routines as a team for a) updating the storyboard, b) updating graphical displays, and c) updating the storyboard. Descriptions for each are provided below.

LEARNING CYCLES

A good learning cycle routine enables the team to move forward quickly and thoughtfully. During the "understanding the system" phase, the team engages in learning cycles crafted to elicit insights about the current system's design. In the learn-in-practice phase, learning cycles focus on testing changes in practice, sometimes on a small scale and other times more broadly.[2] In both cases, well-defined, time-limited cycles that build on each other help the team learn quickly as they navigate the improvement journey.

Although the order of the letters *P D S A* implies a specific order to the steps, they play out differently as a routine. A team Plans an initial PDSA cycle together. The Do then happens outside of the team meeting. When the team comes back together, they usually start by sharing their reflections on the Study part of the cycle and then decide how they are going to Act. Based on this, they Plan the next learning cycle. Thus, although the name implies the logic of a cycle, *P D S A*, in practice the PDSA cadence follows an *S A P D* ordering, except for the very first cycle that gets things rolling.

The structure and time frame of PDSA cycles will vary based on what the team wants to learn and where they are on a PDSA ramp. Early PDSA cycles are often (but not always) short and can be executed quickly by a single person. Later, as the team tests the change in more contexts or at the implement stage, the cycles likely will be longer and more complicated, requiring the coordination of multiple people.

The roles and responsibilities for executing a PDSA also will vary. In some situations, team members may plan and run PDSA cycles independent of each other and share their learning during a huddle or team meeting. In others, team members may plan and execute PDSA cycles together. Finally, team members may plan a PDSA cycle that another individual runs. Whatever the case may be, clearly identifying who is responsible for running each step of the routine and by when is important.

Finally, teams need to decide collectively how and where to document their learning cycles. Teams can adopt or adapt a variety of PDSA forms: some are longer and provide more scaffolds; others are shorter but require more prior knowledge. PDSA forms can be completed online or on paper. In making decisions about documentation, the team will need to balance the ease of sharing learning and personal preferences. For some people, filling out online forms stifles the spirit of inquiry, making it feel like an exercise done for someone else. That said, it makes it easier for the team to collectively see what's being learned. When PSDAs are completed on paper, the inquiry can feel more authentic but raises challenges in sharing the learning with the rest of the team.

Whatever teams decide, they will also need a way to track the PDSA learning over time, especially as the team accumulates more PDSA cycles. As seen in the example of the South African team focused on reducing mother-to-child HIV transmission, the team used an online PDSA tracker to capture a short summary of what was learned from each cycle, which allowed the team to see how their learning evolved over time. The team then updated their storyboard to reflect their new learnings as part of their consolidation routine, which is described in more detail later in the chapter.

When teams develop a productive learning cycle routine, it serves as a flywheel, propelling the team forward. Helping teams learn to use PDSAs skillfully and strategically is one place that teams and team members benefit from having an improvement coach. Table 13.3 describes typical challenges that arise in creating learning cycle routines along with ideas to address the challenges when they occur.

Table 13.3. Common Challenges in the Learning-Cycle Routine

Challenges	Potential Causes	Ways to Address
Tests of change are planned but not completed	When and where the test will be run is not specified clearly	• Take time to work through the logistics of the test while completing the PLAN section. Many PDSA forms include a prompt to encourage logistical planning. • Ensure that the duration of the test is appropriate and clearly specified.
	Unexpected events get in the way	• From time to time, unexpected interruptions such as fire drills, staff shortages, and schedule changes prevent a change from being tested. Often, these are unavoidable. If they occur regularly, it may be worth reraising the question about whether the aim and allocation of resources for improvement is appropriate.
	Forget to collect the necessary data	• Create a data collection form while completing the PLAN section. Paper forms where notes can be jotted down easily are often useful. • Have an improvement coach or teammate help with data collection.
Undocumented Tests of Change	Form is confusing, cumbersome, or inconvenient	• Revisit the PDSA form to see whether adaptations are needed. • Allow team members to complete the PDSA on paper and then upload it to a centralized location.
	Skepticism about the value of documentation	• Have an improvement coach take on documentation at first and gradually transfer the responsibility. • Allow for choice in documentation styles. • Create authentic opportunities to share completed PDSA cycles with others.
PDSAs are not generating learning	Weak or unspecified change ideas	• If a change idea is vague or conceptual, it is not ready to test. Create a prototype of the change before planning the PDSA (see chapter 9). • A team's change ideas sometimes need to be refreshed. When a team finds they are testing reactive, incremental changes instead of fundamental ones, they should return to the methods in chapter 9.

Challenges	Potential Causes	Ways to Address
PDSAs are not generating learning (*continued*)	Overuse of PDSAs	• Distinguish between *tasks* that need to be completed and *tests* that generate learning about a specific change. Scheduling a team meeting or creating a quick survey are usually *tasks* and do not require a PDSA. • Teams often continue running PDSA cycles on a change idea when it is time to implement or abandon.
	Poorly structured PDSA	• Ensure that the size and time frame for the test is appropriate. • Create learning questions that are clear, specific, and relate to the learning objectives of the cycle. • Identify clear predictions and practical data to assess the change ideas. • Close all learning loops, comparing results to predictions and studying unexpected observations before drawing conclusions about what was learned in the cycle.
	Going through the motions	• In the beginning, teams sometimes take a project management approach to their improvement work, treating the steps in a PDSA as tasks that need to be checked off. Keeping conversations about PDSA cycles focused on *learning*, noting the value of failed predictions, can help build an improvement culture within the team. • Compliance orientations often stem from team members' past experience with mandated reforms. The leadership sponsor should work with the team to create a different orientation. • If the team is not curious about what they will learn from the learning cycle, usually something is wrong. Return to the *change ideas, overuse of PDSAs*, and *requirements for documentation*.

DATA ROUTINES

Along with PDSA cycles, teams regularly collect and use data to guide improvement. In chapter 12, we described the family of outcome, process, and balancing measures that teams collect over the course of the project. Teams need regular routines for gathering, entering, and analyzing data so they are available in a timely fashion for team discussions.

Figure 13.2 shows the basic steps of a data routine with guiding questions; each step may need to be broken into more detailed steps, depending on the complexity of the data collection process. It often is useful for teams to work backwards, imagining the data displays they will need and the moments when they will need them. Then they can plan the logistics of gathering and analyzing the data so that they are available at the right time for interpretation.

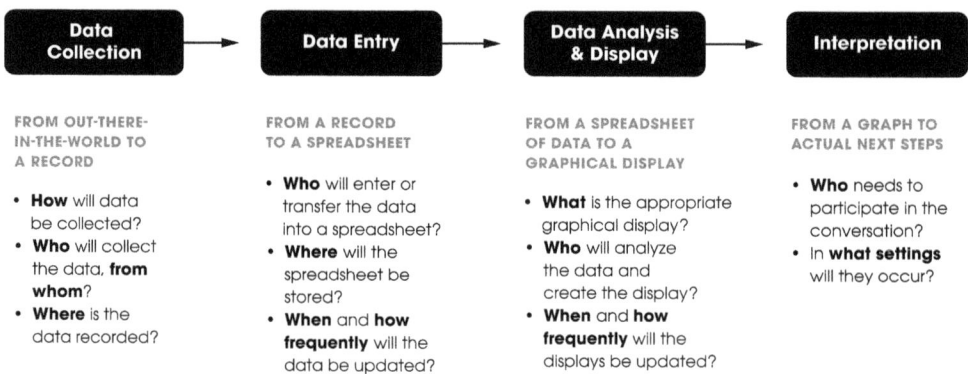

Data Collection	**Data Entry**	**Data Analysis & Display**	**Interpretation**
FROM OUT-THERE-IN-THE-WORLD TO A RECORD	FROM A RECORD TO A SPREADSHEET	FROM A SPREADSHEET OF DATA TO A GRAPHICAL DISPLAY	FROM A GRAPH TO ACTUAL NEXT STEPS
• **How** will data be collected? • **Who** will collect the data, **from whom**? • **Where** is the data recorded?	• **Who** will enter or transfer the data into a spreadsheet? • **Where** will the spreadsheet be stored? • **When** and **how frequently** will the data be updated?	• **What** is the appropriate graphical display? • **Who** will analyze the data and create the display? • **When** and **how frequently** will the displays be updated?	• **Who** needs to participate in the conversation? • In **what settings** will they occur?

Figure 13.2.   Data Routine

Data Collection and Entry

The first task in a data routine is to gather data from wherever it exists and transfer it to a spreadsheet where it can be stored, organized, and analyzed. For measures that draw on existing data, gathering entails pulling the data from the appropriate databases and storing it in an accessible location. The data needed may be in a centralized location, such as an organizational database, or it may require retrieving data from distributed sources such as gradebooks, patient records, or organizational files.

At other times, a team's measures will necessitate collecting new data not currently recorded. Although teams are encouraged to use existing data when possible, sometimes they find themselves without the process or user-experience data they need. In these cases, gathering data requires developing new data collection routines. Teams should design their data collection routines when developing the operational definition of a measure (see chapter 12). That includes deciding who will collect the data at what frequency as well how the data will be collected, including any data collection tools. The challenge is to ensure that data is collected accurately, as intended, especially if there are multiple data collectors.

For both existing measures and new data collection, the data needs to get from where it is recorded to a centralized database where it can be analyzed. When data is collected on paper, data entry is a step often overlooked in the process. It is important for teams to designate who will enter the raw data that has been collected, how frequently it will be entered, and where it will be stored centrally. Even when data is collected in online forms or pulled from existing databases, it can take time to compile it in a format that can support the intended analyses.

Data Analysis

Data analysis entails taking the raw data and formatting it to analyze and create displays that the team can use to assess their progress. The type of analysis and visual display depends on the availability of data and what the team is trying to learn. As recommended in chapter 12, run charts are the most common display used in this phase of the improvement journey, enabling the team to look at change over time. More experienced teams often use Shewhart charts and other complementary forms of data visualization (see appendixes A and B; Provost and Murray 2022; Bennett, Grunow, and Park 2022). Importantly, teams want to look at their family of measures together in a single view to learn how they interrelate (see figure 12.6).

Turning data into measures, and measures into effective visualizations, requires specialized skills and dedicated time. In some cases, improvement coaches or data analysts support teams by creating their data displays for them. When a data analyst external to the team takes the lead on analysis, it is important that the analyst is well versed in the use of measurement for improvement. In addition, the team needs to set clear expectations about what displays are needed and on what time frame to keep up the momentum of learning. Team members still need to develop their internal capability to consume, decipher, and interpret the displays. They should feel ownership of the data, playing an active role in deciding what displays are used and drawing on the analyses to help tell their improvement story.

Interpretation

With analyses in hand, the improvement team is ready to engage in making sense of it, applying their subject matter knowledge to the data. The team should update the data displays in its storyboard regularly, making them readily accessible to everyone on the team. The team should also set aside time to make meaning of the graphs together and decide what to do next (see figure 12.3 for a data conversation protocol). As the team comes to shared interpretations, they add annotations to the graphs, noting, for example, when change ideas were implemented. In some instances, questions will arise that will require follow-up analyses. As we will describe more later in the chapter, one key conversation that requires data is when the team consolidates their learning. Here, the team connects insights from their data and learning cycles to reflect on their theory and decide whether it needs to change.

An important principle in measurement for improvement is to involve those closest to the data in the interpretation. When teams notice unusual variation across units or sites, they should invite people working in those sites to share their interpretations. In addition, the team should always share back data with the people who contributed it. Thus, it is often necessary for some of the work of interpretation to occur outside team meetings.

Table 13.4 describes the data routine for two different measures—one from health care and one from education. Oftentimes teams collect multiple measures, each requiring its own routine. The measures may be available on different time frames and come from different sources. For each measure, it is important to articulate who is responsible for each step and when it needs to happen to ensure greater reliability of the process.

Taken together, data routines are logistically complicated to organize well. This is the primary reason why it is important for teams to identify a parsimonious set of measures and gather just enough data to inform their learning. Overly complicated measurement systems take up all the time available for improvement work. As the quote at the beginning of the last chapter reminds us, "the purpose of measurement for improvement is to speed learning, not slow it down" (Provost and Murray 2022, 53).

Table 13.4. Examples of Data Routines in Practice

Measure	Data Collection	Data Entry	Data Analysis and Display	Interpretation
Central Line–Associated Bloodstream Infections (existing data)	Collected daily. Nurses note when central lines are inserted and the date of an infection when it occurs. Data is entered into a patient's electronic medical record (EMR) during the course of care.	On a monthly basis, the EMR is queried for the numerator (total number of central-line infections) and the denominator (total number of central-line days) of the measure. This data point is entered into the team's spreadsheet.	The central-line infection rate is calculated and displayed on the team's Shewhart chart or run chart.	Team reviews the data monthly to assess the efficacy of the changes they are testing and decide where to focus next.[3]
Student Sense of Self-Efficacy (new data collection)	Collected every six weeks, students complete a one-minute paper survey at end of designated class period. Teacher gives surveys to team lead.	Team lead receives data from all five teachers, then enters it into spreadsheet.	Team lead determines average survey responses for each class. Team lead creates run chart with aggregate (across all classrooms) and small multiples displays (each classroom) for the consolidation meeting.	Team members (five teachers and two student representatives review and discuss data at the consolidation meeting.

Source: Adapted from Bennett, Grunow, and Park 2022, 46.

Table 13.5. Common Challenges in the Data Routine

Challenges	Potential Causes	Ways to Address
Unreliable Data Collection	Data collection is burdensome and time consuming	• Create a simple data collection form with clear directions. • Use a sampling strategy instead of collecting every instance of data. • Pare down the measures that are collected regularly.
Data Is Collected But Not Analyzed	Not knowing which analysis to run or displays to create	• Mock up potential data displays even before data collection begins to decide which display will be most helpful to the team.
	Difficulty formatting data to create the wanted display	• Work with an improvement coach or data specialist to set up the team spreadsheet.
	Unclear responsibilities for entering the data and analysis	• Process map the data routine process for each measure. Clearly specify who is responsible for each step and when each step occurs.
Data Doesn't Provide Useful Information for Learning	Wrong measures	• When data conversations repeatedly fail to produce interesting learning, the team may need to rethink their family of measures. Working with an improvement coach or scanning the improvement literature can help teams identify useful measures for their topic of interest.
	Operational definitions are unclear	• Interpretations of data depend on having clear, shared definitions of what is being measured. When operational definitions are unclear, data displays may not accurately represent what the team cares about. Teams should clarify their operational definitions, specifying clear inclusion and exclusion criteria for all data collected.
	Data quality issues	• To be useful, the data collected must accurately reflect the performance of the system. Developing reliable data collection routines helps ensure data is collected in consistent ways.
	Wrong timing	• When the measures of interest lag or are available infrequently, identify proxy measures or process measures to provide more frequent, timely feedback. • Ensure reliable data routines so that analyses are available in a timely fashion to inform team learning.

CONSOLIDATION

One challenge of organizing a learning journey is deciding where to go next. At any given moment, there usually are multiple potential paths of inquiry and little certainty about which direction will reveal the biggest insights. In a project management approach, the activities are planned in advance and are followed in a specified sequence. In contrast, improvement teams follow the learning. As a result, it is easy for teams to get stuck when deciding which direction to head.

To manage the need for both flexibility and direction in navigating the journey, teams incorporate a routine for consolidating learning into their regular team meetings. It is a chance to step back and reconnect with the larger guiding theory, reflect on the learning to date, and decide where to head next. Using the data from their family of measures, together with their learning from testing changes, the team assesses the evidence for their change ideas and decides where their theory needs to evolve. What is subtracted is as important as what is added. They update their storyboard to capture the learning and decide what should happen in the next "action period" or period of testing (visualized as a dotted arrow in figure 13.1). Designating specific moments, not spaced too far apart, to revisit the big picture, can help teams commit to a particular direction for an action period, knowing they will have a chance soon to pivot later if necessary.[4] Table 13.6 provides a sample agenda for an improvement team consolidation meeting.

It is useful for teams to consolidate learning every four to eight weeks. Consolidation routines can be designated at regular intervals or around natural moments when it makes sense for teams to reset their direction. In schools, for example, the end of quarters, semesters, and school years are natural moments to step back and reset. For teams that are part of a network, an upcoming network meeting creates a natural need to summarize learning and update storyboards in preparation to share with others. Meetings with sponsors can be treated similarly.

Consolidation of learning is one of the moments along the improvement journey when teams need to make collective decisions. They may pursue divergent lines of inquiry during an action period, but during consolidation they consider and discuss the learning together to evolve their shared theory of improvement. As a result, consolidation requires strong conversational capacity. As team members review their data and share their learning, they need to be both candid about what they think and explicit in the evidence they are bringing to bear. Conflicting perspectives is not unusual and can be productive as the team debates the evidence at hand. Hopefully, by this stage of the journey, individual team members also have a better sense of the potential biases and particular beliefs they bring to the table, making these conversations easier and more productive. Setting up the conversation well is important.

In selecting a focus for the next action period, teams have a variety of decisions to make. They need to prioritize their learning goals, identify the most useful methods to address the goals, and decide whether to divide and conquer or pursue a common line of inquiry. This is where the nonlinearity of the improvement journey often reveals itself. When progress has stalled or a team's measures remain stubbornly unchanged, they must decide whether to patiently continue to test, go back to investigating the system, or search for new ideas. When a set of changes generates positive evidence, they must decide whether to spend their resources spreading to new contexts or moving onto another driver in their theory. Often the team has multiple viable paths, but they will need to prioritize given their necessarily limited resources.

Taken together, the improvement routines create a rhythm conducive for team learning. Although most teams and organizations tend to focus on learning the methods and tools when

Table 13.6. Sample Agenda for Consolidation of Learning

Item	Actions
Prework	Team Lead: Organize materials for the meeting—gather PDSAs, make sure the appropriate data displays have been made, ensure that the teams' driver diagram, storyboard, and any other necessary artifacts are readily available. Team Members (individually): Review PDSAs and reflect on . . . • What did you test? What did you learn? What is your evidence? • What was surprising? • Stories of how changes impacted users. • What are the implications for the team's theory?
Shared Purpose and Team Norms	Go-Round Check-In (sample prompts below) • What has been your biggest "improvement win" over the last action period? • Share a word or phrase that captures how you feel about the work over the last action period. • Share an anecdote about a patient/student/family that reminds you of the importance of the work. Review Team Norms Big Picture Orientation (using the team's storyboard) • Review aim and motivation for improvement. • Review the latest version of the driver diagram. • Review learning goal for last action period. • Summarize all the changes tested during the previous action period and how many PDSAs were run on each change idea.
Review Evidence from Last Action Period	Evidence to Review • Learning cycles: Individual team members share reflections on PDSAs. • Family of measures: Review data displays (outcome, key process measures, etc.).
Discuss Findings and Update the Theory[5]	Prompts • What was learned? What's our evidence? • What does the information tell us about the efficacy of the change ideas tested? What is our current degree of belief? What ideas need to be abandoned, adapted, expanded, adopted? • What did we uncover about other parts of the system that might need improving? • What user stories and voices might we want to highlight as part of the journey? Update team's learning in the storyboard and on the driver diagram as necessary.[6]
Determine a Focus for the Next Action Period	Prompts: • Determine focus and key learning goal for the next action period. • What change idea(s) do we want to test next? • If we are ready to expand testing, who do we need to recruit? What is their level of motivation and will? How might we engage them in the journey? • Given what we've learned, are there other activities we need to engage in? (e.g., process mapping, empathy interviews, developing new data collection tools, searching for change ideas). Logistics: Who is going to do what by when?
Summarize and Close	• Update storyboard. • Summarize action items for team. • Plus/delta on the meeting.

they start, the harder shift is embedding effective learning routines into the daily work. When done well, the routines balance rigor with practicality, action, and reflection, and individual and collective learning, enabling the team to learn their way into measurable improvements.

CONCLUSION

The design and redesign of systems is hard work that requires creativity and persistence. In most systems, this work is unaccounted for as people spend most of their time carrying out their assigned responsibilities within the currently designed system. Improvement teams need protected time and space to learn how to shift the system in a different direction. Having reliable routines for collaborating as a team, meeting with leadership, engaging in learning cycles, leveraging data, and consolidating learning helps structure and accelerate this learning. With the support of leadership, teams should set up these improvement routines at the beginning of the journey and embed them into daily work.

A quick cadence of activity really pays off in the learn-in-practice phase of the journey. The team starts with initial ideas for how to change the system to achieve the aim. Their starting theory probably is wrong and definitely is incomplete. By testing changes, reviewing data, and having collective conversations, the team revises their starting hypotheses and develops new ones. The goal is to arrive at a set of changes that move their measures and achieve the aim. When they reach this milestone, they should pause to celebrate. Then they might choose to document their learning in a change package, making it available to others in their organization and beyond. Change packages are described in the next chapter.

VI

HOW DO *WE* GET CHANGES TO WORK ACROSS A DIVERSE SET OF CONTEXTS?

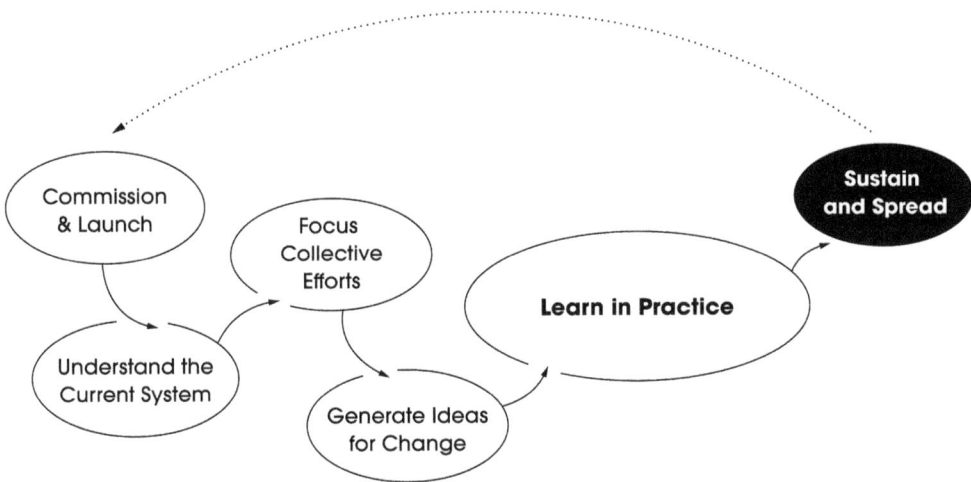

Improvement teams set off on an improvement journey with a specific aim in mind. Through engaging in collective learning, they can discover ways to better meet the needs of the families, communities, and populations they serve. Along with the discovery of promising practices come new challenges and aspirations. For the changes to truly constitute an improvement, they must produce *sustained* improvement. In addition, the excitement generated by success naturally inspires a desire to *spread*. In the *sustain and spread* phase teams ask, "How do *we* get our proven set of changes to work reliably in more places?" This could mean spreading and embedding them in other parts of the organization (e.g., additional classrooms, wards, departments) or to other systems (e.g., districts, hospitals, cities, states, or countries) addressing similar challenges.

An important first step is to codify what the team did, learned, and ultimately accomplished during the journey. One way that teams do this is by creating a change package, which we describe in chapter 14. A change package is an artifact that describes the specific changes that produced the desired outcome and the team's path to get there. The resulting artifact has a variety of uses. First, it captures important knowledge that might otherwise be lost as team members move on to other improvement work or opportunities in their career. Having an artifact helps retain the knowledge of the effective changes and the know-how of implementation. Change packages also serve as a starting place for spread. They give other teams beginning a similar journey a valuable advantage, enabling them to benefit from the steps and missteps of those who have come before them.

Chapter 15 focuses on the spread of ideas. Unfortunately, ideas do not spread naturally just because they are proven effective. Fortunately, research about the spread of innovations provides practical insights that can help teams facilitate the uptake of new ideas. Spread necessitates a new improvement journey, one that shifts its focus from discovering new practices to learning how to bring them to new people and places. The responsibility for spread is taken up by a new team, one that includes people who understand the environments to which the ideas are being spread. This team takes responsibility for designing the spread journey—selecting an aim, assessing the social context where spread will occur, and selecting among various methods for organizing the people involved.

In chapter 16, we come full circle and invite teams to think about an improvement journey from start to finish. We provide guidance for teams on how to plan their journey and offer rubrics they can use to assess their progress both in becoming a high-performing team and in achieving their aim.

Improvement as a journey never ends. We can always make things better for ourselves and for others, everywhere. Documenting and sharing our knowledge with others expands our learning community, accelerating everyone's progress in creating healthier systems for all.

14

Change Packages

Preserving Knowledge, Preparing for Spread

> How do you know that you know something? When you can produce what it is you claim to know.
>
> —Argyris 1993, 3

For many organizations, implementing changes that result in improved outcomes is the end of the improvement journey.[1] Achieving outcomes locally for those they serve is what matters most. Although understandable, this stance is problematic in a couple of ways.

First, it is shortsighted. As we know, systems are not static; they change and evolve constantly, which makes sustaining outcomes tricky. Almost all organizations face a common challenge in maintaining results: the loss of institutional memory. People turn over, and knowledge is lost. New people with different ideas and ways of doing things join the organization. Subsequent variability in practice leads to variation (and often a decline) in performance. This transition is especially acute when leaders change. New leaders recruited from the outside often want to put their stamp on an organization; they may not be aware of or care about damaging the improved, stable outcomes the organization has achieved. As a result, organizations need ways to codify and preserve what works in the face of such inevitable change. Otherwise, they will waste valuable time and resources relearning what works again and again.

Second, focusing solely on one's own organization overlooks the needs of the broader field. The demand for high-quality social services, improved educational outcomes, and superior health care exists elsewhere: in the next district, county, state, or region. Helping our neighbors get better faster is a moral imperative if we hope to achieve better and more equitable experiences at scale. If we know how to get better results, then we have a responsibility to make that knowledge accessible to others. Indeed, if another organization had this information, we would hope they would share it with us.

One way to address both concerns is through a change package, a knowledge repository of what was learned and achieved during a successful improvement journey.[2] This artifact both preserves the story of improvement for the innovating organization and is a valuable starting place for others beginning a similar journey (Bennett 2020, 20; Bennett, Grunow, and Park 2022, 140).

Consider the case of Counties Manukau District Health Board in New Zealand (see chapters 3 and 7). As part of their 20,000 Days campaign, improvement teams were launched with the express aim of reducing hospital stays. Shorter stays and fewer readmissions meant improved outcomes for patients and families while increasing the capacity of the system to serve a growing population. One improvement team at Middlemore Hospital focused their efforts on safer medication outcomes on transfer home (SMOOTH). They sought to ensure that all medications prescribed to patients when discharged from the hospital were reconciled in a way that would prevent harmful interactions that could result in hospital readmission or other adverse events. The team's improvement journey produced stunning results. In one year, 770 medication errors were prevented, 273 of which were graded as "clinically important" and one as "potentially life threatening." This led to a reduction in both the average length of stay for patients and the number of patient readmissions (Lawn et al. 2013).

The story could have ended there and been celebrated as a success, but the team took the added step of documenting their story through a change package. They described the change ideas that led to their success and chronicled their journey in a way that was accessible and easy to understand. Middlemore Hospital retained the narrative of how they achieved what they did for future leaders, staff, and patients. Other hospitals wishing to replicate their success now had a resource to jump-start and accelerate their own improvement journeys (Lawn et al. 2013).[3]

ELEMENTS OF A CHANGE PACKAGE[4]

The specific changes that resulted in the desired outcome lie at the core of a change package. In some instances, a simple list of change ideas and recommended measures for detecting improvement are enough. However, in most cases, including more detailed information about how ideas were tested and implemented is helpful. So are stories about the team's journey and how the work benefited their patients, students, or families. Deciding what to include is usually driven by the intended audience. In most situations, the primary audience is improvement teams pursuing the same or a similar improvement journey in their organization or system. Other stakeholders are important, too, especially those responsible for maintaining the change ideas in practice once implemented.

Table 14.1 contains a complete list of recommended elements for inclusion in a change package. As one might notice, many of the elements named are the same as those found in the charter. However, what is shared in the change package will likely be more comprehensive and look radically different from what was in the original charter given the learning and consolidation that's happened between then and now.

CREATING A CHANGE PACKAGE

For the innovating team, creation of a change package should be cause for celebration. It is a formal, public account of a team's success in improving an important outcome that becomes a part of the organization's institutional memory. Like more formal publications, including academic papers and research articles, it is also an important mechanism for spreading the ideas to other improvement teams and organizations (see chapter 15). For these teams, the change package accelerates their learning. Teams don't need to waste time and resources re-creating the change ideas, theory, and measures from scratch. Instead, they can focus their energy and attention on how to adapt or adopt the ideas into their own contexts. Unfortunately, the practice of creating and disseminating change packages is not widespread in the social sector.

Table 14.1. Elements of a Change Package

Element	Description
Introduction	A brief overview of what's covered in the change package and how it benefits the reader.
Outcomes Achieved	Annotated data displays (Shewhart charts, run charts, etc.) that serve as evidence of improvement of the intended outcome.
Background	Starting conditions of the improvement journey, including baseline performance and important contextual factors (population being served, location, part of the system being addressed, capabilities and capacities of the system, etc.).
Problem Statement	Compelling rationale for why the work was undertaken, how addressing the problem benefits those being served.
Aim (Outcome of Interest)	Clear and common definition of success. Specifies what will be improved, by how much, by when, for whom, and where (see chapter 7).
Measures	Description of measures tied to the aim and theory of improvement used during the journey: outcome, process, process step, and balance measures. May also include measures of network strength for networks and/or team functioning and engagement (e.g., number of learning cycles completed per week, number of improvement huddles held per month, etc.) (see chapters 12 and 13).
Theory of Improvement	Brief overview of what worked to produce the outcomes achieved. Although often displayed as a driver diagram, this can also be a simple list of change ideas that led to the desired outcome (see chapter 10).
Detailed Description of Change Ideas	Extended section of the document highlighting details for each change idea: what was done, what was learned, what evidence was generated, where the idea worked and for whom, and where it did not (the conditions of success). Also includes actionable steps for how to execute the change ideas as well as any key adaptations of the change ideas based on contextual subject matter expertise (see "Use in Practice" section later in this chapter).
Evidence for Change Ideas	May include citations from the academic literature or empirical data generated during the improvement journey. This is a place to describe the degree of belief a team has in their theory and, when needed, in each specific change idea (see "Creating a Change Package" section later in this chapter).
Stories from End Users and Team Members	Narrative experiences are ideally included throughout the change package. Different sections of the change package may include relevant excerpts or quotations from interviews or descriptions of end user and/or team member experiences. Stand-alone stories that highlight the experience of end users and/or team members throughout the improvement journey may also be included.
Contributors to the Work	List of names and roles of everyone involved in the improvement effort, including contributors outside the improvement team. This can help other organizations or teams using the change package have a clearer sense of who may need to be involved in putting the changes into practice. Sometimes included here is a description of resources necessary to accomplish the improvement (e.g., time of individuals and team, financial considerations, etc.).
References	Include any references that other organizations and teams may benefit from in developing their own theories or measurement systems.
Appendixes	Examples of important artifacts are extremely helpful to those adopting/adapting a change package. These include process maps, protocols, checklists, pictures/diagrams, important documented PDSA cycles, data collection tools, sample data displays, and so forth.

It takes additional time, energy, and resources to document the journey. Although some organizations are not willing to make this investment, for most it is an activity that simply gets overlooked as people get caught up in their day-to-day work.

Ideally, creation of a change package should not feel like a separate, stand-alone activity. Instead, it should grow organically as part of the team's rhythms and routines as described in chapter 13. As mentioned earlier, many of the elements of the change package originate in the charter. From there, they evolve and mature as the team learns in practice. This evolution is captured in the storyboard (see chapter 8) as part of the team's consolidation routine (see chapter 13). In tracking the evolution of these elements through the storyboard, the team documents the history of the project as it unfolds. Measures chosen, data collected, and analyses done all provide the evidence for a team's theory in practice and will become useful portions of the final change package. Documented plan-do-study-act (PDSA) cycles, where they exist, serve to reinforce the institutional memory of what was done when, and importantly, what was learned through the process. Inclusion of these key documents in the change package can help bring the story of improvement to life.

Still, an important question remains for teams—when to create a change package. Two potential moments are when the improvement work naturally ends and when measurable progress has been achieved. Even if the aim of the journey isn't reached, if measurable progress was made, a change package that preserves the knowledge of how those gains were realized is helpful for both the innovating team and others interested in tackling a similar aim.

To illustrate this point, we return to the work of Ko Awatea in New Zealand (see chapters 7 and 11). As described earlier, the Ko Awatea improvement team closed the enrollment equity gap in participating early childhood education centers (ECEs) in South Auckland by more than half—from 76 to 89 percent for children of Māori and Pacific Islander descent, as compared to their European-descended peers who were already enrolled at a rate of 97 percent (Tyler, Davies, and Bennett 2018). Although the gap was not completely closed, significant improvement took place—enough so that the team decided to create a change package, codify and publish the learning, and then spread the changes to other centers in the country (Ko Awatea and New Zealand Ministry of Education 2015, 1).

In deciding when to create a change package, one key consideration is the evidence for improvement (Bennett 2020, 21). The question that every team asks when picking up a change package is, "How do we know these ideas even work?" Useful change packages answer this question with empirical evidence that shows the impact of the change ideas on the outcome. To do this, teams can start by looking at the evidence for each change idea to gauge their "degree of belief" (see chapter 11) in its efficacy.

When evaluating the ideas, teams can draw on different types of evidence. The first is any empirical evidence that existed prior to using the change ideas locally. This could include data from a randomized control trial or replication of improved outcomes across multiple sites. As noted in chapter 9, selecting change ideas that already have evidentiary warrant is always a good place for a team to start. The second is evidence generated as part of the local improvement journey, such as a statistical shift in performance on a run chart (see chapter 12 for more on run charts). Again, if a team can replicate improvements in more than one site during the journey, then this should further strengthen the team's degree of belief in the idea. Finally, anecdotal data is another source of evidence that provides important insights not always captured in quantitative data.

Given this, change ideas backed by all three types of evidence would fall on the higher degree of belief side of the continuum, whereas those with only anecdotal evidence from one site, for example, would likely fall more toward the lower end. This is not to say that ideas with lower degree of belief are not important or should not be included in the change package. Authors of the change package should just be transparent about what level of evidence exists for the ideas presented. Then, it is up to the teams interested in using the change package to evaluate the evidence provided and decide which ideas to test in practice, whether to replicate the entirety of the theory presented or adapt it given their local contextual conditions.

In most situations, a team will wait to create a change package until they have identified and tested a set of change ideas that have statistical evidence of moving the aim. However, in some situations during testing, teams may create a smaller "change bundle" consisting of 1–2 change ideas that have moved an important process measure tied to their theory (see chapter 12 for more about process measures) or with qualitative evidence from multiple sources. This usually happens when a team is part of an improvement network working on a common aim. It is an effective way to spread and test ideas across different sites, generating important learning about what works in which contexts. If other improvement teams can replicate similar results in their contexts using the "change bundle," it accelerates the network's progress overall in achieving the aim and engenders a higher degree of belief in the efficacy of the ideas contained therein.

For example, the team from Exemplar Unified focused on increasing the percentage of individualized education program (IEP) goals met (see chapter 8), created a "change bundle" around a process for drafting high-quality IEP goals, an important part of their overall theory. The bundle included a process map as well as protocols and checklists connected to specific steps in the process. A tool to collect data tied to key process measures, such as an average goal quality score and the number of IEPs that included parents as part of the drafting process, was also provided. In addition, the team included guidance about how to carry out the process. The bundle was shared with two other teams in the network who then tested and adapted the process to their contexts.

USE IN PRACTICE

When using a change package, the primary goal of the improvement team is to successfully integrate the change ideas into their own local context. To do so, teams will need to decide the level of fidelity by which they will incorporate the ideas into their systems. Should the ideas in the package be adopted without adaptation to the local environment (high level of fidelity), or can or must they be adapted based on local conditions (lower level of fidelity)? Context matters.[5]

In some instances, change ideas validated by basic science research or successfully replicated under a wide variety of conditions should be adopted "as is" to achieve the best outcomes. In fact, any modifications to the change ideas will negatively affect their ability to achieve the intended results. One example is the prevention of central-line infections (see chapters 12 and 13). Failure to execute the change ideas for prevention with fidelity will increase the chances of an infection occurring. A so-called rigid approach to improvement can at times employ changes to system policy or even law (e.g., state-based seat-belt laws that require seat belts to be worn at all times in a moving vehicle). Such policy changes can facilitate more rapid adoption of changes in practices as they target what Everett Rogers referred to as late majority and laggards (people who actively resist change) with adverse consequences for failing to adopt the change idea (Rogers 2003, 281).[6]

That said, it should be noted that even when a rigid approach to the adoption of change ideas is used, local choices likely will come into play. With central-line infections, inserting and maintaining the central line used to give the patient medicine, fluid, blood, or nutrition must be done with fidelity; however, support to facilitate the execution of these practices may vary locally. For example, to make it easier for practitioners to find the supplies needed for central-line insertions, some hospitals might choose to reorganize their storage closets whereas others might decide to purchase prepackaged materials sold specifically for this purpose (Health Quality & Safety Commission New Zealand and Ko Awatea 2014, 23).

In other instances, the change ideas presented in a change package are a starting set of ideas that need local adaptation to succeed. What worked in rural Colorado may not work the same in urban San Francisco. A good example of flexible adaptation comes from the Building a Teachers Effectiveness Network (BTEN). Improvement leaders in the network agreed that all new teachers needed informal feedback on their instruction at regular intervals (change idea). However, who provided the feedback usually varied by context. In smaller elementary schools where resources were limited, teacher leaders (experienced, respected instructors) were given the time and task of providing such feedback. In large, comprehensive high schools that had different staffing structures and usually many more new teachers, assistant principals, acting as instructional leaders, provided new teachers with consistent informal feedback. The network included these suggestions for adaptation in its change package with the hope that the extra guidance would make it easier for other teams to figure out how to apply the ideas in their own contexts (Carnegie Foundation for the Advancement of Teaching 2015).

As mentioned earlier, teams should draw on subject matter expertise when deciding if and how to adapt a change package. As part of the decision-making process, teams should keep in mind 1) the level of evidence in the change package and 2) the similarity of the local system interested in trying the change package to that of the system where it was developed. When evidence is moderate to low, and/or when the conditions of the originating and adopting systems vary widely, adaptation likely is needed. This is both a pragmatic choice and a relational and strategic one. It is not uncommon for new sites to view change packages with skepticism, especially if they view the originating context as radically different from theirs. It can be helpful when developing a change package for a team to anticipate challenges and potential adaptations to the change package that might make uptake easier.

In either situation, change packages should never be presented as a silver bullet to magically improve outcomes and thus be implemented immediately across the entire organization. The adoption and/or adaptation of a change package locally should be treated as an improvement journey in and of itself with the improvement team engaging in the same routines used to develop, test, and validate the ideas themselves. Given the hesitancy that individuals and organizations naturally display when presented with a new idea, the use of PDSA cycles is helpful in reducing anxiety and resistance to the adoption and adaptation of change packages. Testing the ideas allows people to experience the change, offer feedback, and suggest potential adaptations before moving to full-scale implementation. Because the change package includes suggested measures, people in the organization adopting it can also collect data to see whether the changes they are trying positively impact outcomes in their specific contexts.

Change packages most commonly are developed and used within improvement networks. Networked improvement communities (NICs), collaborative learning networks, and break-through series collaboratives, for example, often invest in the creation of an change package upfront. They also capture changes discovered by teams along the way to spread promising change ideas quickly from one team or network member to another. For long-standing networks, it is important to develop a routine to revise and update the theory, measures, and experiences presented in their change package periodically (annually at a minimum) to reflect the ongoing learning across the network. The network will also need mechanisms to capture valuable learning about how changes can be productively adapted to different local contexts. If the change package doesn't evolve, this is often a signal to the network that learning and improvement have stalled.

CONCLUSION

Knowledge of what works is rarely captured, let alone shared with others. As a result, organizations, networks, and systems are constantly reinventing the wheel, unaware of what's already been learned. Such rework is a waste, slowing progress for communities and individuals served by our social systems. Codifying such knowledge through the creation of change packages can short-circuit this vicious cycle.[7]

Creating a change package is about documenting what was learned during an improvement journey—what worked, for whom, and under what conditions. It preserves knowledge, presents evidence of improvement, and provides a compelling narrative of the improvement journey. Change packages make learning about what works accessible to others. They help fulfill our moral responsibility to capture better, more successful, and more efficient ways of achieving outcomes so others can do the same for the populations they serve. Publication matters. Whether it is in academic journals, or via web-based platforms, sharing the story of improvement is incredibly helpful for other teams starting on their own journeys toward improved outcomes. Ideally, they will build upon, update, refine, and publish/republish their own change packages, strengthening the evidence for the ideas for still others who will follow in their paths. In this way, change packages allow teams to pay it forward, helping subsequent improvement teams launch an accelerated journey focused not on identifying or creating potential solutions but, rather, on spreading known solutions.

15

Organizing for Spread

> I think when people look back at our time, they will be amazed at one thing more than any other. It is this—that we do know more about ourselves now than people did in the past, but that very little of this knowledge has been put into effect.
>
> —Lessing 1987

Redesigning systems is an exhilarating experience, worthy of fanfare and celebration. Creating spaces for people to share their improvement stories and capture the learning for a broader audience is important both for the team and for others interested in taking a similar journey. However, sharing "a better way" will not necessarily lead to the uptake of the ideas in other places. This can be perplexing, particularly for people who have seen firsthand how changes to the system have improved the lives of those it serves. Unfortunately, good ideas, even great ones, do not necessarily spread easily just because they are effective (Rogers 2003).

Take, for example, the rather straightforward innovation of hand washing to decrease the spread of infection in medical practice. It may sound odd at first to pair "hand washing" with "innovative," but the impact of hand washing was once a new discovery. However, more than 150 years later, hand washing still does not happen reliably in many medical settings. Table 15.1 describes the long, slow journey toward the reliable use of hand washing in medical practice.

It can be mystifying how or why a video, meme, or message "goes" viral these days whereas an important lifesaving practice does not. To compound the issue, many changes we seek to spread are significantly more complicated than the seemingly straightforward practice of handwashing. Sutton and Rao call this "the problem of more," and it applies to education, social welfare, and health care. They illustrate how leaders across industries share the common experience of being able to identify instances of remarkable practice, but what "ke[eps] them up at night, and devour[s] their workdays [is] the difficulty of spreading that excellence to more people and more places" (Sutton and Rao 2014, x).

Spreading to new systems is a complex undertaking. Local systems all have some level of difference. Changes that worked somewhere can serve as a useful starting point, but at the same time, making changes work in another system is not a trivial task. In fact, spreading changes is a journey unto itself that usually requires a different team, theory, methods, and tools. Whereas the purpose of a typical improvement journey is to learn what changes work in practice and implement them in a specific department, site, or organization, the goal of a spread journey is to figure out how to get more people to adopt them at a broader scale. This chapter provides guidance for teams that are ready to think about spreading proven practices.

Table 15.1. The History of Hand Washing in Medical Practice

Year	Evidence	Response
1846	Ignaz Semmelweis, a Hungarian doctor working in Vienna General Hospital, establishes a direct link between hand washing and maternal mortality, publishing several studies showing reductions in mortality below 1 percent (Global Handwashing Partnership, n.d.; Centers for Disease Control and Prevention 2000).	Medicine does not yet recognize germ theory. Semmelweis is discredited by the establishment and mocked.
1854	Florence Nightingale, an English nurse, institutes hand washing and other antiseptic measures at Scutari hospital to reduce mortality among injured soldiers during the Crimean War. Mortality drops from 52 percent to less than 20 percent (Global Handwashing Partnership, n.d.; Fee and Garofalo 2011).	Medicine still does not yet recognize germ theory. A dissipation in miasma is credited with the mortality drop. One might speculate that Nightingale's position in the medical system hierarchy given her gender and role as a nurse (as opposed to being a male physician) prevented wide-scale adoption.
1864	Louis Pasteur proposes germ theory and "pasteurization" to kill microorganisms in wine, beer, and milk. He publishes widely between 1866 and 1886.	Because printed journals were the dominant form of communication at the time and not easily accessible, Pasteur's breakthrough science was not widely consumed or put into practice by medical practitioners.
1867	Joseph Lister demonstrates dramatic reductions in infections associated with doctors washing their hands (and instruments used) before and after surgery in a solution containing 5 percent carbolic acid.	"In 1869, at the meetings of the British Association at Leeds, Lister's ideas were mocked" (Huggins et al. n.d.).
1875	Widespread adoption in *surgical medicine* of hand washing and sterilization of instruments using carbolic acid.	Marcus Beck, a personal friend of Lister's, writes a widely used textbook in which he includes antiseptic procedures adopted from Lister. The adoption of Beck's book in medical education propagated adoption of hand washing in surgery.
1962	Mortimer et al. demonstrate the transmission of bacteria between newborns when hospital staff do not wash their hands (Mortimer et al. 1962).	The diffusion of the information relies on reading print journals. The adoption of hand washing is still left to individual decisions made by medical professionals.
1981	The Centers for Disease Control in the United States issues its first *recommendation* on hand hygiene in medicine. The CDC hospital infections program (HIP) offers guidelines for prevention and control of nosocomial infections.	
2002	CDC/Healthcare Infection Control Practices Advisory Committee (HICPAC) *recommends* use of alcohol-based hand rubbing and washing in specific circumstances as the standard of care.	
2018	According to the CDC, in the United States, "On average, healthcare providers *clean their hands less than half of the times they should*. On any given day, about one in 25 hospital patients has at least one healthcare–associated infection" (Centers for Disease Control and Prevention 2016).	

We review the factors that impact the uptake of new ideas and outline the decisions that need to be made in designing a spread strategy. Although spreading improvements is its own distinct line of work, an understanding of key spread concepts and methods is useful for many improvement journeys.[1] Most organizations launch improvement with spread in mind. The initial aim is purposefully scoped down to facilitate learning with an intention to subsequently bring the practices that are discovered to more people and places. Further, improvement teams can draw on the core ideas behind the science of spread anytime they need more people to try a change, whether it's convincing one more person to test an idea or persuading an entire organization to adopt a new practice.

A NOTE ABOUT SPREAD AND SCALE

Before we continue, it is important that we distinguish spread from scale. These terms often are used interchangeably, but they are, in fact, separate albeit interrelated concepts.

Spread: The dissemination of innovations that have been successfully implemented locally across a broader range of contexts.
Scale: Overcoming the institutional inertia and infrastructure issues that arise as new ideas spread to impact outcomes at the larger system level.

When a team seeks to expand the use of a proven literacy practice, for example, part of the challenge will be getting more individual teachers to adopt it (spread). At the same time, widespread use of the literacy practice likely will bump up against existing system structures designed to support the current instruction in place. Even if teachers want to use the new practice, do they have the necessary materials or coaching support, for example, to do so? At a district level, if teachers need new books to support the new practice, they still need to be purchased and distributed to classrooms. Time also needs to be allocated for teachers to receive the coaching support they need. These are issues related to scale, whereas convincing more teachers to adopt the literacy practice is an issue of spread.

If the goal is to embed new practices into the daily work of more places, then organizational leadership needs to think both about how to build the will and motivation for the change (spread) and how to redesign the infrastructure to make the new practice the default way of doing business (scale). In most situations, both are required; however, what an organization decides to emphasize is influenced by the nature of the innovation itself as well as the decision strategy an organization uses in adopting the change, which we will talk about in more detail later in the chapter. Because the activities used to scale a change are similar to those described in implementation (e.g., new policies and procedures, resourcing, education, and training), we will spend most of this chapter on spread.

GETTING READY TO SPREAD

Organizing for spread presumes the identification of a set of practices worthy of dissemination. That is, a set of practices has been proven to work somewhere. Although this might seem obvious, we highlight this point because it is not uncommon for organizations to hold big, bold aspirations for large-scale impact with undeveloped ideas about how to get there. As described in chapter 14, a change package that includes evidence-based practices, along with stories and resources for their practical application in other places (Bennett 2020; Bennett, Grunow, and Park 2022, 140–47), is a good place to start.

Once an organization has identified the practices to spread, then leadership can commission and launch a new journey. In most cases, this means recruiting a new team to lead the effort. The spread team is responsible for designing the spread journey and supporting the people, teams, and sites where the practices are being spread. Like an improvement team, a spread team includes a sponsor, a senior leader who oversees the initiative, and a team lead who manages the day-to-day work. The team also includes someone from the original improvement team or a person knowledgeable about the changes being spread as well as representatives from the departments, sites, or organizations to which the ideas are being disseminated (Langley et al. 2009, 198–99).

As part of the planning process, the spread team usually engages in four central activities: deciding on the size of the spread effort, assessing the change ideas for strengths and weaknesses regarding spread, learning about the social context where spread is to occur, and choosing a method relevant to the intended size of the effort and consistent with the resources available.

DETERMINING THE SIZE OF THE SPREAD EFFORT

One of the team's first tasks is to set a new aim. Although the same questions apply when crafting an aim statement for a spread effort—What will be improved? By how much? By when? For whom and where?—the one that often requires the most deliberation is where. More specifically, how many places do you expect to adopt the new ideas (i.e., what is the target population)? For example, Ko Awatea began by working on attendance and enrollment in seven early childhood education centers in Auckland (see chapter 7). Once they discovered how to improve attendance in these seven centers, they turned their attention to spreading these changes to the rest of the forty-nine early childhood education centers on the North Island.[2]

The size of spread depends on the capacity to support new people to take on the change and the will and excitement of those involved. Given this, it is helpful, whenever possible, to begin a spread effort with the ultimate target population in mind. This enables the team to backwards plan the successive waves of spread. For Ko Awatea, their goal was to impact the experiences of children across the country. They planned to get there in three waves: seven centers in Auckland, then forty-nine on the North Island, then all the centers on both islands.

Of course, there is no guarantee that things will go according to plan. Moving to the next stage should not occur based on an arbitrary time line but, rather, when the conditions have been met to warrant spread. Still, keeping the next step in mind can help teams establish the relationships, know-how, and infrastructure they will need to get there.

THE SCIENCE OF SPREAD

With an aim and set of changes in hand, the spread team is ready to think about *how* to bring the practices to new people in ways that facilitate their uptake. Here it is useful to take a slight detour into the science of spread. In this science are many practical lessons that help teams devise an effective strategy for spread.

Understanding spread starts with the observation that some innovations are adopted quicker than others. The cell phone spread rapidly. Meanwhile, the Dvorak keyboard—a keyboard that makes typing easier and more efficient, never succeeded in replacing the QWERTY keyboards we use today. The question is why? What makes some innovations spread broadly, whereas others, even seemingly advantageous ones, fail to do so?

These were the questions that fascinated sociologist and communication theorist Everett Rogers. He summarized the research in this area in his book *Diffusion of Innovations* (Rogers 2003). This seminal book is long, and at the same time, it conveys many clear, practical insights about why some innovations spread and others do not. For this reason, we aim to provide an accessible summary here. Rogers defined an innovation as "an idea, practice or object perceived as new by an individual or other unit of adoption" (Rogers 2003, 36). For our purposes, the diffusion of innovation is synonymous with the spread of changes.

In his book, Rogers described five factors that influence the spread of an innovation. They are presented as a theory of spread in figure 15.1.

To understand the theory, it is useful to imagine what happens when a person takes on something new. The individual first must become aware of the innovation, then form an opinion about it, decide whether to try it or reject it, try it out (perhaps), and then either commit to its use or reject it. To be adopted, the innovation must make it through all the steps. By better understanding how people make decisions about whether to adopt an innovation, we can better shepherd innovations through the process.

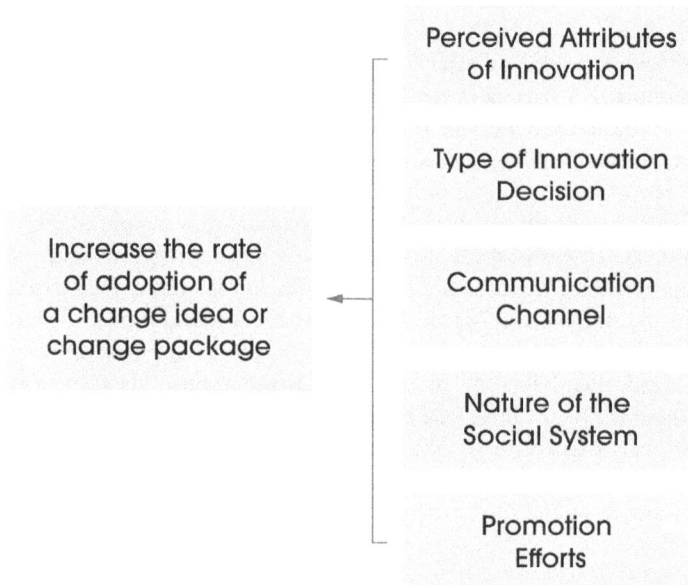

Figure 15.1. "Drivers" of the Diffusion of Innovations
Source: Rogers 2003, 222

How Do People Perceive the Changes?

As is true with many theories, some drivers carry more weight than others in explaining the diffusion of innovation. According to Rogers, the nature of the innovation itself has the biggest impact on the rate of adoption. After people learn of a new idea, they form an opinion about it. Rogers highlights five attributes of innovation that predict how favorably an innovation will be perceived (see table 15.2).

During the improvement journey, teams work tirelessly to amass evidence of efficacy for their change ideas. That said, when organizing spread efforts, it is also useful to assess the change ideas based on these perceptual attributes.[3] In some cases, teams can take steps to enhance the spreadability of their change ideas. In-person visits or videos can allow people to observe new practices. Small-scale tests can help with trialability. Supporting materials can be created to reduce unnecessary complexity. Some changes can be adapted to local contexts or built into systems to make them more compatible and less cumbersome to use.

Table 15.2. Attributes of Innovations That Influence Their Adoption[4]

Relative Advantage	"Relative advantage is the degree to which an innovation is perceived as better than the idea it supersedes" (Rogers 2003, 15). Here, the empirical value of the idea is not what is at stake but, rather, an individual's reaction to it. A mountain of evidence could exist, but if a person doesn't perceive value, then the change idea may be rejected.
Compatibility	"Compatibility is the degree to which an innovation is perceived as consistent with the existing values, past experiences, and needs of potential adopters" (Rogers 2003, 15). People are always asking themselves, does this fit with my beliefs? My experiences? Do I need this? If they decide they don't, then it is unlikely they will take up the innovation even if there is a clear benefit in doing so.[5]
Complexity	"Complexity is the degree to which an innovation is perceived as relatively difficult to understand and to use" (Rogers 2003, 16). Is the innovation simple or intuitive enough to understand and use with minimal effort, or does it require learning new information or skills? Not surprisingly, innovations that are easier to understand and pick up are adopted more quickly.
Trialability	"Trialability is the degree to which an innovation may be experimented with on a limited basis" (Rogers 2003, 16). In chapter 11, we noted that one objective of a PDSA might be to "give individuals an opportunity to try a change in practice before adopting it as the new status quo" (see table 11.5). The adage "try before you buy" reminds us that individuals may need the opportunity to wrestle with the relative advantage, compatibility, and complexity of the idea without the pressure of coercion or accountability associated with implementation.
Observability	"Observability is the degree to which the results of an innovation are visible to others" (Rogers 2003, 16). Can others see the value or impact of a change idea on an outcome? Perhaps more than the other perceived attributes, this is where evidence of impact matters. Improvement teams that have invested in collection, analysis, and display of data and personal testimonies of those who have used or been positively impacted by the change idea(s) will find spreading the ideas easier. Even better is giving people the chance to observe the practice in action.

Source: Rogers 2003, 15–16.

Of course, some changes that teams want to spread will simply not rate high on one or more of the attributes. For example, changing instructional practice in education is notoriously difficult to do. It is complex, often has low relative advantage in the early stages, takes a long time to demonstrate impact, and often requires shifting relationships between teachers and students in ways that are not immediately compatible with local norms. As a result, the team may strategically pair changes that are easier to spread with more difficult ones to get early wins and build momentum for change. Or they may need to limit the size and/or time frame in which they intend to spread.

Communication Channels

How people learn about an innovation also matters. Which communication strategy is most useful depends on where people are in deciding to adopt an innovation. Rogers defines communication channels as "the means by which messages get from one individual to another" (Rogers 2003, 18). In the hand-washing example, print journals were an early communication channel used to disseminate information and evidence supporting the practice. However, the journals only reached a select, albeit important, audience. The idea of hand washing spread more broadly through interpersonal communication. Joseph Lister's personal relationship with influencer Marcus Beck was key in getting hand washing to be taken up in surgical practice.

Successful spread efforts will leverage communication channels not only to raise awareness of a change idea but also to create an appropriate context for persuasion. They will bring together people who have not yet adopted the idea with those who have. When people perceive the person to be like them, the communication will be more effective (Rogers 2003, 306). Teachers are more likely to persuade other teachers. Contrast this with many change efforts where administrators try to message, convince, or cajole teachers into new practices only to see their efforts bear little to no fruit.

The importance of interpersonal communication leads to the next factor influencing the spread of change—the social system. Changes are not spread onto a blank canvas; rather, they are interjected into an existing social environment with structures, relationships, and norms. Understanding the existing social structure can help teams tap into the existing sources of energy, relationships, and communication channels to facilitate spread.

The Social System

Compared to other forms of decision making, what makes innovation decisions unique is "the perceived newness of an innovation, and the uncertainty associated with this newness" (Rogers 2003, 168). For any given innovation, people will vary in how they react to the uncertainty. Some move quickly from learning about an innovation to trying it, whereas others require more time. This variation should be expected. In perhaps the most renowned part of his theory, Rogers delineates five "adopter categories" to describe the willingness with which people embrace a particular innovation (see figure 15.2).

Importantly, the adopter categories are intended to describe people's orientation to a particular innovation and are not labels to describe inherent characteristics of people. Each of us is an early adopter of certain innovations and traditionalists with respect to others. Innovators are often the first to learn about a particular practice and do not need assurances before trying

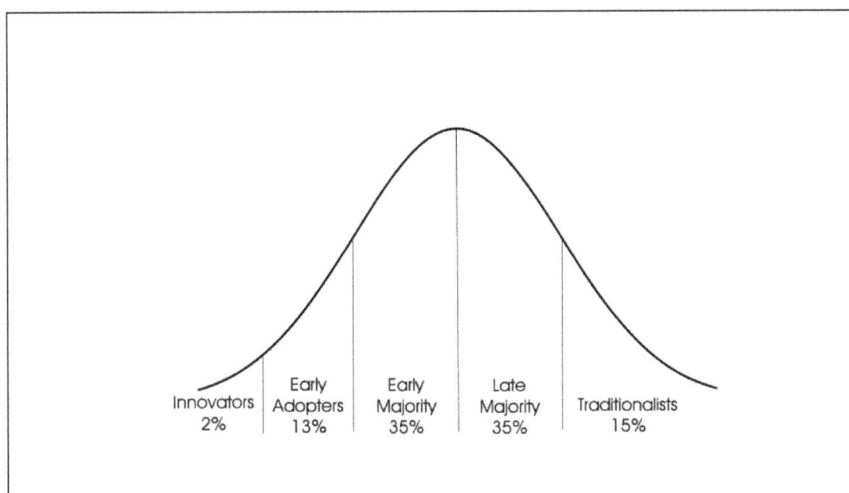

Figure 15.2.   Adopter Categories
Source: Rogers 2003, 281

it out. Early adopters are the "first followers" and are important for making the innovation seem less of a fringe idea. The early majority tend to "wait and see" but will adopt an innovation after a period of deliberation. The late majority are more skeptical; they will only adopt once uncertainty has been minimized. Finally, traditionalists prefer the way things are currently done, willing to change only when the existing ways of working are removed.

In change efforts, it is not unusual to complain about those who are slow or resistant to change. Instead of focusing energy on those who resist, spread efforts should focus on finding early adopters, leveraging their leadership to make the changes more observable, and reducing the uncertainty for others. Once enough individuals have adopted the innovation, it often increases the likelihood that others will follow suit.

Opinion leaders and social influencers are also important for the spread of new practices. These are people who hold sway over others, sometimes because of positional authority; however, more often they are informal leaders found in unexpected places. One way to find opinion leaders is to simply ask a handful of people, "When you need advice, who do you ask?" After a few rounds, it is often possible to identify a handful of connectors to whom many frequently turn.

For spread, it is helpful to identify both the opinion leaders and the early adopters and actively involve them in spreading the change. Sometimes these people are the same; sometimes they're different. Both will have communication networks that will shape how others perceive the innovation. These networks include formal structures (units, grade-level teams) and informal relationships (e.g., friendships). Tapping into existing communication structures can help in spreading change.

Finally, the structure and cultural norms of a social system will influence the rate of spread. In hierarchical systems, communication boundaries prevent ideas from moving from one part of the organization to another. In these cases, new collaborative structures are needed to facilitate the communication necessary for spread. Social systems also have norms. For example, some have norms of transparency and experimentation, encouraging people to "give it a try," providing fertile ground for innovation adoptions. Other systems may be more opaque, engendering fear and operating from a place of compliance and accountability. In these places, it is essential to create safe spaces that allow for experimentation with new ideas.

The Promotion of Change

Another component of Rogers's theory deals with the question of who is responsible for introducing the changes to new people. Rogers refers to these people as "change agents" (Rogers 2003, 365). When teams are tasked with spreading changes, they become, by definition, change agents. Understanding what this role entails can be helpful in successfully spreading change ideas.

Change agents are catalysts. Sometimes they raise awareness, other times they develop capability, and in still other instances they serve as persuaders, intentionally cultivating relationships to encourage the adoption of ideas. What they do depends on their relationship to the people and system taking on the change. If they are seen as credible and like those in the new context, they can play key roles in persuading others. They can also draw on their personal networks and work with key opinion leaders. Using change agents to support "local champions" can help spread the innovation, particularly if the changes are perceived as being "brought in from the outside."

Type of Innovation Decision

Thus far, we have mostly focused on what influences individuals to accept or reject a new practice. It is worth noting, however, that not all innovation decisions are made by individuals, especially in the context of organizations. With some innovations, individuals can choose to adopt or reject an innovation regardless of what others in the organization decide. These are known as optional innovation decisions. Individual teachers can decide whether to use a certain technology in their classroom, and individual doctors can decide whether to integrate a new treatment into their practice. Collective innovation decisions are made by consensus among the members of a system. A school may decide to try a conflict-resolution program together, or a surgical department may choose to implement a surgical safety checklist. With authority-based innovation decisions, a small group of key leaders choose for the organization as a whole; for example, when leadership at a hospital or health-care insurance provider selects the use of one drug over another after careful consideration and mandates compliance to its use by its provider network.

The type of innovation decision that an organization selects will influence how quickly innovations are adopted and whether they are sustained. For example, optional innovation decisions usually are the slowest, but sometimes they increase the likelihood that new practices will be sustained because individuals likely will adopt them out of intrinsic motivation. Authority-based decisions likely will be taken up more quickly, especially if there is a consequence for not complying.

However, even if an organization makes an authority-based decision to adopt, it doesn't mean that implementation will follow directly. For example, seat-belt or hand-washing policies can be adopted and mandated at a state or organizational level, but ultimately individuals must decide to adopt the practice as part of their daily lives. As a result, it is important to know who the relevant decision makers are for any given innovation and what they need to adopt the decision.

As mentioned earlier, sometimes individuals want to adopt a change, but they are slow to do so because specific challenges get in the way. For example, they might not understand how to execute the new practice, or a technological barrier gets in the way. Here is where adoption shifts from being an issue of spread to that of scale. As we described earlier, scaling touches on issues of implementation and sustainability, whereas spread deals with convincing people and organizations to adopt a change. In these situations, redesigning the system infrastructure will facilitate its uptake by making it easier to adopt the change, helping to save time and effort. In some instances, the organization can remove the need to decide at all, integrating the change into the way the system operates. In these situations, people do not even realize they are adopting a change. For example, technology systems can integrate dropdown menus that guide doctors to prescribe the right dose of antibiotics.

METHODS FOR SPREAD

Understanding the attributes that impact the spread of new practices can help leaders design spread efforts that are more likely to be successful. They should assess the spreadability of the practices in their change package and determine how each decision to adopt should be made. They need to understand the existing social system where they intend to spread and identify opinion leaders, early adopters and communication structures that can be leveraged to facilitate the uptake of new ideas. These assessments often cause teams to revisit the aim of their spread effort and the people who need to be involved.

Along with a set of changes and aim, spread plans also include the selection of a method for organizing the people engaged. In the words of McCannon, Massoud, and Alyesh, there are "many ways to many." Table 15.3, adapted from McCannon, Massoud, and Alyesh, describes multiple structures that can be used. The choice of method will depend on the nature of the changes and the social system where adoption is desired.

Each method depicted has advantages and disadvantages in promoting the uptake of a known best practice. Teams needing to decide which method is right for them should consider:

- How many sites, locations, or individuals they hope will adopt the practice.
- What resources they have available to support their spread efforts (e.g., time, money, expertise, volunteers).
- The duration of the spread work, including how quickly the team needs adoption of the change to occur.
- The simplicity or complexity of the practice the team seeks to spread.

For example, Target CLAB Zero, a national collaborative in New Zealand that focused on reducing central line–associated bloodstream infections (see chapter 12) chose a breakthrough series collaborative (BTSC) as its spread strategy. They chose this method because the intervention was well defined and moderately complex, meaning intensive care units (ICUs) needed to reliably execute two bundles of five changes each for every patient in need. Further, the size of spread was relatively moderate—twenty-five ICUs across the country.

Table 15.3. Methods for Spread

Method	Description	Nature of the Intervention	Audience Dimensions	Resources	Time Frame
Natural Diffusion	An organic, unguided spread of concepts, innovations, or knowledge through social networks, cultural exchanges, or everyday interactions among individuals and groups.	Any	Any	Low	Years to decades
Breakthrough Series Collaborative (BTSC)	A structured, time-limited approach to spread, developed by the Institute for Healthcare Improvement, that brings together 10–100 teams from different organizations to implement innovative solutions to complex problems in their contexts.	Moderate to complex intervention	Scale of tens to hundreds of sites; often skilled practitioners	Moderate to high	6–18 months
Extension Agent	A professional who serves as a liaison between research institutions and local communities, providing research-based information and expertise to address agricultural, environmental, and other relevant issues in the community.	Moderate to complex practices	Scale of tens to hundreds of sites; actors are geographically disparate or cannot come together easily	Moderate	Indefinite
Wedge and Spread or Wave Sequence	Used to promote an innovation or idea in systems containing nested, interdependent organizations (e.g., primary, secondary, and tertiary care in a health-care system; or elementary, middle, high school, and district levels in an education system). Individual wedges that include representatives from each level are targeted for reliable adoption of a change before a team moves on to the "next" wedge in the system.	Complex, multi-actor interventions	Tens to hundreds of organizations	Moderate to high	Months to years
Campaign	An approach to spread that entails orchestrating a well-structured, collaborative initiative, using a range of advocacy and engagement strategies, to propagate and amplify a particular social cause, program, or innovation within the broader community and stakeholder network.	Well-documented, straightforward, and evidence-based interventions	Scale of hundreds to thousands of sites; large audience representing a significant portion of the whole (e.g., one or two steps removed from full scale	Moderate to high	12–24 months
Grassroots Organizing	Grassroots organizing is a bottom-up, community-driven approach to mobilizing individuals and groups at the local level to collectively advocate for social, political, or environmental change.	Simple to moderate	Tens to tens of thousands of individuals	Low to moderate	Months to years

Source: Adapted from McGregor, Mansoud, and Aleesh 2015.

The Ministry of Health, which launched the collaborative, sought to accomplish this spread strategy in eighteen months (Gray et al. 2015).

Community Solutions, on the other hand, chose to launch the 100,000 Homes Campaign as their spread strategy with the goal of finding permanent housing for one hundred thousand homeless people in fifty-five cities in the United States in three years. Drawing on earlier work done in New York City, the organization sought to spread two core practices that could be applied universally in different contexts: developing a homeless registry (a database that tracked information about the homeless people in a given community) and using a vulnerability index (an assessment tool used to identify the homeless people most at risk). Together, these two practices allowed a community to track and assess their homeless population, identify their specific needs, and prioritize resources and services accordingly (Soule et al. n.d.).

By the nature of bringing changes to more people and places, spread efforts often fall toward the more complex end of the improvement initiatives continuum (see figure 3.1) and require multiple teams to execute. As a result, they often require ample resources in the form of time, leadership, and money. Commissioning and launching multiple teams as part of a spread initiative also requires more extensive planning, given that more people need to be brought on board simultaneously. Like any other improvement journey, spread will require learning. Knowledge management routines and easy-to-use measurement systems will be critical for learning across a larger group of people.[6] These will help the team see which spread strategies are working and, more important, which ones are not.

CONCLUSION

Discovering a set of practices that measurably improves a system's performance naturally prompts a desire to spread them to new places. Spread is messy work. Practices do not spread simply because they are effective. They experience different rates of adoption across different social contexts. Much more is known about the spread of innovations than is typically used in practice. It is particularly helpful to remember the insight from Rogers that "diffusion is fundamentally a social process" (Rogers 2003, 35). How people learn about an innovation, who they learn it from, and how they are invited to try it out impacts the likelihood that they will decide to adopt it. Understanding the science of spread can help teams navigate the messy path of bringing new practices to a broader set of people and organizations.

Spreading proven practices requires a new improvement journey, one that often takes more time and resources than the initial effort. Teams taking on the responsibility for spread begin by developing a spread strategy. They determine an aim, assess the changes and social context, and select an appropriate method for organizing spread. The people and organizations participating in spread efforts benefit by starting with a set of proven practices, but still, they must learn how to adapt the practices to their unique local context. No matter how good the ideas or the strategy, the successful spread of ideas is never assured. Like all improvement journeys, persistence, curiosity, and a system for learning will be critical resources along the way.

16

Guiding the Journey

Learn your way into improvement.

A journey predicated on learning will need to be flexible. What is learned in one learning cycle, action period, or phase of the work influences what happens next. At the same time, infinite flexibility can be paralyzing, leaving open too many options for what direction to head. As a scaffold, we described throughout this book the phases of a journey as they typically unfold:

- commission and launch a team,
- work together to understand the current system,
- decide where to focus collectively,
- generate ideas for change,
- learn your way into improvements by testing ideas in practice, and
- think forward to sustaining and spreading the changes that prove efficacious.

One of the trickiest parts of organizing a learning journey is knowing when to move from one phase to the next. Learning generates excitement. Teams uncover insights about how their systems work (or don't), which opens different paths to learn more. On one level, this is an important indication that the journey is succeeding, enlivening the collective learning that lies at the heart of improvement science. At the same time, it can lead teams down tangents that take them away from their intended goal. Interesting discoveries can be easy to confuse with progress. The team can find themselves walking around a mountain when the real goal is to reach the top.

This chapter focuses on ways to guide the improvement journey as it unfolds. This starts with creating a plan for how the team will move through the phases from the starting point to measurable improvement. Along the way, the team can use two assessment tools—the project progress score and team rubric—to reflect on where they are in the journey and what pivots they might need to make to reach their intended destination.

BACKWARDS MAPPING THE IMPROVEMENT JOURNEY

Successful improvement journeys achieve three objectives. First, they demonstrate measurable progress toward the aim. This is the most obvious and important indicator of success.[1] Second, successful improvement projects capture how outcomes were improved. Along with the graphs that show improved performance, the team identifies and documents the changes they believe resulted in the improvements. The evidence for the changes will continue to build—or be challenged—through attempts to replicate the findings in new contexts. Finally, an improvement journey develops valuable, reusable improvement capabilities that can be applied to new problems and opportunities. Engaging in improvement, team members will develop new lenses, new relationships, and new skills that will help them pursue change in the future. This can be true even when teams fail to make measurable progress on their aim but generate useful learning that will help them with their next attempt. Measurable improvement, practical know-how, and improvement capabilities are all resources that make improvement worth the investment.

Teams should begin an improvement journey with the end in mind. In the commissioning phase, as the focus is being selected and time lines are being established, it is often useful to backwards map the phases of work that will help the team reach their intended goals. Here, when an experienced improvement coach can be helpful in designing a journey that meets the organizational needs. Creating an improvement journey plan begins by establishing the overall time frame for the project. Improvement journeys vary in their duration. The time frame depends on the complexity of the project and the amount of time leadership is willing to allocate. Next, the available time is divided into phases with designated time frames for each phase. Creating a visual representation of the time line can serve as a useful anchor point for leaders and team members alike. Teams can use the phases in the order they were presented across this book as a starting point for designing a journey. Not all the phases deserve the same amount of time, and the phases naturally overlap. For example, teams specify an aim either as the culmination of the phase dedicated to understanding the system or in a "chartering phase" in which they select an aim and generate changes at the same time (see chapter 8). Table 16.1 provides guidance on how to divide an improvement project into phases.

Table 16.1. Guidance on the Duration of Each Phase of the Improvement Journey

Phase of Improvement Journey	Example Project Lasting 24 Months
Commission and Launch	2 months (varies from 1 to 3 months)
Understand the Current System	3 months (varies from 0 to 6 months)
Charter Improvement • Focus Collective Effort • Generate Ideas for Change	1 month (varies from 1 meeting to 6 weeks)
Learn in Practice	16 months (varies from 12 to 18 months)
Sustain and Plan for Spread	2 months (varies from 1 to 3 months)

The most important part of creating an improvement journey plan is protecting the time for learning in practice. This is the heart of the journey, the phase in which the team will learn the most about how to redesign the system to achieve their aims. Allocating two-thirds of the time available to this phase is a good rule of thumb. The rest of the plan can be built around what is needed to set up powerful learning in practice.

The biggest mistake that teams make is getting stuck in the "understanding the system" phase. Sometimes organizations purposely slow down and spend time here to build valuable relational capacity and common systems understandings across diverse stakeholders that previously worked in silos. More often, teams unintentionally get stuck here, unsure of when they understand enough, and remain tentative about putting a stake in the ground and declaring an aim. Creating an overall improvement journey plan with time-delimited phases can help teams avoid arriving at the end of the allocated time with enlightened understandings but no meaningful change.

Table 16.1 should be treated only as a starting point for planning a journey. In reality, a team's time line and path will look different depending on the problem they are trying to solve. One key differentiating factor will be the type of improvement project the team is taking on. As explained previously, improvement projects can involve a) designing something new, b) improving something that exists, or c) spreading successful practices from one place to the next. Projects that focus on improving existing processes may follow the phases in the order described. When teams start off already having diagnosed that they have a situation that requires new design or spread, a different ordering is needed. Design projects start with an aim, focus upfront on designing new changes, and then learn what happens when new practices are put in place. From there, learning cycles can be used to address problems that emerge. Spread projects begin with an aim and changes in mind. They move quickly to learning in practice, taking time to investigate the system as the need arises.

Beyond the type of project, there are different ways to structure a learning journey and different needs depending on the starting context. For some teams, more time learning in practice is needed; for others, more time sourcing change ideas may be required. Teams will need to design their unique time line to align with the resources allocated and the specific nuances of their project.

Figure 16.1 visualizes the improvement journey for three different teams whose work has been described throughout the book.

- The Exemplar school district set out to improve outcomes for students with disabilities by joining a network that had already selected a focus. Still, they spent time understanding the specific outcomes and experiences of special education students in their context. They could move quickly from there to setting a specific aim, identifying changes, and learning in practice. Once they discovered useful changes, they captured them in a change bundle for others to use while moving on to a new project.
- The SMOOTH team proposed to leadership a project focused on improving the safety of medication use. Once the project was approved, they worked to understand the current system and create a charter at the same time. They made important discoveries through learning in practice and paused toward the end of the allocated time to capture their learning for others to use.
- Finally, the Shasta team described in chapter 5, set out to improve literacy outcomes across an entire county. They dedicated a phase of work to understand the system through which they identified first-grade fluency as a high-leverage place to start. They then launched improvement teams of first-grade teachers who focused on learning how to improve formative assessment practices and small-group instruction. This work generated enough momentum that the county decided to continue to work with teams on a new focus.

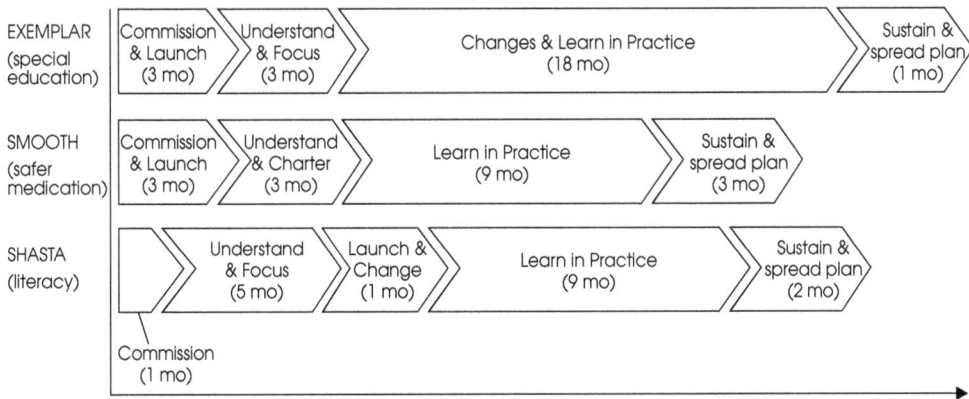

Figure 16.1. Planning the Improvement Journey

The nature of learning journeys is that they take you in unexpected directions. Having a plan and set of milestones upfront can be helpful for organizing the work. Learning consolidations and sponsor check-ins can be scheduled around key decision points, helping the team transition from one phase to another. Equally important is flexibility. A team may arrive at a milestone and decide they need to revise their plans, spending more time in a particular phase or moving in a different direction. The outline of the journey can help the team see the implications of these decisions and reformulate their plans so they can follow the learning and still make it to their destination.

For many teams, the prospect of a journey that is not linear can be difficult to manage. Having a sense of where they are, whether they are progressing—even when it feels like they are not—can help teams maintain momentum and focus. The project progress score and team rubric are two tools that help teams reflect and take stock of their progress as their journey unfolds.

PROJECT PROGRESS SCORE

The Project Progress Score (PPS) is a rubric that supports teams in reflecting on their progress toward their aim (see table 16.2). The rubric can be applied to improvement projects with different aims and those in different industries. It provides a common language to communicate progress made toward improvement.

The rubric is organized using a scale that ranges from 0.5—indicating an intention to engage—to 5.0—indicating outstanding sustainable results. When using the rubric, it is important to note that it is a cumulative scale. Each step of the rubric builds on the elements that precede it. To achieve a 2.5, a team needs to have met the criteria for a score of 0.5, 1.0, 1.5, 2.0, as well as the criteria for the score of 2.5. The aim and outcome measures for the project serve as the main reference point for determining when results have been achieved. A 3.5 indicates demonstrable improvement in at least one of the team's family of measures. Improvement in the outcome measure is required for 4.0 and beyond. Projects with larger, more ambitious aims will move up the scale more slowly than more narrowly scoped ones.

The project progress score is meant to be used as a self-assessment. At times teams calibrate their score with an improvement coach, but mostly the tool exists to give improvement teams the chance to examine their work and assess their own progress. Teams discuss where they think they are, provide evidence for their assessment, and ultimately develop a consensus viewpoint. Ideally, teams would track their progress up the scale as they would

Table 16.2.   Project Progress Score

Project Progress Score	Operational Definition of Project Progress Score
0.5 **Intent to Participate**	A general focus area has been identified, but a specific project has not been selected or the team formed.
1.0 **Team Established**	Team has been identified, but no work has been accomplished. The team has chosen a specific area to investigate.
1.5 **Planning Has Begun**	Organization of the project structure has begun (i.e., meetings are scheduled, required resources and support are identified, tools/materials are gathered, etc.).
2.0 **Activity but No Tests**	Initial learning has begun: investigation about the problem, collection of baseline data, development of initial theory of improvement, and so forth.
2.5 **Tests but No Improvement**	Initial testing cycles have begun. Some measures have been established to track progress. Data displays have been created.
3.0 **Modest Improvement**	Completed tests of changes have produced meaningful learning relevant to the theory of improvement identified in the team's charter. Anecdotal evidence of improvement exists.
3.5 **Improvement**	Testing continues, and additional improvement in project measures toward goals is seen.
4.0 **Significant Improvement**	Expected results are achieved for the identified population or subsystem. Support for implementation has begun (training, documentation of practices, establishment of standard work routines, etc.).
4.5 **Sustainable Improvement**	Data on key measures indicate sustainability of the improvement (i.e., 9–12 data points over time at the new level of performance).
5.0 **Outstanding Sustainable Results**	Project goals and expected results have been accomplished. Organizational changes have been made to accommodate new practices and make the changes permanent.

Source: Bennett, Grunow, and Park 2022, 78–79.

any other measure, over time and graphically. As they do so, it's important to remember that there are no good or bad scores here, just a reflection of where the team currently is with reference to what they set out to achieve.

Progress along the project progress score scale is not expected to move at the same pace (see figure 16.2). Teams move quickly in the early stages as they commission, launch, and begin to engage in improvement work. Progress through the middle of the scale proceeds more slowly. Learning takes time. Plateauing at a score of 3.0 is common until evidence accumulates to indicate that changes are resulting in real improvement for the system or process that is the focus of the project. Once a project achieves a score of 3.5, it is often a relatively rapid ascent to a score of 4 or higher. Often achieving such a score is a matter of patience, waiting for the data to unfold and indicate sustained change. However, if improvement teams have not taken

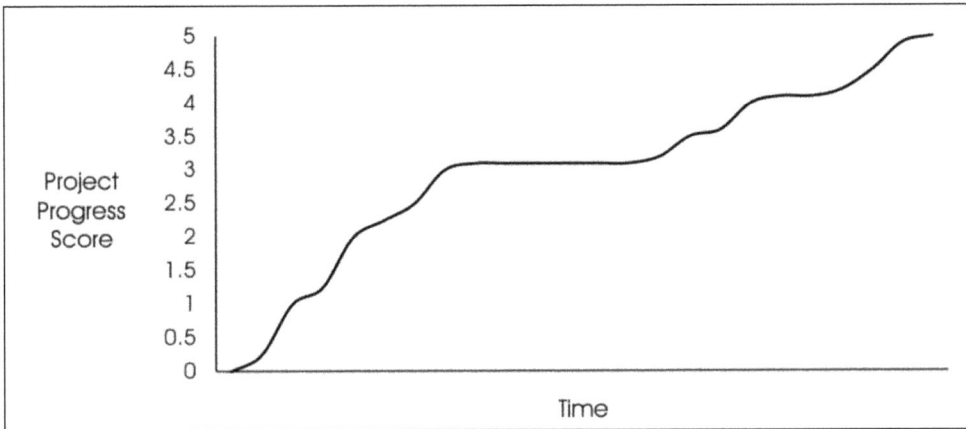

Figure 16.2. Example of Project Progress for an Improvement Team

the steps associated with implementation (see chapter 11), backsliding can occur, and teams may see their improvements devolve as the inertia of the system pushes back against their efforts or focus shifts prematurely to other system priorities.

As teams use the project progress score, they should remember that it is not a judgment, nor does it capture whether they are learning. It simply prompts a reflection on where they are on the journey and where they need to go.

TEAM RUBRIC

In addition to reflecting on the progress of their project, teams also benefit from reflecting on how they are working together as a team. The improvement team rubric in table 16.3 is built around seven core elements that enable collective improvement work. Leadership support, conversational capacity, and effective team rhythms are established at the beginning when improvement is commissioned and launched (chapters 3 and 4). They must continue, not atrophy, for the work to be successful. Inquiry and data propel team learning across the journey. Teams also need quality change ideas based on strong subject matter knowledge when they start testing changes in practice. Well-structured plan-do-study-act (PDSA) cycles focused on ideas that have little potential will fail to produce meaningful learning. Finally, the team will need to reflect regularly on their work with an equity lens, asking themselves whether they are looking for ways that their system is producing differential impact and how the voice of the user is integrated into their work.

The team rubric is intended to be used by teams and coaches to reflect on how they are functioning as an improvement team. The team should take time to celebrate strengths and skills they have developed together. They can also use the rubric in moments when it feels like learning has stalled to diagnose what kind of support would be useful.

Teams and coaches often use the project progress score and team rubric together. The project progress score provides the long view, helping the team think about their progress toward their aim. The team rubric provides more of a formative assessment, helping teams think about their collective learning and how to strengthen it. Teams can set aside time during consolidation moments to engage in these two reflections. Coaches can use the two instruments to think about their coaching and track the progress of the multiple teams that they coach.[2]

Table 16.3.   Improvement Team Rubric

	1 *Red Flag*	2 *Potential Barrier*	3 *Adequate*	4 *Accelerator*
Leadership Support	• Improvement work not connected to organizational priorities • Insufficient allocation of time and/or resources			• Direct tie to organizational priorities; sustained focus • Appropriate time and resources • Regular leader check-ins and barriers removed
Conversational Capacity	• 1–2 people dominate • Disconnected, stilted, safe, or defensive talk			• Equitable talk • Actively build on and challenge each other's assumptions
Rhythm of Learning	• Inconsistent participation of team members • Infrequent, inconsistent, and one-off activities			• Active participation of team members • Efficient and frequent data, testing, and meeting routines
Quality of Change Ideas	• Weak change ideas			• Evidence-based change ideas • Change ideas target high-leverage problems
Productive Inquiry (learning cycles)	• Rote, mechanistic use of PDSAs • No documentation of learning			• Strategic use of PDSAs that produce relevant learning • Reliable documentation • Updating of common theory based on learning
Use of Data	• Little or no use of quantitative or qualitative data			• Regular and efficient use of data to guide learning
Equity Focus	• Silence about inequities • Blaming			• Explicit equity focus • Locate inequities in the system and take responsibility

Source: Bennett, Grunow, and Park 2022, 80.

CONCLUSION

Leaders commission improvement work, and teams set out on a learning journey, all hopeful of what they might accomplish. Achieving the aim will require an openness to discovery and willingness to adapt to new learning when the system responds to changes in surprising ways. After all, if we knew the steps to improved outcomes, we would not need to go on an improvement journey in the first place. A careful balance of planning and flexibility is key to managing the inherent uncertainty. At the beginning of the journey, mapping out how to allocate the time across the phases can help teams maintain forward momentum. Treating the plan not as a rigid set of steps to be followed but, rather as an initial sketch, enables the team to follow the learning where it leads. At regular moments when teams think about what to do next, the project progress score and team rubric can help them look internally, recognizing strengths and deciding what is needed. Along the way, teams get better and better at navigating the winding path that is improvement.

Conclusion

Improvement begins with a powerful inspiration for what can be accomplished. Powerful inspirations are not in short supply in health care, education, and social welfare; these are organizations whose central purpose is to promote the well-being of individuals and communities. Hundreds and thousands of nurses, teachers, social workers, and many more, dedicate their lives to this purpose every single day. Occasionally, society remembers to appreciate their commitment.

And yet, despite these efforts, long-standing, persistent gaps remain between the bold visions we have for all and the sobering reality that those visions are only realized for some. An estimated five hundred thousand people experience homelessness on a given night, eleven million children live in poverty, 7.1 percent of seniors sixty and older are food insecure, and 25 percent of teens today are diagnosed with a mental health condition (Community Solutions n.d.; Children's Defense Fund 2019; Feeding America 2019; Thrive Teen 2023). And this is just in the United States of America.

We wrote this book to provide a practical way forward: teams, drawing on improvement science, actively engaged in redesigning the systems in which they work. Throughout, we drew on examples of teams around the world learning their way into better outcomes: increasing access to early childhood education, providing lifesaving care to people living with HIV, and reducing childhood food insecurity, to name a few. And more teams in different fields are using improvement science to address a host of other issues we all care about collectively, including increasing college access, reducing infant mortality, interrupting the school-to-prison pipeline, and reducing child neglect.

Poverty, hunger, homelessness, and inequitable access to quality education and health care are complex systems issues. Making progress in addressing these issues is generational work. Redesigning and ultimately transforming our systems will require action on multiple fronts—shifting policies, rethinking organizational practice, changing resource flows, interrupting power dynamics, leveraging relationships, and challenging belief systems.

Although we recognize that the use of improvement science to tackle such complex issues has skeptics, we see it as a useful addition to the array of approaches needed to make progress. We believe this primarily because improvement science is fueled by a natural resource: the human capability for collective learning. In most organizations, learning capability is highly underused. Thinking critically and finding solutions all too often are left to leaders, researchers, policy makers, and external evaluators.

Meanwhile, frontline workers and those who must navigate the system to receive the care they deserve waste their time and energy inventing "work-arounds" to do their jobs and get what they need. Organizational leaders further squander this natural resource when they overlook the creativity, knowledge, and expertise that everyone in the system could bring to the table if asked. Finally, most social sector organizations have limited resources to close the gaps between what's needed and what's delivered. Even with access to unlimited resources, it is unlikely that pouring more resources into the same way of working would result in the outcomes we seek. Given these constraints, it seems like a good bet for organizations to double down on the natural resources they do have—dedicated professionals, communities, and families—to leverage collaborative learning in a disciplined way to redesign their shared systems from the inside out.

In addition, improvement science is practical. The core methods and tools are simple to learn and can be used by everyone in the system. This is why they are often foregrounded when people are introduced to the approach. However, although the methods and tools are necessary, they are insufficient and not the stars of the show. Their utility is in their ability to enliven collective learning. When done well, process mapping can help people see how their work is interdependent. An accessible data display can spark a rich conversation that highlights different perspectives about why the system operates the way it does. Crafting an aim statement raises conversations about what is important to whom. Planning or debriefing a plan-do-study-act (PDSA) cycle sets up conversations that surface assumptions and create the space for them to be reconsidered. As seen in these examples, the real star of improvement is making meaning collectively; it is in knowing that the sum of our collective knowledge is greater than that of any one individual—no matter their position on an organizational chart.

Improvement science provides a frame for people to learn together—equal parts technical, relational, and personal. The technical aspects provide practical methods and tools to investigate our systems and organize and introduce change while generating data, both quantitative and qualitative, that can drive joint learning. The relational attributes have the potential to shift power dynamics between leaders and workers, practitioners and researchers, institutions and families, by valuing the expertise everyone has to contribute and promoting collective ownership of the work. The personal habits of improvement require people to engage in honest self-reflection, take responsibility for their actions, and show up in potentially different ways, shifting from knowers and mandators to learners and collaborators. These three attributes together drive collective learning and systems change.

It's also what's needed to pursue arguably the most important redesign challenges that health care, education, and social welfare institutions face: creating more equitable systems that extend the securities and freedoms that some enjoy to everyone. Admittedly, improvement science has not always had equity as its central and explicit focus; it has not always been the primary value on the handle of the magnifying glass used to direct improvement efforts. That said, improvement work *can* be equity centered. The underlying disciplines that inform the theory of improvement science—understanding variation, appreciating systems, investing in the human side of change, and building new knowledge through collective inquiry—are highly relevant when it comes to creating more equitable systems.

The improvement practices can be leveraged as well. Across the improvement journey we have attempted to point out the specific moments where teams can use the improvement practices in the pursuit of equity. Teams can set aims strategically to meet the needs of those who historically have been underserved and disaggregate their data to see whether their efforts are interrupting the disproportionate outcomes our systems are producing. They can use a variety of methods to find and weed out inequitable practices embedded in our systems, even when those working within are doing so with the best of intentions. Through collaboration and conversations, teams can surface and shift away from deficit orientations holding the current status quo in place. When done with intentionality, the improvement practices provide teams with a practical way forward to discover how to redesign systems so that their outcomes are no longer predictably unequal.

In order for improvement to represent a meaningful step forward, it must go beyond a focus on producing more equitable outcomes; as Brandi Hinnant-Crawford reminds us, it must also embrace an equity-centered process. This means asking questions about who has a seat at the improvement table and how their contributions are valued. This is easy to say and harder to do. It takes intentional work, recognizing the ways in which we often unwittingly perpetuate unjust systems despite our stated values and intentions.

"There requires a significant amount of humility and the sharing of power for the improvement process to be equitable. You have to recognize the people [who] may not have your training or your degrees may have the definition of the problem as well as the ingenuity to develop the right solution. And so giving that up is hard for folks" (Hinnant-Crawford 2022).

Given this, perhaps the most important contribution that improvement science can offer to the pursuit of equity is a context and a space that can be leveraged to engage in authentic collaboration among educators, health-care providers, social-welfare professionals, and the individuals and communities they serve.

Our colleague and friend Louis Gomez once told us, "You write what you know, and you teach what you want to learn." For the past decade, we have spent a good portion of our time together teaching improvement to teams in the social sector, using it as an opportunity to wrestle with the ideas and deepen our understanding of the approach. In writing this book, we have attempted to consolidate what we've learned in the hope that it will help others working to create more equitable systems. At the same time, we know that our knowledge is incomplete and will continue to evolve.

This is also true of the field of improvement science. As more teams and organizations take up this approach, apply it to their local context, and share the practical knowledge they gain along the way, our collective learning about how to get to better outcomes as a field will evolve as well. As a result, we will all get smarter together, strengthening our collective ability to transform our social systems.

For us, the leading edge of improvement science is pushing the boundaries of our social systems. Donella Meadows, the brilliant systems thinker whose ideas we have pulled on for much of the book, reminds us that the world is a system where everything is interconnected. "The lesson of boundaries is hard even for systems thinkers to get. There is no single, legitimate boundary to draw around a system. We have to invent boundaries for our sanity; and boundaries can produce problems when we forget that we've artificially created them" (Meadows 2008, 97).

Some of the most exciting improvement work happening now is in cross-sector initiatives that bring together teams and organizations from education, health care, social welfare, and the communities they serve to learn collectively.

This is the future of improvement: standing together humbly and with curiosity, wondering what we can accomplish together, what changes we can make, and how we will know when we have arrived.

Acknowledgments

This book is the product of a system. As authors, our ideas have been shaped by significant experiences and relationships. Some are specifically mentioned below; many more are not. We are grateful to all.

First, and foremost, we would like to thank all the people and organizations that have invited us along on their improvement journeys, sharing their aspirations, their work, their systems, and their stories. Working with multiple organizations and across many fields affords us a broad view. However, much of our learning depends on frontline teams that are deeply rooted in a place, lending their energy and intellect to improve outcomes for those they serve. We owe a special thanks to all the faces behind the improvement cases that are shared throughout the book. You have made the ideas of improvement come alive in ways that we hope will inspire others.

We are particularly indebted to the wisdom of Lloyd Provost and Uma Kotagal, who have shaped our improvement thinking and practice more than anyone else. We appreciate every opportunity to learn from you and feel lucky to call you mentors and friends.

The original push to write this book came from Mark Kerr, and his enthusiasm helped us take the plunge. A set of close colleagues provided critical feedback along the way, helping us see places where the ideas were unclear, incomplete, or not yet useful. Thank you especially to Lloyd Provost, Louis Gomez, Brandi Hinnant-Crawford, Ben Daley, Kelly McMahon, Taqwanda Hailey, Sarah Lundy, Amar Shah, Brittany Gollins, and Sola Takahashi for reading early drafts and offering critical insights.

Our own learning about improvement science would not have been possible were it not for experiences we had while working with the Institute for Healthcare Improvement and the Carnegie Foundation for the Advancement of Teaching. The colleagues and experiences that these organizations provided widened our horizons, pushed our thinking, and gave us incredible learning opportunities. Don Berwick and Tony Bryk played pivotal roles in creating a space for improvement science in our respective fields, affording us career paths that otherwise would have been unavailable. The pioneering work of the Associates in Process Improvement and Cincinnati Children's Hospital Medical Center, combined with their generosity in sharing their expertise with us, has shaped our understanding of improvement in important ways. We send our thanks to the multiple co-learners and coconspirators we have met through these organizations.

Finally, this book is the product of a fifteen-year partnership among the three authors. Writing a book pushed that partnership to a new level. We are grateful to each other for the time, patience, good humor, and perseverance necessary to complete this work.

Appendix A

An Introduction to Shewhart Charts

The most important challenge faced by leaders of organizations, departments, and teams is prediction. Understanding what is likely to come next is a great deal more important than what has come before. How many patients can I expect to show up in my emergency department next week? How many teachers can I expect to be absent from my school next week? How many people will my census reveal as newly unhoused in my community? Questions such as these, big and small, have profound consequences for how we manage (and mismanage) as well as improve our systems. Understanding variation, one of the four domains of improvement science discussed in chapter 1, has the potential to provide improvement teams with deep insights and to predict what comes next.

Most people would agree that variation is everywhere in the world. In the natural world, we have cataloged more than 380,000 variations of plants (World Flora Online n.d.); in the mechanical world, we can name hundreds of different types of cars in production. People vary in everything from height to location, from language to experience. Importantly, processes and systems vary in their ability to meet the needs of the people they serve. As we saw in chapter 7, the rate of maternal mortality varies between race groups in the United States, as do educational outcomes (see chapter 1). Variation in outcomes doesn't just occur between people; it also occurs over time and can display important predictive patterns for what we can expect people to experience if we know how to look (see chapter 5 on understanding hospital discharges). What matters to improvement leaders and improvement teams is the ability to distinguish between variation that is expected, that is common, given the design of our systems, and variation that is unexpected and out of the ordinary, in either good ways (think bright spotting, chapter 9) or in ways we would like to eliminate.

In the 1920s, a physicist, engineer, and statistician, Walter Shewhart, turned toward the problem of prediction. Using his context as a laboratory for learning, he leveraged aspects of both descriptive and inferential statistics to create the control chart method, today commonly known as Shewhart charts, statistical process control charts, or control charts. This style of analysis is concerned primarily with distinguishing between two types of variation.

The first type of variation Shewhart referred to as common cause (or chance cause) variation. He wrote that "any unknown cause of a phenomenon will be termed a chance cause"

(Shewhart 1931/1980, 7). Provost and Murray would clarify this definition further, writing, "Common causes—those causes that are inherent in the system (process or product) over time, affect everyone working in the system, and affecting all outcomes of the system" (Provost and Murray 2022, 124).

The second type of variation present in systems Shewhart referred to as assignable (or special) (Shewhart 1931/1980, 14). We can define these as "Special Causes—those causes that are not part of the system (process or product) all the time or do not affect everyone but arise because of specific circumstances" (Provost and Murray 2022, 124). Importantly, systems and processes that display only common causes of variation are said to be stable and predictable into the near future. Those displaying special causes of variation are unstable and unpredictable. Learning and explanation about the reasons behind this unusual variation in performance is needed.

Imagine your morning commute; perhaps each day you record how much time it takes to get to work. Some days might be 25 minutes, others 26 minutes, still others 31 minutes. What creates this variation in commute time? Invariably people will answer with "the time I leave the house" or "regular traffic on my normal route." These are examples of common causes; they apply every day you go to work. There will be some variation, but what if, expecting to spend twenty-seven minutes on your commute, you found yourself in traffic for forty-five minutes one day? You would similarly expect an explanation for this variance from the norm. Perhaps there was a traffic accident on the bridge, or road construction to repair the surface of the street, or a lane closure. Certainly, there would be an explanation, an assignable or special cause that wasn't there all the time and wasn't predictable on the day you experienced the delay.

In developing this form of analysis, Walter Shewhart created a variety of charts, each specific to a different type of data. Some data falls along a continuous scale: time, money, and workload, for example, can be subdivided continuously. Think about hours, minutes, seconds, and so on. Other things either happen or they do not. Percentages are good examples of this. In the social sector, we use both with some frequency. Is a person unhoused (percentage of the population experiencing homelessness)? How many times did patients fall in our clinic this month (rate of falls)? What is the average score for our school or district on our state math proficiency exam (a continuous measure described by an average)? Each of these is important to leaders and teams because in answering the question we obtain valuable information about how to manage the system.

Despite there being many types of Shewhart charts, all are interpreted using the same set of rules connected to patterns of variation of the observed data. Highlighted in table A.1 are the rules used to distinguish between the presence of either common cause variation or special cause variation in the data set.

At first glance, all Shewhart charts have some distinguishing characteristics. Each is described by up to four elements: the data points, representing the observed data being plotted; the centerline, describing the central tendency of the data plotted (or a portion thereof); and an upper and/or lower limit, which describe the expected variation from the data plotted if that data were being generated by a process or system that displays only common causes of variation. Data falling outside the limits or displaying the patterns described in table A.1 indicate that special causes of variation likely are affecting the performance of the process or system measure being studied. It is important to note that Walter Shewhart insisted that all the data examined be plotted visually in the order in which it was collected because the order might contain important patterns indicating the presence of special causes of variation present in the measure of interest.

Table A.1. Rules for the Detection of Special Cause Variation[1]

Rule	Example
1—Any point outside the limits.	A point exactly on a control limit is not considered outside the limit. When there is no lower or upper control limit, rule 1 does not apply to the side missing the limit.
2—Shift. A run of eight or more points in a row above (shift up) or below (shift down) the centerline.	A point exactly on the centerline does not cancel or count toward a shift.
3—Trend. Six or more consecutive points increasing (trend up) or decreasing (trend down).	Ties between two consecutive points do not cancel or add to a trend. When Shewhart charts have varying limits due to varying numbers of measurements within subgroups, then rule 3 is optional.
4—Two out of three consecutive points near (outer one-third) a limit.	When there is no lower or upper limit, rule 4 usually is not applied to the side missing the limit.
5—Fifteen consecutive points close (inner one-third of the limits) to the centerline.	

Source: Rules for detecting special cause variation (Provost and Murray 2022, 135).

These rules provide leaders and improvement teams with the ability to distinguish important types of variation (common and special) present in their systems. The ability to make this distinction directs how and where improvement occurs. For example, during the stage when improvement teams are working to understand the current system, it is imperative to know whether subgroups (e.g., locations, time periods) differ from each other because of common or special causes of variation. If the causes are common, then fundamental redesign of the system is the only way to improve performance. If special causes are at work, understanding what they are is a critical first step to improvement.

Will reactive changes repair a system to a steady acceptable state, or will fundamental changes be needed to both correct for special causes of variation and to change the average performance of a system to something more desirable? If we observe special causes in a good way, what do we do with that data? This was the case in Arizona (chapter 9), where a team focused on increasing the rate of FAFSA completions used Shewhart charts to discover three schools that were outperforming the rest of their system. Like the team in Arizona, we might learn from and replicate the practices generating such positive deviance to strengthen our systems overall (see chapter 9 for more).

In practice, Shewhart charts are useful throughout the improvement journey, from diagnosis (understanding the current system), to setting aims with an understanding of the common cause variation and average performance we desire (focusing collective efforts), to where special causes might be bright spots worth replicating (generating ideas for change), to where special causes might be statistical evidence that improvement is occurring (learning in practice), to where a common cause state at the level of performance desired indicates a stable, predictable system delivering the intended outcome for a community (sustaining), to time periods when Shewhart charts can help us learn about the uptake of change across a variety of different environments (spread). Their visual nature makes them accessible to everyone, including those without deep statistical knowledge, democratizing the use of quantitative data that too often has been a source of power held over organizations, communities, and groups.

Failing to distinguish between common and special causes of variation in our systems carries significant risks and potential wasteful efforts. Leaders and teams who do not understand or appreciate these differences might overreact to variation they see in their data. Frequently this occurs when people perceive high or low values at a given location or for a specific subgroup as being important or unusual, thinking corrective action is needed when the variation they are seeing is common, indicating no cause for concern or (often more likely) that the whole system needs redesign and corrective action at the point noticed will not result in the desired improvement. Another circumstance in failing to understand common and special cause variation occurs when people fail to perceive variation where important differences are occurring. Just such a circumstance occurred in the Arizona case; leaders nearly missed the opportunity to learn from a bright spot because the person who had created the conditions for the unusually high level of FAFSA completions had lost confidence in the system to notice and was on the verge of leaving the position. These types of hidden losses frequently can occur when leaders of systems and of improvement are unaware of common and special causes of variation in performance.

A more detailed explanation of Shewhart charts is beyond the scope of this text. Readers are encouraged to examine *The Health Care Data Guide: Learning from Data for Improvement* by Provost and Murray (2022) for more on applying Shewhart's theory of variation in the context of social service organizations.

Appendix B

An Overview of Run Charts

A run chart is one of the more accessible and useful statistical tools available to improvement teams trying to understand variation in their systems and, ultimately, trying to answer the question, "how do we know that a change is an improvement?" In its most frequently used form, a run chart plots data as it occurs over time (e.g., in real time, daily, weekly, monthly). The plot of data is usually a line graph (see figure B.1). What distinguishes run charts from more simple line graphs is the addition of a median line, describing the middle value of the data being plotted (Ott 1975, 40; Provost and Murray 2022, 77; Bennett, Grunow, and Park 2022, 183).

The addition of this simple statistic, the median, provides a wealth of insight into the data being plotted. When improvement teams first launch, they are encouraged to investigate their system, and one way to do that is to analyze historically available data. Prior to any change they might introduce, the team can learn about the historic performance of their systems and can use that information to predict future performance of their system should no change occur (i.e., change ideas tested in practice fail to have their intended impact on improving outcomes). The run chart takes advantage of this "baseline" data. A median is calculated for

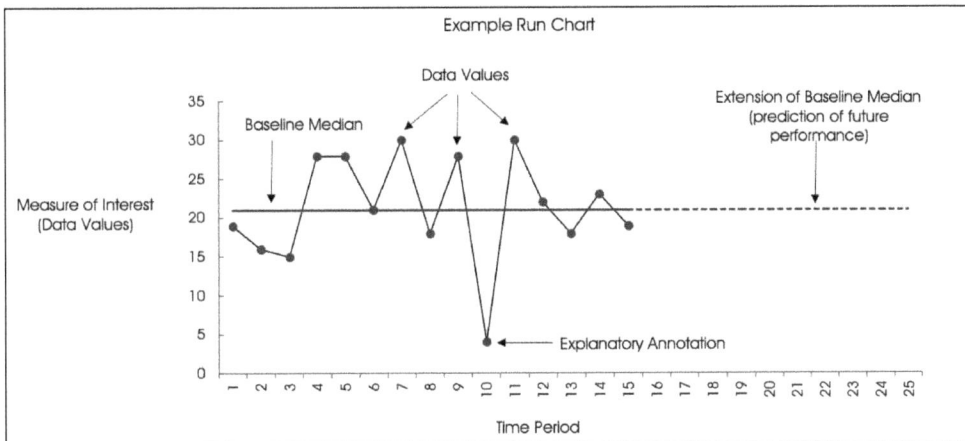

Figure B.1. Elements of a Run Chart

225

the baseline period, then plotted on the chart, and "extended" into the future as a prediction of future performance. Remember, the median is the middle value of the data being plotted. By definition, half the data will fall above and half below the median value. In a future without change, all future values should fall randomly to one side of the median or the other in equal proportions. If future data deviates in some way from this random pattern, the team can observe such a change because they have a baseline median as a guide.

Ideally, such deviations are due to a change the team made in practice. Annotation, linking changes to when they occurred in time, noted on the chart, can help teams increase their degree of belief that the change ideas they are testing in practice are impacting the system in statistically observable ways. However, the reverse is also true; if a change is tested and no change is detected in the performance of the measure targeted for improvement, then teams have disconfirming evidence suggesting the change idea didn't work as intended, and they may need to move to a different change idea. The detectable deviations from baseline can be described using four run chart rules for detecting nonrandom variation (see table B.1).

GUIDANCE FOR USE

Run charts are useful precisely because they are so simple. They don't require users to understand complex statistical computations or to interpret tables of numbers divorced from the interventions they are trying in practice. The interpretation is primarily visual, but the rules are based on probabilities, and so there is guidance for teams about their use to ensure that improvement teams are getting the most from the tool when they apply it.

To use run charts effectively, improvement teams first need to develop and define a measure that is meaningful to their improvement journey. As described in chapter 12, this might be an outcome measure directly tied to a team's aim statement or it might be a process, process step, or balance measure. Typically, the measure chosen to be plotted on a run chart is directly linked to the problem, opportunity, or theory on which a team is focused. Importantly, the measure chosen should capture data occurring independently. That is a statistical way of saying that data at one point in time (or at one location) does not influence the performance of the data at the next point in time (or location). Data that is not independent includes such things as weight. If a person weighs 150 pounds today, it is very likely that he will weigh a similar amount tomorrow. The measure of his weight from one day to the next is not independent, so it would not be a good choice of measure for a run chart. Conversely, the grade point average of one student can be considered independent from that of another student. We would not have any expectation that the grades given to one student would overlap with those of another.

Because the median is so important for detecting nonrandom variation in future performance, it is important to collect enough baseline data to calculate a baseline median that reflects the historic variation in the performance of the system under study. Ten data points is the recommended minimum for creation of a baseline median. In classroom settings, using weekly quizzes and daily exit tickets this might mean from ten days to ten weeks; in healthcare and public-health settings, using monthly measures the baseline period would be ten months, less than a year. In some instances, when data is collected just once per year, as with some educational outcome data, this would mean a ten-year baseline (data spanning this duration is common at the state and federal levels in the United States). When less data is used, it is possible that the baseline median calculated won't reflect the performance of the system ac-

Table B.1. Four Rules for Detecting Nonrandom Variation on a Run Chart

Rule	Example
Shift Six or more consecutive values all above or all below the median.	 *Note:* Values falling on the median do not count toward or against a shift (i.e., they are ignored).
Trend Five or more consecutive values all increasing or all decreasing.	 *Note:* If two consecutive values are the same, for the purpose of counting, the second value is ignored; it neither makes nor breaks the trend.
Too Many or Too Few Runs Occurs when the data line crosses the median line too many or too few times to be considered random (see table B.2).[1]	 | Total # of data points	Min # of runs	Max # of runs	Actual # of runs
---	---	---	---
23	7	17	18	 *Note:* Some data values may fall directly on the median line; these are ignored for the purpose of counting the total values for consideration in determining too many or too few runs.
Astronomical Value The subjective application of subject matter expertise to detect a single value that is blatantly or obviously different from the other data values present on the chart.	 *Note:* This is a non-probability–based rule depending on the application of subject matter expertise.

Source: Provost and Murray 2022, 89–97; Bennett, Grunow, and Park 2022, 187–93.

curately (i.e., enough data may not be present to ensure that the median calculated represents the actual middle value of performance for the measure or system).[2] Above ten data points, the median is unlikely to fluctuate with the addition of new data. It has settled down and is a reasonable estimate of the middle value of the measure of systems performance.

Once baseline data is collected and plotted alongside the baseline median, the run chart should be updated with every new data point collected. Doing so will allow improvement teams to detect changes in performance if and as they occur.

When a shift occurs in the data, the baseline median plotted is no longer a useful prediction of future performance. After ten data points, including those comprising the shift, are available, calculate a new median for what is known as a new phase on the run chart. This new median should then be extended into the future as a prediction of future performance.

Although run charts are easy, straightforward statistical tools that can be applied to measures of almost every improvement journey, they do have drawbacks. Three important weaknesses are:

1. *Astronomical values*—The nature of a median is that its calculation is unaffected by very large or very small values in a data set: 9, 10, and 11 have the same median (10) as 9, 10, and 100 (10). Run charts can't detect large variations from data point to data point. As a result, such large variations in performance can only be interpreted as such by subject-matter experts engaged in conversations about the data they are plotting. For this reason, teams are encouraged to use Shewhart charts (see rule 1, appendix A) to understand individual data values that deviate in unusual ways from the baseline performance of a measure.
2. *Probability-based rules for interpretation and the amount of data collected*—Run charts work as a statistical tool by leveraging probabilities. For example, the probability of six consecutive data values all falling to one side of the median can be calculated by multiplying the probability of one value falling to one side of the median six times ($0.5 \times 0.5 \times 0.5 \times 0.5 \times 0.5 \times 0.5 = 0.01$). In plain English, the likelihood that six data values will fall to one side of the median happening by chance is about $1/100$ (i.e., very unlikely; hence the shift rule). But as the size of a data set increases beyond thirty data values, the probabilities of observing shifts, trends, and too few and too many runs begin to change. As a result, it is not recommended that teams use a run chart with more than thirty data values. Once 20–30 data values are available for analysis, improvement teams are encouraged to switch from a run chart to a Shewhart chart (see appendix A).
3. *Percentages*—Percentages are calculated values, as opposed to observed values. For example, $1/10 = 10\%$ (one observed value), $10/100 = 10\%$ (ten observed values), $100/1000 = 10\%$ (one hundred observed values). In each instance, we have a data point = 10%, but those percentages don't behave in the same way. If we observe one more value, things look very different: $2/10 = 20\%$, $11/100 = 11\%$, and $101/1000 = 10.1\%$. The amount of raw data matters. Unfortunately, run charts cannot distinguish between percentages calculated with small denominators and those calculated with large denominators. As a result, it is recommended that all data values plotted on a run chart have roughly equal denominator sizes (i.e., not varying by more than 25 percent in size from the average denominator size).

Although run charts are simple to create and use, like any tool, there is room for nuisance in their application, more than can be explored here. For more on run charts and special considerations for their use, improvement teams are encouraged to consult *The Health Care Data Guide: Learning from Data for Improvement* by Provost and Murray (2022).

Table B.2. Determining the Presence of Too Many or Too Few Runs on a Run Chart

Total number of data points displayed on the run chart (excluding any data points falling exactly on the median).	Minimum number of runs needed for random variation. (If there are fewer than this number, nonrandom variation is detected.)	Maximum number of runs allowed for random variation. (If there are more than this number, nonrandom variation is detected.)
10	3	9
11	3	10
12	3	11
13	4	11
14	4	12
15	5	12
16	5	13
17	5	13
18	6	14
19	6	15
20	6	16
21	7	16
22	7	17
23	7	17
24	8	18
25	8	18
26	9	19
27	10	19
28	10	20
29	10	20
30	11	21

Source: Provost and Murray 2022, 92; Bennett, Grunow, and Park 2022, 191.

Appendix C

Improvement Habits

Habits are things we do regularly without consciously thinking about it. While not easy, existing habits can evolve, new habits can be created, and old habits can be discarded. In improvement, there are eight major mental habits that we look for and encourage in improvement team members. (Bennett, Grunow, and Park 2022, 19).

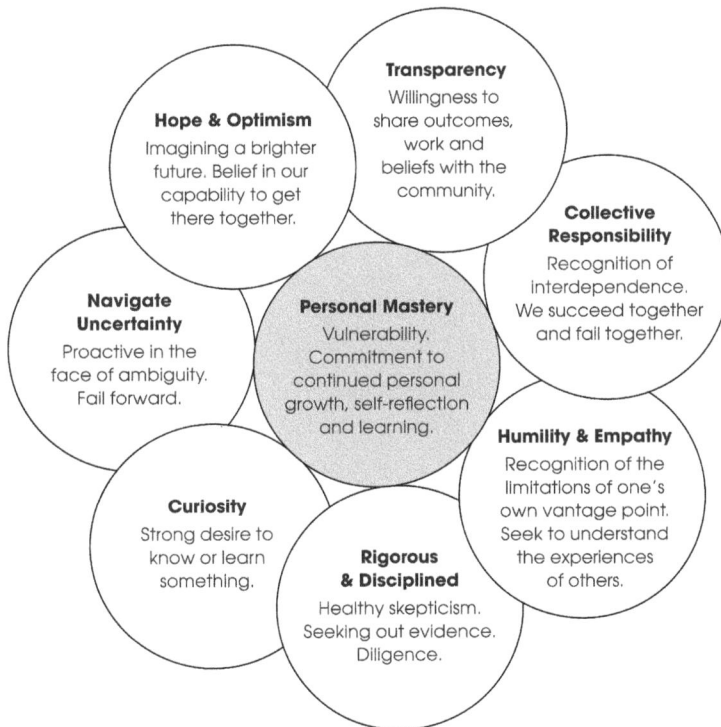

Figure C.1.   Improvement Habits
Source: Bennett, Grunow and Park 2022, 19

Notes

INTRODUCTION

1. For examples of reports with compelling calls to action in education and health care, see *To Err Is Human: Building a Safer Health Care in America* (Institute of Medicine and Committee on Quality of Health Care in America 2000); *Crossing the Quality Chasm: A New Health System for the 21st Century* (Institute of Medicine and Committee on Quality of Health Care in America 2001); and *A Nation at Risk: The Imperative for Educational Reform* (U.S. Department of Education 1983).

2. Alicia Grunow.

3. There is a technical distinction between the terms "improvement science" and "quality improvement" that we are choosing to smooth over here. Quality improvement is the umbrella field encompassing all methodologies concerned with approaches, methods, and tools to change processes, products, and services to better match the needs of customers. Improvement science is one specific branch within the field of quality improvement based on the theoretical assumptions described in the text box. Statistician and management expert W. Edwards Deming is credited with launching the broader field of quality improvement, and his ideas led directly to the definition of improvement science. The first to use the term "improvement science" were those who worked directly with Deming, Langley et al. in their 1996 book *The Improvement Guide*, and it was further described by Perla, Provost, and Parry in 2013.

Technically, some improvement methodologies the reader may have heard of such as lean, Six Sigma, implementation science, and so forth, do not draw on the same theoretical foundations articulated in the science of improvement, but they would be considered quality improvement approaches. Practitioners focused on improvement of their systems are likely to encounter both the terms "quality improvement" and "improvement science." While distinguishing between the two has important implications for theory translating to practice, the authors recognize that many will find drawing strict boundaries unnecessary or even unhelpful when working with their teams. Practically, the tools and methods may overlap. Therefore, we use the term "improvement science" colloquially to refer to the field as well as technically to the theory that backstops the methods and tools presented throughout this book.

In some contexts, particularly in education, the term "continuous improvement" is preferred over "improvement science." In the larger improvement literature, continuous improvement is often used more narrowly to refer to important efforts to continually make changes to existing practices but not necessarily including designing new practices, often called innovation. Therefore, we prefer the term improvement science in which design, improvement, and spread are all included. However, it is the practice and not the language that ultimately matters. Teams and organizations should use the language that works in their context.

4. For example, R. A. Fisher at Rothamsted Agricultural Experiment Station in the United Kingdom and Walter Shewhart at Bell Laboratories in the United States in the 1920s, as well as the Japanese Union of Scientists and Engineers in the late 1940s.

5. Improvement organizations use improvement science as their primary management framework in contrast with organizations managed in more traditional ways such as management by objective, autocratic management, or laissez-faire management.

CHAPTER 1

1. Note: the stated purpose of a system is not always its actual or *common purpose*. As Meadows writes, "Purposes are deduced from behavior, not from rhetoric or stated goals" (Meadows 2008, 14).

2. Systems have been defined in many ways in the literature. Senge defines systems as "a perceived whole whose elements 'hang together' because they continually affect each other over time and operate toward a common purpose" (Senge et al. 1994). Meadows defines systems twice: "A system is a set of things—people, cells, molecules or whatever—interconnected in such a way that they produce their own pattern of behavior over time" and "an interconnected set of elements that is coherently organized in a way that achieves something" (Meadows 2008). Langley et al. define systems as "an interdependent group of items, people, or processes with a common purpose" (Langley et al. 2009). Our definition summarizes these, borrowing important ideas and language to do so.

3. In his seminal article, "Public Good, Private Goods: The American Struggle over Educational Goals" (1997), education historian David Labaree identifies "three alternative goals for American education that have been at the root of educational conflicts over the years: democratic equality (schools should focus on preparing citizens), social efficiency (they should focus on training workers) and social mobility (they should prepare individuals to compete for social positions)."

4. A number of systems frameworks that organizations might choose to adopt focus directly on equity. Two notable frameworks are Kania, Kramer, and Senge's "Six Conditions of Systems Change" and the National Equity Project's "Lens of Systemic Oppression" (Kania, Kramer, and Senge 2018; National Equity Project 2020). Both draw attention to the interactions among individual, interpersonal, and organizational factors. The social systems we intend to improve can also be described as complex under Snowden's Cynefin Framework, containing interactions that are nonlinear with "the whole being greater than the sum of its parts" (Snowden and Boone 2007).

5. Systems-thinking scholars sometimes refer to the term "mental models": "habits of thought—deeply held beliefs and assumptions and taken for granted ways of operating that influence how we think, what we do, and how we talk" (Kania, Kramer, and Senge 2018). The authors here equate the term "mental models" with beliefs and mind-sets.

6. Cystic fibrosis: "From 2000 to 2010, median forced expiratory volume in 1 s increased from 81.7% to 100.1% predicted and median body mass index increased from the 35th to the 55th percentile." Surgical site infections: "The Class I and II SSI rate decreased from 1.5 per 100 procedure days at baseline to 0.54 per 100 procedure days, a 64% reduction" (Institute for Healthcare Improvement 2005; Siracusa et al. 2014; Ryckman et al. 2009).

7. The authors distinguish between capacity—having the resources (time, human, financial) necessary to accomplish something—and capability—having the knowledge of how to do something—throughout this text.

8. For more on Cincinnati Children's transformational journey, see "Being the Best at Getting Better," a conversation between Uma Kotagal, MD, and Amy Compton-Phillips, MD, published in the *NEJM Catalyst* in 2016; and *Harvard Business Review* case study "Cincinnati Children's Hospital Medical Center" by Tucker and Edmondson (2009/2011).

9. The diagram in figure 1.2 is an adaptation of the diagram published by Langley et al. 2009, which includes values on the handle of a "lens" useful for examining systems targeted for improvement efforts.

10. These four types of improvement knowledge were described as the Systems of Profound Knowledge by W. Edwards Deming (Deming 1993/2000).

In *Learning to Improve*, the authors organize the discussion of improvement science in education using six principles: 1) be problem focused and user centered, 2) attend to variability, 3) see the system, 4) embrace measurement, 5) learn through disciplined inquiry, and 6) organize as networks. The six principles were inspired by and can be cross walked to the four domains of improvement knowledge. However, the focus on networks is an addition, and the importance of the "human side of change" is not emphasized. Either framework can be useful, depending on the purpose or discussion.

11. W. Edwards Deming referred to this as Theory of Knowledge, a term coined by American philosopher C. I. Lewis in his book *Mind and the World Order: Outline of a Theory of Knowledge*. Lewis is often credited with helping define "Conceptual Pragmatism" within the field of philosophy (Lewis 1956).

12. This definition of equity is adapted from definitions provided by Aguilar in Coaching for Equity and from the National Equity Project (https://www.nationalequityproject.org/). We acknowledge that people and organizations define equity in different ways. For this book, we use this definition.

13. For an example of racial disparities in health care, see Weinstein et al. (2017). For documentation of racial disparities in education, see Reardon, Kalogrides, and Shores (2019).

14. "Intersectionality means the examination of race, sex, class, national origin, and sexual orientation and how their combinations play out in various settings" (Delgado and Stefancic 2000, 51).

15. Improvement science in health care has a history of focusing on these dimensions of quality: safe, effective, patient centered, timely, efficient, and equitable (Committee on Quality of Health Care in America and Institute of Medicine 2001, 39). However, only in recent years have practitioners turned their attention toward the final dimension—equitable—using the science of improvement to reduce inequities long present in our systems.

16. Although certain types of expertise are often associated with specific role groups (e.g., academics and research knowledge, organizational leaders, and professional knowledge), we recognize that individuals often bring multiple types of knowledge to the table and should not be limited in sharing what they know based on a specific role they play.

17. See note 3 in the introduction on classifying differing methodologies. See also *Improvement Science at Your Fingertips* for a time line cataloging the emergence of different methodologies (Bennett, Grunow, and Park 2022, 9).

18. The authors choose to bold the word "we" in each question of the Model for Improvement, a departure from its original instantiation, to emphasize the inclusive nature of the improvement journey. The idea of equity of voice and a consistent return to the question of "Who is at the table?" during the entire improvement journey occurs throughout the text. This small change is a reminder to not lose sight of this important relational perspective.

19. The Carnegie Foundation, in its book *Learning to Improve*, which introduces improvement science to the field of education, made changes to the wording and organization of the Model for Improvement. Many organizations have put into common use this modification of the original, which states the questions this way: "What specifically are we trying to accomplish?," "What changes might we introduce and why?," and "How will we know that a change is actually an improvement?" (Bryk et al. 2015, 114). Teams should use the wording that works best for them. In addition, some teams find it helpful to change the order of the three questions of the Model

for Improvement. The authors recommend doing this whenever it is helpful but note that for any improvement journey in time it will be very important to formulate answers to all three questions.

20. The same framework can also be used to structure more complicated analytic designs such as times series and factorial designs.

21. One advantage of using the improvement journey map is that it creates space to apply many different improvement tools that may be relevant during specific phases. We will introduce several key tools for each phase throughout the book, but it will not be an exhaustive list.

22. An interesting side note on "understanding the current system" as a distinct step. The need to understand the current system was not overlooked by the authors of *The Improvement Guide*. Around the time that the Model for Improvement was being developed, improvement professionals had a long history of analyzing the current system. In fact, teams often got stuck in the analysis phase of the work.

In creating the Model for Improvement, the authors intentionally biased the method toward learning by doing to avoid the tendency toward analysis paralysis. They locate methods for understanding the system in chapter 6: "Developing a Change." Thirty years after the invention of the Model for Improvement, it is more common for improvement professionals to start by doing, forgetting to dedicate time to understand what is currently happening. After working for years in the social sector, we have chosen to put this step back in as an important starting place.

The tendency toward "solutionitis" in the social sector is still strong, and the authors find it useful to emphasize the need to slow down and investigate at the start of a journey. However, the tendency toward "analysis paralysis" is still real and should be mitigated against.

23. Useful references on the dynamics and difficulty of changing teaching practice generally and mathematics practice specifically include *The Teaching Gap* (Stigler and Hiebert 2009), *Tinkering Towards Utopia* (Tyack and Cuban 1995), and "A Revolution in One Classroom" (Cohen 1990).

PART I

1. For a description of habits that embody an improvement culture, see appendix C.

CHAPTER 2

1. In their article, Liebman and Cruikshank (2017) describe various governance (leadership) models in the education sector. Bureaucratic governance structures rely on top-down, command-and-control methods where the front line implements programs as prescribed by leadership. This is a typical form of governance based on distrust of the worker and operating on fear that can be traced back to the birth of the modern manager in the Industrial Revolution (Edmonson 2012). In contrast, professionalism or craft governance models emphasize the autonomy of professionals (such as physicians or teachers) to make decisions based on their clinical expertise. Evolutionary learning, which aligns most closely to improvement science, "employs flexible governance structures supporting iterative improvement processes that respond to problems and variable circumstances as they arise" (Liebman and Cruikshank 2017, 416). In this model, centralized managers and frontline workers share decision-making authority. Managers set the general direction and goals for the organization and create the conditions necessary for frontline workers to own the day-to-day operations to engage in problem solving. As leaders assume improvement science ways of working, the implied shift of governance model is one of the most subtle yet important shifts. For a summary of the tensions that improvement teams face, see Cohen-Vogel, Harrison, and Cohen-Vogel 2022, 325–47.

2. Authors who study learning organizations highlight the importance of teaming in organizational learning. Organizations learn, not through individuals getting smarter but through collectives getting smarter (Senge 1990; Katzenbach and Smith 1993; Edmondson 2012).

3. A particularly poignant example from Richard Elmore: "Only about one in ten teacher teams that I observe functions at a level that would result in any improvement of instructional practice and student learning in the classroom" (Troen and Boles 2012, xv).

4. More specifically, the key tool that supports improvement teams is the Model for Improvement (see chapter 1). In answering the first two questions in the Model for Improvement—What specifically are we trying to accomplish? How will we know if a change is an improvement?—teams commit to a common aim and a common set of measures to discipline conversations about whether they are getting there. The articulation of "change ideas" and the PDSA cycle to test ideas in practice provide the team with a common "working approach" to guide team learning.

5. Katzenbach and Smith (1993) are careful to highlight that the point is not to turn every small group into a highperforming team. To be sure, working groups are a functional way of addressing many organizational tasks, such as sharing information or making decisions. This classification is useful in providing a language to describe different ways small groups tend to work together.

6. Our experience in combination with reading the research on teams suggests that 4–6 persons is an ideal size. The research literature on teams consistently supports the notion that larger team sizes pose co-

ordination challenges that get in the way of team performance. Katzenbach and Smith note that smaller teams are more likely than larger teams to successfully work through "individual, functional, and hierarchical differences toward a common plan and hold themselves jointly accountable for results" (Katzenbach and Smith 1993, 42). In addition, Edmondson, Dillon, and Roloff, citing Sarin and McDermott (2003), note, "Team size was negatively related to learning, possibly because of the additional challenge of coordinating and communicating among more people" (Edmondson, Dillon, and Roloff 2007, 21).

7. Some organizations will also give the key supports a name, such as an "advisory group." This can help balance the intention of being inclusive while still empowering a specific team.

8. As teams evolve from real to high-performing teams, leadership responsibilities tend to become more distributed across the team (Katzenbach and Smith 1993, 79). However, early in the life of a team a designated team lead serves the critical role described.

9. An individualized education program (IEP) is a plan or program developed to ensure that a child with an identified disability who is attending an elementary or secondary educational institution receives specialized instruction and related services.

CHAPTER 3

1. Guidance on how to create the centralized infrastructure required to effectively support an improvement network is an important topic but beyond the scope of this book. For more on improvement networks, see "The Breakthrough Series: IHI's Collaborative Model for Achieving Breakthrough Improvement " (Institute for Healthcare Improvement 2003); and *Learning to Improve* (Bryk et al. 2015); and "Building a Learning Healthcare System Network: Modules" (James M. Anderson Center for Health Systems Excellence 2020). However, improvement networks depend on high-functioning improvement teams across local contexts. The guidance in this book is relevant for those responsible for leading and supporting those teams.

2. In his book *The Fifth Discipline* (1990), Peter Senge calls this common dynamic in organizations "shifting the burden" (Senge 1990). In this dynamic, organizations respond quickly with seemingly obvious solutions to a problem. Often these quick fixes address the symptoms of a problem, not the problem itself. What's more, in providing short-term relief to the problem, they impede investments in "fundamental solutions" that attack its root cause. Recognizing this tendency (and then avoiding it) can help leaders and teams productively lead systems change.

3. This power imbalance can occur whenever an individual engaged in the work—a team lead, coach, researcher, doctor—is perceived as "the expert."

CHAPTER 4

1. This point was popularized with Bruce W. Tuckman in 1965. His article Developmental Sequence in Small Groups" described in easy-to-remember language the "Stages of Group Development." These included forming, storming, norming, performing, and adjourning (Tuckman 1965, 384–99).

2. In sharing stories, it is important to be aware that storytelling should be invitational. Care should be taken to avoid "tokenizing" people in marginalized groups or giving them the responsibility to teach others about their experiences.

3. We focus on conversations about race in the context of equity-focused improvement because of the prevalence of race-based drivers of inequity in the health care and education sectors in the United States. When the focus of improvement work seeks to interrupt inequities based on other characteristics such as gender, disability, or language, teams also need to build their conversational capacity to take on hard topics specific to the focus area.

4. For an overview of how huddles are used in health care to manage complexity, support quality improvement, and promote high reliability, see *Health Care Huddles: Managing Complexity to Achieve High Reliability* (Provost et al. 2015).

PART II

1. Over the years, the guidance on the need for an explicit phase dedicated to understanding the system as part of the journey has oscillated. Some improvement approaches, such as Lean and the Toyota Production System, place a heavy emphasis on understanding the system to pinpoint the exact root causes of a problem. The implied assumption behind this approach is that once the root causes are known, the necessary changes become self-evident and just need to be implemented and monitored. However, one of the observations of the authors of *The Improvement Guide* was the tendency of improvement teams to get bogged down in analysis paralysis (Langley et al. 2009, 142). They too believed in the importance of understanding the system but developed a different approach that emphasized trying to change the system as a way to understand it. The theory implied here is that when you make a change to the system, you provoke it in ways that allow the system to reveal itself. Based on our experiences, we have chosen to put this step back in as an important starting place. The tendency toward "solutionitis" in the social sector is still strong, and we find it useful for teams to investigate the system as part of the journey, while mitigating the tendency toward analysis paralysis.

CHAPTER 5

1. Figure 5.1 displays a cross-sectional analysis of literacy outcomes; it is a snapshot that compares the outcomes of students in different grade levels at a single point in time. The shortcomings of cross-sectional analyses are that they conflate growth and cohort differences. A more sophisticated analysis of literacy outcomes would take a longitudinal view, enabling the team to follow the growth trajectories of cohorts of students over time. In this instance, a longitudinal analysis could determine whether the same students who struggle with literacy in middle school showed signs of struggle as early as third grade. The downside of longitudinal analyses is that they are difficult to produce, requiring more advanced data skills and sophisticated data systems that link student data over time. For this team, the more readily available cross-sectional view of data presented in figure 5.1, along with their professional experience, provided enough information to convince them they should be working on early-grade literacy.

2. "Persons who had experienced four or more categories of childhood exposure, compared to those who had experienced none, had 4- to 12-fold increased health risks for alcoholism, drug abuse, depression, and suicide attempt; a 2- to 4-fold increase in smoking, poor self-rated health, ≥50 sexual intercourse partners, and sexually transmitted disease; and a 1.4- to 1.6-fold increase in physical inactivity and severe obesity" (Felitti et al. 1998, 245).

3. Fluency refers to an individual's ability to read with speed, accuracy, and proper phrasing and expression. Fluency is correlated to reading comprehension; to understand what they read, students need to be able to read fluently, whether they are reading aloud or silently.

4. Formative assessment refers to a variety of methods educators use to evaluate students' current understanding of specific concepts, learning needs, and academic progress. The information is used to inform ongoing instruction and student learning.

5. Peter Senge describes the importance of being able to hold "creative tension" between a vision and the current reality as one of the five core disciplines of a learning organization. He calls this discipline "personal mastery" (Senge 1990). Recognizing the gaps between the current reality and visions is inherently uncomfortable; as a result, a human tendency is to release the tension—either by not facing the current reality or by collapsing the vision down to what already is. Investigating the system requires counteracting that tendency, both holding onto the vision and facing into the current reality at the same time.

6. All that said, if teams do not like the language of problems, they can substitute the term "opportunities." Some teams use the informal, made-up term "probletunity."

7. We use data throughout the text in a broad sense to include both quantitative and qualitative data. Data can be defined as "documented observations or the results of performing a measurement process.

The concept of data refers to strings or patterns of characters that describe some aspect of the world" (Provost and Murray 2022). In improvement work, data includes qualitative data generated through empathy methods, documented observations of practice, feedback from stakeholders (including end users) as well as from such quantitative sources as historically available measures and project measures.

8. Learning cycles that focus on investigation can be structured as plan-do-study-act cycles (see chapter 11) as is suggested in *The Improvement Guide* (Langley et al. 2009). Most people associate PDSA cycles with testing changes, so we avoid using the term here, opting instead for the more general term "learning cycle." When the investigative cycle is structured as a PDSA, the *planning* involves specifying a question along with the method and data that will be used to answer it. *Doing* entails collecting or finding the data. The *study* entails analyzing and making sense of the data collected (e.g., creating a chart, pulling out key insights from empathy methods, marking up a process map). In the *act* portion, teams decide what to do next.

9. Researchers typically define chronic absenteeism as missing more than 10 percent of school days. Chronic absenteeism has been linked to lower levels of achievement using a range of academic outcomes (Attendance Works 2018).

10. For more about Community Design Partners, see https://www.communitydesignpartners.com.

11. This example describes a six-month-long, district-wide effort to understand chronic absenteeism. The same sort of process could be used on a much smaller scale by a single team in a single school. The inclusion of a wide set of stakeholders afforded the district the opportunity to build common understandings and collect a great deal of data. As a trade-off, it took more resources and time.

12. It is worth noting again that conducting one hundred empathy interviews is an exceptional effort. The perceived need to get a comprehensive view can be an unnecessary barrier to seeking the users' perspectives. Teams can learn a great deal by conducting a handful of empathy interviews, which can be accomplished within a single week.

13. The creation of headlines proceeds much in the same way as an affinity analysis. Interviews are examined for themes, and then themes are grouped together. For more on headlining, see *Improvement Science at Your Fingertips: A Resource Guide for Coaches of Improvement* (Bennett, Grunow, and Park 2022, 85–86).

14. These themes can also be summarized using affinity analysis and/or a cause-and-effect diagram, which we will describe in chapter 6.

15. Improvement teams should exercise caution in making meaning from very small sample sizes as they may not be representative of the experience of most end users. The choice of who to interview and how many interviews to conduct should be informed by subject matter experts on the team to mitigate for this possible eventuality.

16. For more guidance and specific protocols on empathy methods, see *Improvement Science at Your Fingertips* (Bennett, Grunow, and Park 2022, 83–87).

17. Data is analyzed here using Shewhart control charts. Shewhart charts analyze data looking for "common causes" and "special causes" of variation in data. Common causes are defined as "those causes that are inherent in the system (process or product) all the time, affect everyone working in the system, and affecting all outcomes of the system" (Provost and Murray 2022, 124). "Common causes" of variation differ from "special causes" and are defined as "those causes that are not part of the system (process or product) all the time or do not affect everyone, but arise because of specific circumstances" (Provost and Murray 2022, 124). Specific patterns are used to detect special cause variation (see *The Health Care Data Guide: Learning from Data for Improvement* by Murray and Provost [2022]), one of which is the oscillating pattern seen in figure 5.3. For a brief explanation of Shewhart charts, see appendix A.

18. The days that were "unusually low" were identified as "special causes" by a Shewhart chart. For more on Shewhart charts, see appendix A.

19. In chapter 1, we describe a system as "an interconnected set of elements that is coherently organized in a way that achieves something." Organizational practices are only one kind of element that makes up a system. Structures, power dynamics, and beliefs also come into play. There are numerous tools and methodologies for mapping systems more broadly (e.g., causal loop diagrams, linkage of processes, stakeholder maps, iceberg model, and so forth). There are situations where systems mapping

may be useful for a team, particularly for long-term, complex improvement efforts where stakeholders are working together for the first time. However, for most teams starting by mapping key practices is a more accessible and useful starting point even though it is not a good method to see the whole system.

20. KwaZulu-Natal is roughly the size of Indiana.

21. The hospital team described in this case was part of a large improvement network made up of 16 hospitals and 264 primary care clinics across the province. The two-year initiative, the 20,000 Lives campaign, was launched by Professor Nigel Rollins in partnership with the Institute for Healthcare Improvement with the aim of reducing the mother-to-child HIV transmission rate from 21 percent of births to <5 percent (Institute for Healthcare Improvement 2008).

22. For an excellent treatment on the role of organizational routines in creating racial inequities in schools, see Lewis and Diamond 2015; Diamond and Gomez 2023.

23. Teams can choose to create a simple system map at this point. The simplest way to do this is to list each process on a sticky note and arrange them on a board (or slide) along with the outcome. Arrows can be added to represent important interconnections between processes. This system map can then be used to prioritize processes and/or interconnections to further explore.

24. In analyzing the process, it can be helpful to start by defining quality for the process. Quality can refer to any number of dimensions from how long a process takes, to its rate of success, to its reliability when applied across contexts, to fairness when applied to diverse populations.

25. One variation on a process map that can be useful in analyzing the current system is the "process failure analysis." In this version, teams create a basic process map with a level of detail of about 5–7 steps. Below each step, the team can record ways in which the step breaks down. Above each step teams can record change ideas as they occur. For more on process failures analysis, see *Improvement Science at Your Fingertips: A Resource Guide for Coaches of Improvement* (Bennett, Grunow, and Park 2022).

26. The learning agenda format is fashioned after a K-W-L chart that has been used since the 1980s to structure independent learning in classrooms (*K* for know, *W* for want, and *L* for learned).

CHAPTER 6

1. We choose the terms "leverage points" and "cause-and-effect analysis" over "root causes" and "root-cause analysis" for analyzing social systems. In manufacturing, it is often possible to identify a singular root cause (i.e., a specific machine) that is responsible for a high number of defects. However, social systems are dynamic, and it is not always possible to identify factors a team can isolate and remove. Looking for "leverage points" that are actionable and might tilt the system in a healthier direction feels like a more accurate depiction of social systems improvement. That said, from a practical perspective teams should use the language they prefer.

2. Both these tools are part of the original seven basic tools for quality highlighted by Dr. Kaoru Ishikawa in his now classic book *Guide to Quality Control* (Ishikawa 1982).

3. Oftentimes, the cause categories are identified through logically grouping causes according to themes generated by the team studying the system. Some teams find it useful to use standard categories for the cause categories. Historically these are materials, methods, equipment, measurement, environment, and people (Bennett, Grunow, and Park 2022, 122). However, Brandi Hinnant-Crawford offers a different and useful list for the field of education: structural causes, organizational causes, policy causes, ideological causes, capacity causes, historical causes, resources causes, and practice/pedagogical causes (Hinnant-Crawford 2020, 53).

4. The "five whys" protocol, attributed to Tachii Ohno, is often used in facilitating identification of "root causes" (Hinnant-Crawford 2020, 50–51). This protocol prompts people to take a cause they identify and ask "why" multiple times until they get beneath the symptoms of a problem to more of a root cause. It's not always necessary to ask why exactly five times; rather, the idea is that people ask why until they get to something that feels like a key cause and yet is still actionable. Getting to "poverty" as a cause, for example, is not particularly useful as what action to take on poverty is not readily apparent.

5. The example in this section is a continuation of the case from chapter 5 and represents the work of Community Design Partners.

6. Quality management scholar Joseph Juran coined the phrase "Pareto principle" after observing a natural phenomenon that occurs in a group of data where a "vital few" factors rather than the "trivial many" contribute to the bulk of an effect (Pyzdek and DeFeo 2019).

7. It's worth noting that the Pareto principle applies specifically to the frequency of occurrence. At times something may be rare but important. A Pareto analysis can't reveal these situations; instead, subject matter expertise must be used to pick up on these cause categories.

8. This analysis came out of early work done by the Carnegie Foundation for the Advancement of Teaching as part of the Carnegie Math Pathways. To learn more about this work, see https://carnegiemath pathways.org/.

9. This example of a Pareto analysis, like many, does not conform perfectly to the 80:20 rule. If you follow the line graph, you will notice it takes four of the cause categories to get to 80 percent (84 percent, to be exact). In other words, 67 percent of the causes (four out of six) are responsible for 80 percent of the problem. This does not make the analysis any less useful, however. The value of the Pareto analysis is not in conforming to the 80:20 rule but in helping teams see which causes are more prevalent than others.

10. The seminal article on cognitive biases was written by Tversky and Kahneman in 1974. Since then, cognitive researchers have explored, named, and demonstrated many cognitive biases. In the table, we choose six well-established cognitive biases that are particularly relevant for improvement work. The definitions in the table are adapted from Decision Lab's easy-to-use online resource (Biases, *The Decision Lab*).

The reader may be surprised that "implicit bias" is not listed in the table of cognitive biases. Implicit bias generally refers to "negative attitudes or judgments, of which one is not consciously aware, against a specific social group." Implicit-bias training has become a popular component of organizational training programs focused on diversity and inclusion. It is omitted here not due to irrelevance; that all of us have unconscious prejudices is not in doubt. However, from a cognitive bias perspective, the biases listed in table 6.1 explain how people often unconsciously "form negative attitudes or judgments against a social group." From an equity perspective, the attention only on unconscious attitudes is problematic; both implicit and explicit beliefs about groups of people are important to examine (for more, see Goldhill 2017).

11. The ladder of inference was first published by organizational learning expert Chris Argyris. It was popularized in Peter Senge's *The Fifth Discipline* (1990).

12. The larger cultural narrative that we are rational, objective human beings also gets in the way of recognizing the limitations of our own thinking. Social psychologist Lee Ross, in fact, coined the term "naive realism" to describe this bias: "[we] believe our perception of the world reflects it exactly as it is, unbiased and unfiltered. We don't think our emotions, past experiences, or cultural identity affect the way we perceive the world and thus believe others see it in the same way as we do" (The Decision Lab n.d.).

CHAPTER 7

1. According to the National College Attainment Network (NCAN), summer melt is "the phenomenon of college-intending students who have applied to, been accepted by, and made a deposit to a college or university, but fail to matriculate to that college (or any other) in the fall following their high school graduation" (Ash 2021).

2. Between January and June 2014, the overall median enrollment at the early childhood education centers increased from 76.4 to 88.9 percent; overall median attendance increased from 44.9 to 59.2 percent (Tyler, Davies, and Bennett 2018).

3. The Red Cross is an example of holding a general "aim" while remaining committed to focusing on the specific needs of the subset of the community experiencing disproportionally worse outcomes. Around the globe the Red Cross and Red Crescent are known to be apolitical: "The global Red Cross

and Red Crescent Movement—including the American Red Cross—utilizes the emblem to signify our promise of voluntary, neutral and impartial assistance to all people in need, regardless of race, religion or citizenship status" (American Red Cross 2020).

4. How we think about setting this target is what differentiates an aim statement from SMART goals and objectives as they are typically used in organizations. Traditionally, SMART goals are defined as specific, measurable, attainable, relevant, and time bound. Aim statements are similar to SMART goals with one important distinction. The targets set in aim statements should be ambitious, not attainable. SMART goals most often have been used in accountability frames, where there are negative consequences if the target isn't met. Because of this, organizations tend to set safe incremental targets that are "attainable" that don't necessarily require redesign of the system to achieve as opposed to "ambitious" goals that do require fundamental change to the system.

PART IV

1. Organizational learning scholar Chris Argyris identifies "defensive reasoning" as the key barrier to organizational learning. Defensive reasoning is the tendency of people in organizations to keep their assumptions, inferences, and conclusions private or tacit. This is a deeply socialized self-protection mechanism that allows people to avoid the social threat that arises when we are wrong or we have inconsistencies between our beliefs and actions. It also produces a "closed loop," preventing learning. Argyris argues that organizational learning requires flipping this dynamic, creating conditions where premises and inferences can be made explicit and tested in the world of practice. The ladder of inference, described in chapter 6, is a helpful tool teams can use to help make this flip.

CHAPTER 9

1. Peter Skillman, Ted 2006 Design Challenge. https://www.youtube.com/watch?v=1p5sBzMtB3Q.

2. From "Why Group Brainstorming Is a Waste of Time," *Harvard Business Review*, 2015: "The most widely used method to spark group creativity is *brainstorming*, a technique first introduced by Alex Osborn, a real life 'Mad Man,' in the 1950s. Brainstorming is based on four rules: (a) generate as many ideas as possible; (b) prioritize unusual or original ideas; (c) combine and refine the ideas generated; and (d) abstain from criticism during the exercise. The process, which should be informal and unstructured, is based on two old psychological premises. First, that the mere presence of others can have motivating effects on an individual's performance. Second, that quantity (eventually) leads to quality" (Chamorro-Premuzic 2015).

3. The methods listed in table 9.1 are conceptually different but not necessarily separate in practice. For example, you may apply logical thinking when trying to learn from end users or while applying change concepts. They are listed separately here to inspire different entry points for generating ideas for change.

4. New Visions for Public Schools has managed a network of high schools for the New York City Department of Education since 1989. More on this case can be found in Sharon Greenberg and Anthony Bryk, "Supporting Improvement through an Analytic Hub," in Bryk 2020, 47–75.

5. FAFSA stands for the Free Application for Federal Student Aid.

6. On the surface, this may seem like an obvious change. However, many high schools rely on general communication blasts and school-wide events to support students and families with the college application process. They do not necessarily have ways to track and proactively manage students' progress on key milestones in the college application process (such as college selection, FAFSA completion, and applications).

7. Positive deviance, a phrase coined by John and Monique Sternin, refers to examples that lie outside the system in a good way (Pascale, Sternin, and Sternin 2010). How do we know if an example really is

beyond what we would expect from a system's performance? In the 1920s this question was answered in situations where data is available by Walter Shewhart, a physicist and statistician who created statistical process control (SPC) methods (Shewhart 1931/1980). The mathematical methods he created are used to understand the expected performance of a process or system in the future given its past performance. The methods distinguish between common causes and special causes of variation in systems. Special causes are applicable here, as they are explainable causes that apply at a specific location, to a specific group or subgroup, or at a particular time causing performance to fall beyond the bounds of a systems design. For more on the use of statistical process control methods, see appendix A. In the case of the Sternins, the discovery of positive deviance was generated by using qualitative methods of observation and was made possible because the Sternins lived close to the population experiencing malnutrition.

8. In his book *Democratizing Innovation*, MIT professor Eric von Hippel lays out the argument for why lead users—those ahead of most users in their identification of problems and development and use of solutions—are a particularly valuable source of innovation (von Hippel 2005). He focuses mostly on organizations looking to develop new products. His website includes resources for finding and engaging lead users in innovation (von Hippel n.d.).

9. Expert convenings and ninety-day cycles are two other methods for generating change ideas that are related to scanning. In an expert convening, research, professional, and out-of-field experts are brought together to generate and prioritize an initial set of change ideas. These experts can also help select appropriate improvement measures. (For more on expert convenings, see Institute for Healthcare Improvement 2003, 5; High Tech High Graduate School of Education n.d.). A ninety--day cycle is a time-bound innovation routine that structures the scanning and initial testing of promising ideas on a specific topic. (For more on ninety-day cycles, see Martin and Mate 2018). For large improvement efforts—such as networks—engaging in a ninety-day cycle or an expert convening is recommended to ensure that the community starts with strong change ideas. However, expert convenings and ninety-day cycles are often too resource intensive for most team-based improvement efforts.

10. As described by Andrea Kabacenell during a presentation at Institute for Healthcare Improvement's Innovation College, July 30, 2012.

11. Edward de Bono invented the term "lateral thinking" in 1967 as a way of distinguishing between all types of creative thinking (the creation of art, the writing of music, etc.) and creative thinking specifically concerned with "changing concepts and perceptions." "Lateral thinking is *pattern switching in an asymmetric patterning system*" (italics present in the original). It is "based on the behavior of patterning systems," particularly "self-organizing information systems" (de Bono 1999, 121–22). This term and underlying theory serve as the basis for creativity methods broadly known as "provocation techniques or methods."

12. Their complete list of change concepts can be found in *The Improvement Guide* alongside an extended appendix detailing examples of use in practice (Langley et al. 2009, 132, 357–408).

13. The change concept can either be chosen purposefully by the team or randomly to spur creative thinking. To assist teams in choosing concepts that are relevant for their scenario, the authors group concepts into categories such as "concepts useful for the design or redesign of a process or system, or for a product or service." They also have included distinctions for concepts that are specifically useful for eliminating quality problems, expanding expectations, and increasing demand, managing people, and reducing costs while maintaining or improving quality (Langley et al. 2009, 361–63).

14. Many readers will recognize this tool as being related or similar to PICK (Possible, Implement, Challenge, Kill) charts. The authors prefer the language of Effort-Impact Charts and so use it here. In practice, these tools work in similar ways for improvement teams.

15. Recognizing the importance of translating research to practice, Yeager et al. (2016) conducted a study on the use of design-thinking (prototyping and testing) in improving the effectiveness of growth mindset interventions targeted at ninth-grade students entering high school. The researchers found that interventions revised through a user-centered design process with students "were more effective in changing proxy outcomes such as beliefs and short-term behaviors than the researcher's initial materials. Furthermore, the intervention increased core course grades for previously low-achieving students."

16. Although a repeat study has not been carried out since then, examples persist. In 1993, research demonstrated the ineffectiveness of phenylephrine, a common decongestant found in over-the-counter cold medication. It took until 2023 for the Food and Drug Administration to conclude that the research was indeed correct (Hendeles 1993; Jewett 2023). It remains to be seen if pharmaceutical companies will apply this research to the formulation of their products.

17. Whenever possible, it is useful for teams to have a subject matter expert as a key resource (see figure 1.1). Ideally, this subject matter expert would speak the language of improvement and be well versed in the latest research on a particular topic. Subject matter experts help the team locate research and key practices, make sense of outcomes, and provide feedback on focus areas and specific change ideas.

18. The pitfalls discussed come from a mixture of literature and the authors' experiences working with teams. Various references to these pitfalls can be found throughout (Langley et al. 2009).

CHAPTER 10

1. To learn more about the continuing work of Un Buen Comienzo, see https://fundacionoportuni dad.cl/un-buen-comienzo/.

2. The evaluation was designed as a randomized control trial. Sixty-four schools were assigned randomly to either the treatment group (receiving the Un Buen Comienzo professional development program) or a control group. Three cohorts of students were followed through the prekindergarten and kindergarten years. At regular intervals, data was collected on a) the quality of classroom interactions (using the CLASS observation tool), b) the language development of the children (using Woodcock-Muñoz assessments), c) students' social-emotional development (using surveys), and d) attendance. Data was collected from both the control group and the treatment group and compared. To get good estimates of the program's effects, program staff were instructed not to change the program across the four years of the evaluation. For more information, see chapter 2 of *Un Buen Comienzo para los Niños de Chile* (Treviño, Aguirre, and Varela 2018).

3. The social structure of Un Buen Comienzo shifted over time. As described, it began as a program that was delivered to schools. When they first switched to an improvement approach in 2011, they supported individual schools to set aims and engage in continuous improvement. Subsequently, they added a network component, periodically gathering school teams in learning sessions to exchange ideas (Arbour et al. 2023).

4. Driver diagrams were first introduced through an example in *The Improvement Guide* (Langley et al. 2009, 286) with the methodological approach explicated by Bennett and Provost in 2015.

5. As the improvement initiative continued, local government officials also became involved to align all levels of the system.

6. As we will discuss later in the chapter, a team's theory changes over time. Un Buen Comienzo updated and rearranged their theory every year based on learning. The version in figure 10.1 corresponds (imperfectly) to the version that existed in 2014–2015. Small adjustments have been made to demonstrate the conventions of a driver diagram and make it simpler to read.

7. Schools saw significant increases in two out of their three measures of oral language development. On average, in oral comprehension and emergent writing, students ended kindergarten at a level expected of a child that is six years, five months, and six years, eleven months, respectively. These ending points represent more than a year of extra development than their peers in comparison classrooms. Interestingly, they did not see similar movement in their third outcome measure: vocabulary. For more on the experimental design that produced these results, see chapter 7 in *Un Buen Comienzo para los Niños de Chile* (Treviño, Aguirre, and Varela 2018, 257).

8. Secondary drivers can be difficult to use well. Their application can result in an ever-expanding, overcomplicated theory that not only does not focus efforts but obscures, rather than facilitates, the ability to see the link between the aim and the change ideas. It is often useful to start without secondary drivers; then only add them when the theory is that more than one "actionable place," when improved,

will result in the desired movement of a primary driver. When used, secondary drivers should further organize change ideas according to their project impact pathway.

9. For some projects, a driver diagram is not the most useful way to capture the improvement team's theory. When the focus of the improvement work is designing or redesigning a single process, a process map annotated with change ideas may be a better way to organize ideas. For projects where changes are sequenced across a time dimension or in specific phases, a "pipeline" visual might be more useful. Examples of pipeline projects include improving college access (where changes need to occur from students' junior year to the summer after senior year), or improvements in hiring (where changes are spread across phases of posting positions, applying, interviewing, and selecting).

10. In these rural areas, children often walk long distances to go to school. The school buildings are often poorly heated and insulated. Parents expressed that one reason they keep children home during the winter months is to avoid their children being wet and cold throughout the school day.

11. In the words of W. Edwards Deming, "a goal that lies beyond the means of its accomplishment will lead to discouragement, frustration, demoralization. In other words, there must be a method to achieve an aim" (Deming 2000, 41).

12. In these rural areas, children often walk long distances to go to school. The school buildings are often poorly heated and insulated. Parents expressed that one reason they keep children home during the winter months is to avoid their children being wet and cold throughout the school day.

13. It is often useful to keep a "slide" that comes after a team's driver diagram to capture change ideas they are "saving for later." This can help teams let go of keeping too many changes on the diagram itself.

14. One trick in using a driver diagram is recognizing what it is not. Driver diagrams are not meant to capture all the system elements that impact the aim, only the highest leverage. They also are not the right tool to show how all the system's elements are interrelated. Instead, they impose a somewhat artificial linearity, using arrows to show only the main causal hypotheses so they can be tested in practice. For teams that struggle to prioritize, it can be helpful to first map the system using tools specific to that purpose (e.g., linkage of process, causal loop diagrams, etc.), including the broader array of interrelated systems components that impact the outcome. Then the driver diagram can be used subsequently to prioritize where a change will be targeted.

15. As we describe in chapter 13, it is important that these consolidation moments be scheduled to allow for time to come to an updated shared theory together. When team members update the theory individually, a "versioning problem" often exists, and the theory ceases to be shared. When it's updated, the new theory is labeled with a date and updated in the team's storyboard. It can be useful to keep a separate "document" where all the versions of the team's theory are included.

16. Teams will usually update their theory more often than once per year. In this case, because multiple schools were involved, the Un Buen Comienzo team made major updates to the theory annually in alignment with the school calendar. Schools had their own versions of the driver diagram to represent the learning in their context. These were updated more frequently: twice a year or in some circumstances quarterly.

PART V

1. In the journey map, the learn-in-practice oval is the largest for a reason. Over the course of the journey, teams should expect to spend roughly two-thirds or more of their time in this phase.

CHAPTER 11

1. It is possible to critique the team, with the benefit of hindsight bias (see chapter 6 for more on how people think), for not understanding the problem before testing a change. However, the team had experiential knowledge as members of the community, and testing a change on a small scale with the in-

tention of learning can be an excellent method, whether or not the assumptions they made were correct. In this case, the team deliberately chose as the driver a staff member from the community who, when stopping by to pick up children for school, could prompt conversations with families about keeping their children home, as in an empathy interview. Putting their hypothesis to the test, they were able to test their assumptions about the problem (which turned out to be incorrect) and uncover the barriers to attendance that families were experiencing.

2. Typically, improvement teams use a PDSA template to plan and record the learning from their experiments.

3. As described in chapter 5, teams can also use PDSA cycles to investigate their system. The "plan" section of an investigative PDSA cycle is structured by a question to explore instead of a change idea to be tested.

4. Before abandoning, the team should make sure the idea had been well executed during the test. Teams do not want to draw the wrong conclusion about the efficacy of a change idea if it was not carried out fully or as intended.

5. In other cases, the team may learn relatively little about the change they tried, but through their observations they open a new path that they did not previously imagine. The first PDSA in the opening case is an example of learning that comes from observation. The casual conversations Jon had with the parents, which were not explicitly part of the plan of the PDSA cycle, produced the most important discovery—that not having lunch to send was a key barrier to attendance. In practice, we often refer to this as "learning that comes in from the side." Be ready for these unexpected learnings; often, they are an avenue for powerful insights.

6. We would describe these types of failures as "intelligent failures" as described in Amy Edmondson's book *Right Kind of Wrong: The Science of Failing Well* (2023). Intelligent failures involve "careful thinking, don't cause unnecessary harm, and generate useful learning that advances our knowledge" (11).

7. In a study of 122 middle school math teachers (Jackson, Gibbons, and Sharpe 2017), the researchers found that "most teachers did not view all their students as capable of participating in rigorous mathematical activity. Most teachers attributed at least some of their students' difficulty to inherent traits of the students or deficits in their families or communities, and most described lowering the cognitive demand of an activity if they perceived that students were facing difficulty." This highlights the pernicious effects of deficit thinking and its impact on teacher behavior. PDSAs, therefore, can serve as powerful ways to unearth implicit beliefs, blind spots, and deficit orientations so they can be challenged.

8. An ostomy is a way for bodily waste to pass through a surgically created opening on the abdomen into a "pouch" or "ostomy bag" on the outside of the body or a surgically created internal pouch. https://www.ostomy.org/what-is-an-ostomy/.

9. Antiretroviral medications are those prescribed to people living with HIV. They suppress the HIV virus, allowing people to live normal, healthy lives.

10. Their success was so notable that the improvement team was given an opportunity to share it at a national HIV conference, encouraging other hospitals facing the same challenge to adopt their model to reduce the chronic-care burden hospital-based clinics were experiencing (Bennett et al. 2007).

11. The one to five to twenty-five to all rule of thumb was developed by Tom Nolan, a leading improvement expert and a partner in the Associates for Process Improvement. As is true with most rules of thumb, it need not be followed literally to carry useful wisdom. Start quickly with one. Move from one to five to see whether your design works in more than one place. The jump to twenty-five can feel big, but it forces learning about what is needed to support change on a larger scale. Use this knowledge to implement well in all settings, paying attention to whether the improvement is sustained. Scaling up by multiples helps structure the necessary learning and safeguards against investing in boutique solutions that are not doable at the desired scale.

12. Using sequential planned experimentation (also known as complex PDSA cycles) to understand the interaction effects of multiple changes being made simultaneously is a good example; it is a technique used with some frequency in medicine. See *Quality Improvement through Planned Experimentation* (Moen, Nolan, and Provost 2012) for more on this topic.

13. In both examples depicted in this chapter, "implementation" was pursued at two levels. Level 1: each primary health center or early learning center had to learn how to embed successful change ideas into their local organization's way of working. Each site engaged in its own PDSA ramp, moving from small-scale testing to implementation of a given practice at their site. Level 2: in a parallel fashion, the sites depicted in these cases were part of a network focused on a singular aim intent on learning from each other. The shared learning was also structured as a ramp with change ideas first tested in one PHC or early learning center and then subsequently spread to all the PHCs or early learning centers in the network. It is fairly common when improvement teams work within nested organizational structures that implementation activities will be needed on multiple levels.

14. Degree of belief as a concept refers to the belief individuals hold that a prediction will be correct. This differs from statistical significance (are two things different from each other) and statistical confidence (belief that the observed value from some sample is within range of the actual value). "One's degree of belief in a prediction depends on two considerations: (1) the extent to which the prediction can be supported by evidence, and (2) the similarity between the conditions under which the evidence was obtained and the conditions to which the prediction applies" (Langley et al. 2009, 141).

15. A fourth dimension that can be taken into consideration when determining the scale of the test is the *capacity* of the organization, department, or team to execute the change. *Capacity* includes individual skills to execute the change well (often called capability) and the "space" to take on the change (e.g., time, band width, and resources). Promising changes often fail in organizations because of inadequate attention to these dimensions. Inquiry is a useful way to build skills necessary to execute change well. Inquiry can also be used to free up organizational space. In *Learning to Improve*, a figure similar to 11.8 was used, with "limited and strong capacity" replacing the cost of failure dimension (Bryk et al. 2015, 120). In reality, all four conditions—will, confidence, capacity, and cost of failure—are important to consider when determining the appropriate scale of a test.

16. As we will see in chapter 15, the ability to try an "innovation" on a small scale also increases its spreadability.

17. For greater detail on addressing these common systems components during implementation, consult *The Improvement Guide: A Practical Approach to Enhancing Organizational Performance* (Langley et al. 2009, 180–84).

CHAPTER 12

1. We can think of data as all possible available observations that can be made of our physical, behavioral, and perceptual worlds (Provost and Murray 2022, 27–29).

2. In their book *Street Data: A Next-Generation Model for Equity, Pedagogy, and School Transformation* (2021), Safir, Dugan, and Wilson use the term "satellite data" when referring to "broad-brush quantitative measures" in contrast with street data, "qualitative, systematic, and experiential data that emerges at eye level," which encompasses the stories, anecdotes, experiences, and emotion from the community.

3. In the example presented, "percent proficient in oral language" represents the outcome measure, while "scores on CLASS observation," "time spent on language," and "percent attendance" represent process measures. The Un Buen Comienzo team did not actively pursue a balance measure; however, "time spent on play" is included to provide the reader with an example of what an appropriate balance measure could be given this context.

4. From a practical perspective, when a team decides they need to work on a different outcome measure, it is helpful to consider this a new improvement project. As such, they must return to crafting a new aim and charter as well as engaging in the other phases of the improvement journey.

5. It is also possible to identify *process step measures* one layer below the process measure. These are the individual steps or actions accomplished in sequence to complete a process. Identifying process step measures can be helpful in cases where a particular step in a process or delay between steps is considered high leverage and is the focus of a series of PDSA cycles (e.g., delays between assessment and placement).

A measure at this level affords the improvement team a focal point in a process where they can observe whether a change applied over time improves that step (or set of steps) captured by the measure. These measures, if used, are tracked for the duration of focus on the process or step being improved.

6. *Evidence* is a specific kind of information; information "that can be used to support a hypothesis by testing it. Thus, all evidence is information, but not all information is evidence." Evidence entails a comparison with standards, across time or between groups (Dammann 2019).

7. Most improvement is informed by graphs (run charts and Shewhart charts) unfolding over time. More frequent observations are advantageous for understanding whether improvement is occurring. If possible, it is helpful for teams to have data they can summarize and plot weekly or monthly in the case of process measures; monthly or quarterly in the case of outcome measures. This can mean using data collection mechanisms that observe or collect data daily. In some industries, such as education, traditional outcome data is only available once per year, making it difficult for improvement teams to use such data effectively. Instead, they will depend on more frequently occurring processes to give them early indications as to when improvement is occurring, as with the Un Buen Comienzo example.

8. The lack of process measures in education has led some to call for the development of more "practical measures," which can be defined as those "collected, analyzed, and used within the daily work lives of practitioners. They are also 'practical' in that they reflect practice—in that they act as sensing mechanisms at the level at which work is carried out" (WestEd 2023).

9. Brandon Bennett.

10. Adapted from Target CLAB Zero (Health Quality & Safety Commission New Zealand and Ko Awatea 2014).

11. Collaborative documents provide greater detail that can be accommodated here, such as the operational definition of terms contained in the definition (e.g., operational definition of a "great vessel").

12. This is an example of a *systematic random sample*. Case managers choose a random starting point and a sample of IEPs using systematic, evenly spaced intervals. Other sampling strategies include *judgment sampling* in which individuals or items are chosen based on the expertise—or judgment—of subject matter experts; and *convenience sampling* in which samples are chosen based on what data is most readily available. For more on sampling strategies, see Provost and Murray 2022, 53–58. The utility of sampling is summed up in the authors' opening sentence on sampling: "The purpose of measurement for improvement is to speed learning, not slow it down."

13. Graphical representations require quantitative data. Qualitative data can be turned into quantitative data. An example of this translation occurs in the Pareto analysis presented in chapter 6 on understanding where community college math students are lost from the system. The moment when students left the system (qualitative data) was graphed by counting the number of students at that moment in the system (quantitative data).

14. Creating easy-to-interpret data visualizations takes some work, but creating such visualizations can prevent most confusion about what is happening and where a team should go next. The authors recommend several sources for learning more (Bennett et al. 2022; Tufte 2001; Tukey 1977).

15. Percent licensed places attended is defined as the percentage of total licensed hours for which children were present in the early education center. For example, if a center was licensed to provide twelve hundred hours per week (space for thirty full-time learners attending forty hours per week), and for eight hundred of those hours students were onsite (twenty full-time learners or some combination of part-time learners), then the percent of licensed places attended would be equal to 800/1200 hours × 100 = 66.66%.

CHAPTER 13

1. According to Boudett and City, the authors of *Meeting Wise: Making the Most of Collaborative Time for Educators* (2014), if teams want to establish meetings as "powerful learning spaces," they should con-

sider the four aspects of meetings: purpose, process, preparation, and pacing. To download a Meeting Wise agenda template, see https://datawise.gse.harvard.edu/meeting-wise-resources.

2. As mentioned in chapter 5, learning cycles that focus on testing changes and those that focus on investigating the system can use the same PDSA structure.

3. For an example of a lifesaving use of a Shewhart chart (see appendix A) to detect and respond to unwanted changes in CLABSI rates, see "An Unexpected Increase in Catheter-Associated Bloodstream Infections at a Children's Hospital following Introduction of the Spiros Closed Male Connector" (Wheeler et al. 2012, 48–50).

4. Teams have a similar need for consolidation when they focus on understanding the system (chapters 5 and 6). They review the evidence from investigation cycles, come to new collective hypotheses about the root causes of the current outcomes (sometimes summarized in a cause-and-effect diagram), and decide what to do next. The key decision during this phase is agreeing whether they need to continue to investigate or they are ready to set an aim and create the team's charter.

5. How the information is organized or documented when it is synthesized can be done using a variety of methods—affinity diagrams, heat maps, matrix diagrams, Shewhart charts, and so on. Whatever method is used, the primary goal is to be able to see patterns, trends, or themes.

6. The team should then revisit its theory of improvement and make any necessary revisions—add, drop, or modify change ideas, driver(s), or process steps—given what is discussed. A team does not necessarily need to revise their theory every time they have a consolidation meeting. In the case of networks where multiple improvement teams likely are testing a common theory, then that theory more likely will be revised every 4–6 months by a centralized team based on the consolidated learning of all the teams over 2–3 action periods.

CHAPTER 14

1. For more on when and how to make permanent changes to systems, see the section on implementation in chapter 11.

2. Other ways of disseminating learning from improvement journeys include formal publications in academic journals, the creation of case studies, and presentations at national and international conferences.

3. A copy of the SMOOTH change package can be downloaded at https://koawatea.countiesmanukau.health.nz/assets/Blog/teamcounties/b47f92206a/SMOOTH-HTG-Final-March-2014.pdf. Accessed July 31, 2023.

4. For improvement efforts that are focused on spread, a change package is created at the beginning of the journey. For example, in a Breakthrough Series Collaborative model subject matter experts craft a starting change package for participating teams. These packages are developed for both technical and relational reasons. Technically, it is desired that participating teams have the best evidence available to them at the start; and relationally, the package limits teams' choice of where to start their improvement journey. These change packages can look different than what is described here. In some cases, they are simply a list of change ideas; in others, a change bundle or toolkit (as with the insertion and maintenance bundles for CLABSI, see chapter 12); in still others, a driver diagram alone. Importantly, as with all change packages, the evidence for these various iterations varies from weak to strong. In all contexts, communicating the level of evidence is a key feature of a change package.

5. Readers are encouraged to consult *Scaling up Excellence*, chapter 2, for more on the question of high fidelity versus low fidelity in the adoption of change (Sutton and Rao 2014, 33–63).

6. For more on what drives the adoption of change ideas, see chapter 15 on organizing for spread.

7. Industry journals, including recent examples like the BMJ open journal, have been created and maintained for precisely this reason (*BMJ Open* n.d.). Their mission has been to make public and accessible learning that is happening across a field, including learning about what is producing improvements in practice.

CHAPTER 15

1. Indeed, although we introduce a few key spread concepts and methods in this chapter, organizations taking on a spread journey should explore the extensive body of knowledge on the topic to support their efforts. A complete treatment of spreading and scaling effective practices is beyond the scope of this book.

2. In the second phase of the work, Ko Awatea took on two parallel improvement efforts. One effort focused on the spread of the effective practices to the forty-nine centers. The other engaged the original seven centers to work toward improving oral language outcomes, which was the "big-dot goal" they set out to achieve (see chapter 7 for more on big-dot goals and proximal aims).

3. In *The Improvement Guide*, the authors suggest rating changes on each of the attributes using a scale from 1 = weak to 5 = strong (Langley et al. 2009, 201). In thinking forward to spread, teams can consider these attributes when generating and selecting change ideas. See chapter 9 for more on sourcing change ideas.

4. Rogers notes that these attributes are not independent of each other but, rather, overlap. For example, a change may be observable because it is triable. However, each attribute highlights a useful dimension for thinking about the spreadability of a change.

5. One author encountered this issue as a key barrier when trying to spread a set of change ideas that prevented central-line infections to intensive care units (ICUs) across New Zealand. A key prevention technique was for the doctor inserting the central line to wear gloves, a mask, a gown, and a surgical cap and for the patient to be covered in a full drape (except for the exact site where the line would be placed). This change was designed to create sterile conditions for the insertion of the line. Some doctors in the country balked at the idea. They had been placing central lines for years, sometimes decades, and personally had not experienced a patient becoming infected in the absence of these things. These lived experiences were likely true, not just professional posturing; after all, central-line infections were fairly rare. Unfortunately, they are often fatal when they occur. For these doctors, the change ideas were perceived as being incompatible with their beliefs and experiences, even though the scientific evidence for their use was undeniable.

6. For more on organizing spread initiatives, see *The Improvement Guide* (Langley et al. 2009, 196; Massoud et al. 2006; Nolan et al. 2005).

CHAPTER 16

1. For many teams, demonstrating improvement for the system can occur even when the aim of the project is not reached. Remember the New Zealand team focused on closing the disparity gap in access to early education for children from Māori and Pacific Islander families. They didn't meet their aim, but they did close the gap by more than half, a major improvement for those early learning centers. Teams will know they have improved when they can demonstrate a statistical shift on a run chart (see chapter 12) or produce special cause variation on a Shewhart chart (see appendix A).

2. One final reflection tool that some teams and coaches find helpful is the "Improvement Habits" included in appendix C. These habits of mind attempt to capture the dispositions and ways of thinking characteristics of an improvement culture. Framework overload is a real danger, which is why we do not include it here as a regular routine. The important point is that teams will want to reflect regularly on how they are working together. The instrument that guides this reflection is less important than making the time and space to talk about the team functioning.

APPENDIX A

1. Data displayed on Shewhart charts can be used to examine a measure unfolding over time. When this is the case, all five rules for interpretation can be used to determine the presence or absence of special cause variation. Data comparing other types of subgroups, such as location, race category, or role category, where time is not present on the horizontal axis, only use rule 1—any point outside the limits—to detect the presence of special cause variation in a data set. Time-ordered data that is not independent (i.e., displays a high degree of autocorrelation) similarly can only be interpreted using rule 1—any point outside the limits. For more on why this is the case, see Provost and Murray (2022).

APPENDIX B

1. See table B.2 for guidance on using the rule of too many or too few runs for determining random variation on a run chart.

2. Some teams will not have the ability to collect and analyze ten data points prior to making changes in their systems. This should not impede their learning, teams should instead work with the data they do have, understand the potential limitations of having less data, and lean more heavily on the subject matter experts on their teams to help them understand the baseline performance of their measures of interest.

References

Aguilar, Elena. 2016. *The Art of Coaching Teams: Building Resilient Communities That Transform Schools*. Hoboken, NJ: Wiley.

———. 2020. *Coaching for Equity: Conversations That Change Practice*. Hoboken, NJ: Wiley.

Ahlström, Joakim. 2014. *How to Succeed with Continuous Improvement: A Primer for Becoming the Best in the World*. New York: McGraw-Hill Education.

All Children Thrive Learning Network Team. 2022. *The System to Achieve Food Equity (SAFE): Year One Report*.

Allensworth, Elaine M., and John Q. Easton. 2007. "What Matters for Staying On-Track and Graduating in Chicago Public High Schools: A Closer Look at Course Grades, Failures, and Attendance in the Freshman Year," 1–68. Chicago: Consortium on Chicago School Research at the University of Chicago.

American Red Cross. 2020. "Red Cross Emblem Symbolizes Neutrality, Impartiality." https://www.redcross.org/about-us/news-and-events/news/2020/red-cross-emblem-symbolizes-neutrality-impartiality.html.

Applewhite, E. J., and Richard B. Fuller. 1982. *Synergetics: Explorations in the Geometry of Thinking*. New York: Macmillan.

Arbour, Mary Catherine, Carolina Soto, Yanira Alée, Sidney Atwood, Pablo Muñoz, and Marcela Marzolo. 2023. "Absenteeism Prevention in Preschools in Chile: Impact from a Quasi-Experimental Evaluation of 2011–2017 Ministry of Education Data." *Frontiers in Education* 7 (January). https://doi.org/10.3389/feduc.2022.975092.

Arbour, Mary Catherine, Hirokazu Yoshikawa, John Willett, Christina Weiland, Catherine Snow, Susana Mendive, M. Clara Barata, and Ernesto Treviño. 2016. "Experimental Impacts of a Preschool Intervention in Chile on Children's Language Outcomes: Moderation by Student Absenteeism." *Journal of Research on Educational Effectiveness* 9, no. 1 (June): 117–49. https://doi.org/10.1080/19345747.2015.1109013.

Argyris, Chris. 1990. *Overcoming Organizational Defenses: Facilitating Organizational Learning*. Boston: Allyn and Bacon.

———. 1993. *Knowledge for Action: A Guide to Overcoming Barriers to Organizational Change*. Hoboken, NJ: Wiley.

———. 1999. *On Organizational Learning*. New York: Blackwell Business.

Argyris, Chris, Robert D. Putnam, and Diana M. Smith. 1985. *Action Science*. Hoboken, NJ: Wiley.

Ash, Ainsley. 2021. "Stopping Summer Melt Starts in the Spring." National College Attainment Network. https://www.ncan.org/news/559403/Stopping-Summer-Melt-Starts-in-the-Spring.htm.

ASQ. n.d. "What Is FMEA? Failure Mode and Effects Analysis." Accessed August 6, 2023. https://asq.org/quality-resources/fmea.

Attendance Works. 2018. "Seminal Research." Attendance Works. https://www.attendanceworks.org/research/seminal-research/.

Badger, Emily, and Kevin Quealy. 2017. "How Effective Is Your School District? A New Measure Shows Where Students Learn the Most." *New York Times*, December 5, 2017. https://www.nytimes.com/interactive/2017/12/05/upshot/a-better-way-to-compare-public-schools.html.

Balas, Andrew E., and Suzanne A. Boren. 2000. "Managing Clinical Knowledge for Health Care Improvement." *Yearbook of Medical Informatics*, 65–70.

Barnard-Brak, L., and D. Lechtenberger. 2010. "Student IEP Participation and Academic Achievement Across Time." *Remedial and Special Education* 31, no. 5 (September/October): 343–349. http://capacity-resource.middletownautism.com/wp-content/uploads/sites/6/2017/03/iep-article.pdf.

Beck, Andrew F., Adrienne W. Henize, Ting T. Qiu, Bin Huang, Yin Zhang, Melissa D. Klein, Donita Parrish, Elaine E. Fink, and Robert S. Khan. 2022. "Reductions in Hospitalizations among Children Referred to a Primary Care-Based Medical-Legal Partnership." *Health Affairs* 41, no. 3 (March): 341–49. https://doi.org/10.1377/hlthaff.2021.00905.

Bennett, Brandon. 2018. "Branching Out: Use Measurement Trees to Determine Whether Your Improvement Efforts Are Paying Off." *Quality Progress* 51, no. 9 (September): 18–23. https://asq.org/quality-progress/articles/branching-out?id=83db0cd0e97e4fca855caae3194fed74.

———. 2020. "Special Delivery: Change Packages Are a Powerful Starting Point for Sharing Ideas That Work." *Quality Progress* 53, no. 1 (January): 18–24.

Bennett, Brandon, Alicia Grunow, and Sandra Park. 2022. *Improvement Science at Your Fingertips: A Resource Guide for Coaches of Improvement*. San Francisco: ISC LLC.

Bennett, Brandon, Linda Dlamini, Ellen Mkize, Steve Reid, and Pierre Barker. 2007. "The 8 Steps to Successful Down Referral: Opening the Door to a PHC Driven ARV Program." Conference poster, Third South African AIDS Conference, Durban, South Africa.

Bennett, Brandon, and Lloyd Provost. 2015. "What's Your Theory? Driver Diagram Serves as Tool for Building and Testing Theories of Improvement." *Quality Progress* 48, no. 7 (July): 36–43.

Bergerum, Carolina, Agneta K. Engström, Johan Thor, and Maria Wolmesjö. 2020. "Patient Involvement in Quality Improvement—a 'Tug of War' or a Dialogue in a Learning Process to Improve Healthcare." *BMC Heath Services Research* 20, no. 1115 (12): 1–13. https://doi.org/10.1186/s12913-020-05970-4.

"Best Children's Hospitals/Top Pediatric Hospital Rankings/US News Best Hospitals." *U.S. News Health*. Accessed July 13, 2022. https://health.usnews.com/best-hospitals/pediatric-rankings.

Black, Paul, and Dylan William. 1998. "Assessment and Classroom Learning." *Assessment and Classroom Learning, Assessment in Education: Principles, Policy & Practice* 5, no. 1 (March): 7–74. https://www.gla.ac.uk/t4/learningandteaching/files/PGCTHE/BlackandWiliam1998.pdf.

BMJ Open. n.d. Accessed October 7, 2023. https://bmjopen.bmj.com/.

Boudett, Kathryn P., and Elizabeth A. City. 2014. *Meeting Wise: Making the Most of Collaborative Time for Educators*. Cambridge, MA: Harvard Education Press.

Brown, Brené. 2018. *Dare to Lead: Brave Work. Tough Conversations. Whole Hearts*. New York: Random House.

———. 2021. *Atlas of the Heart: Mapping Meaningful Connection and the Language of Human Experience*. London: Vermilion.

Bruner, Charles, Anne Discher, and Hedy Change. 2011. "Chronic Elementary Absenteeism: A Problem Hidden in Plain Sight," a research brief from Attendance Works and Child & Family Policy Center.

Bryk, Anthony S. 2020. *Improvement in Action: Advancing Quality in America's Schools*. Cambridge, MA: Harvard Education Press.

Bryk, Anthony S., Louis M. Gomez, Alicia Grunow, and Paul G. LeMahieu. 2015. *Learning to Improve: How America's Schools Can Get Better at Getting Better.* Cambridge, MA: Harvard Education Press.

Bryk, Anthony, and Barbara Schneider. 2004. *Trust in Schools: A Core Resource for Improvement.* New York: Russell Sage Foundation.

"Un Buen Comienzo—Fundación Educacional Oportunidad." n.d. Accessed October 7, 2023. https://fundacionoportunidad.cl/un-buen-comienzo/.

Caillier, Stacey. 2022. "Improvement Science in Education—a Tool for Our Collective Liberation." HTH Unboxed. https://hthunboxed.org/unboxed_posts/improvement-as-a-tool-for-our-collective-liberation-an-interview-with-dr-brandi-hinnant-crawford/.

Carnegie Foundation for the Advancement of Teaching. 2015. "Building a Teaching Effectiveness Network." Appendixes to the Year 4 final report to the Gates Foundation, B1–B25.

Centers for Disease Control and Prevention. 2000. "CDC Newsroom Archive." https://www.cdc.gov/media/pressrel/r2k0306c.htm.

———. 2008. HIV AIDS Surveillance Report, 2006, vol. 18. Atlanta: U.S. Department of Health and Human Services.

———. 2016. "What You May Not Know about Hand Hygiene—and Really Should." https://blogs.cdc.gov/publichealthmatters/2016/05/what-you-may-not-know-about-hand-hygiene/.

Chamorro-Premuzic, Tomas. 2015. "Why Group Brainstorming Is a Waste of Time." *Harvard Business Review.* https://hbr.org/2015/03/why-group-brainstorming-is-a-waste-of-time.

Children's Defense Fund. 2023. https://www.childrensdefense.org/tools-and-resources/the-state-of-americas-children/.

Cincinnati Children's Hospital Medical Center. n.d. "Learning Networks/Anderson Center." Cincinnati Children's Hospital. Accessed March 15, 2022. https://www.cincinnatichildrens.org/research/divisions/j/anderson-center/learning-networks.

Cohen, D. 1990. "A Revolution in One Classroom: The Case of Mrs. Oublier." *Educational Evaluation and Policy Analysis* 12 (3): 311–29. https://doi.org/10.2307/1164355.

Cohen-Vogel, Lora, Christopher Harrison, and David Cohen-Vogel. 2022. "On Teams: Exploring Variation in the Social Organization of Improvement Research in Education." In *The Foundational Handbook on Improvement Research in Education*, edited by Donald J. Peurach, Jennifer L. Russell, Lora Cohen-Vogel, and William R. Penuel, 325–47. Lanham, MD: Rowman & Littlefield.

Committee on Quality of Health Care in America, and Institute of Medicine. 2001. *Crossing the Quality Chasm: A New Health System for the 21st Century.* Washington, DC: National Academies Press.

Community Design Partners. 2020. *BEYOND High School Student-Centered Transition Supports during COVID.*

Community Solutions. n.d. "The Challenge." Accessed October 8, 2023. https://community.solutions/the-challenge/.

Compton-Phillips, Amy. 2016. "'Being the Best at Getting Better'—Creating a Culture of Change." NEJM Catalyst. https://catalyst.nejm.org/doi/full/10.1056/CAT.17.0491.

Conron, K., and B. Wilson. 2019. *LGBTQ Youth of Color Impacted by the Child Welfare and Juvenile Justice System: A Research Agenda.* Los Angeles: Williams Institute, UCLA School of Law.

Dammann, Olaf. 2019. "Data, Information, Evidence, and Knowledge." *Online Journal of Public Health Informatics* 10, no. 3 (March): e224. https://doi.org/10.5210/ojphi.v10i3.9631.

David, Jennie G., Alexander Jofriet, Michael Seid, and Peter A. Margolis. 2018. "'A Guide to Gutsy Living': Patient-Driven Development of a Pediatric Ostomy Toolkit." *Pediatrics* 141, no. 5 (May): 1–7. e20172789.

de Bono, Edward. 1991, rev. 2018. "The Teaching of Creative Thinking." https://www.debono.com/teaching-creative-thinking-1.

———. 1992. *Serious Creativity: Using the Power of Lateral Thinking to Create New Ideas.* New York: HarperBusiness.

———. 1999. *Six Thinking Hats.* Boston: Little, Brown.

The Decision Lab. n.d. "Naive Realism." Accessed July 5, 2023. https://thedecisionlab.com/biases/naive-realism.

Delgado, Richard, and Jean Stefancic, eds. 2000. *Critical Race Theory: The Cutting Edge*. Philadelphia: Temple University Press.

Deming, W. Edwards. 1992. *Shaping America's Future III: Proceedings of the National Forum on Transforming Our System of Educating Youth with W. Edwards Deming*. Bloomington, IN: National Education Service.

————. 2000. *The New Economics: For Industry, Government, Education*. Cambridge, MA: MIT Press.

————. 2000. *Out of the Crisis*. Cambridge, MA: MIT Press.

Diamond, John B., and Louis M. Gomez. 2023. "Disrupting White Supremacy and Anti-Black Racism in Educational Organizations." *Educational Researcher* 20, no. 10 (March): 1–9.

Diamond, John B., and Amanda E. Lewis. 2015. *Despite the Best Intentions: How Racial Inequality Thrives in Good Schools*. Oxford: Oxford University Press.

DuFour, Richard, Rebecca DuFour, Robert Eaker, Thomas W. Many, and Mike Mattos. 2016. *Learning by Doing: A Handbook for Professional Learning Communities at Work*. 3rd ed. Bloomington, IN: Solution Tree.

Dweck, Carol S. 2006. *Mindset: The New Psychology of Success*. New York: Random House.

Edmondson, Amy C. 2012. *Teaming: How Organizations Learn, Innovate, and Compete in the Knowledge Economy*. Hoboken, NJ: Wiley.

————. 2023. *Right Kind of Wrong: The Science of Failing Well*. New York: Atria Books.

Edmondson, Amy C., James R. Dillon, and Kathryn S. Roloff. 2007. "Three Perspectives on Team Learning: Outcome Improvement, Task Mastery, and Group Process." *Academy of Management Annals* 1, no. 1 (December). https://doi.org/10.5465/078559811.

Edmonson, Amy, and Anita Tucker. 2009. "Cincinnati Children's Hospital Medical Center," case study. Harvard Business Review. https://store.hbr.org/product/cincinnati-children-s-hospital-medical-center/609109.

Ericsson, K. Anders, and Neil Charness. 1994. "Expert Performance: Its Structure and Acquisition." *American Psychologist* 49, no. 8 (August): 725–47. https://doi.org/10.1037/0003-066X.49.8.725.

Fahle, Erin M., Sean F. Reardon, Demetra Kalogrides, Ericka S. Weathers, and Heewon Jang. 2020. "Racial Segregation and School Poverty in the United States, 1999–2016." *Race and Social Problems* 12 (March): 42–56. https://doi.org/10.1007/s12552-019-09277-w.

Fee, Elizabeth, and Mary E. Garofalo. 2011. "Florence Nightingale and the Crimean War." *American Journal of Public Health* 101, no. 5 (May): 776. https://doi.org/10.2105/AJPH.2009.188607.

Feeding America. 2019. "The State of Hunger in 2021." https://www.feedingamerica.org/research/state-senior-hunger?_ga=2.30167679.1334601650.1696110222-1495072131.1695062803.

————. 2022. "Map the Meal Gap." *An Analysis of County and Congressional District Food Insecurity and County Food Cost in the United States in 2020*. In Technical Brief.

Felitti, Vincent J., Robert F. Anda, Dale Nordenberg, David F. Williamson, Alison M. Spitz, Valerie Edwards, Mary P. Koss, and James S. Marks. 1998. "Relationship of Childhood Abuse and Household Dysfunction to Many of the Leading Causes of Death in Adults." *American Journal of Preventative Medicine* 14, no. 4: 245–58.

Feltman, Charles. 2021. *The Thin Book of Trust: An Essential Primer for Building Trust at Work*. Edited by Sue A. Hammond. Bend, OR: Thin Book.

Feynman, Richard P., Robert B. Leighton, and Matthew Sands. 2011. *The Feynman Lectures on Physics*. Boxed set: New Millennium ed. New York: Basic Books.

Forrester, Jay W. 1973. *World Dynamics*. 2nd ed. Cambridge, MA: Wright-Allen Press.

Gawande, Atul. 2012. "How Do We Heal Medicine?" Video. Ted Conferences. https://www.ted.com/talks/atul_gawande_how_do_we_heal_medicine.

Gerstein, R., D. Compton, C. Compton, J. Dimino, L. Santoro, S. Linan-Thompson, and W. D. Tilly. 2009. "Assisting Students Struggling with Reading: Response to Intervention and Multi-Tier Intervention for Reading in the Primary Grades. A Practice Guide." Washington, DC: Institute of Education Sciences, What Works Clearinghouse. https://ies.ed.gov/ncee/wwc/practiceguide/3.

Global Handwashing Partnership. n.d. "History." Accessed August 6, 2023. https://globalhandwashing.org/about-handwashing/history-of-handwashing/.

Godfrey, A. Blanton. 1996. "National Demonstration Project in Quality Improvement in Health Care." *Quality Digest*, September 1996. https://www.qualitydigest.com/sep96/health.html.

Goldhill, Olivia. 2017. "Implicit Bias Trainings Are Used to Fight Racism, but IAT Science Is Flawed." Quartz. https://qz.com/1144504/the-world-is-relying-on-a-flawed-psychological-test-to-fight-racism.

goShadow. 2019. "Shadowing the Patient for a Better Care Experience." https://www.goshadow.org/post/shadowing-the-patient-for-a-better-care-experience.

Gray, Jonathon, Suzanne Proudfoot, Maxine Power, Brandon Bennett, Sue Wells, and Mary Sneddon. 2015. "Target CLAB Zero: A National Improvement Collaborative to Reduce Central Line–Associated Bacteraemia in New Zealand Intensive Care Units." *New Zealand Medical Journal* 128 (1421): 13–21. https://pubmed.ncbi.nlm.nih.gov/26370751/.

Greene, Andy, and Roberto Parada. 2014. "Stephen King: The Rolling Stone Interview." *Rolling Stone*, October 31, 2014. https://www.rollingstone.com/culture/culture-features/stephen-king-the-rolling-stone-interview-191529/.

Gottman, J. M. 2011. *The Science of Trust: Emotional Attunement for Couples*. New York: Norton.

Grooms, Jevay. 2020. "No Home and No Acceptance: Exploring the Intersectionality of Sexual/Gender Identities (LBGTQ) and Race in the Foster Care System." *Review of Black Political Economy* 47 (2): 177–93. https://doi.org/10.1177/0034644620911381.

Gwen, Kostal, and Amar Shah. 2021. "Putting Improvement in Everyone's Hands: Opening Up Healthcare Improvement by Simplifying, Supporting and Refocusing on Core Purpose." *British Journal of Healthcare Management* 27, no. 2 (February): 1–6. https://doi.org/10.12968/bjhc.2020.0189.

Harder, Ben. "Best Children's Hospitals 2023–2024 Honor Roll and Overview." *US News and World Report*. June 21, 2023. https://health.usnews.com/health-news/best-childrens-hospitals/articles/best-childrens-hospitals-honor-roll-and-overview.

Health Quality & Safety Commission New Zealand and Ko Awatea. 2014. "Target CLAB Zero: Central Line Associated Bacteraemia." CLABSI Change Package. Auckland: Health Quality & Safety Commission New Zealand.

Heath, Chip, and Karla Starr. 2022. Making Numbers Count: The Art and Science of Communicating Numbers. New York: Avid Reader/Simon & Schuster.

Hendeles, Leslie. 1993. "Selecting a Decongestant." Pharmacotherapy 13 (6, pt. 2): 129S–46S.

High Tech High Graduate School of Education. n.d. "Expert Convening." Accessed July 13, 2023. https://hthgse.edu/resources/expert-convening/.

High Tech High Unboxed. 2022. "Improvement as a Tool for Our Collective Liberation, with Dr. Brandi Hinnant-Crawford." https://hthunboxed.org/podcasts/s3e14-improvement-as-a-tool-for-our-collective-liberation-with-dr-brandi-hinnant-crawford/.

Hill, Latoya, Samantha Artiga, and Usha Ranji. 2022. "Racial Disparities in Maternal and Infant Health: Current Status and Efforts to Address Them." Kaiser Family Foundation. https://www.kff.org/racial-equity-and-health-policy/issue-brief/racial-disparities-in-maternal-and-infant-health-current-status-and-efforts-to-address-them/#.

Hinnant-Crawford, Brandi N. 2020. *Improvement Science in Education: A Primer*. Gorham, ME: Myers Education.

———. 2022. "Improvement as a Tool for Our Collective Liberation." HTH Unboxed. https://hthunboxed.org/podcasts/s03e14-improvement-as-a-tool-for-our-collective-liberation-with-dr-brandi-hinnant-crawford/.

Hoffman, Kelly M., Sophie Trawalter, Jordan R. Axt, and M. N. Oliver. 2016. "Racial Bias in Pain Assessment and Treatment Recommendations, and False Beliefs about Biological Difference between Blacks and Whites." *Proceedings of the National Academy of Sciences of the United States of America* 113 (16): 4296–4301. https://doi.org/10.1073/pnas.1516047113.

Huggins, William, W. D. Sparkes, Thomas Annan, John Erichsen, and Joseph Lister. n.d. "Joseph Lister." Wikipedia. Accessed August 6, 2023. https://en.wikipedia.org/wiki/Joseph_Lister#cite_ref-25.

IDEO. 2019. "Why Everyone Should Prototype (Not Just Designers)." https://www.ideou.com/blogs /inspiration/why-everyone-should-prototype-not-just-designers.

———. n.d. "Brainstorming—IDEO U." Accessed July 12, 2023. https://www.ideou.com/pages /brainstorming.

ImproveCareNow, Patient Advisory Council. 2015. "The Ostomy Toolkit: A Guide to Gutsy Living." https://www.improvecarenow.org/the_ostomy_toolkit.

Institute for Healthcare Improvement. 2003. "The Breakthrough Series: IHI's Collaborative Model for Achieving Breakthrough Improvement." http://www.ihi.org/resources/Pages/IHIWhitePapers/The BreakthroughSeriesIHIsCollaborativeModelforAchievingBreakthroughImprovement.aspx.

———. 2005. "Pursuing Perfection: Report from Cincinnati Children's on Improving Family-Centered Care for Cystic Fibrosis Patients/IHI." Institute for Healthcare Improvement.

———. 2008. "Preventing Mother-to-Child Transmission of HIV in South Africa/IHI." Institute for Healthcare Improvement.

———. n.d. "History/IHI." Accessed March 15, 2022. http://www.ihi.org/about/Pages/History.aspx.

Institute of Medicine and Committee on Quality of Health Care in America. 2000. *To Err Is Human: Building a Safer Health System*. Edited by Janet M. Corrigan, Linda T. Kohn, and Molla S. Donaldson. Washington, DC: National Academies Press.

———. 2001. *Crossing the Quality Chasm: A New Health System for the 21st Century*. Washington, DC: National Academies Press.

Ishikawa, Kaoru, ed. 1982. *Guide to Quality Control*. Tokyo: Asian Productivity Organization.

Jackson, K., L. Gibbons, and C. J. Sharpe. 2017. "Teachers' Views of Students' Mathematical Capabilities: Challenges and Possibilities for Ambitious Reform." *Teachers College Record* 119, no. 1: 1–43. https://doi.org/10.1177/016146811711900708.

James M. Anderson Center for Health Systems Excellence. 2020. "Building a Learning Healthcare System Network Modules." https://www.cincinnatichildrens.org/research/divisions/j/anderson-center /learning-networks.

Jewett, Christina. 2023. "Why the F.D.A. Took So Long to Tackle a Disputed Cold Remedy." *New York Times*, September 17, 2023. https://www.nytimes.com/2023/09/15/health/fda-cold-medicine -decongestant.html.

Kahneman, Daniel. 2011. *Thinking, Fast and Slow*. New York: Farrar, Straus & Giroux.

Kahneman, Daniel, Olivier Sibony, and Cass R. Sunstein. 2021. *Noise: A Flaw in Human Judgment*. Boston: Little, Brown Spark.

Kania, John, Mark Kramer, and Peter Senge. 2018. "The Water of Systems Change." Whitepaper. FSG. www.fsg.org.

Katzenbach, Jon R., and Douglas K. Smith. 2015. *The Wisdom of Teams: Creating the High-Performance Organization*. Boston: Harvard Business Review Press.

Kenney, Charles. 2008. *The Best Practice: How the New Quality Movement Is Transforming Medicine*. New York: PublicAffairs. Langley, Gerald J., Ronald D. Moen, Kevin M. Nolan, Kotagal, Uma R., and Amy Compton-Phillips. 2016. "'Being the Best at Getting Better'—Creating a Culture of Change." *NEJM Catalyst* (June). https://catalyst.nejm.org/doi/full/10.1056/CAT.17.0491.

Kim, Daniel H. 1999. "Introduction to Systems Thinking." https://thesystemsthinker.com/introduc tion-to-systems-thinking/.

Kline, Patrick M., Evan K. Rose, and Christopher R. Walters. 2021. "Systemic Discrimination among Large U.S. Employers." NBER Working Paper Series No. 29053 (July).

Ko Awatea and New Zealand Ministry of Education. 2015. "Early Childhood Education Change Package." Auckland: Ko Awatea.

Koch, Richard. 1998. *The 80/20 Principle: The Secret of Achieving More with Less*. Boston: Nicholas Brealey.

Kostal, Gwen, and Amar Shah. 2021. "Putting Improvement in Everyone's Hands: Opening Up Healthcare Improvement by Simplifying, Supporting and Refocusing on Core Purpose." *British Journal of Healthcare Management* 27, no. 2 (February): 1–6. https://doi.org/10.12968/bjhc.2020.0189.

Labaree, David. 1997. "Private Goods, Public Goods: The American Struggle over Educational Goals." *American Educational Research Journal* 34, no. 1 (Spring): 39–81.

Ladson-Billings, Gloria. 2006. "From the Achievement Gap to the Education Debt: Understanding Achievement in U.S. Schools." *Educational Researcher* 35, no. 7 (October): 3–12.

———. 2007. "Pushing Past the Achievement Gap: An Essay on the Language of Deficit." *Journal of Negro Education* 76 (3): 316–23.

Langley, Gerald J., Ronald D. Moen, Kevin M. Nolan, Thomas W. Nolan, Clifford L. Norman, and Lloyd P. Provost. 2009. *The Improvement Guide: A Practical Approach to Enhancing Organizational Performance.* 2nd ed. Hoboken, NJ: Wiley.

Lawn, Rebecca, Sanjoy Nand, Monique Davies, Nisha Bangs, Doreen Liow, Ahmed Marmoush, Sonia Varma, and Ian Hutchby. 2013. "SMOOTH Collaborative." Safer Medication Outcomes on Transfer Home Change Package, 1. Counties Manukau Health and Ko Awatea. https://koawatea.counties manukau.health.nz/assets/Blog/teamcounties/b47f92206a/SMOOTH-HTG-Final-March-2014.pdf.

Lessing, Doris. 1987. *Prisons We Choose to Live Inside.* New York: HarperCollins.

Lewis, Amanda E., and John B. Diamond. 2015. *Despite the Best Intentions: How Racial Inequality Thrives in Good Schools.* Oxford: Oxford University Press.

Lewis, Clarence I. 1956. *Mind and the World Order: Outline of a Theory of Knowledge.* Garden City, NY: Dover.

Liebman, James, and Elizabeth Cruikshank. 2017. "Governance of Steel and Kryptonite Politics in Contemporary Public Education Reform." *Florida Law Review* 69 (2): 365–463.

"List of Cognitive Biases and Heuristics." n.d. The Decision Lab. Accessed March 3, 2023. https://thedecisionlab.com/biases-index.

LUMA Institute. n.d. "Fly-on-the-Wall Observation." Accessed November 2, 2022. https://www.luma -institute.com/fly-on-the-wall-observation/.

Martin, L. A., and K. Mate. 2018. "IHI Innovation System." Boston: Institute for Healthcare Improvement.

Massoud, M. R., G. A. Nielson, K. Nolan, M. W. Schall, and C. Sevin. 2006. "A Framework for Spread: From Local Improvements to System-Wide Change." IHI Innovation Series white paper. Boston: Institute for Healthcare Improvement.

McCannon, Joe, M. Rashad Massoud, and Abigail Z. Alyesh. 2016. "Many Ways to Many: A Brief Compendium of Networked Learning Methods." *Stanford Social Innovation Review* (October). https://ssir.org/articles/entry/many_ways_to_many.

Meadows, Donella H. 2008. *Thinking in Systems: A Primer.* Edited by Diana Wright. Chelsea, VT: Chelsea Green.

Merriam-Webster. 2023. "Innovation," definition and meaning. https://www.merriam-webster.com/dic tionary/innovation.

Middleton, Lesley, Diana Dowdle, Luis Villa, and Jonathon Gray. 2019. "Saving 20000 Days and Beyond: A Realist Evaluation of Two Quality Improvement Campaigns to Manage Hospital Demand in a New Zealand District Health Board." *BMJ Open Quality* (December): 1–10. http://doi.10.1136 /bmjoq-2018-000374.

Middleton, Lesley, David Mason, Luis Villa, Jacqueline Cumming, and Janet McDonald. 2014. "Evaluation of the 20,000 Days Campaign." Report for Counties Manukau District Health Board. https://www.wgtn.ac.nz/sog/about/news/news-archives/2014-news-archived/new-hsrc-report-evaluation-of -the-20,000-days-campaign/Evaluation-of-the-20000-Days-Campaign.pdf.

Moen, Ronald, Thomas W. Nolan, and Lloyd P. Provost. 2012. *Quality Improvement through Planned Experimentation 3/E.* New York: McGraw-Hill Education.

Moen, Ronald D., and Clifford L. Norman. 2010. "Circling Back: Clearing Up Myths about the Deming Cycle and Seeing How It Keeps Evolving." *Quality Progress* (November): 22–28.

Mondale, Sarah, and Sarah Patton, executive producers. 2001. *School: The Story of American Public Education*. Stone Lantern Films. https://stonelanternfilms.org/school-series/.

Moore, David S. 2007. *The Basic Practice of Statistics*. New York: Freeman.

Mortimer, E. A., Jr., P. J. Lipsitz, E. Wolinsky, A. J. Gonzaga, and C. H. Rammelkamp Jr. 1962. "Transmission of Staphylococci between Newborns: Importance of the Hands to Personnel." *American Journal of Diseases of Children* 104 (September): 289–95. https://doi.org/10.1001/archpedi.1962.02080030291012.

Morton, M. H., G. M. Samuels, A. Dworsky, and S. Patel. 2018. *Missed Opportunities: LGBTQ Youth Homelessness in America*. Chicago: Chapin Hall at the University of Chicago.

National Equity Project. 2020. "The Lens of Systemic Oppression." https://www.nationalequityproject.org/frameworks/lens-of-systemic-oppression?gclid=CjwKCAjw_b6WBhAQEiwAp4HyIBCgMUItr8U-x4hvM3T3ifSAHLlo-QPV7MJaUQu-Y0RylHmmAIpzKBoCujsQAvD_BwE.

National Institutes of Health. 2022. "Eugenics and Scientific Racism." National Human Genome Research Institute. https://www.genome.gov/about-genomics/fact-sheets/Eugenics-and-Scientific-Racism.

Nolan, Kevin, Marie W. Schall, Fabiane Erb, and Thomas Nolan. 2005. "Using a Framework for Spread: The Case of Patient Access in the Veterans Health Administration." *Joint Commission Journal on Quality and Patient Safety* 31, no. 6 (June): 339–47. https://doi.org/10.1016/s1553-7250(05)31045-2.

Oakes, Jeannie. 2005. *Keeping Track: How Schools Structure Inequality*. New Haven, CT: Yale University Press.

O'Day, Jennifer A., and Marshall S. Smith. 2019. *Opportunity for All: A Framework for Quality and Equality in Education*. Cambridge, MA: Harvard Education Press.

Ott, Ellis R. 1975. *Process Quality Control: Troubleshooting and Interpretation of Data*. New York: McGraw-Hill.

Oxford Languages Dictionary. 2023. https://www.google.com/search?q=define+theory&sxsrf=AB5stBgFVxmVdmcCPqBRrBXiKYyEhJrUuw%3A1689626836595&ei=1Ki1ZPT7I8vokPIPqqChoA4&ved=0ahUKEwj0tZe7zpaAAxVLNEQIHSpQCOQQ4dUDCBE&uact=5&oq=define+theory&gs_lp=Egxnd3Mtd2l6LXNlcnAiDWRlZmluZSB0aGVvcnkDBAjGIoFGCc.

pablopicasso.org. n.d. "15 Pablo Picasso Fun Facts." Accessed August 6, 2023. https://www.pablopicasso.org/picasso-facts.jsp.

Pascale, Richard, Jerry Sternin, and Monique Sternin. 2010. *The Power of Positive Deviance: How Unlikely Innovators Solve the World's Toughest Problems*. Boston: Harvard Business Press.

Patterson, Kerry, Joseph Grenny, Ron McMillan, and Al Switzler. 2012. *Crucial Conversations: Tools for Talking When Stakes Are High*. 2nd ed. New York: McGraw-Hill Education.

Perla, Rocco J., Lloyd P. Provost, and Sandy K. Murray. 2011. "The Run Chart: A Simple Analytical Tool for Learning from Variation in Healthcare Processes." *BMJ Quality & Safety* 20, no. 1 (January): 46–51. https://doi.org/10.1136/bmjqs.2009.037895.

Perla, Rocco J., Lloyd P. Provost, and Gareth J. Parry. 2013. "Seven Propositions of the Science of Improvement: Exploring Foundations." *Quality Management in Health Care* 22(3): 170–86.

Pileggi, Molly, Lindsey Liu, and Alyn Turner. 2020. "Back on Track: How Off-Track Ninth Graders Progressed in Later Years of High School, Class of 2017 and 2018." Philadelphia: Philadelphia Education Research Consortium.

Provost, Lloyd P., and Sandra K. Murray. 2022. *The Health Care Data Guide: Learning from Data for Improvement*. Hoboken, NJ: Wiley.

Provost, Shannon M., Holly J. Lanham, Luci K. Leykum, Reuben R. McDaniel Jr., and Jacquelin Pugh. 2015. "Health Care Huddles: Managing Complexity to Achieve High Reliability." *Health Care Management Review* 40, no. 1 (January/March): 2–12. https://doi.org/10.1097/HMR.0000000000000009.

Pyzdek, Thomas, and Joseph A. DeFeo. 2019. "Pareto Principle (80/20 Rule) & Pareto Analysis Guide." Juran. https://www.juran.com/blog/a-guide-to-the-pareto-principle-80-20-rule-pareto-analysis/.

Reardon, S., D. Kalogrides, and K. Shores. 2019. "The Geography of Racial/Ethnic Test Score Gaps." *American Journal of Sociology* 124 (4).

Rogers, Everett M. 2003. *Diffusion of Innovations*. 5th ed. New York: Free Press.

Rollins, Nigel, Kristy Little, Similo Mzolo, Christiane Horwood, and Marie-Louise Newell. 2007. "Surveillance of Mother-to-Child Transmission Prevention Programmes at Immunization Clinics: The Case for Universal Screening." *AIDS* 21, no. 10 (June): 1341–47. https://doi.org/10.1097/QAD.0b013e32814db7d4.

Ryckman, Frederick C., Pamela J. Schoettker, Kathryn R. Hays, Beverly L. Connelly, Rebecca L. Blacklidge, Cindi A. Bedinghaus, Mary L. Sorter, Lloyd C. Friend, and Uma R. Kotagal. 2009. "Reducing Surgical Site Infections at a Pediatric Academic Medical Center." *Joint Commission Journal on Quality and Patient Safety* 35, no. 4 (April): 192–98. https://doi.org/10.1016/S1553-7250(09)35026-6.

Safir, Shane, Jamila Dugan, and Carrie Wilson. 2021. *Street Data: A Next-Generation Model for Equity, Pedagogy, and School Transformation*. Thousand Oaks, CA: Corwin.

Samuel, Joyce P., Alyssa Burgart, Susan H. Wootton, David Magnus, John D. Lantos, and Jon E. Tyson. 2016. "Randomized n-of-1 Trials: Quality Improvement, Research, or Both?" *Pediatrics* 138, no. 2 (August): 1–5. e20161103.

Sarin, S., and C. McDermott. 2003. "The Effect of Team Leader Characteristics on Learning, Knowledge Application, and Performance of Cross-Functional New Product Development Teams." *Decision Sciences* 34 (4): 707–39.

Schneiderman, Arthur M. 1988. "Setting Quality Goals." *Quality Progress* 21, no. 4 (April): 51–57.

Schoberer, Daniela, Helga E. Breimaier, Julia Zuschnegg, Thomas Findling, Susanna Schaffer, and Tamara Archan. 2021. "Fall Prevention in Hospitals and Nursing Homes: Clinical Practice Guideline." *Worldviews on Evidence-Based Nursing* 19, no. 2 (March): 86–93. https://doi.org/10.1111/wvn.12571.

Senge, Peter M. 1990. *The Fifth Discipline: The Art and Practice of the Learning Organization*. New York: Doubleday/Currency.

Senge, Peter, Art Kleiner, Charlotte Roberts, Richard Ross, and Bryan Smith. 1994. *The Fifth Discipline Fieldbook*. New York: Doubleday/Currency.

Senge, P., and O. Scharmer. 2001. "Community Action Research." In Handbook of Action Research: Participative Inquiry and Practice, edited by Peter Reason and Hilary Bradbury-Huang. Thousand Oaks, CA: Sage. https://doi.org/10.1046/j.1365-2648.2001.0668a.x.

Shamash, Emily. 2020. "Staying Warm and Comfortable during Infusions." https://www.improvecarenow.org/staying_warm_and_comfortable_during_infusions.

Shasta Strengthening Families Collaborative. n.d. "Shasta County ACE Study and Data." Accessed March 1, 2024. https://shastastrengtheningfamilies.org/shasta-county-ace-study/.

Shewhart, Walter A. 1980. *Economic Control of Quality of Manufactured Product*. Milwaukee, WI: American Society for Quality Control.

Shook, John. 2008. *Managing to Learn: Using the A3 Management Process to Solve Problems, Gain Agreement, Mentor and Lead*. Boston: Lean Enterprise Institute.

Singleton, Glenn E. 2015. *Courageous Conversations about Race: A Field Guide for Achieving Equity in Schools*. Thousand Oaks, CA: Sage.

Singleton, Glenn E., and Curtis Linton, eds. 2006. *Courageous Conversations about Race: A Field Guide for Achieving Equity in Schools*. Thousand Oaks, CA: Sage.

Siracusa, Christopher M., Jeanne L. Weiland, James D. Acton, Amitra K. Chima, Barbara A. Chini, Andrea J. Hoberman, J. Denise Wetzel, Raouf S. Amin, and Gary L. McPhail. 2014. "The Impact of Transforming Delivery on Cystic Fibrosis Outcomes: A Decade of Quality Improvement at Cincinnati Children's Hospital." *BMJ Quality and Safety* 23: i56–i63. https://doi.org/10.1136/bmjqs-2013-002361.

Skiba, Russell J., Alfredo J. Artiles, Elizabeth B. Kozleski, Daniel J. Losen, and Elizabeth G. Harry. 2016. "Risks and Consequences of Oversimplifying Educational Inequities: A Response to Morgan et al." *Educational Researcher* 45 (3): 221–25.

Skiba, Russell J., Robert H. Horner, Choong-Geun Chung, M. K. Rausch, Seth L. May, and Tary Tobin. 2011. "Race Is Not Neutral: A National Investigation of African American and Latino Disproportionality in School Discipline." *School Psychology Review* 40 (1): 85–107. https://doi.org/10.1080/02 796015.2011.12087730.

Skiba, R. J., A. B. Simmons, S. Ritter, A. C. Gibb, M. K. Rausch, J. Cuadrado, and C. G. Chung. 2008. "Achieving Equity in Special Education: History, Status, and Current Challenges." *Exceptional Children* 74 (3): 264–68.

Skillman, Peter. n.d. "Spaghetti Tower Design Challenge." Peter Skillman Design. Accessed July 12, 2023. http://www.peterskillmandesign.com/spaghetti-tower-design-challenge/2019/2/9/peter-skill man-marshmallow-design-challenge.

Snowden, David J., and Mary E. Boone. 2007. "A Leader's Framework for Decision Making." *Harvard Business Review* (November): 1–9.

Solberg, Leif, Gordon Mosser, and Sharon McDonald. 1997. "The Three Faces of Performance Measurement: Improvement, Accountability, and Research." *Journal on Quality Improvement* 23, no. 3 (March): 135–47. https://pubmed.ncbi.nlm.nih.gov/9103968/.

Soto, Ivannia. 2012. *ELL Shadowing as a Catalyst for Change*. Thousand Oaks, CA: Sage.

Soule, Sarah, Huggy Rao, Robert Sutton, and Davina Drabkin. n.d. "The 100,000 Homes Campaign." Stanford Graduate School of Business. Accessed October 8, 2023. https://www.gsb.stanford.edu/ faculty-research/case-studies/100000-homes-campaign.

Stanford d. school. n.d. "Shadow a Student Challenge—Stanford d.school." Accessed November 2, 2022. https://dschool.stanford.edu/shadow-a-student-k12.

Stewart, Jon. 2015. "Jon Stewart on His 'Daily Show' Run: 'It So Far Exceeded My Expectations.'" NPR: Fresh Air. https://www.npr.org/programs/fresh-air/2015/08/06/429851717/fresh-air-for-au gust-6-2015.

Stigler, James W., and James Hiebert. 2009. *The Teaching Gap: Best Ideas from the World's Teachers for Improving Education in the Classroom*. New York: Free Press.

Stroh, David P. 2015. *Systems Thinking for Social Change: A Practical Guide to Solving Complex Problems, Avoiding Unintended Consequences, and Achieving Lasting Results*. Chelsea, VT: Chelsea Green.

Sutton, Robert I., and Hayagreeva Rao. 2014. *Scaling Up Excellence: Getting to More without Settling for Less*. New York: Crown.

Tague, Nancy R. 2015. *Quality Toolbox*. (Indian Subcontinent Edition). New Delhi: Infotech Standards India PV. Limited.

Thrive Teen. 2023. "Teen Mental Health Statistics in 2023—ThriveTeen." https://thriveteen.com/teen -mental-health-statistics/.

Tolman, Charles W., Rene Van Hezewijk, Frances Cherry, and Ian Lubeck, eds. 1996. *Problems of Theoretical Psychology*. Concord, Ontario, Canada: Captus.

Treviño, Ernesto, Elisa Aguirre, and Carla Varela, eds. 2018. *Un Buen Comienzo para los niños de Chile*. Santiago: Ediciones Universidad Diego Portales.

Troen, Vivian, and Katherine Boles. 2012. *The Power of Teacher Teams: With Cases, Analyses, and Strategies for Success*. Thousand Oaks, CA: Corwin.

Tucker, Anita L., and Amy C. Edmondson. 2009. "Cincinnati Children's Hospital Medical Center." Harvard Business School Case 609-109 (June; revised April 2011).

Tuckman, Bruce W. 1965. "Developmental Sequence in Small Groups." *Psychological Bulletin* 63 (6): 384–99.

Tufte, Edward. 2001. *The Visual Display of Quantitative Information*. 2nd ed. Cheshire, CT: Graphics Press.

Tukey, John. 1977. *Exploratory Data Analysis*. Boston: Addison-Wesley.

Tversky, Amos, and Daniel Kahneman. 1974. "Judgments under Uncertainty: Heuristics and Biases." *Science* 185: 1124–31.

Tyack, David B., and Larry Cuban. 1995. *Tinkering toward Utopia: A Century of Public School Reform*. Cambridge, MA: Harvard University Press.

Tyler, Jilly, Monique Davies, and Brandon Bennett. 2018. "Increasing Early Childhood Education En-rolment and Attendance Rates in South Auckland, New Zealand." *New Zealand International Research in Early Childhood Education Journal* 21 (1): 100–111.

U.S. Department of Education. 1983. *A Nation at Risk: The Imperative for Educational Reform*. Wash-ington, DC: U.S. Government Printing Office.

von Hippel, Eric. 2005. *Democratizing Innovation*. Cambridge, MA: MIT Press.

———. n.d. Accessed July 15, 2023. https://evhippel.mit.edu/.

Weber, Craig. 2013. *Conversational Capacity: The Secret to Building Successful Teams That Perform When the Pressure Is On*. New York: McGraw-Hill Education.

Weinstein, James N., Amy B. Geller, Yamrot Negussie, and Alina Baciu, eds. 2017. *Communities in Ac-tion: Pathways to Health Equity*. Washington, DC: National Academies Press.

WestEd. 2023. "FAQs." Math Practical Measurement. https://mpm.wested.org/.

———. n.d. Carnegie Math Pathways. Accessed October 8, 2023. https://carnegiemathpathways.org/.

Wheatley, Margaret J. 2009. *Turning to One Another: Simple Conversations to Restore Hope to the Future*. Oakland, CA: Berrett-Koehler.

Wheeler, Derek S., Mary Jo Giaconne, Nancy Hutchinson, Mary Haygood, Kathy Demmel, Maria T. Britto, Peter A. Margolis, and Lloyd P. Provost. 2012. "An Unexpected Increase in Catheter-Associated Bloodstream Infections at a Children's Hospital Following Introduction of the Spiros Closed Male Connector." *American Journal of Infection Control* 40 (February): 48–50. https://doi.org/10.1016/j.ajic.2011.02.015.

Wilkerson, Isabel. 2020. *Caste: The Origins of Our Discontents*. New York: Random House.

World Flora Online. n.d. Accessed July 17, 2023. https://www.worldfloraonline.org/.

Yeager, D., C. Romero, D. Paunesku, C. S. Hulleman, B. Schneider, B. Hinojosa, H. Y. Lee, et al. 2016. "Using Design Thinking to Improve Psychology Interventions: The Case of the Growth Mindset dur-ing the Transition to High School." *Journal of Educational Psychology* 108 (3): 374–91.

Yoshikawa, Hirokazu, Diana Leyva, Catherine E. Snow, Ernesto Treviño, Clara M. Barata, Christina Weiland, Celia J. Gomez, et al. 2015. "Experimental Impacts of a Teacher Professional Development Program in Chile on Preschool Classroom Quality and Child Outcomes." *Developmental Psychology* 51, no. 3: 309–22. https://doi.org/10.1037/a0038785.

Index

About the Authors

Alicia Grunow is cofounder of the Improvement Collective, a company that partners with organizations to improve a wide variety of outcomes that impact children and families. She trains teams, coaches, and leaders on the application of improvement science methods and helps people design improvement initiatives to get tangible results. She coauthored the seminal book *Learning to Improve: How America's Schools Can Get Better at Getting Better*. Alicia began her career as a bilingual teacher and holds a PhD in education from Stanford University.

Sandra Park is a cofounder of the Improvement Collective where she trains improvement coaches and advises large-scale education networks and projects. She led one of the first improvement networks to apply improvement science in the field of education at the Carnegie Foundation. Sandra previously taught elementary school in Oregon, Maryland, and Washington, DC and was director of programs at First Graduate in San Francisco. She holds a PhD in education policy from The University of California, Berkeley and an Improvement Advisor certificate from the Institute for Healthcare Improvement.

Brandon Bennett is an advisor, teacher, and author who helps organizations in health care, education, and social welfare improve outcomes for the communities and individuals they serve. As the founder of ISC LLC, he teaches advanced improvement methods and partners on a range of global initiatives including disease-specific processes, academic outcomes for students with disabilities, and country-wide improvement efforts. Brandon has a BS in psychology from the University of California, Davis and an MPH from Loma Linda University School of Public Health, specializing in global health. He is the author of several results-based and methodological papers on the application of improvement science methods and has been a featured speaker at quality conferences around the world.